CONIECTANEA BIBLICA · NEW TESTAMENT SERIES 8

CHRYS C. CARAGOUNIS

The Ephesian
Mysterion

MEANING AND CONTENT

CWK GLEERUP

CWK Gleerup is the imprint for the scientific and scholarly publications of
LiberLäromedel Lund

Doctoral Thesis at Uppsala University 1977

Printed in Sweden by Carl Bloms Boktryckeri AB, Lund   ISBN   91-40-04417-3

εἰς ἔπαινον δόξης τῆς χάριτος αὐτοῦ

Eph 1: 6

To my Mother
To Sophie and our Children

CONTENTS

Abbreviations IX

Chapter I. Μυστήριον: The Scope of its Meaning and Application .... 1— 34
1. The Problem 1
2. The Eleusinian Mysteries .... 3— 19
   A. The Age 3
   B. The Provenance 4
   C. A Comparative Study of Ὄργια, Τελετή, Μυστήρια .... 5— 19
      i. Ὄργια, Τελετή, Μυστήρια as Designations of the Mysteries
         throughout Antiquity 5
      ii. Ὄργια 6
      iii. Τελετή 7
      iv. Μυστήρια 9
          a. The Meaning of Derivatives 10
          b. Ἄρρητα and Ἀπόρρητα in Relation to the Mysteries 11
          c. Some Historical Considerations 11
          d. The Content of the Mysteries and its Import 14
          e. Some Reflections on the Meaning of the Ceremonies 18
3. The Subsequent History of the Term Prior to the NT .... 20— 26
   A. Μυστήριον in Philosophy .... 20— 21
      i. Plato 20
      ii. Philo 21
   B. Μυστήριον in Secular Use .... 21— 22
      i. Of Ordinary Secrets 21
      ii. In Medicine 22
   C. Μυστήριον in the LXX .... 22— 23
      i. Apocrypha 22
      ii. Daniel 23
   D. Μυστήριον in the Pseudepigrapha .... 23— 26
      i. Various Pseudepigraphical Books 23
      ii. I Enoch 24
4. The use of Μυστήριον in the NT .... 26— 30
5. The use of Μυστήριον in the Early Christian Authors .... 31— 32
6. Conclusions .... 32— 34

Chapter II. Some Peculiar Features in Ephesians .... 35— 56
1. Some Statistical Observations .... 35— 38
   A. Parentheses — Digressions .... 35— 36
   B. The Major Divisions 36
   C. Eulogy, Doxology, Prayers .... 36— 38
2. The Eulogy .... 39— 52
   A. The Genre .... 39— 41
   B. A Hymn? .... 41— 45

VIII

C. The Delimitation, Position and Function of the Eulogy .... 45— 52
   i. Comparison with Eulogies in OT and Judaism 48
   ii. Focus (semantic) 48
   iii. Climax 49
   iv. Contents prefiguring the entire Epistle 50
3. Prayers .... 52— 55
4. The Digression of 3: 2—13 .... 55— 56

Chapter III. An Analysis of the larger Semantic units of Eph 1—3 .... 57— 78
A. Semantic Considerations .... 57— 59
B. An Analysis of the Sections and Paragraphs of Eph 1—3 .... 59— 77

Chapter IV. A Propositional Analysis of 1: 3—10 and 3: 1—13 .... 78—116
A. Some Preliminary Remarks 78
B. Analysis of 1: 3—10 .... 78— 96
C. Analysis of 3: 1—13 .... 96—112
   i. The Context: the Prayer of 3: 1, 14—19 96
   ii. The *Mysterion* Digression of 3: 2—13 .... 96—112
D. Concluding Remarks .... 112—113
E. A Propositional Display of Eph 1: 3—10 .... 113—114
F. A Propositional Display of Eph 3: 1—13 .... 114—116

Chapter V. The Ephesian *Mysterion* and its Background Usage .... 117—135
1. Summarising Ch. IV .... 117—118
2. The Mystery Religions .... 119—120
3. Gnosticism .... 120—121
4. The OT .... 121—126
   Daniel 121
   i. General Considerations 121
   ii. The Image 122
   iii. The Visions of Chs. 7 and 8 122
   iv. A Comparison between the Dan רז and the Eph *Mysterion* 123
5. The Pseudepigrapha .... 126—129
   I Enoch .... 127—129
6. The Qumran Writings .... 129—133
7. Conclusion .... 134—135

Chapter VI. Μυστήριον in Ephesians .... 136—161
1. The 'Εν-dimension in Eph as a Reference Point .... 136—137
2. The Supreme End in View .... 138—139
3. The Σύν-state of the Gentiles .... 139—142
4. The Author's Role .... 142—143
5. The Cosmic *Anakephalaiōsis* .... 143—146
6. Excursuses .... 146—161
   A. 'Εν τοῖς 'Επουρανίοις .... 146—152
   B. 'Εν Χριστῷ, κτλ. .... 152—157
   C. 'Αρχαί, 'Εξουσίαι, κτλ. .... 157—161

Bibliography .... 162—183

Indices .... 184—199
   I. Index of Authors .... 184—186
   II. Index of Reference Works 188
   III. Index of Passages .... 189—199

ABBREVIATIONS

(Of Periodicals and Series)

AB=The Anchor Bible, N.Y., London.
AGSU=Arbeiten zur Geschichte des Spätjudentums und Urchristentums, Leiden.
AJA=American Journal of Archeology, Princeton.
AJT=The American Journal of Theology, Chicago.
AnBib=Analecta Biblica, Rome.
ANS=Auslegung neutestamentlicher Schriften, Zürich.
ArchRW=Archiv für Religionswissenschaft, Leipzig, Berlin.
ΑρχΔ=᾽Αρχαιολογικὸν Δελτίον, ᾽Αθῆναι.
ΑρχΕφ=᾽Αρχαιολογικὴ ᾽Εφημερίς, ᾽Αθῆναι.
ASNU=Acta Seminarii, Neotestamentici Upsaliensis, Uppsala.
ATR=Anglican Theological Review, Evanston.
AUL=Acta Universitet, Lund.
AY=Athens Yearbook, Athens.
ΒΕΠ=Βιβλιοθήκη ῾Ελλήνων Πατέρων καὶ ᾽Εκκλησιαστικῶν Συγγραφέων, ᾽Αθῆναι,
BETS=Bulletin of the Evangelical Theological Society, Wheaton Ill.
BFCTL=Bibliothèque de la Facultè Catholique de Théologie de Lyon, Lyon.
BHTh=Beiträge zur historischen Theologie, Tübingen.
BhZNW=Beihefte zur Zeitschrift für die neutestamentliche Wissenschaft und die
   Kunde der älteren Kirche, Giessen, Berlin.
BICS=Bulletin of the Institute for Classical Studies, London.
Bib=Biblica, Rome.
BKT: BC=Beiträge zur Kontroverstheologie (Beiheft zur Catholica Nr. 1), Münster.
BL=Bibel und Leben, Düsseldorf.
BNTC=Black's New Testament Commentaries, London.
BS=Bibliotheca Sacra, Dallas.
BT=The Bible Translator, London.
BT=Bibliotheca Teubneriana, Leipzig.
BU=Biblische Untersuchungen, Regensburg.
BWANT=Beiträge zur Wissenschaft vom Alten und Neuen Testament, Stuttgart.
BZ=Biblische Zeitschrift, Paderborn.
CB:NTS=Coniectanea Biblica: NT Series, Lund.
CBQ=The Catholic Biblical Quarterly, Washington.
CGT=The Cambridge Greek Testament, Cambridge.
CMG=Corpus Medicorum Gaecorum, Leipzig.
CN=Coniectanea Neotestamentica, Lund.
CNEB=Cambridge Bible Commentary: NEB, Cambridge.
ConcTM=Concordia Theological Monthly, St. Louis, Missouri.
CR=The Classical Review, London.
EGT=Expositor's Greek Testament, Grand Rapids.
EPRO=Etudes Préliminaires aux Religions Orientales dans l'empire Romain, Leiden.
Eran=Eranos: Acta philologica Suecana, Uppsala, Hauniae.

ET=Expository Times, Aberdeen, Edinburgh
ETL=Ephemerides Theologicae Lovanienses, Louvain.
EvTh=Evangelische Theologie, München.
ΕφΑρχ='Εφημερὶς 'Αρχαιολογική (περίοδος τρίτη 1883—1909), 'Αθῆναι.
FRLANT=Forschungen zur Religion und Literatur des Alten und Neuen Testaments, Göttingen.
GCS=Die Griechischen Christlichen Schriftsteller, Leipzig.
GeistLeb=Geist und Leben, Würzburg.
Glot=Glotta, Zeitschrift für griechische und lateinische Sprache, Göttingen.
Herm=Hermeneia, Philadelphia.
HNT=Hand-Commentar zum Neuen Testament, Leipzig.
Hesp=Hesperia, Cambridge, Mass.
HSNT=Die Heilige Schrift Neuen Testaments, Nördlingen.
HTKNT=Herders Theologischer Kommentar zum Neuen Testament, Basel etc.
HTR=Harvard Theological Review, Cambridge, Mass.
HUCA=Hebrew Union College Annual, Cincinnati.
ICC=International Critical Commentary, Edinburgh.
ILGL=International Library of General Linguistics, München.
JBL=Journal of Biblical Literature, Philadelphia, Missoula.
JHS=Journal of Hellenic Studies, London.
JKPh=Jahrbuch für die Klassische Philologie, Suppl., Leipzig.
JR=The Journal of Religion, Chicago.
JTS=The Journal of Theological Studies, London.
KAT=Kommentar zum Alten Testament, Gütersloh.
KEKNT=Kritisch-Exegetischer Kommentar über das Neue Testament, Göttingen.
Lat=Latomus, Brussels.
LCL=Loeb Classical Library, London.
Ling=Linguistics.
MNTC=The Moffat New Testament Commentary, London, N.Y.
MPG=J. P. Migny, Patrologia Graeca, Paris, 1857—66.
MPL=J. P. Migny, Patrologia Latina, Paris.
MThZ=Münchener Theologische Zeitschrift, München.
NCB=New Clarendon Bible, Oxford.
NF=Neutestamentliche Forschungen, Gütersloh.
NICNT=The New International Commentary on the New Testament, Grand Rapids.
Nov T=Novum Testamentum, Leiden.
NTD=Das Neue Testament Deutsch, Göttingen.
NTS=New Testament Studies, Cambridge.
NTS:M=New Testament Studies, Monograph Series, Cambridge.
NTSR=New Testament for Spiritual Reading, N.Y.
OCT=Oxford Classical Texts, Oxford.
OTL=Old Testament Library, London.
PNT=Die Prediking van het Nieuwe Testament, Nijkerk.
PVTG=Pseudepigrapha Veteris Testamenti Graece, Leiden.
QD=Quaestiones Disputatae, Freiburg.
RAC=Reallexicon für Antike und Christentum, Stuttgart.
RB=Revue Biblique, Paris.
RecB=Recherches Bibliques, Louvain.
REG=Revue des Etudes Grecques, Paris.
RGG=Die Religion in Geschichte und Gegenwart, Tübingen.

RHR=Revue de l'Histoire des Religions, Paris.
SANT=Studien zum Alten und Neuen Testament.
SB=Stuttgarter Bibelstudien, Stuttgart.
SBL=Society of Biblical Literature, Diss. Series, Missoula.
SBM=Stuttgarter Biblische Monographien, Stuttgart.
SC=Sources Chrétiennes, Paris.
ScJT=Scottish Journal of Theology, Edinburgh.
SE=Studia Evangelica, Berlin.
SEÅ=Svensk Exegetisk Årsbok, Lund.
SH=Scripta Hierosolymitana, Jerusalem.
SNT=Studien zum NT, Gütersloh.
STK=Svensk Teologisk Kvartalskrift, Lund.
SUNT=Studien zur Umwelt des Neuen Testaments, Göttingen.
TB=Theologische Blätter, Leipzig, Bonn.
TBC=Torch Bible Commentaries, London.
TC=Theological Collections, London.
TDNT=Theological Dictionary of the New Testament, Grand Rapids.
TL=Theologische Literaturzeitung, Halle, Berlin.
TNTC=Tyndale New Testament Commentaries, London.
TS=Theological Studies, Baltimore.
TSK=Theologische Studien und Kritiken, Hamburg, Gotha, Leipzig, Berlin.
TT=Theology Today, Princeton.
TTs=Teologisk Tidsskrift, København.
TU=Texte und Untersuchungen, Berlin.
TZ=Theologische Zeitschrift, Basel.
UNT=Untersuchungen zum Neuen Testament, Leipzig.
USR=Union Seminary Review.
VF=Verkündigung und Forschung, München.
VT=Vetus Testamentum, Leiden.
WD=Wort und Dienst (Jahrbuch der Theologischen Schule, Bethel), bei Bielefeld.
WMANT=Wissenschaftliche Monographien zum Alten und Neuen Testament, Neu-
    kirchen.
WSB=Wuppertaler Studiebibel, Wuppertal.
ZNW=Zeitschrift für die neutestamentliche Wissenschaft und die Kunde der älteren
    Kirche, Giessen, Berlin.
ZKT=Zeitschrift für Katholische Theologie, Innsbruck.

CHAPTER I

ΜΥΣΤΗΡΙΟΝ: THE SCOPE OF ITS MEANING AND APPLICATION

1. THE PROBLEM

The term μυστήριον occurs 28× in the NT.[1] In class. and post-class. Greek literature the pl. is usually a designation of certain secret cults, known as Mystery Religions. The word is customarily derived from μύω = *to close the eyes* (or even the mouth).[2] The closing of the mouth is understood of the silence which the μύστης was enjoined, and this in turn is thought to give the characteristic colouring of the rites and the definitive meaning of μυστήριον, i.e. secrecy. NT scholars thus generally take it as a designation of God's secret (plan) which in OT times was kept *secret/hidden* but which in the NT has been revealed.[3] Moreover, many scholars state unequivocally that our term expresses solely the idea of that which is *secret* and has no reference whatsoever to the idea of the *mysterious* or *incomprehensible*.[4]

---

[1] I.e. including I Cor 2:1 with P⁴⁶ *vid.* ℵ* A C etc., *GNT, WH* as against the reading μαρτύριον in ℵᶜ B D G P Ψ 33 etc., *ΚΔ*, Nest. Cf. Metzger, *TC*, *ad loc.*, and see *infra* I, 5, note *ad loc.* Hartman, *SEÅ*, 1974, 112 says, "Possibly, the general theme of God's hidden wisdom from 1:18 and onwards could be taken as a reason for choosing 'mystery'."

[2] Robinson, 234 points out that "μύσας means 'with the eyes shut'; and though the word is sometimes used by transference also of the shutting of the mouth, it is always necessary that the word 'mouth' should be expressly added in order to give this meaning".

[3] E.g. Alford, 138 (cf. also vol. II, 434); Robinson, 30 f., 39, 76, 234—40; Salmond, 258, 303; Robertson, *PI*, 67; Moule, *CPh*, 81 f. (though he concedes the sense of 'secret' or 'mysterious' for I Cor 15:51; Rev 1:20; 17:5, 7); Mackay, *GO*, 81 ff.; Geldenhuys, *Lk*, 246; Murray, *Rm*, II, 91 ff.; Grosheide, *1C*, 64; Morris, *1—2Th*, 228; Bruce, *Col*, 218; Ladd, *JK*, 220; Anderson-Scott, *CAP*, 127; Chafer, *ELDC*, 97 ff.; Bruce, *Rm*, 283; Taylor, *Mk*, 255; Hodge, 45 f.; Mitton, *EE*, 86 ff. (though he sometimes conflates the senses of 'secret' and 'perplexity'); Barrett, *Rm*, 222 f.; Kelly, *Past*, 82 f.; Dodd, *Rm*, 182, 244; Scott, *Col*, 32 f.; Caird, *Rev*, 128; Barrett, *1C*, 315, 380.

Many Germans translate μυστήριον with 'Geheimnis' but make no further qualifying comments on the term as such: e.g. Dibelius, *Kol-Eph-Ph*; Lohmeyer, *Kol-Ph*; Althaus, *Rm*; Wendland, *1—2K* (has 'geheimnisvoll'); Conzelmann, *Eph*; Oepke, *1—2Th*; Conzelmann, *Kol*; Schlier, 60; Gnilka, 76 ff.; Gaugler, 46.

[4] The originator, or at least the authority on which English scholarship has based its definition of μυστήριον in the NT, seems to be Bishop Lightfoot, who in his comm.

The rendering of μυστήριον with the Eng. *secret* or Ger. *Geheimnis* (for which there were other Gk. terms available, e.g. κρυπτόν, κρύφιον, ἀπόκρυφον) does injustice to the scope of the meaning of our term.[5]

The close occurrence of μυστήριον with words like ἀποκεκρυμμένον (Eph 3: 9; Col 1: 26) renders the sense of *secret* very unlikely since it is pointless to speak of a *hidden secret (plan)*. The noun *secret* cannot be qualified by the adj. *hidden*. Consequently, it is also inappropriate to speak of a *revealed secret,* since the *secret* is dissolved in the process of revelation. And yet the NT speaks of a hidden and of a revealed μυστήριον,

The task of this ch. will be to examine the use of our term from hoary antiquity to post-NT times and cover the main provinces of its application — Mystery Religions, Philosophy, Secular use, Magic, Gnosticism, LXX, Pseudepigrapha and Early Christian writers — in order to ascertain its basic meaning, the shifts of meaning it underwent and the connotations it bore in a given context.

The earliest references of μυστήριον are concerned with the Mystery Religions, and in particular, the Eleusinian Mysteries which were among the oldest in Greece [6] and certainly the most renowned. Hence, I shall concentrate on these since they can adequately account for the shaping of the meaning and the associations of our term.

---

on *Col* and on *Phlm*, 168 expresses himself on the subject thus: "The idea of *secrecy* or *reserve* disappears when μυστήριον is adopted into the Christian vocabulary by St. Paul and the word signifies simply 'a truth which was once hidden but now is revealed', a truth which without special revelation would have been unknown. Of the nature of the truth itself the word says nothing. It may be transcendental, incomprehensible, mystical, mysterious, in the modern sense of the term (I Cor 15: 51; Eph 5: 32); but this idea is quite *accidental* (ital. mine) and must be gathered from the special circumstances of the case, for it cannot be inferred from the word itself." Abbott, who has helped standardize this view of our term, in his comm. largely follows the Bishop of Durham: "We must be on our guard" he says on p. 15, "against importing into this word (as is done by some expositors) the meaning of the Eng. 'mystery', as in Shakespeare's 'Mysteries which heaven will not have earth to know'. It signifies simply 'a truth once hidden but now revealed'. The truth may be 'mysterious', in the modern sense, but that is not implied by the word (so Lightfoot also, who, however, refers to I Cor 15: 51 and Eph 5: 32 as instances of this accidental idea; but see *post*)". Abbott warmly defends the sense of *secret* in Gk., Lat., and NT usage, overlooking all evidence to the contrary, such as has been here amassed. He even proceeds to correct Lightfoot's minimal concession of 'mysterious' for Eph 5: 32: "It does not mean a 'mysterious thing or saying' . . . 'hiddeness' is the whole of its meaning" (174).

[5] Many European langs. lacking a native term to express the idea of the *mysterious* have borrowed and adapted the Gk. term. This circumstance is in itself a pointer against the equation of μυστήριον with 'secret', for example.

[6] Cf. Plut., *Frg.* 24 (=Hipp., *Phil.* 5, 20) πρὸ γὰρ τῶν Ἐλευσινίων μυστηρίων ἔστιν ἐν τῇ Φλιοῦντι τῆς λεγομένης Μεγάλης ὄργια.

2. THE ELEUSINIAN MYSTERIES

A. The Age

Noack's [7] hypothesis, followed by many, that the worship of Demeter was originally practised before an altar,[8] and that the first Temple to Demeter (distinct from the later *Telesteria*) was built in the VIII B.C. has been proved wrong by the more recent excavations of Kourouniotes,[9] Travlos,[10] and Mylonas.[11] Though Eleusis was actually inhabited in the Middle Bronze Age or Middle Helladic period (c. 1950—1600 B.C.),[12] there is no evidence of any Mystery cult [13] until the late Helladic II and III 1500—1110 B.C.) to which period are assigned the remains of the earliest Temple (a structure of about 10.20×7.10 m., external measurements) discovered by Kourouniotes [14] in 1931—32. These dates form precisely the limits of the period to which tradition assigns the establishment of Demeter's cult in Eleusis. Both Apollodorus and the *Parian Chronicle* lead to the conclusion that Demeter came to Eleusis sometime in the second half of the XVth cent. B.C.[15]

Despite the possibility that the Mysteries were practised in Mycenaean times, apart from one short inscription in *Linear B* on an amphora found under the Lesser Propylaea,[16] no texts in that script have been unearthed in Eleusis. Among the tablets in *Linear B* from Knossos, Pylos and Mycenae, neither the name *Demeter* nor the word μυστήριον have been attested beyond doubt.[17] The disappointing conclusion of Mylonas is that "No

---

[7] Noack, *EBEH*. His conclusions were based on Philios' work.

[8] Followed by Kern, *RG*, II, 192 "Die Dromena, die zuerst im Freien stattfanden", though Deubner, *WEM*, 17 states "Dass die δρώμενα einstmals im Freien vor sich gingen . . . ist eine sehr zweifelhafte Vermutung".

[9] Kourouniotes, *ArchRW*, 1935, 52—78; Αρχ Δ, 1930—5 (Parartema); *El*, I, 1932; Αρχ Δ, 1933—5.

[10] Travlos, *Hesp*, 1949; Εφ Αρχ, 1951.

[11] Mylonas, ΠΕ; *HDSE*; *EEM*.

[12] Mylonas, *AJA*, 1932; *AJA*, 1936, 415—31; *IEE*, I, 127; Kourouniotes—Mylonas, *AJA*, 1933, 271—86.

[13] See *IEE*, I, 100 and 103 for a photograph of a ritual *kernos* with ten cups — a vessel characteristic of the Eleusinian Mysteries — belonging to the Proto-Cycladic culture of Philakopi Polis I (2200—2000 B.C.) and cf. Mylonas, *EEM*, 17.

[14] Kourouniotes, *ArchRW*, 1935, 52—78.

[15] See Mylonas, *EEM*, 14, 33.

[16] Found by Kourouniotes and Threpsiades, and first published and interpreted by Mylonas in *AJA*, 1936, 415—31, and Εφ Αρχ, 1936, 61—100, as παῖς-κόρη, which interpretation, however, is invalidated by the values given to the script by Ventris.

[17] Ventris and Chadwick, *JHS*, 1953, 97 at first suggested that *da-ma-te DA 40* could mean *Demeter*, but later in *DMG*, 241 f. withdrew it and said that Webster, *BICS*, 1954, 13 and Furumark, *Eran*, 1954, 39 ff. accepted the meaning of *Damater* (Corn-

artistic or epigraphical evidence has come to light which could be associated definitely with our Goddesses . . . Only the remains at Eleusis and the Gk. tradition prove the existence of the cult in that remote age and on our site".[18]

B. The Provenance

The provenance of the Mysteries has been a matter of debate. Herodotus had equated Demeter with Isis and derived the Mysteries from Egypt.[19] Foucart[20] maintained, mainly on the basis of the similarities between the eleusinian myth and the myth of Isis and Osiris,[21] an Egyptian origin, very popular for a time, till the falacy of his thesis was exposed by Picard[22] who showed the lack of contact between the two places.[23] Picard himself advanced a Kretan origin[24] in which he had been preceded by Persson's theory of a Minoan derivation.[25] Kern considered the Mysteries pre-hellenic, connected not with Egypt but with the Orphic and Samothrasian ones and patterned on Kretan prototypes themselves derived from Asia Minor.[26] Mylonas shows that all these theories of origin are based on outdated reports of excavation, which have in very large measure been invalidated by the latest diggings.[27] "Thus far", he concludes,[28] "while we

land). Webster, *Lat*, 1957, 531—6 says it is "still permissible to find Demeter in the thirteenth cent. Pylos and to suppose that an abbreviation of her name signified an ammount of land under corn". In his *MH*, Webster is certain that "Demeter was worshipped in Pylos in the thirteenth cent." (43 f.) and that "the King was 'initiated' there" (124 ff.).On the other hand, Mylonas as late as 1970 (*IEE*, I, 298) as well as in a private conversation with the present author, in Mycenae in Aug. 1973, stated that no Mycenaean evidence has yet come to light relating to Demeter. Cf. also Chadwick, *DLB*, 125 f.

With regard to μυστήριον Palmer, *IMGT*, 260 and 435 equates the *Linear B* word *te-ri-ja* (which he reads as *mu-te-ri-ja*) with μυστήριον and says it is the name of a festival. In the same conversation Mylonas rejected Palmer's emendation.

[18] Mylonas, *EEM*, 53.

[19] Hdt. II, 59, 156, 171. See also II, 122 f.

[20] Foucart, *ME*, 20—40.

[21] Plut., *Is-Os*.

[22] Picard, *REG*, 1927, 321—30.

[23] Cf. Zijderveld, Tε, 21 "Waarschijnlijk echter kent de Aeg. godsdienst geen mysteriën in den zin dien de Grieken daaran hechten". Besides, a word equivalent with μυστήριον is unknown in Egyptian (Zijderveld, Tε, 101).

[24] Picard, *RP*.

[25] Persson, *ArchRW*, 1922, 287—309. Nilsson, *MMR*, 279 ff., 506, 558 f.; *ArchRW*, 1935, 109 f. supposes Cretan influence. Deubner, *AF*, 71 autochthonous origin.

[26] Kern, *RG*, I, 135, 143 f.; II, 185.

[27] Mylonas, *EEM*, 16—9. So also Kourouniotes, *ArchRW*, 1935, 54: "Aber das schöne Bild, das uns da (sc. in Noack) gegeben wird, muss nach den Resultaten unserer letzten Ausgrabungen modifiziert werden".

[28] *EEM*, 20.

can prove from which sections of the Mediterranean world the cult did not come, we cannot prove decisively where it did originate . . . It is obvious that we favour a North Greek origin".[29]

The results of the foregoing discussion seem to indicate that the Eleusinian Mysteries were probably instituted after the middle of the second millenium B.C. and that they were very probably of Gk. origin. Consequently, they form the most important basis for the investigation of the meaning of our word. The presumption is also made that μυστήριον is an indiginous Gk. word.

C. A Comparative Study of Ὄργια, Τελετή and Μυστήρια

Strangely enough, neither Homer nor Hesiod mention the Mysteries.[30] However, the aetiological myth of the institution of the rites, which is at the same time their earliest literary evidence, is contained in the so-called Homeric *Hymn to Demeter*, which is dated nowadays in the late VII B.C. Significantly, the word μυστήριον is not contained in this work,[31] the rite being designated by the word ὄργια. Like μυστήριον, ὄργια occurs neither in Homer nor in Hesiod. Besides ὄργια and μυστήρια the word τελετή is also applied to the Mysteries.

i. Ὄργια. Τελετή and Μυστήρια as Designations of the Mysteries throughout Antiquity

The three terms are used throughout antiquity as designations of various mystery rites [32] and of the Eleusinian Mysteries in particular.[33] They are

---

[29] "Der Name Eleusis . . ." says Kerenyi, *ME*, 36, "bezieht sich im günstigen Sinne auf die Unterwelt, ist mit 'Ort der Ankunft' zu übersetzen und als die glückliche Ankunft zu verstehen: grammatisch wird es durch Akzent und Flexion von éleusis, 'Ankunft' unterschieden, doch er gehört ebenso wie dieser mit *Elysion*, der bezeichnung der Gefilder der Seligen, nach der Regel des griechischen Ablautes zusammen." Nilsson, *MMR*, 520 ff. maintains that Eleusis is a pre-Hellenic name.

[30] This 'strangeness' is considerably diminished when we consider that the Mysteries were, in the archaic age, but a humble agrarian cult, despised by the aristocracy of Athens and that their popularity saw its first blooming in late VI B.C. when Pisistratus built a *Telesterion* on a hitherto unprecedented scale (See Mylonas, *EEM*, 78 ff.). Hesiod is, of course, acquainted with the abduction of Persephone by Plouton (cf. *Th.* 912 ff) and Homer is aware that Persephone rules at the side of *Hades* in the underworld (*Il.* and *Od. passim*).

[31] Its first occurrence is in Heracl., *Frg.* 14: τίσι δὴ μαντεύεται Ἡράκλειτος ὁ Ἐφέσιος; νυκτιπόλοις, μάγοις, βάκχοις, λήναις, μύσταις, τούτοις ἀπειλεῖ τὰ μετὰ θάνατον, τούτοις μαντεύεται τὸ πῦρ· τὰ γὰρ νομιζόμενα κατὰ ἀνθρώπους μυστήρια ἀνιερωστὶ μυοῦνται.

[32] E.g. Ὄργια: Aes., *Sep. Th.* 179; Soph., *Tr.* 765; Hdt. II, 51; V, 61; Apoll. Rh.,

all often used by the same author[34] and occasionally in the same passage.[35] The significance of these facts is that it is not possible to consider one term as replacing another wholly synonymous word[36] and that their collateral use indicates that the terms, though referring to the same rite, most likely describe different aspects of it.[37]

ii. Ὄργια

The word ὄργιον is etymologically related to words like ἔρδω, ῥέζω, ἔργον, ἐργάζομαι, ὄργανον, a group of words whose basic significance is that of *act, performance, work*. Accordingly, in complete confirmity to its etymology, ὄργια is used in close conjunction with ἔρδω in its very first occurrence in Gk. lit.[38] and at that, in the most fundamental passage of the institution of the Eleusinian Mysteries: ὄργια δ᾽ αὐτὴ ἐγὼν ὑποθήσομαι, ὡς ἂν ἔπειτα εὐαγέως ἔρδοντες ἐμὸν νόον ἱλάσκοισθε (*Hymn*, 273 ff.). The ptc. of ἔρδω defines the meaning of ὄργια as certain ritual acts or performances.

The only other occurrence of ὄργια in the *Hymn* is more difficult: δεῖξεν · · · δρησμοσύνην θ᾽ ἱερῶν καὶ ἐπέφραδεν ὄργια πᾶσι . . . σεμνά, τά τ᾽ οὔπως ἔστι παρεξίμεν οὔτε πυθέσθαι οὔτ᾽ ἀχέειν· μέγα γάρ τι θεῶν σέβας ἰσχάνει αὐδήν (*Hymn*, 474—9). The word δρησμοσύνη=δρηστοσύνη, of the same root as δράω, bears the sense of *act, performance*, but is here more immediately connected with ἱερά rather than ὄργια. The use of ἐπέφραδεν need not imply that ὄργια were some sort of teachings; the goddess first showed the sacred ritual as a whole (δρησμοσύνην θ᾽ἱερῶν — possibly with accompanying gestures) and then explained in detail the various acts (ἐπέφραδεν ὄργια) that would constitute her Mysteries. The last two lines of the quota-

---

Argon. I. 920; Theocr., *Id.* 26, 13; Plut., *Frg.* 24, 212; Luc., *Salt.* 15; Τελετή: Eur., *Bac.* 20 f.; Aristl., *Rh.* 2, 24, 2; Pl., *Euthd.* 277 d; Apolld. *Bib* II, 2, 2; Plut., *Mor.* 360 F; Paus. I, 2, 5; Luc., *Pseud.* 5; Μυστήρια: Aes., *Frg.* 479; Hdt. II, 51; Apolld., *Bib.* I, 3, 2; Plut., *Mor.* 417 A; Paus. IX, 30, 4 f.

[33] E.g. Ὄργια: *Hymn*, 273; Ar., *Ra.* 386; Plut., *Frg.* 212; Clem. Al., *Protr.* 2; Τελετή: Ar., *Pax*, 413—20; Plut., *Mor.* 360 F; Paus. I, 37, 4; 38, 3; Clem. Al., *Protr.* 2; Μυστήρια: Heracl., *Frg.* 14; Aes., *Frg.* 479; Eur., *Supp.* 173; Apolld., *Bib.* II, 5, 12; Plut., *Mor.* 21; Luc., *Herm.* 4.

[34] E.g. Soph., *Tr.* 765; *Frg.* 943; Ar., *Th.* 948; *Pl.* 1013; Apolld., *Bib.* III, 5, 1; II, 5, 12; Paus. IX, 25, 5—9; 30, 4—5 (cf. Plut., *Vit.* 711—2).

[35] E.g. Plut., *Mor.* 417 A; 422 C; *Frg.* 24; Luc., *Salt.* 15; *Demon.* 11; Hipp., *Phil.* V, 7; Cl. Al., *Protr.* 2.

[36] Hence I cannot accept V. d. Burg's conclusion (in AΔO, 103) that ὄργια "zich niet kunnen handhaven tegenover μυστήρια en τελετή.

[37] Besides these three standard terms occur also ἱερά (*Hymn*, 481 f.; Hdt. VIII, 65) and δρώμενα (Paus. V, 10, 1).

[38] But see V. d. Burg, AΔO, 94.

tion are of particular interest, but they shall be noted below in another connection.

The next instances in point of date are Aes., *Sep. Th.* 179 and Soph., *Tr.* 765; *Ant.* 1013. In Hdt. II, 51 we read: ὅστις δὲ τὰ Καβείρων ὄργια μεμύηται, τὰ Σαμοθρήικες ἐπιτελέουσι . . . οὗτος ὡνὴρ οἶδε τὸ λέγω. In view of the vb. ἐπιτελεῖν, ὄργια must be given its regular sense of *performances*. In Ar., *Ra.* 356 the ὄργια of the Muses are certain dance-performances: ἢ γενναίων ὄργια Μουσῶν μήτ᾽ εἶδεν μήτ᾽ ἐχόρευσεν. Similarly further on ὄργια is met as a title of Demeter in the context of dance and play: Δήμητερ ἁγνῶν ὀργίων ἄνασσα . . . σῷζε τὸν σαυτῆς χορόν . . . παῖσαί τε καὶ χορεῦσαι (*Ra.* 386 ff.). In another quotation from Aristophanes games forms part of the ὄργια: ἄγε νῦν ἡμεῖς παίσωμεν ἅπερ νόμος ἐνθάδε ταῖσι γυναιξίν, ὅταν ὄργια σεμνὰ θεοῖν ἱεραῖς ὥραις ἀνέχωμεν (*Th.* 947 f.).

Euripides uses ὄργια of Dionysus' rites: τοιγάρ νιν αὐτὰς ἐκ δόμων ᾤστρησ᾽ ἐγὼ μανίαις, ὄρος δ᾽ οἰκοῦσι παράκοποι φρενῶν· σκευήν τ᾽ ἔχειν ἠνάγκασ᾽ ὀργίων ἐμῶν.[39] In a context like this involving the wild gesticulations of the μαινάδες in the Bacchic orgies the word ὄργια reaches its most coloured usage — a usage which contributed, together with the ὄργια Ἀφροδίτης, to the negative ring which the word gradually came to carry, that of *acts of profligacy or debauchery*.[40]

iii. Τελετή

The earliest occurrences of τελετή [41] seem to be found in Pin., *Ol.* III, 41: ὅτι πλείσταισι βροτῶν ξεινίαις αὐτοὺς ἐποίχονται τραπέζαις, εὐσεβεῖ γνώμᾳ φυλάσσοντες μακάρων τελετάς — of the *Theoxenia* held at Agrigentum in honour of the Dioscuri. Again: πλεῖστα νικάσαντά σε καὶ τελεταῖς ὡρίαις ἐν Παλλάδος εἶδον — referring to the *Panathenaean* festival at Athens. In Hdt. II, 171 we read: καὶ τῆς Δήμητρος τελετῆς πέρι, τὴν οἱ Ἕλληνες θεσμοφόρια καλέουσι. Neither the *Theoxenia*, nor the *Panathenaea*, nor the *Thesmophoria* were strictly speaking Mysteries. Hence, in these instances τελετή is used in the sense of celebration or ceremony.[42] Of a Scythian king-initiate we read: μέλοντι δὲ οἱ ἐς χεῖρας ἄγεσθαι τὴν τελετὴν ἐγένετο φάσμα μέγιστον (i.e. his house caught fire) . . . Σκύλης δὲ οὐδὲν τούτου εἵνεκα ἧσσον ἐπετέλεσε τὴν τελετήν (Hdt. IV, 79). His reverence was such that even the burning down of his palace could not hinder him from completing the performance of the ritual.

---

[39] Eur., *Bac.* 32 ff. Cf. also *ibid.* 78 ff.: τά τε ματρὸς μεγάλας ὄργια Κυβέλας θεμιτεύων, ἀνὰ θύρσον τε τινάσσων, κισσῷ τε στεφανωθεὶς Διόνυσον θεραπεύει,

[40] For more material on ὄργια see V. d. Burg, ΑΔΟ,, 91—124.

[41] The Ps-Homeric *Batr.* 303: καὶ πολέμου τελετὴ μονοημέρου ἐξετελέσθη,

[42] So Zijderveld, Τε, 9.

8

In *Bac.* 20 f. Euripides calls Dionysus' rites τελεταί: ἐς τήνδε πρῶτον ἦλθον Ἑλλήνων πόλιν, τἀκεῖ χορεύσας καὶ καταστήσας ἐμὰς τελετάς, ἵν' εἴην ἐμφανὴς δαίμων βροτοῖς — the sense being simply that of celebration. Likewise, in *Bac.* 72 ff. we have: ὦ μάκαρ, ὅστις εὐδαίμων τελετὰς θεῶν εἰδὼς βιοτὰν ἁγιστεύει καὶ θιασεύεται ψυχὰν ἐν ὄρεσσι βακχεύων ὁσίοις καθαρμοῖσιν — of divine celebrations or ceremonies in general and of Dionysus' own in particular.

In Ar., *Pax* 411—20 the sun and the moon plot to destroy the Athenians who do not honour them in order to give their celebrations or sacred ceremonies to the barbarians who do so: διὰ τοῦτ' εἰκότως βούλοιντ' ἂν ἡμᾶς πάντας ἐξολωλέναι, ἵνα τὰς τελετὰς λάβοιεν αὐτοὶ τῶν θεῶν . . . πρὸς ταῦτ' ὦ φίλ' Ἑρμῆ ξύλλαβε ἡμῖν προθύμως τήνδε καὶ ξυνέλκυσον, καί σοι τὰ μεγάλ' ἡμεῖς Παναθήναι' ἄξομεν πάσας τε τὰς ἄλλας τελετὰς τὰς τῶν θεῶν, μυστήρι' Ἑρμῆ, Διπόλει', Ἀδώνεια. In both places τελετή covers the whole pageant, ritual sacrifices, divine service which make up the ἑορτή of the deity. The Μυστήρια along with the Παναθήναια, Διπόλεια and Ἀδώνεια is one of the τελεταί.[43] In fact the Mysteries are ἡ τιμιωτάτη πασῶν τελετή (Aristl., *Rh.* II, 24, 2).

Ancient tradition credited Orpheus with the invention of divine ceremonies: Ὀρφεὺς μὲν γὰρ τελετάς θ' ἡμῖν κατέδειξε φόνων τ' ἀπέχεσθαι, Μουσαῖος δ' ἐξακέσεις τε νόσων καὶ χρησμούς, Ἡσίοδος δὲ γῆς ἐργασίας, καρπῶν ὥρας, ἀρότους.[44] Similarly, in Demosthenes: ὁ τὰς ἁγιωτάτας ἡμῖν τελετὰς καταδείξας Ὀρφεύς.[45] Both of these instances refer to celebrations and worship in general, though Euripides ascribes to Orpheus in particular the showing of the Mysteries to men: μυστηρίων τε τῶν ἀπορρήτων φανὰς ἔδειξεν Ὀρφεύς.[46]

Of the two terms τελετή is the wider one covering the Mysteries as well as other celebrations, while ὄργια is normally confined to the Mysteries. Etymologically τελετή is linked with τελέω, *to perform, to complete, to make perfect* (cf. τέλειος).[47] The initiate who had completed his initiation was called τετελεσμένος (*rited, perfected*), while the Initiation Hall, the locus of both the *Anaktoron* of the Deity (i.e. the holy of holies with the *Hiera*) and the Hierophant's throne, was called τελεστήριον. It was the

---

[43] Cf. Zijderveld, Τε, 15 f. for a similar understanding of τελετή: "Deze plaats is dus een voorbeeld hoe τελετή dient om religieuze plechtigheden van verschillend karakter".

[44] Ar., *Ra.* 1032 ff. See also *ibid.* 368 of Dionysus' τελεταί,

[45] Dem. 772. Popular etym. derived θρησκεία from Θρᾶξ, the national denomination of Orpheus, its founder, Cf. *OF*, 37; *Et. Mag.* 455, 10; Greg. N., *Or.* 39 (in *MPG*, 36, 340); *Sui.* s.v.

[46] Eur., *Rh.* 942. Also *OF*, 37.

[47] Zijderveld, Τε. 37 states "De oorspronkelijke *algemeene beteekenis: uitvoering, voltrekking,* zonder sacrale bijbeteekenis, schijnt aleen beward te zijn Batr. 305" (=303), and cf. 6 f. Cf. further Harrison, *CR*, 1914, 36—8.

sanctuary in which the ceremony took place. The term τελετή accordingly views the rites as a procedure in which the worshippers offer their worship and sacrifices to the deity. The ritual is considered as a whole and in its religious significance. The term denotes the totality of the sacred ceremony performed in honour of a divinity. Therefore, it can be applied to any festival or celebration, secret or otherwise (so Plut., *Frg.* 212). Ὄργια, on the other hand, considers the rite as the aggregate of various acts or events performed by the participants (cf. e.g. the Dionysiac orgies in which the Mainads' active part comes to the fore), with the emphasis placed more on the aspect of things performed rather than on the religious significance of the rite as a whole.[48]

Now if ὄργια and τελετή each describe the Mysteries from one particular point of view, it is not unreasonable to suppose that the term μυστήριον also, may describe a third aspect of the Mysteries.

iv. Μυστήρια

With regard to the etymology of μυστήριον we lack the felicity we enjoy in the case of ὄργια and τελετή· Here, suddenly all becomes dark and impenetrable. The mass of explanations that has reached us is almost mere guesswork.[49]

Therefore, the only knowledge we may hope to attain is of the kind

---

[48] Cf. Kern, *RG*, II, 187: "Das Word ὄργια . . . kommt von einem Stam, der 'tun' bedeutet . . . Neben ὄργια sind Telete (τελετή, τελεταί) und Mysterien (μυστήριον, μυστήρια) (Bd. I, 136) die griechischen Bezeichnungen für Weihen: oft werden sie völlig synonym gebraucht, wenn auch τελετή zunächst nur die Vollendung einer Hand-lung bedeutet! Sie wird aber schon sehr früh und zwar meist im Plural auf eine gottes-dienstliche Handlung bezogen . . . der Begriff Telete (ist) von Mysterien oft völlig fernzuhalten", and adds in a n. "Vgl. Kühner—Blass, Ausf. Gramm., I, 2, 425. Ὄργια bedeutet also ursprünglich dasselbe wie δρώμενα".

[49] Thus, the Sch. of Ar., *Ra.* 456 writes: μυστήρια δὲ ἐκλήθη παρὰ τὸ τοὺς ἀκούοντας μυεῖν τὸ στόμα καὶ μηδενὶ ταῦτα ἐξηγεῖσθαι, μύειν δὲ ἐστὶ τὸ κλείειν τὸ στόμα. In similar fashion the Sch. of Soph., *OC*, 1051 (p. 445) says: ἐπεὶ ἄρρητα τὰ μυστήρια καὶ καθόπερ κλεισὶν ἡ γλῶσσα κατείληπται ὑπὲρ τοῦ μὴ ἐξενεγκεῖν.

The ancients themselves could only make guesses about the derivation of the word. Thus, some of them, acc. to Cl. Al., *Protr.* 2, derived it from the μύσος shown to Dionysus; others from a certain Μυοῦς of Attica; and others still from the late μυθήρια — a word created to explain the etym. of μυστήριον! (*Et. Mag.*, 595, 48). Ath. III, 98 d attributed to Diod. Sic, the jesting etym. τὰς τῶν μυῶν διεκδύσεις μυστήρια ἐκάλει ὅτι τοὺς μῦς τηρεῖ. All this, as Bornkamm, *TDNT*, IV, 803 remarks, "demon-strates the uncertainty" felt, though Frisk, *GEW*, II, s.v., undeterred by this confusion, accepts the traditional etym. from μύω. So also does Krämer, *WD*, 1959, 121—5. Nevertheless in view of this perplexity (see Kern, *RG*, I, 136) it is wiser to leave the question of the etym. open, and not work out the etym. of μυστήριον from the order to the initiates *to keep their mouth shut* with respect to the secret they had experienced.

that relates to the connotative meaning of the term. Now the connotative meaning of a term sometimes overshadows its denotative meaning and becomes the dominant meaning associated with it in the minds of people. I want to suggest that μυστήριον is a notable example of this, i.e. no matter which root it derives from, the term was from its earliest occurrences in lit. associated with the idea of the *unfathomable, impenetrable, incomprehensible.* Unfortunately, it is not possible to discover this or any other connotative meaning by examining the context of its various occurrences. The reason is that the term is a technical one as a designation of Mystery rites. So everyone who heard or read it knew exactly how to understand it. The context is accordingly of no help here. But pointers to such associations, it is deemed, can be discovered by considering certain terms occurring in close association with it (e.g. ἄρρητος), some historical circumstances of the cult, the contents of the rite, and the total impression it made on the initiates. These factors may be inconclusive if considered individually, but taken collectively yield a cumulative evidence that makes the meaning advocated here, to say the least, very probable.

a. The Meaning of Derivatives

In post-class. times we find the adj. μυστηριώδης [50] used in the sense of something *mysterious, incomprehensible:* τὴν δὲ μεγάλη καὶ μυστηριώδη καὶ ἄπιστον . . . ἀρχὴν τοῦ δόγματος ὀκνῶ μὲν ἔτι τῷ λόγῳ κινεῖν. [51] The *Sch.* of Lucian uses the noun μυστηριωδία [52] in a similar sense, while in Mod. Gk. the adv. μυστηριωδῶς means *mysteriously.* It is significant that in the subsequent development words formed from the stem μυστικ- generally refer to what is *secret,* [53] while words formed from the stem μυστηρ- generally have the sense of the *mysterious.* [54] It cannot be controverted that the adj. μυστηριώδης (mysterious) and the adv. μυστηριωδῶς (mysteriously) were developed out of the term μυστήριον because that term had latent the idea of the mysterious. At least it had such associations that rendered it the most suitable word from which to derive the words desired, for it is absurd to maintain that μυστήριον meant only *secret* and that suddenly Plutarch created the adj. μυστηριώδης from μυστήριον with the adj. carrying a different sense. [55]

---

[50] E.g. Plut., *Mor.* 10e; as equivalent to the Eng. *mysterious.*

[51] Plut., *Mor.* 996 b (great, incomprehensible, incredible).

[52] Sch. on Luc., *Lex.* 10: ἀρρητοποιοὺς διασύρων εἶπε τοὺς τελεστὰς διὰ τήν μυστηριωδίαν αὐτῶν. Cf. ΔΔ, s.v.

[53] E.g. μυστικόν, μυστικότης.

[54] E.g. μυστηριώδης, μυστηριώδια, μυστηριωδῶς.

[55] For a similar development in the case of ὀψώνιον, see Caragounis, *NovT,* 1974, 35—57.

b. Ἄρρητα and Ἀπόρρητα in relation to the Mysteries

It is worthy of note that the Lexicographer Hesychius (s.v.) defines μυστήρια as ἄρρητα καὶ ἀνεξήγητα and the Sch. of Sophocles says ἄρρητα τὰ μυστήρια.[56] The term ἄρρητος is distinguished from ἀπόρρητος in that while the latter denotes something whose utterance is prohibited, hence, something to be kept a secret, the former denotes that which cannot be uttered or described, ineffable, or, that which it is not proper to divulge because of its sacred or divine nature. For ἀπόρρητον the following may be cited: ἀπόρρητα ποιησάμενοι (Hdt. IX, 94), τ᾽ ἀπόρρητ᾽ ἔφη (Ar., Ec. 442), ἀπόρρητον φλόγα θύουσα (Eur., IT 1331). Ἀπόρρητον (in Philosophy) is evidenced in the sense of the indescribable: ἀλλ᾽ ἔστιν ἀδιανόητόν τε καὶ ἄρρητον καὶ ἄφθεγκτον καὶ ἄλογον (Pl., Soph. 238 c), and in its sacred character: ἄρρητα ἱρά (Hdt. VI, 135), ἄρρητοι ἱροεργίαι (Hdt. V, 83), πῶς δῆτα λέγω λόγον ἄρρητον (Soph., Aj. 214). Tiresias is described by Oedipus as one who can observe what may be taught and what may not be uttered, what is heavenly and what is earthly: διδακτά τε ἄρρητά τ᾽ οὐράνιά τε καὶ χθονοστιβῆ (Soph., OT 301). It is to be noted that the chiasmus relates διδακτά to χθονοστιβῆ and ἄρρητα to οὐράνια thus accentuating their ineffable nature. By the same token the Mysteries of Demeter and Kore are called ἄρρητα ἱερά (Xen., Hell. VI, 3, 6), Kore herself is the ἄρρητος κόρη,[57] and again it is said of Mother and Daughter ἄχραντα ἀρρήτων θέσμια (IG, III, 713) — the ἄχραντα θέσμια being their Mysteries. The μυστήρια are ἄρρητα because they are σεμνά; but they are σεμνά because they are the Mysteries of Demeter and Kore who are themselves σεμναί and ἁγναί, and as such too holy, too divine, too ineffable to be described by mortal lips, to be searched out by the νοῦς of man, or to be made the subject of human conversation.[58]

c. Some historical Considerations

According to ancient tradition[59] all non-Eleusinians were at first excluded from the Mysteries. In the days of Erechtheus the first war between Athens and Eleusis broke out which resulted in the subjection of the Eleusinians, who nevertheless, succeded in keeping the performance

---

[56] Sch. Soph., OC, 1051. Cf. infra I, 5 (under Hipp.).

[57] Eur., Frg. 63. Cf. also id., Hel. 1307: τὰς . . . ἀρρήτου κούρας.

[58] See infra I, 2, C, iv, c. The term ἀπόρρητος is also applied to the Mysteries, not synonymously with ἄρρητος, indeed, but in order to bring out the prohibition of their disclosure appropriate to their nature of ἄρρητα: μυστηρίων τε τῶν ἀπορρήτων φανὰς ἔδειξεν Ὀρφεύς (Eur., Rh. 943) and τὰ ἀπόρρητα τῆς κατὰ τὰ μυστήρια τελετῆς (SIG, 873, 9). See further V. d. Burg, ΑΔΟ, 5—51.

[59] Apolld., Bib. II, 5, 12.

of the Mysteries to themselves.[60] The Eleusinians who had evidently regained their independence during the unstable years which followed Erechtheus' death, were subdued afresh by the exploits of Theseus, but once again managed to keep the Mysteries in their hands.[61]

The connection of Athens with the Eleusinian cult becomes more probable at the time of the fifth Olympiad (760 B.C.) when following a general famine the Delphic Oracle directed the Athenians to sacrifice to Demeter on behalf of all Greeks — the festival being termed *Proerosia*.[62] By the time of Solon (c. 640—561) the connection is a fact for we hear of a law of Solon's with regard to the celebration of the Mysteries.[63] Gradually all Greeks were allowed to participate in them [64] while after the Roman conquest of Greece the Mysteries assumed universal character.[65]

The interesting point in this historical survey is the tenacity with which the Eleusinians clung to their Mysteries. Although bereft of their liberty, they were determined that nobody should find out the mysterious secret of their Goddesses! Almost to the very end of the long history of the cult, the Hierophants were chosen from the house of Eumolpos,[66] the original

---

[60] *Ibid.* III, 15, 4; Paus. I, 36, 4; 38, 3. It is not clear if this implies the debarment of the Athenians from the Mysteries or simply the reservation of the conduct of the Mysteries to the Eumolpids and the Kerykes. Apolld., *Bib.* III, 14, 7 stated that after the death of Erichthonius and during the reign of his son Pandion, Demeter and Dionysus came to Attica: ἀλλὰ Δήμητρα μὲν Κελεὸς (εἰς τὴν Ἐλευσῖνα) ὑπεδέξατο, Διόνυσον δὲ Ἰκάριος. However, the *Par. Chr.* (Jacoby, *MP*, 6 f.) relates that Demeter came to Athens in the reign of Erechtheus (i.e. 1409—8 B.C.).

[61] Mylonas, *EEM*, 29. See also 24—9 for a delineation of the struggles between Eleusis and Athens.

[62] Isocr., *Pan.* IV, 31; *Sui.* s. v. εἰρεσιώνη and προηροσία. Also *SIG*, 83.

[63] And., *Myst.* 111; also Oliver, *Hesp*, 1935, 21 ff., and Mylonas, *EEM*, 63 f. The celebration took place yearly, but every fourth year it was held with special splendour (cf. ΕφΑρχ, 1883, 123, and 1887, 36).

[64] I.e. by the second half of the VI B.C. Cf. Hdt. VIII, 65, and see Mylonas, *EEM*, 77 and 248. The violation by Demetrius Poliorketes (Plut., *Dem.* 24) did not consist in his desire as a Macedonian to be initiated, but in his demand to be initiated at once in both the Lesser Mysteries of Agrae and the Greater Mysteries of Eleusis, a demand which led the Athenians to change by decree the name of the current month temporarily into that of *Boedromion*, so that the initiation might take place.

[65] With the opening of the Mysteries to all Greeks and finally to Romans as well, certain safeguards became necessary in order to protect the purity of the rites Decharme, *EM*, II, 456). The πρόρρησις (Isocr., *Pan.* IV, 157; Sch. Ar., *Ra.* 369) was directed against murderers, wizards, and, after the destruction of Eleusis by the Persians in 480—79 B.C., against barbarians as well (see Kern, *RG*, II, 197, and Mylonas, EEM, 247 ff.). Apollonius Tyaneus was rejected because he was a wizard (Philst., *Vit. Ap.* IV, 18). Nero himself abstained from visiting Eleusis since a likely refusal to initiate him would have been mortifying (Suet., *Nero* c, 34, 4).

[66] The last Hierophant, at the close of the IV A. D., was a Thespian, a priest of Mithras, acc. to Eun., *Vit. Soph.* (Maximos), 52 ff.

practiser of the Mysteries,[67] and the secrets of their rites were confided orally to their successors. A situation like this might easily have given rise to the word μυστήριον as a term created or applied to express the intriguing character of the sealed rites, either by those to whom admittance was denied, or even by the Athenians themselves whose sense of awe was enhanced by the very privilege of participation extended to them. The *Hymn* assures us that the element of the divine or *numinous* permeated the rites of Demeter: σεμνά, τά τ᾽ οὔπως ἔστι παρεξίμεν οὔτε πυθέσθαι οὔτ᾽ ἀχέειν· μέγα γάρ τι θεῶν σέβας ἰσχάνει αὐδήν.[68] The adj. σεμνός which qualifies these rites is connected with σέβομαι and bears the sense of *reverent, dignified, august, awful*. Demeter herself is styled σεμνή[69] as well as ἁγνή,[70] both terms of personal qualities expressing otherwordliness, or unapproachability, which by transference are applied also to her rites.[71] The rest of our quotation describes the feeling of divine dread which hovers over the Mysteries and which in a mysterious way arrests every attempt to profane them by disclosing their divine substance to mortal men.

This evidence suggests that what struck those unsophisticated people was not merely the element of *secrecy*, but more especially the element of *mysterious secrecy*.[72] It is thus very possible that when this word was first applied to the awful Mysteries of the august Goddesses — possibly hitherto known as ὄργια and perhaps also τελετή — it was to express the idea of the mysterious, the intriguing which many felt to be a fitting description of the character of the cult.

We get an important, if otherwise faint, glimpse of the mysterious nature of the Eleusinian Mysteries when we try to reconstruct the procedure of the rites from the scattered hints in ancient authors. The fact that no connected account has reached us would seem to be an eloquent testimony to their mysterious character.[73] Here only a few of the more significant events can be touched upon.

---

[67] I.e. one of the original founders of the cult, see *Hymn*, 475.

[68] *Hymn*, 478 f. where, however, we have ὄργια not μυστήρια.

[69] *Hymn*, 486 (where she is also αἰδοῖα); so also, the terrible Erinyes in e.g. Soph., *Aj.* 837; *OC*, 90, 458.

[70] *Hymn*, 203, 439; cf. Ar., *Ra.* 386 f. So also Persephone, *Hymn*, 337; Paus. IV, 33, 4.

[71] E.g. Soph., *Frg.* 943: σεμνά τῆς σῆς παρθένου μυστήρια· Eur., *Hipp.* 25; *Supp.* 470 λύσαντα σεμνά στεμμάτων μυστήρια. Cf. also Hdn. VIII, 7, 4: σεμνόν μυστήριον.

[72] The concept of the mysterious or numinous occurs generally in all primitive societies.

[73] Some scholars hold that no secret has been handed down simply because there was no secret to transmit.

d. The Content of the Mysteries and its Import

The first prerequisite for participation was initiation into the Lesser Mysteries of Agrae.[74] Following that in an exclusive gathering on the 16th *Boedromion* in the *Eleusinion* Hall in Athens,[75] the *Hierokeryx*, in the presence of the Hierophant and the *Dadouchos*,[76] proclaimed the πρόρρησις which was directed against all undesirables.[77] The following day, called ἅλαδε μύσται, the candidates for initiation bathed ritually in the bay of Phalerum and washed each his sacrificial piglet, which was sacrificed probably on the same day. After the sacrifice on behalf of the city on the 17th and the arrival of Asclepius on the 18th *Boedromion*[78] the crowd of initiates started on their mystic procession to Eleusis on the Sacred Way.[79] Despite the week-long fast and the 22 klm. long road, the members of the *pompe* showed amazing physical endurance, high spirits and a mood of festivity. This was due to their being mystically strengthened by the presence of the *Hiera*, the divine personification of the processional joviality in *Iacchos* whose statue led the train,[80] and by their meditation upon the august Goddesses whose favours they would soon experience.

Several strange events transpired on the way, events which to the initates were full of mystic import. One of them was called *krokosis* and involved the tying of a ribbon of saffron colour on the right hand and the left leg of each initiate by the dwellers of a certain vicinity they passed (Paus., I, 38, 2).[81] Its meaning is not known; "perhaps it protected the initiates against evil spirits".[82] The magical and mystical import were present also in another happening, the *gephyrismoi* which occurred on the bridge of Kephisos, the rivulet east of Eleusis.[83] Men with heads covered took their heart's fill in throwing insults at the most prominent

---

[74] Iambl., *Protr.* 2: πρὸ τῶν μεγάλων μυστηρίων τά μικρὰ παραδοτέον. Also *IG*, I², 6: 93, 96,; 313, 144; II², 1672: 4. Cf. also Cl. Al., *Str.* IV, 3, 1; Sdh.: Ar., *Pl.* 845, 1013: καὶ ἔστι τὰ μικρὰ ὥσπερ προκάθαρσις καὶ προάγευσις τῶν μεγάλων.

[75] See Travlos, *PDAA*, 198 ff.

[76] On the Eleusinian functionaries see Clinton, *SOEM*.

[77] Isocr., *Pan.* IV, 157; Sch.: Ar., *Ra.* 369.

[78] The latter was observed since 421 B.C. when Asclepius' cult was established in Athens.

[79] See *SIG*, 885 for direction of procedure.

[80] Cf. the initiates' cry: Ἴαχχ', ὦ Ἴαχχε (Ar., *Ra.* 324 f.). Also Hdt. VIII, 65.

[81] *Anecd. Gr.* I, 273, 25. Deubner, *AF*, 77 thinks this rite took place at an earlier juncture at Athens to avoid delay on the road.

[82] Mylonas, *EEM*, 256; so Deubner, *AF*, 76 f.

[83] Str. IX, 400 places the event on the Athenian Kephisus, while Foucart, *ME*, 335 and Mylonas, *EEM*, 256 with Hesychius prefer the Eleusinian rivulet. Tzetzes (Sch.: Ar., *Pl.* 1013) said that the Athenian women, travelling to the Mysteries on carriages, railed at one another in imitation of the incident between Demeter and Iambe.

citizen-initiates.[84] Again, we ask, What was the purpose? Possibly, *apotropaic*, to protect from the jealousy of evil spirits through humility, says Mylonas. The day ended probably with the *kernophoria*, a dance performed by the women-initiates with the mystic *kernos* on their head after which the μύσται gave themselves up to night-long revel as depicted on the *Niinion* tablet.[85]

The initiation proper took place on the nights of the 20th—21st and 21st—22nd *Boedromion*. Then transpired the three aspects of the τελετή, the δρώμενα, the λεγόμενα and the δεικνύμενα. It is generally held that the δρώμενα [86] must have been a re-enactment of the Eleusinian myth: the abduction of Persephone,[87] the sorrow and search of Demeter, and the re-union of Mother and Daughter. Prof. Mylonas draws attention to the *Ploutonion*, the two caves north of the *Telesterion*, the larger of which contained in part the small Temple of Plouto, while the little one had a small elliptic opening at the side from the outside of which six steps led below to a pit. Tradition identified the caves with the portals of *Hades*.[88]

The μύσται who had shared Demeter's fast had come to identify themselves with the embittered Mother: their heart was rent as they observed her 'come' to Eleusis and sit on the mirthless stone (ἀγέλαστος πέτρα) disconsolate and dejected.[89] When the signal was given with torch in hand they would rush through the space between the sacred buildings, along corridors and up stairs within the holy precinct, in the pitch darkness of the night,[90] imagining themselves to be traversing the portals and corridors of Hades, as in a herculean attempt to find Persephone and bring her to her grieving Mother. This mimick search would surely prove

---

[84] Hesych. s.v. γεφυρίς, γεφυρισταί.

[85] Cf. Kourouniotes, ΑρχΕφ, 1937, 224. For a coloured photogr. see *IEE*, III: 2, 276.

[86] For a study of this term see V. d. Burg, ΑΔΟ, 52—90.

[87] Cf. Tert., *Ad. Nat.* 2, 7; Athenag. 32, 1: τὰ πάθη αὐτῶν (sc. τῶν θεῶν) δεικνύουσιν μυστήρια; Cl. Al., *Protr.* 2. Cf. Harrison, *PGR*, 567.

[88] E.g. *Orph. hymn. ad Pl.* (*OH*, 115).

[89] "Such a pageant", observes Mylonas, *EEM*, 261 f., "accompanied with music, singing, and measured steps, but with very few explanatory words and with no dialogue, could have been very impressive and condusive of those feelings of awe, sorrow, despair, and joy which could, as in a tragedy, bring about a *katharsis*." For the place of dance in the Mysteries, see Luc., *Salt.* 15.

[90] Cf. the words of Them. after Plut. preserved in a *frg.* in Stob., *Ecl.* 4: πλάναι καὶ περίδρομοι κοπώδεις καὶ διὰ σκότους τινὲς ὕποπτοι πορεῖαι καὶ ἀτέλεστοι, Cf. Plut., *Mor.* 360 F. Noack, *EBEH*, 237 says, "Die Vorstellung des παθεῖν, des τρόμος, des φρικῶδες, also irgenwelche quälende und erschütternde Eindrücke, denen die Mysten ausgesetzt waren, die sie in der Nacht erlebten und durch die sie innerlich beschwert wurden bis zur äussersten seelischen Spannung, erscheint so notwendig und ist von Aristoteles an bis zu den Kirchenvätern wiederholt ausgedrückt worden das sich entsprechende Vorgänge nicht einfach ausscheiden lassen".

fruitless, its only value being on the psychological plane [91] in intensifying in them the desire to find Kore, in hightening their expectations, though for the archaic mind mere participation in the sorrows of a god or goddess might have meant an inestimably great merit with the gods. And at the peak of their emotions Persephone would emerge, probably from the hole at the side of the small cave as from the underworld,[92] and with shouts of joy and exultation [93] be escorted by the elated μύσται to the *Telesterion* in the *Anaktoron* of which she would re-unite with her Mother.[94]

The mysterious element is seen in the λεγόμενα too. While on the one hand it was imperative that the initiate should understand Greek [95] to follow that the Hierophant said, yet on the other hand, Aristotle witnessed (*apud* Synesius) that τοὺς τετελεσμένους οὐ μαθεῖν τι δεῖν ἀλλὰ παθεῖν καὶ διατεθῆναι δηλονότι γινομένους ἐπιτηδείους.[96] Most probably the words of the Hierophant were not long discourses but short liturgical formulae (Mylonas).[97]

The nature of the δεικνύμενα (the ἱερά contained in the κίσται) which formed the climax of the rites, has caused much disputation among

---

[91] Cf. Farnell, *CGS*, III, 192 "Through their psychological results, through the abiding influences, that may be produced *on will and feeling* by a solemn, majestic and long-sustained ceremony."

[92] Cf. Al., *Protr.* 2: Δηὼ (sc. Demeter) δὲ καὶ Κόρη δρᾶμα ἤδη ἐγενέσθην μυστικόν, καὶ τὴν πλάνην καὶ τὴν ἁρπαγὴν καὶ τὸ πένθος αὐταῖν Ἐλευσὶς δᾳδουχεῖ.

[93] Cf. Nilsson, *ArchRW*, 1935, "ihr Rückkehr wird mit Freude und Jubel begrüsst".

[94] Many scholars (e.g. Foucart, Noack, Nilsson, Deubner, Wehrli) have assumed the existence of an *Hieros Gamos* in Eleusis, basing it on the formula in Procl., *Tim.* 293 c (=Hipp., *Phil.* V, 7, 34) ὕε, κύε as representing the cry of the initiates while the Hierophant and the Priestess of Demeter held their sacred marriage, as well as on the Hierophant's cultic cry, ἱερὸν ἔτεκε πότνια κοῦρον Βριμὼ Βριμόν (Hipp., *Phil.* V, 8), taken fron the Naasene Sermon, and hence not very dependable as a witness) variously interpreted of Ploutos (=wealth), or, of the initiate's new birth; as well as on a hint in Ast., *Hom.* X. Against this is to be set the information that the Hierophant had castrated himself (Hipp., *Phil.* V, 8), the condition that the μύσται abstained from sexual intercourse in the days of the rites, and the general nature of the Mysteries which were said to be ὄργια or μυστήρια ἀγνά and σεμνά. For further arguments against this hypothesis, see Mylonas, *EEM*, 270 ff., 311 ff., and on the testimony of the Fathers, see Mylonas, *AY*, 1959, *passim*.

[95] Therefore anyone who could not understand Gk. was not accepted for initiation. Sop., (*Rh. Gr. 8*) preserves the story, actually a dream, of a boy who had performed all the rites, but had failed to hear what the Hierophant said, and was considered, on that account, as uninitiated.

[96] Syn. Dion. 10; Cl. Al., *Str.* V, 11; Plut., *Mor.* 22.

[97] Foucart, *ME*, 423 suggests that the λεγόμενα consisted in teachings useful in the underworld, as we find in the Egyp. Book of the Dead. But this theory has been shown to be untenable archeologically.

modern scholars.[1] It is the one aspect of the rites about which we know absolutely nothing.[2] A ζόφος ἠερόεις hovers over it. The most sacred objects of the Eleusinian cult were tabu; no uninitiated person was to know of their nature.[3] Gods and men together watched day and night over their

---

[1] Speculation has taken wide dimensions with respect to the nature of the ἱερά. Dieterich, *ML*, 125 f. and *ME*, 110 f., on the basis of the *synthema* ἐνήστευσα, ἔπιον τὸν κυκεῶνα, ἔλαβον ἐκ κίστης, ἐργασάμενος ἀπεθέμην εἰς κάλαθον καὶ ἐκ καλάθου εἰς κίστην preserved in Cl. Al., *Protr.* 2, concluded that the ἱερά must have been a phalus with which the μύστης performed a symbolic act of union with the goddess, which issued into his rebirth as her child (*ME*, 55). Pringsheim, *GEK*, 59 objected that the phalus could not represent Demeter. Körte, *ArchRW*, 1915, followed by Noack, *EBEH*, 228 ff. and Kern, *RG*, II, 193, rejected Lobeck's emendation (*Agl.* 25) from ἐργασάμενος to ἐγγευσάμενος and suggested that what the μύστης took from the cist was a female pudenda which he slid up and down his body, while Kern, *GMKZ*, 10 added that he even held a sham sexual intercourse with it. Many reacted against this hypothesis. See Wehrli, *ArchRW*, 1934, 81 ff. Deubner, *AF*, 81 ff. has given the essential arguments against it. Picard, *RHR*, 1927, 237 ff. combined Dieterich's and Körte's hypotheses claiming that the cist contained a phalus while the κάλαθος a κτείς with which the μύστης through manipulation, had a mystical union with Dionysus and Demeter. Deubner, *AF*, 82 maintains, however, that "Es kann also nicht zugegeben werden, dass der Ritus mit der κίστη notwendig ein Pudendum gewesen müsse", while Nilsson, *ArchRW*, 1935, 122 f. with Pringsheim thinks that the κάλαθος of Clement's *synthema* belonged to Demeter's rites in the Alexandrian Eleusis, which the venerable Father had confused with the Attic one. In a long appendix Mylonas, *EEM*, 287—316, shows quite conclusively that Clement's statement did not apply to our Mysteries, but to those near Alexandria, and that the nature of the ἱερά is still totally unknown to us. All manipulation theories, it would seem, are groundless, since the μύσται were not only men but also children and even women! Besides the two goddesses (as well as their Mysteries) were often characterized as ἀγναί and σεμναί.

[2] Soph., *OC*, 1051 ff.: χρυσέα κλῇς ἐπὶ γλώσσᾳ βέβακε προσπόλων Εὐμολπιδᾶν.

[3] Cf. Diod. Sic. II, 62, 8: οὐ θέμις τοῖς ἀμυήτοις ἱστορεῖν τὰ κατὰ μέρος; also V, 49, 5; Apoll. Rh., *Argon.* I, 920 (of Cabeiric Myst.). The γραφὴ ἀσεβείας was directed against all those who sacriligiously divulged or mimicked the Mysteries: Sop., (*Rh. Gr.* 117, 13): ἐὰν τις τὰ μυστήρια εἴπη τιμωρείσθω; Isocr., *De Big.* 347: εἰ τις εἰς τὰ μυστήρια φαίνοιτ' ἐξαμαρτάνων· Ps-Lys. VI, 51: λέγειν τῇ φωνῇ τὰ ἀπόρρητα. The grand expedition to Sicily (415—3 B.C.) came to an inglorious end when its most competent general, Alcibiades, was deprived of his command through the indictment that in a party with his friends he had profanely played the Hierophant when he shows the ἱερά: Lys. 14, 42; Thuc. VI, 28; Xen., *Hell.* I, 4, 14; Plut., *Alc.* 19—22; And., *Myst.* 11; Paus. I, 2, 5. See Παπαχατζῆ. ΠΕΠ, I, 157. Andocides himself (*Myst.* 10, 19 ff.) was another suspect; Aeschylus almost lost his life under the same accusation, Aristl., *EN*, III, 1, 17. A price was set on the head of Diagoras of Melus for making the Mysteries known, Ar., *Av.* 1073 f.; *Ra.* 320; Jos., *Ap.* II, 266, while Orpheus, the first teacher of the Mysteries, was bolted to death by Zeus, *OF*, 123: κεραυνωθῆναι δὲ αὐτὸν τῶν λόγων ἔνεκα ὧν ἐδίδασκεν ἐν τοῖς μυστηρίοις οὐ πρότερον ἀκηκοότας ἀνθρώπους. On the silence enjoined, see further Soph., *OC*, 1050 ff.; Aes., *Frg.* 302, 218; Ar., *Eq.* 282; Isocr., *De Big.* 6; Ael., *Frg.* 12; 58, 8; Liv. 31, 14; Hor., *Od.* III, 2, 25 ff.; Diog. Laert. II, 8, 101; Paus. I, 2, 5; 37, 4; 38, 7.

sanctity and vented their wrath in abundance on the violators.[4] The ὄργια or μυστήρια were truly σεμνά!

With the accomplishment of this part of the ceremony, the initiation was complete[5] and the μύστης was styled τετελεσμένος. The experience made a deep impression on him, and he returned home with feelings of dread and in a mood oriented to the chthonian realms whose rites he had witnessed.[6] The fear of death had been diminished and at least the hope, if not the belief, in after-life was deeply rooted in him. The result, according to Diodorus Siculus, was γίνεσθαι . . . εὐσεβεστέρους καὶ δικαιοτέρους καὶ κατὰ πᾶν βελτίονας ἑαυτῶν τοὺς τῶν μυστηρίων κοινωνήσαντας.[7] In this manner the Mysteries held their spell on the people.[8]

e. Some Reflections on the Meaning of the Ceremonies

Such a result could be achieved either by magical or mysterious actions, as the ancient world very well knew.[9] The staging of the rites in the night was no doubt part of the plan. Such nights, about which there is the

---

[4] Cf. *Hymn* 478 f.: σεμνά, τά τ᾽ οὔπως ἔστι παρεξίμεν οὔτε πυθέσθαι οὔτ᾽ ἀχέειν· μέγα γάρ τι θεῶν σέβας ἰσχάνει αὐδήν. See Liv. 33, 14; *Sui.* s.v. ἱεροφάντης, Ael., *Frg.* 58, 8.

[5] The ἐποπτεία, the highest degree of initiation, was apparently voluntary. Again, what objects were shown is a matter of debate. A number of scholars accept the information of Hipp., *Phil.* V, 8: Ἀθηναῖοι μυοῦντες Ἐλευσίνια καὶ ἐπιδεικνύντες τοῖς ἐποπτεύουσι τὸ μέγα καὶ θαυμαστὸν καὶ τελειότατον ἐποπτικὸν ἐκεῖ μυστήριον ἐν σιωπῇ, τεθερισμένον στάχυν. See Wehrli, *ArchRW*, 1934, 90. But this is improbable. The χλοερὸς στάχυς τεθερισμένος applied to Attis. Besides, most of these scholars also hold the manipulation theory with the in-built contradiction that while the manipulation of the ἱερά, if it existed, was a δρώμενον, the opening of the cist was a δεικνύμενον, revealing an arbitrary mixing together of the two different parts of the τελετή. Furthermore, after the supposed union of the μύστης with the Deity with all its emotional impact on the worshipper the showing of a mere στάχυς τεθερισμένος must have been a most extraordinary anticlimax.

[6] Cf. Deubner, *AF*, 78 f.

[7] Diod. Sic. V, 49; Also Ar., *Ra.* 457 ff.: ὅσοι μεμυήμεθ᾽ εὐσεβή τε διήγομεν τρόπον περὶ τοὺς ξένους καὶ τοὺς ἰδιώτας.

[8] Cf. Aes., *Frg.* 479 (in Ar., *Ra.* 887): εἶναί με τῶν σῶν ἄξιον μυστηρίων. the *Hymn* (480 ff.) spoke of the bliss of the initiates: ὄλβιος, ὅς τάδ᾽ ὄπωπεν ἐπιχθονίων ἀνθρώπων· ὅς δ᾽ ἀτελὴς ἱερῶν ὅς τ᾽ ἄμμορος, οὔποθ᾽ ὁμοίων αἶσαν ἔχει φθίμενός περ ὑπὸ ζόφῳ ἠερόεντι, and Pindar (*Frg.* 114) commemorated it on the grave of an Athenian initiate: ὄλβιος ὅστις ἰδὼν κεῖν᾽ εἶσ᾽ ὑπὸ χθόν· οἶδε μέν βίου τελευτὰν οἶδε δὲ διόσδοτον ἀρχάν. Similarly Soph., *Frg.* 753: ὡς τρὶς ὄλβιοι κεῖνοι βροτῶν, οἱ ταῦτα δερχθέντες τέλη μολώσ᾽ ἐς ¨Αιδου· τοῖσδε γὰρ μόνοις ἐκεῖ, ζῆν ἔστι, τοῖς δ᾽ ἄλλοισι πάντ᾽ ἐκεῖ κακά, cf. Plut., *Mor.* 21; Pl., *Res.* 363 c; Ar., *Ra.* 455 ff. The hierarchy of Eleusis assured mankind not only that their rites afforded the only way to salvation (Plut., *Mor.* 22; Diog. Laert. VI, 39) but also of the consequent punishment of the uninitiated (Pl., *Ap.* 41 a; *Phd.* 69 d; Paus. X, 31, 9).

[9] So Deubner, *AF*, 79.

greatest paucity in ancient authors, were called μυστηριώτιδες.[10] The aim of the δρώμενα most probably was to arouse the emotions of the participants and condition them for the other two aspects of the rites. The complext of buildings as revealed by archeology together with the two caves and the traditions attached to them, composed an ideal setting [11] for the mysterious ceremonies. They were all carefully calculated to produce the desired frame of mind [12] into which certain ritual formulae were poured which no-one could really understand.[13]

But it actually mattered little to the initiate that he could not comprehend exactly what was being said; he could hardly have expected this of himself in such a mysterious setting where the goddess of cultivable land and the divinities of the underworld extended to him their benevolence and favours and assured him of their salvific intentions.

The strangeness of the objects exhibited was intended to put the final touch on the mysterious.[14] Indeed, it may be supposed that had the initiate been able to understand exactly what was taking place, had he grasped the meaning of the Hierophant's words, and had he been able to identify the objects of the δεικνύμενα, the mystery would probably have vanished.[15] The soul of the Mysteries was their mysterious, impenetrable, inscrutable nature: the taunting situation that while the μύστης participated (at least in part) in all the aspects of the rites [16] and was 'supposed' to follow all that was taking place, yet was never quite able to fathom the inner meaning of the whole. But this was probably what gave him the satisfaction he looked for. His inability to penetrate the mysterious character of the rites was no doubt a proof to him of the presence of the divine in the rites, and therefore he could rest assured that he had somehow come in touch with or gazed at the august Mistresses of the Eleusinian Mysteries.[17]

---

[10] Mylonas, *EEM*, 258.

[11] Cf. Noack, *EBEH*, 236, "Wo es so sehr auf die phychologische Entspannung und Lösung einer seelischen Disposition, einer hochgradischen Erregung ankam, war die *Einheit des Ortes* für die gesamten Ablauf der Feier — λυσιπόνων τελετάν, Pin., frg. 131 — unerlässlich. Und das Gebäude hat auch nichts anderes gestattet."

[12] Cf. the silence witnessed: ὥσπερ ἐν μυστηρίοις ἐσιώπων Philst., *Vit. Ap.* I, 15. Also Ach. Tat. I, 11; Lib., *Plethr.* 6 (=*Or.* X, 6).

[13] Cf. Theodt., *Ther.* I, 721: ὁ δέ ἱεροφάντης μόνος οἶδεν τῶν γινομένων τὸν λόγον, καὶ οἷς ἄν δοκιμάσῃ καταμηνύει, and Iambl., *Myst.* 7, 1: μυστικῶν καὶ ἀποπεκρυμμένων καὶ ἀφανῶν νοήσεων.

[14] Mylonas, *EEM*, 273 f. supposes these objects to have been relics from Mycenaean times.

[15] Was it not ultimately due to scepticism that some of the more enlightened minds (e.g. Aeschylus, Alcibiades) unravelled or parodied the Mysteries ? See *supra* n. 3.

[16] Though Nilsson, *GFR*, 43 denies that the initiates had any part in the δρώμενα.

[17] Cf. Kern, *RG*, I, 136, "Dass es (sc. μυστήριον) in späterer Zeit (i.e. post archaic =class. not hellen.) allgemein die Bedeutung eines geheimnisvollen und dunklen Gottesdienstes gehabt hat, steht fest". To the same effect Anrich, *AM*, 32—4.

3. THE SUBSEQUENT HISTORY OF THE TERM PRIOR TO THE NT

A. Μυστήριον in Philosophy

i. Plato

When we leave the sphere of the Mysteries and enter that of Philosophy, our attention is drawn to an important circumstance. By the time of Plato the term μυστήριον is applied no longer exclusively to the Mysteries but in a neutral sense, so to speak, which Philosophy can readily utilize. The term itself occurs only twice in Plato (*Men.* 76 e; *Tht.* 156 a) though references and allusions to the Mysteries are frequent.[18] For example, Diotima's instruction to Socrates [19] about the nature of true Beauty and the philosopher's gradual ascent to its apprehension (i.e. his 'initiation' into its mysteries) is couched in Mystery terminology and ideas. We observe here the tendency to use μυστήριον in a metaphorical sense of the philosopher's intellectual flights in his effort to understand and explain the nature of true Being, true Beauty, or the Divine. Once again, the application is to divine things — since Philosophy is divine — but with the difference that this time the μυστήριον addresses itself to man's intellect rather than to his emotions, as was the case in the Eleusinian Mysteries. The μυστήριον is no longer dark and mysterious ritualism, but philosophical problems, often related in some way to the nature of God, to which only the highest of Plato's three classes of men — those in whom the λογιστικόν prevails [20] — can be admitted. The rest have an innate incapacity for the comprehension of philosophical language. In *Tht.* 156 a Plato designates as μυστήρια certain deep teachings of Protagoras: ἄλλοι δὲ πολὺ κομψότεροι, ὧν μέλλω σοι τὰ μυστήρια λέγειν. The 'mysteries' are not readily intelligible to anyone: the non-specialist has to rely on the specialist, the 'initiated' philosopher, so to speak, to explain them. In *Men.* 76 e Socrates, who is about to reveal the character of true Virtue, plays on the cultic and philosophical applications of μυστήριον: [20a] ἀναγκαῖόν σοι ἀπιέναι πρὸ τῶν μυστηρίων, ἀλλ᾽ εἰ περιμείναις τε καὶ μυηθείης (i.e. into the 'mysteries' of Virtue).[21]

---

[18] E.g. *Phdr.* 249 a—250 c; *Gor.* 497 c; *Symp.* 210—11.

[19] Pl., *Symp.* 201 d—212 a.

[20] This division occurs first in *Res.* 439 d ff.; it recurs in a myth in *Phdr.* 253 c ff.; and appears in *Tim.* and *Pol.*

[20a] Evidently the Mysteries were about to be celebrated before which Meno had said he must depart.

[21] Similarly Plut., *Mor.* 422 c.

ii. Philo

The platonizing Philo Judaeus makes a similar use of our term when he designates thereby the exalted and infallible teachings about Being — teachings which transcend the human mind (cf. ὁ δ᾽ ἄρα οὐδὲ τῷ νῷ καταληπτός, *De Imm.* XIII, 62) but which can be mediated through a companion, *viz.*, personified Truth: παρ᾽ ἧς μυηθέντες τὰ περὶ τοῦ ὄντος ἀψευδῆ μυστήρια (*ibid.* XIII, 61). Again after discussing the nature of Virtue allegorized from OT persons and events, he appeals, as an Hierophant (cf. ἱεροφαντήσομεν, *Cher.* XII, 42) to the 'initiated': ταῦτα, ὦ μύσται κεκαθαρμένοι τὰ ὦτα, ὡς ἱερὰ ὄντος μυστήρια ψυχαῖς ταῖς ἑαυτῶν παραδέχεσθε καὶ μηδενὶ τῶν ἀμυήτων ἐκλαλήσητε (*Cher.* XIV, 48). He himself owes the knowledge of these mysteries to other Hierophants like Moses and Jeremiah: καὶ γὰρ ἐγὼ παρὰ Μωυσεῖ τῷ θεοφιλεῖ μυηθεὶς τὰ μεγάλα μυστήρια ὅμως αὖθις Ἱερεμίαν τὸν προφήτην ἰδὼν καὶ γνούς, ὅτι οὐ μόνον μύστης ἐστιν ἀλλὰ καὶ ἱεροφάντης ἱκανός, οὐκ ὤκνησα φοιτῆσαι πρὸς αὐτόν.[22]

B. Μυστήριον in Secular Use

i. Of Ordinary Secrets

The tendency to secularize our term reaches its furthermost point in Menander who reduced its meaning to that of a mere secret: μυστήριον σου μὴ κατείπῃς τῷ φίλῳ.[23] Such a use was, in many respects, a logical one, since as we saw above, μυστήριον contains the element of secrecy. Soranus required a good many virtues of an accomplished midwife because she was to be entrusted with the μυστήρια βίου,[24] and the LXX uses it repeatedly in this sense (se below).

The cultic and philosophical usage of that which is hard-to-understand, the obscure, was also secularized. Mnesimachus was apparently intrigued by what transpired when man fell asleep and described sleep, in Eleusinian terminology,[25] as constituting the 'Lesser Mysteries' in relation to death which constituted the 'Greater Mysteries': ὕπνος τὰ μικρὰ τοῦ θανάτου μυστήρια,[26] while Soranus (*Gyn.* I, 4) spoke of superstitious beliefs as συνηθές τι μυστήριον καὶ βιωτικὴν θρησκείαν.

---

[22] *Ibid.* 14, 49. "For Philo and the Christian Alexandrians", says Bornkamm, *TDNT*, IV, 809, "the Bible is the Book of Mysteries; its figures and events conceal Mysteries appointed only for initiates". On Philo and the Mysteries, see Cerfaux, *RLC*, I, 65—112; Lagrange's review in *RB*, 1925, 150—2; Wolfson, *Ph*, I, 36—53; Mack, *LS*, 108 f.

[23] Men., *Inc.* 168 (*CAF*, III, 200).

[24] Sor., *Gyn.* 1, 3; also 1, 4: ἐν τῷ βίῳ μυστηρίων μετέχειν.

[25] Cf. Iambl., *Protr.* 2: πρὸ τῶν μεγάλων μυστηρίων τὰ μικρὰ παραδοτέον. Also *IG*, I², 6: 93, 96; Pl., *Gor.* 497 c.

[26] Mnes., *Frg.* 11 (=Plut., *Mor.* 107 e; *CAF*, II, 442). Cf. Lidzbarski, *JBM*, 168: "Das Mysterium des Todes ist der Schlaf."

ii. In Medicine

The Medical Aretaeus (*CD*, II, 7) described a prescription for medicine as τοὐμὸν τὸ μυστήριον, probably in the sense, 'The secret is mine', while another physician, Alexander Trall. (V, 4) witnessed for a coughing medicament the appelation τὸ μυστήριον καλούμενον. What the motivation was is hard to say.[27]

C. Μυστήριον in the LXX [28]

i. Apocrypha

The LXX witnessed both the religious and secular usages of both an ordinary secret and a mystery. For the religious sense we have two instances in Wis 14: 15 καὶ παρέδωκε τοῖς ὑποχειρίοις μυστήρια καὶ τελετάς, and ἢ γὰρ τεκνοφόνους τελετάς, ἢ κρύφια μυστήρια.[29] The sense of an ordinary human secret is clearly evidenced: μυστήριον βασιλέως καλὸν κρύψαι, τὰ δὲ ἔργα τοῦ Θεοῦ ἀνακαλύπτειν ἐνδόξως (Tob 12: 7). Sirach attaches supreme importance to the keeping of friends' secrets: ὁ ἀποκαλύπτων μυστήρια ἀπώλεσε πίστιν, καὶ οὐ μὴ εὕρῃ φίλον πρὸς τὴν ψυχὴν αὐτοῦ.[30] In II Mac 13: 21 the traitor Rhodokos προσήγγειλε τὰ μυστήρια τοῖς πολεμίοις, while Nebuchadrezzar declared to his leading subjects τὸ μυστήριον τῆς βουλῆς αὐτοῦ (Jdt 2: 2) — i.e. his secret design.

Another group of passages is concerned with the thoughts and counsels

---

[27] Quite naturally a term with such associations could not fail to be exploited by magical authors. In their usage the meaning oscillates between what is hidden or secret and what is mysterious or unintelligible. E.g. *PGM*, 12, 313 ff.: ὃ καὶ ἔχε ἐν ἀποκρύφῳ ὡς μεγαλομυστήριον, κρύβε, κρύβε, *PGM*, 1, 130 f.; the so-called Mithras Liturgy (=*PGM*, 4, 719 ff.): παλινγενόμενος ἀπογίγνομαι· αὐξανόμενος καὶ αὐξηθεὶς τελευτῶ, ἀπὸ γενέσεως ζωογόνου γενόμενος, εἰς ἀπογενεσίαν ἀναλυθεὶς πορεύομαι, ὡς σύ (sc. the deity) ἔκτισας, ὡς σὺ ἐνομοθέτησας καὶ ἐποίησας μυστήριον, *PGM*, 13, 27: ἄρξαι λέγειν τὴν στήλην καὶ τὸ μυστήριον τοῦ Θεοῦ ὅ ἐστιν κάνθαρος (title of a book: cf. Reitzenstein, *HM*, 242, and Schneider, *TSK*, 1932, 255); *PML*, 10, 19: δότε πνεῦμα τῷ ὑπ' ἐμοῦ κατασκευασμένῳ μυστηρίῳ.
The Gnostics availed themselves of the term a great deal in order to stress the character of their esoteric doctrines. The μυστήριον is not a mere secret here, but a spiritual, unrevealed 'truth'. In *Poem.* μυστήριον occurs just once in the sense of something stupendous or awe-inspiring: ὁ δὲ Ποιμάνδρης εἶπε, τοῦτό ἐστι τὸ κεκρυμμένον μυστήριον μέχρι τῆσδε τῆς ἡμέρας, ἡ γὰρ φύσις ἐπιμιγεῖσα τῷ ἀνθρώπῳ ἤνεγκε τι θαῦμα θαυμασιώτατον (*CH*, I, 16). Cf. also Reitzenstein, *HM*, 242. In the Naasene Sermon (as reconstructed by Reitzenstein from Hipp., *Phil.* V) μυστήριον occurs 17 X in combination with very suggestive adjs. See *infra* I, 5.

[28] For μυστήριον in other OT *VV* see Schneider, *TSK*, 1932, 257 f.

[29] Wis 14: 23. Note that in this and in the previous quotation τελεταί are distinguished from μυστήρια. In this passage μυστήρια is qualified by the adj. κρύφιος.

[30] Sir 27: 16. Also 27: 17, 21; 22: 22.

of God, and the context would seem to imply that μυστήριον expresses the inexplorable or unfathomable character of His purposes and will. Thus the author of Wisdom (2: 22) says of the wicked οὐκ ἔγνωσαν μυστήρια Θεοῦ, and in 6: 22 he proposes to disclose the mysteries connected with wisdom [31] and its nature: οὐκ ἀποκρύψω ὑμῖν μυστήρια, ἀλλ᾽ ἀπ᾽ ἀρχῆς γενέσεως ἐξιχνιάσω, καὶ θήσω εἰς τὸ ἐμφανὲς τὴν γνῶσιν αὐτῆς. [32]

ii. Daniel

The nine occurrences in Daniel translating the Aram. (orig. Persian) רז, cannot obviously have the meaning of secret. The μυστήριον relates not only to the interpretation of the dream but to the dream itself as well; the king demands not only its explanation but also the delineation of it. The unfortunate subjects are puzzled by all this while Daniel confesses that οἰκτιρμοὺς ἐζήτουν παρὰ τοῦ Θεοῦ τοῦ οὐρανοῦ ὑπὲρ τοῦ μυστηρίου τούτου (2: 18). The whole thing was a mystery to him till it was solved one night in a vision: ἐν ὁράματι τῆς νυκτὸς τὸ μυστήριον ἀπεκαλύφθη (2: 19). Bold in contrast to the bewildered magicians he declares: τὸ μυστήριον ὃ ὁ βασιλεὺς ἐπερωτᾷ, οὐκ ἔστι σοφῶν, μάγων, ἐπαοιδῶν, γαζαρηνῶν ἀναγγεῖλαι τῷ βασιλεῖ· ἀλλ᾽ ἢ ἔστι Θεὸς ἐν οὐρανῷ ἀποκαλύπτων μυστήρια (2: 27 f.). Daniel disclaims all credit for his understanding of the mystery; he is aware of a divine influence upon him which makes possible such 'super-human' knowledge: ἐμοὶ δὲ οὐκ ἐν σοφίᾳ τῇ οὔσῃ ἐν ἐμοὶ παρὰ πάντας τοὺς ζῶντας τὸ μυστήριον τοῦτο ἀπεκαλύφθη (2: 30). The nature of the Danielic μυστήριον is no doubt that of the mysterious purposes of God regarding the last days. God alone knows them and reveals them in His own time, way and measure to His chosen ones. [33]

D. Μυστήριον in the Pseudepigrapha [34]

i. Various Pseudepigraphical Books

The tendency of the LXX to push into the background the religious application of μυστήριον is carried even further in the Pseudepigrapha which, as a rule, illustrate only the secular senses of *secret* and

---

[31] Cf. Brown, *SB*, 9: "It is in Sirach that for the first time we meet wisdom as an agent of God in revealing mysteries".

[32] Cf. Sinaitic *suppl.* in Sir. 3: 19 (Heb. סוד; passage omitted in LXX): ἀλλὰ πραέσιν ἀποκαλύπτει τὰ μυστήρια αὐτοῦ.

[33] The remaining instances in Dan are 2: 29, 47 (*bis*); 4: 6. All LXX references have been cited.

[34] Some of the works quoted in this section are from the Christian era. However, since the discussion is not so much the background of the NT μυστήριον as the historical semantic development of the word, I feel uninhibited in the use of this material.

mysterious.[35] Of the first type the following are some exx.: ἀλλ' ἔκλαιον ἐν κρυφῇ ἡμέρας πολλὰς διὰ τὸν Ἰωσήφ· ἐφοβούμην γὰρ τοὺς ἀδελφούς μου, ὅτι συνέθεντο πάντες ὅστις ἐξείπῃ τὸ μυστήριον ἀναιρεθῆναι αὐτόν (*Test Z* 1:6); ἐγὼ δὲ μωραινόμενος τῇ μέθῃ ἐδήλωσα τὰ μυστήρια τῆς καρδίας μου;[36] μὴ ἀκούσῃ ἐν μάχῃ ἀλλότριος τὸ μυστήριόν σου.[37] Of the second type an obvious instance is: καὶ ἦν μυστήριον φαινόμενον ἐν τῷ τεκεῖν τὴν Θάμαρ[38] — of the mysterious or curious phonomenon attending Thamar's delivery. More often μυστήριον defines God's purpose and will: "so as to proclaim unto mortals the mysteries of God".[39] In *IV Ez* 12:36 we have: "Thou alone hast been found worthy to learn this mystery of the Most High"; further on, "Though shalt teach them to the wise of the people whose hearts thou knowest are able to comprehend and keep all these mysteries (12:38); and again, "The Most High has revealed many secrets unto thee" (10:38). The Lat. has *mysteria multa*, while the Syr. has *r'z' sgy*" and the Eth. *mestîr ḥebu'* (=hidden mystery).[40] In similar fashion Levi is to act as the mouthpiece of God in declaring His mysteries to men.[41] In *III Bar* 1:6 the angel promises to show "other mysteries greater than these"; "the mysteries of God" (1:8), and "the greater mysteries" (2:5), while in *Slav En* Enoch has access to that from which even the angels have been debarred: "Hear, Enoch, and take these my words, for not to my angels have I told my secret".[42]

ii. I Enoch

The evidence of *I En* is of particular interest.[43] In the earlier Gk. frgs.[44] μυστήριον is the heavenly mystery or secret betrayed by the Watchers to

---

[35] A possible ref. to the Mysteries is *II Bar* 60:1 where Charles has 'mysteries' and Kautzsch 'Mysterien'.

[36] *Test J* 12:3, 4, 6 (in Morfill's retrans. from the Slav.).

[37] *Test G* 6:5, which, however, Charles regards as a Christian interpolation. Other instances are: *Test J* 16:4 (cf. also Morfil's retrans.); *Ps Sol* 14:5 "secrets of the heart" (Charles); *Ahik* 2:53 (Ar.) "secret of thy friend" (Charles). In *Sent Phoc* 229 the phrase ταῦτα δικαιοσύνης μυστήρια characterizes a long list of moral advices (in Denis, *FP*, 156).

[38] *Test J* 12:4 (in Morfill's retran.).

[39] *Sib Or* 3:812; Kautzsch (3:811) 'göttliche Rätsel'.

[40] In *II Bar* 48:3, "Thou revealest not Thy mysteries to many", the Syr. has similarly *r'zyk*. So also in *II Bar* 81:4.

[41] *Test L* 2:10. Cf. further 7:4 and Morfill's retran.

[42] *II En* 24:3 (Version A). Version B: "And to my angels I have not made known my secret". In *Ahik* 5:7 we have 'secrets and riddles' and in 8:37 'the mysteries and the secrets'. Cf. further *Vit Ad Ev* 21:1 and 34:1 (on both, MS C).

[43] Of *I En* we possess in Gk. only one portion at the beginning and two at the end. A number of Aram. frgs. discovered in Quamran Cave IV, were recently published by Milik. These frgs. represent chiely the Book of the Watchers (1—36), the Astro-

womankind.[45] In the middle sections of the work for which there is neither Gk. nor Aram.,[46] the idea of the mysterious, the incomprehensible recurs frequently: e.g. "Deep are all Thy secrets and innumerable, and Thy righteousness is beyond reckoning".[47] More important are the final Gk. frgs. Before his departure Enoch prophesies judgments on the sinners and blessings on the just. This knowledge which he terms a μυστήριον comes from the heavenly tablets which he has read (103, 2 f.). Further on he expatiates with regard to the sinners, "I know this mystery, that sinners will alter and pervert the words of righteousness in many ways",[48] and with regard to the righteous: καὶ πάλιν ἐγὼ γινώσκω μυστήριον δεύτερον, ὅτι δικαίοις καὶ ὁσίοις καὶ φρονίμοις δοθήσονται αἱ βίβλοι μου εἰς χαρὰν ἀληθείας, καὶ αὐτοὶ πιστεύσουσιν αὐταῖς καὶ ἐν αὐταῖς χαρήσονται καὶ ἀγαλλιάσονται πάντες

---

nomical Book (72—82) and the Dream-Visions (83—90). For the rest of the text we are dependent on an Ethiopic tran., extand for the whole work. This acc. to Milik (BE, 88) is not reliable in details. In the Gk frgs. the word μυστήριον occurs only 7 × (plus 2 × in frgs. preserved in Sync.; the 2 other instances in Sync. are parallels to the above 7 cases). In Charles' tran. we have three related terms: 'mystery' 6 × (4 × of which translate the Gk. μυστήριον; for the two other instances the Gk. is lost, but the Eth. implies that the Gk. read μυστήριον); 'secret' 38 × (2 × of which translate the Gk. μυστήριον; the seventh occurrence of μυστήριον is omitted in Charles); and 'hidden' 19 ×. The instructive point here is the behaviour of the Eth. Charles' aggregate of 'mystery', 'secret' and 'hidden' is 63 ×. The Eth. uses only two words to translate all these instances; the one is ḥebu' (=secret) and the other is mesṭīr — an adaptation of the Gk. μυστήριον. (For these figures I have consulted the ed. of Flemming, BHÄT). All the instances of Charles' 'hidden' and all but one of 'secret' are in Eth. represented by the term ḥebu'. For the one occurrence in which Charles has 'secret' for the Eth. mesṭīr, the Gk. is lost. The two instances where Charles has 'mystery /-ies' for which the Gk. is lost, the Eth. has mesṭīr. Of the 7 instances of the Gk. μυστήριον the Eth. has mesṭīr 5 × and ḥebu' 2 ×. In one other case where the Gk. has the adv. μυστηριακῶς the Eth. has 'in secret' and is followed by Charles. The evidence suggests that the Eth. translator felt that the indigenous word ḥebu' (=secret) was not always a proper translation for the Gk. μυστήριον and was, accordingly led to adopt an adapted form of the Gk. term. The implication is that the Eth. translator sensed two different meanings in μυστήριον — or at least two slightly different nuances — for the expression of which he used sometimes ḥebu' and sometimes the naturalized mesṭīr. That the two terms bear two different senses is implied in IV Ez 10: 38 where the Eth. term qualifies the Gk. one — mesṭīr ḥebu' (=hidden', or 'secret mystery').

[44] I En 16: 3. See also 8: 3; 9: 6; 10: 7, and Sync. ad loci.

[45] The contents of this μυστήριον are delineated in I En 8: 1—4.

[46] Milik, BE, 91 f. considers that the Parables are "a Christian Greek composition".

[47] Charles' tran. of I En 63: 3. Bornkamm, TDNT, IV, 815 translates 'mysteries'. See also I En 63: 3 a; 51: 3. In 90: 1 the Eth. has mesṭīr.

[48] Ibid. 104: 10 (Charles' tran.). At this point the Gk. has a lacuna of two lines, but there can be no doubt that it read μυστήριον, cf. vs. 12.

οἱ δίκαιοι μαθεῖν ἐξ αὐτῶν πάσας τὰς ὁδοὺς τῆς ἀληθείας.[49] It is impossible to reduce every occurrence of μυστήριον or of 'secret' (in Charles, *AP*) in *I En* to the sense of a mere *secret*.

4. THE USE OF ΜΥΣΤΗΡΙΟΝ IN THE NT

In the NT our term is applied to a wide variety of concepts, though its basic significance, running as a current through all these instances, seems to be but one — the emphasis on the mysterious element in each concept. In this sense it may be said that terminologically μυστήριον is used uniformly in the NT bearing its original denotation, or — since we are uncertain of its etymology — its earliest associations, i.e. in the Eleusinian Mysteries. A possible exception is Rev 1: 20 where μυστήριον has been taken to denote the 'symbolic meaning'[50] of the stars and the lampstands. The Gk. sentence is, however, incomplete. As it stands, the best we can make of it is to say that μυστήριον signifies that which requires explanation with regard to the stars and lampstands.

The rest of the NT occurrences might be grouped in several ways: a) acc. to the order of occurrence; b) acc. to date to show the development of concepts; c) in groups of synoptic, pauline and non-pauline instances; d) in two main groups, one comprising all references to the plan of God, and the other all other occurrences, which are admittedly, of very diverse character — or even with minor refinements; e) in groups acc. to the adjs. or vbs. used correlatively with μυστήριον to exhibit the contextual texture of various associations with our word, as well as in several other ways. All of these methods of grouping, however, are beset with problems peculiar to each one of them. Thus, whatever rudimentary grouping the following discussion may chance to evince will be for purposes of convenience and conciseness.

The only synoptic occurrence (Mt 13: 11 = Mk 4: 11 = Lk 8: 10) speaks of the μυστήρια τῆς βασιλείας τῶν οὐρανῶν.[51] The μυστήρια are given to the knowledge of some (δέδοται γνῶναι) while from others they are withheld (οὐ δέδοται).[52] This 'giving' consists in the divine ability to understand.

---

[49] *I En* 104: 12—3. Similarly in the Noachic frg. (106: 19). The Gk. frg. again has a lacuna at this point; however, the Eth. reads *mesṭir* in all of the last four instances.

[50] By e.g. Brown, *SB*, 36; Bornkamm, *TDNT*, IV, 824, 'hidden sense'; Charles, *Rev*, 34, 'secret meaning'.

[51] Mk has the sg. Cerfaux, *NTS*, 1956, 241 thinks the pl. is more original, but cf. Brown, *SB*, 33. See Drury's interpretation (*JTS*, 1973, 367—79) and Bowker's criticism (*JTS*, 1974, 300—17).

[52] I adhere to Mt on account of its fuller context. Schneider, *TSK*, 262 thinks Mt's account is the original one.

In other words, though the μυστήρια are seen and heard by both classes of men (vv. 13, 16), they are understood only by those on whom the divine grace operates.[53] They are, consequently, not apprehensible by mere human intelligence. Hence, the meaning ought not to be *secret*, but *that which is above human comprehension.*

In I Cor 13: 2 τὰ μυστήρια πάντα include all that is a riddle to man, in short, everything that transcends his power of conceiving, whether related to divine or human matters.[54] Similarly, in I Cor 14: 2 οὐδεὶς γὰρ ἀκούει means 'no-one understands' and the phrase ἐν πνεύματι δὲ λαλεῖ μυστήρια discloses the character of that which is uttered by the glossolalist in the presence of those unpossessed of the charisma of speaking or interpreting tongues. What they hear is to them a mystery![55] In I Cor 15: 51 Paul concludes his discussion of the deeply misunderstood subject of the resurrection of the dead by calling attention to some peculiar events which will attend it: ἰδοὺ μυστήριον ὑμῖν λέγω.[56]

The passage of II Th 2: 7 is fraught with difficulties. Nontheless, we may note that the core of the μυστήριον ἀνομίας are the person and work of the ἄνομος who, for the time being operates in concealment or disguise. His coming and actions are inspired and effected through Satan ἐν πάσῃ δυνάμει καὶ σημείοις καὶ τέρασιν ψεύδους (vs 9).[57] The mystery will be solved when at the *parousia* of Christ the lawless one will be stripped off (ἀποκαλυφθήσεται, vs. 8) and his real character will become evident to all.

The great harlot of Rev 17: 3 ff. bears on her forehead the title μυστήριον (vs. 5).[58] The seer is greatly astonished and the angel interposes to solve the mystery: Διὰ τί ἐθαύμασας; ἐγὼ ἐρῶ σοι τὸ μυστήριον τῆς γυναικὸς καὶ τοῦ θηρίου (vs. 7). The second mention of μυστήριον would seem to have the

---

[53] For Johansson, *STK*, 1940, 10 ff., 24, 38, this μυστήριον is identical with Christ's messianic character which is first revealed after his betrayal. See also Arvedson, *MC*, *passim*.

[54] Kennedy, *PMR*, 168; Brown, *SB*, 46 and Grosheide, *1C*, 304 think the reference is to religious matters alone.

[55] Brown, *SB*, 47 thinks μυστήριον here means 'hidden truths', while Coppens, *PQ*, 137 translates 'mysteriously'. It is more likely that πνεύματι refers to the human spirit (cf. vs. 15) which bubbles up utterances incomprehensible to others. Cf. Grosheide, *1C*, 318: "There is a possibility to speak *in the spirit*, i.e. without the co-operation of the mind (understanding)". Barret, *1C*, 130 has "riddles with no solution".

[56] Cf. Mitton, *EE*, 87.

[57] Cf. Brown, *SB*, 39, "We believe that *mysterion* is employed primarily to signify the mysterious disposition of divine providence whereby evil is allowed to exist and work in the world. The economy of evil (like the economy of divine salvation) is a mystery because it is the work of a supernatural being, beyond human knowledge", and adds in a note "As both V. Soden . . . and Deden . . . point out, the eschatological context also surrounds the Satanic activity with mystery atmosphere".

[58] I.e. 'the hidden significance of her appearance'.

28

sense 'I will tell you the (symbolic) meaning [59] of the woman and the beast'. But the element of bewilderment, of puzzling permeates the passage: the inhabitants of the earth will be deeply astonished (θαυμασθήσονται, vs. 8), the comprehension of it challenges a νοῦς ἔχων σοφίαν (vs. 9), the interpretation itself is a riddle (vv. 9—12), and the witness of the vision himself is filled with awe (vs. 7).

When in Eph 6: 19 the author asks for prayer ἵνα μοι δοθῇ λόγος ἐν ἀνοίξει τοῦ στόματός μου, ἐν παρρησίᾳ γνωρίσαι τὸ μυστήριον τοῦ εὐαγγελίου, he is not troubled about proper words to declare an easily understood *secret*, but strains about for appropriate and adequate forms and words to express the inexpressible.[60]

In I Cor 4: 1 as well as in Rm 16: 25 and Rev 10: 7 the context does not make the sense of the mysterious obvious at first sight; however, after further consideration, we observe that οἰκονόμοι μυστηρίων has a backward look on ch. 2,[61] that Rm 16: 25 refers exactly to the same thing as Eph 3,[62] and Rev 10: 7 to the whole burden of that book,[63] i.e. to God's mysterious designs.

The μυστήριον of Rm 11: 25 relates to the peculiar nature of God's economy whereby the offer of salvation to the Gentiles involves somehow the temporary (ἄχρις οὗ) and partial (ἀπὸ μέρους) rejection of Israel (or of the gospel by Israel). At the end, however, Israel too shall be lavished God's grace.[64] It is the overpowering of this vision that elicits from Paul the exclamation ὦ βάθος πλούτου καὶ σοφίας καὶ γνώσεως! ὡς ἀνεξεραύνητα καὶ ἀνεξιχνίαστα! τίς ἔγνω νοῦν Κυρίου! The adjs. ἀνεξεραύνητα and ἀνεξιχνίαστα alone are decisive for the sense of the *mysterious*.[65]

In I Cor 2 the rather unassociated use of μυστήριον in vs. 1 [66] becomes

---

[59] So Brown, *SB*, 37; Bornkamm, *TDNT*, IV, 823 has 'secret', while Caird, *Rev*, 214 translates "I will explain to you the symbolism of the woman".

[60] So too in = Col 4: 3 which, however, Mitton, *EE*, 89 relates to Col 1: 26 f. The contextual pars. to Eph 6: 18 ff. are too obvious to be brushed aside.

[61] Prümm, *Bib*, 1956, 139 holds that the pl. is a literary variant of the great Mystery.

[62] So Brown, *SB*, 51, "God's mysterious plan hidden from ages past". Similarly, Dewailly, *SEÅ*, 1966, 114—21.

[63] Cf. Brown, *SB*, 38: "Here we have a different use of mystery — no longer a symbol (i.e. as in 1: 20), but the mysterious will of God for the end time". Caird, *Rev*, renders with 'secret purpose'.

[64] See Schlier's interpretation in *ZK*, 243 f.

[65] So Bornkamm, *TDNT*, IV, 822 f.

[66] The *v. l.* μαρτύριον though represented by equally strong MS support, seems less probable. The preferred reading μυστήριον, on the other hand, involves the question as to whether a use of μυστήριον identical with that in Eph 4: 19=Col 4: 3 could have been possible at so early a date in Paul's career. It is rejected recently by Grosheide, *1C*, 58 and Barrett, *1C*, 37 *et al.* Among its advocates are: Weiss, *1K*; Lietz-

more defined as we proceed. The σοφία τοῦ αἰῶνος τούτου is juxtaposed to Θεοῦ σοφίαν. The latter is disclosed in a deep mystery (ἐν μυστηρίῳ),[67] which the ἄρχοντες τοῦ αἰῶνος τούτου fail to understand and so crucify the great Subject of the μυστήριον of vs. 1. The μυστήριον has its origin in the depths of God, so there is only one who can really instruct men in it, viz., the Holy Spirit which searches (ἐραυνᾷ) and knows (ἔγνωκεν) τὰ βάθη τοῦ Θεοῦ. This means that knowledge of the μυστήριον can be acquired only by revelation[68] through the Spirit by him who possesses it, i.e., the πνευματικός. On the contrary, the μυστήριον is rejected as foolish by the ψυχικός who is quite incapable of its apprehension ὅτι πνευματικῶς ἀνακρίνεται. The note of wonder, of exclamation, before such a mystery is sounded again: τίς γὰρ ἔγνω νοῦν Κυρίου!

In Eph 1: 9 acquaintance with the μυστήριον τοῦ θελήματος αὐτοῦ implies a more than adequate endowment (ἐπερίσσευσεν) ἐν πάσῃ σοφίᾳ καὶ φρονήσει. The mystery which deals with the universal anakephalaiōsis in Christ stands hierarchically above the other μυστήριον concepts in this Epistle and includes them as parts of a whole.[69] The μυστήριον of ch. 3 which has been withheld from the men of the past, has been revealed now to the apostles and prophets (vs. 5).[70] The magnitude of it is such that under its impact the author is made to feel his insignificance. He styles himself, in contravention of grammar, as ἐλαχιστότερος πάντων ἁγίων, characterizes the μυστήριον as ἀνεξιχνίαστον πλοῦτος and qualifies it by the adj. ἀποκεκρυμμένον, thereby setting forth its inscrutable nature.[71]

mann, 1K; Schneider, TSK, 1932, 265; Hering, 1C; Bornkamm, TDNT, IV, 819; Wilckens, WT, 45; Funk, LHWG, 295; Brown, SB, 49; Coppens, PQ, 146.

[67] The passage is confessedly difficult. Dupont, Gn, 137 and Lyonnet, Bib, 1954, 495 render the phrase "in announcing a mystery", but Mitton, EE, 87 observes that "the chief interest is in 'wisdom', and the reference to 'mystery' is incidental", while Coppens, PQ, 143 ff. suggests "it is a divine wisdom, mysterious and hidden". Ἐν μυστηρίῳ can be connected either with Θεοῦ σοφίαν locatively, or, with λαλοῦμεν characterizing the nature of the Christian message. The latter alt. would seem to find support in vv. 10 ff. On the connection of μυστήριον with τέλειος, see Schneider, TSK, 1932, 266 f. and Prümm, Bib, 1963, 76—92.

[68] Cf. Gaugler, 46.

[69] Bieder, TZ, 1955, 330 points to the three gens. with μυστήριον: of the will of God (1:9), of Christ (3:4), and of the Gospel (6:19 and says they form a unified theme: the mystery of God's will effected through Christ and proclaimed in the Gospel. Schlier, 61 f. remarks that "das Geheimnis . . . das Geheimnis Gottes in Christus, seiner Weisheit, das Geheimnis Christi als seiner Weisheit und das Geheimnis der Kirche als des Leibes Christi und seiner Weisheit ist, aber nicht als drei Mysteria, sondern als eines und dasselbe". See also id., ZK, 299—307.

[70] Mitton, EE, 85 compares this vs. with Col 1:26 and remarks "a most surprising modification" in the interests of "the Church hierarchy".

[71] Chrysostom understands it similarly: εἰ ὁ πλοῦτος αὐτοῦ ἀνεξιχνίαστος, καὶ μετὰ τὸ φανῆναι, πολλῷ μᾶλλον ἡ οὐσία. Εἰ μυστήριον ἔτι ἐστί, πολλῷ μᾶλλον πρὸ τοῦ

Similarly, in Col 1: 26 τὸ μυστήριον τὸ ἀποκεκρυμμένον is defined in more detail in vs. 27: τί τὸ πλοῦτος τῆς δόξης τοῦ μυστηρίου τούτου ἐν τοῖς ἔθνεσιν, ὅ ἐστιν Χριστὸς ἐν ὑμῖν, ἡ ἐλπὶς τῆς δόξης. Here the μυστήριον is not merely Christ and His event, but His indwelling in the believers.[72] Acc. to 2: 2 f. πάντες οἱ θησαυροὶ τῆς σοφίας καὶ γνώσεως lie hidden (ἀπόκρυφοι) in the μυστήριον which is equated with Christ. Once again we get an idea of the nature of the μυστήριον: its chief characteristic is its infinity and inexplorability.

In Eph 5: 32 the μυστήριον has been interpreted of the conjugal union,[73] but the author here no doubt refers it primarily to the union of Christ and the Church.[74] But this union is not a great *secret* for it has been openly proclaimed; it is a deep mystery, unsearchable and inexplicable, for it involves, in some sense, the union of God and man.[75]

In I Tm 3: 9 τὸ μυστήριον τῆς πίστεως exhibits a development which was in many respects a logical inference from the earlier usage in defining the purposes of God. The μυστήριον here (together with πίστις, itself used in a developed sense) refers to the whole *corpus* of Christian teaching and the mystery it enwraps.[76] The εὐσεβείας μυστήριον involves at once the most significant and incomprehensible items of the Christ event,[77] precisely those events which must have been a 'holy mystery' to every believer (cf. ἔχοντας τὸ μυστήριον τῆς πίστεως ἐν καθαρᾷ συνειδήσει).[78]

γνωρισθῆναι. Μυστήριον γὰρ αὐτὸ διὰ τοῦτο καλεῖ, ἐπειδὴ μηδὲ ἄγγελοι ᾔδεσαν, μηδὲ τινὶ δῆλον ἦν (Comm. Eph., *ad loc.*).

[72] Some, to be sure, would translate 'Christ among you' (e.g. C. F. D. Moule, *CPh*, 83, 86; Lohse, *CPh*, 73) but such an understanding is improbable. The NT speaks often of the indwelling of Christ in the fathful. It is this indwelling that guarantees the believers' eschatological exaltation. Lightfoot, *CPh*, 169 says, "'within you' . . . more probable interpretation as suggested by Rm 8: 10, II Cor 13: 5, Gal 4: 19; cf. Eph 3: 17"; Mitton, *EE*, 88 similarly, "The emphasis is far more on Christ and His indwelling than upon the inclusion of the Gentiles". Schneider, *TSK*, 1932, 270 says, "Der Ausdruck χριστὸς ἐν ὑμῖν ist durchaus realistisch zu fassen: es ist der in den Gläubigen wohnende Christus"; Schlier, 61 'Christus in uns'.

[73] Esp. by Roman Catholics.

[74] Brown, *SB*, 65 f. says the μυστήριον "refers to a scriptural passage which contains a deeper meaning than that which appears at first sight". So also Robinson, 126; Abbott, *Col*, 175; Bornkamm, *TDNT*, IV, 823; Bruce, 119; Mussner, *PQ*, 162. Bieder, *MCM*, says the great mystery deals with a holy Eros between Christ and the Church; Schlier, 262, "ein Typus auf Christus und die Ekklesia".

[75] Cf. I Cor 6: 17 ὁ δὲ κολλώμενος τῷ Κυρίῳ ἕν πνεῦμά ἐστιν. See V. Soden, *ZNW*, 1911, 194.

[76] Cf. Brown, *SB*, 67: "We may say that the mystery of faith is what is believed, as the mystery of the gospel is what is preached".

[77] It is, in fact, in the last analysis, identical with His Person. So Bieder, *MCM*; Kelly, *Past.* 89 f.; Barrett, *Past*, 65 f. On εὐσέβεια see Foerster, *NTS*, 1958—9, 213—8.

[78] Cf. Barrett, *Past*, 66.

5. THE USE OF ΜΥΣΤΗΡΙΟΝ IN THE EARLY CHRISTIAN AUTHORS

The evidence which the early Christian writers afford is important in two respects: for their own understanding of the term and for their understanding of the biblical use of it.

Ignatius (Eph 19: 1) calls the virginity of Mary, her childbirth and the death of Christ τρία μυστήρια κραυγῆς, ἅτινα ἐν ἡσυχίᾳ Θεοῦ ἐπράχθη. Though the first could be described as a secret, her childbirth and especially the death of Christ were anything but a secret. Ignatius' meaning was *mysterious*. Similarly, the death of Christ is a μυστήριον δι᾽ οὗ ἐλάβομεν τὸ πιστεύειν (*Id.*, Magn 9: 2).

A difficult case is πᾶς δὲ προφήτης δεδοκιμασμένος, ἀληθινός, ποιῶν εἰς μυστήριον κοσμικὸν ἐκκλησίας (*Did* 11: 11). Whatever be the meaning of κοσμικός here, μυστήριον can hardly mean a *secret*.[79]

Diognetus is told τὸ δὲ τῆς ἰδίας αὐτῶν (sc. of the Christians) θεοσεβείας μυστήριον μὴ προσδοκήσῃς δύνασθαι παρὰ ἀνθρώπου μαθειν.[80] The reason for this disappointing statement is the nature of the μυστήριον: οὐδὲ ἀνθρωπίνων οἰκονομίαν μυστηρίων πεπίστευνται ἀλλ᾽ αὐτὸς (sc. ὁ Θεός) . . . ἀπ᾽ οὐρανῶν τὴν ἀλήθειαν καὶ τὸν λόγον τὸν ἅγιον καὶ ἀπερινόητον ἀνθρώποις ἐνίδρυσε καὶ ἐγκατεστήριξε ταῖς καρδίαις αὐτῶν (*Ibid.*, 7: 1 f.). We note that the μυστήρια imply a λόγος ἀπερινόητος.[81] Again we read that while the unbelievers failed to understand the Logos (cf. μὴ νοούμενος) those who were deemed faithful ἔγνωσαν πατρὸς μυστήρια[82] — perhaps an allusion to the syn. occurrences.

Justin's τὸ μυστήριον τοῦ προβάτου (Dial 40: 1) is identical in meaning with Rev 1: 20. Justin speaks of the μυστήριον τοῦ Χριστοῦ (44: 2), and of the μυστήριον τοῦ σταυροῦ (134: 5; 138: 2) in the sense of that which is beyond human comprehension, as the following citation makes plain: (ἡμεῖς) οἵτινες διὰ τοῦ ἐξουθενημένου καὶ ὀνείδους μεστοῦ μυστηρίου τοῦ σταυροῦ κληθέντες ὑπὸ Θεοῦ . . . ὑπομένομεν (131: 2). Again for Justin τὸ πάθος τοῦ Χριστοῦ is a σωτήριον μυστήριον (74: 3) by which God saves man. He also speaks of certain OT events as οἰκονομία μυστηρίων (134: 2; 141: 4). A clear instance of the significance of the term for Justin is: ἀλλ᾽ ὅταν ἐγὼ ζητῶν ἐπαπορήσω, τότε τοῦ μυστηρίου τῶν Χριστιανῶν ἀνακράζω τὸ θαῦμα, ὅτι ὑπὲρ νοῦν, ὑπὲρ λόγον, ὑπὲρ κατάληψιν κτιστῆς φύσεως τὰ ἡμέτερα (*EOO*, 16).[83]

---

[79]. See *BAG*, s. v.

[80] *Diogn* 4, 6. We have here perhaps an allusion to I Tm 3: 16, though it should be noted that the writer uses θεοσέβεια not εὐσέβεια.

[81] Cf. Epiph., *Haer* 31, 5, 3, μνείαν ποιοῦμαι μυστηρίων πρὸς ὑμᾶς, οὔτε ἀρχαῖς οὔτε ἐξουσίαις οὔτε ὑποταγαῖς οὔτε πάσῃ συγχύσει περινοηθῆναι δυναμένων.

[82] *Diogn* 11: 2. Cf. also 10: 7 μυστήριον Θεοῦ.

[83] This writing is considered spurious. Whoever the actual author was, its evidence for the meaning of our term is important.

Irenaeus proposes to expose the 'monstrous and deep mysteries' of the Gnostics in order to protect from error those who cannot comprehend them and discern their pernicious nature: ἡγησάμην . . . μηνῦσαί σοι, ἀγαπητὲ, τὰ τερατώδη καὶ βαθέα μυστήρια, ἃ οὐ πάντες χωροῦσιν, ἐπεὶ μὴ πάντες τὸν ἐγκέφαλον ἐξεπτύκασιν.[84]

Hippolytus in describing the heresy of the Naasenes, makes copious quotations from a tractate of theirs in which the term μυστήριον appears a great many times. The adjs. used to qualify our term are most revealing of the meaning intended: κεκρυμμένον μυστήριον ἐν σιωπῇ (Phil., V, 8); κρυπτὰ καὶ ἀπόρρητα μυστήρια (V: 7); μέγα καὶ κρύφιον καὶ ὅλων ἄγνωστον μυστήριον κεκαλυμμένον καὶ ἀνακεκαλυμμένον (V, 7); μέγα καὶ θαυμαστὸν καὶ τελειότατον μυστήριον (V, 8); μυστήριον ἄρρητον (V, 8); ἄρρητα μυστήρια (V, 8 (3 ×)); κρύφιον καὶ ἄρρητον τῆς μακαρίας μυστήριον ἡδονῆς, V, 7); μέγα καὶ ἄρρητον μυστήριον (V, 7—8 (bis)). In his work again Noëtus (4), the mutual indwelling of the Father and Son during the later's incarnation is considered a mystery: ἐδείκνυε μυστήριον οἰκονομίας, ὅτι σεσαρκωμένου τοῦ Λόγου, καὶ ἐνανθρωπήσαντος, ὁ Πατὴρ ἦν ἐν τῷ Υἱῷ, καὶ ὁ Υἱὸς ἐν τῷ Πατρί.

Clement of Alexandria has been quoted repeatedly in connection with the Eleusinian Mysteries. Like the Christian authors before him, he regards the incarnation of Christ a divine mystery: σαρκὶ ἐνδυθεὶς (μυστήριον θεῖον τοῦτο) τὸν ὄφιν ἐχειρώσατο . . . ὦ θαύματος μυστικοῦ! (Protr., 9). The mystery terminology especially appealed to him, despite his merciless and occasionally misapplied judgments on the Mysteries. He put it to use [85] when discussing a higher Christian knowledge to which one must, as it were, be initiated: ὦ τῶν ἁγίων ὡς ἀληθῶς μυστηρίων, ὦ φωτὸς ἀκηράτου· δᾳδουχοῦμαι τοὺς οὐρανοὺς καὶ τὸν Θεὸν ἐποπτεῦσαι . . . ταῦτα τῶν ἐμῶν μυστηρίων βακχεύματα (Protr., 12). Again he speaks of those who reject the scriptures without first taking time to delve deep into its mysteries: μὴ γὰρ μαθόντες τὰ τῆς γνώσεως τῆς ἐκκλησιαστικῆς μυστήρια μηδὲ χωρήσαντες τὸ μεγαλεῖον τῆς ἀληθείας, μέχρι τοῦ βάθους τῶν πραγμάτων κατελθεῖν ἀπορραθυμήσαντες, ἐξ ἐπιπολῆς ἀναγνόντες παρεπέμψαντο τὰς γραφάς (Str., 7: 16).

6. CONCLUSIONS

The first and foremost conclusion of this study is that the orig. meaning of μυστήριον was that of the *hard-to-understand*, the *incomprehensible*, the *mysterious*, which meaning it has preserved in all subsequent times

---

[84] Iren., Ad Hear, Proem, 2. Cf. also I, 21, 4: μὴ δεῖν τὸ τῆς ἀρρήτου καὶ ἀοράτου δυνάμεως μυστήριον δι᾽ ὁρατῶν καὶ φθαρτῶν ἐπιτελεῖσθαι κτισμάτων, καὶ τῶν ἀνενοήτων καὶ ἀσωμάτων δι᾽ αἰσθητῶν καὶ σωματικῶν.

[85] Cf. Prümm, ZKT, 1937, 398: "Von den 91 Fällen, in denen das Hauptwort μυστήριον bei Klemens vorkommt, handelt es sich bei einem Drittel unmittelbar um die heidnischen Mysterienkulte". See further Marsh, JTS, 1936, 64—80.

to the present day. During the course of its history its semasiological stream sometimes became broader and shallower with its meaning being thinned down to a mere *secret*; at other junctures again, the banks of the 'stream' drew together, its bed sank deep and its contents assumed a dark impenetrable appearance, with its meaning shifting back to the *mysterious*.

The term seems to be a κατ' ἐξοχήν religious one, and it is not surprising that it never lost its religious character during its long history. In the religion of Eleusis the μυστήρια is a divine drama (δρᾶμα, δρώμενα, δράω): ἀγνά (holy), σεμνά (awful) and ἄρρητα (ineffable), which it is given to man to witness under very special circumstances and with the utmost of solemnity. The drama's sanctity may not be violated, its contents not divulged to outsiders, its scenes not mimicked or parodied even by the very μύσται. The drama entails participation in divine sorrow and pain with a resulting *katharsis* in the μύστης a divine revelation of the most intimate nature, a vision of things indescribable (ἄρρητα καὶ ἀνεξήγητα). It is a *mysterium tremendum*! The vision is overwhelming.[86] The impact of the divine is immense.[87] It is to be seriously doubted whether the μύστης had any clear conception of what really transpired in the most solemn moment of the ceremony, or could give a rational account of what he had witnessed under the effects of divine presence. The drama, the revelation, the vision were μυστήρια ἄρρητα — mysteries beyond description. What was apprehended was the outward contours of the vision; the rest, the core, remained unrevealed. I maintain, therefore, that *mysteriousness* was the element which our term expressed in the Eleusinian Mysteries and not merely *secrecy*.[88] Herein lies the great legacy of Eleusis for the NT.

By the time the term reaches the NT is has already been used in the domain of Philosophy, Magic, Apocalypticism. Its usage has ceased to be the sole prerogative of cultic religion. Where it does not bear the 'attenuated' sense of *secret*, or is not applied to the Mysteries, it is generally

---

[86] Cf. Lucius' description of his experience in Ap., *Met.* 11, 23, and see Griffiths, *IB*, 294 ff.

[87] We know, for example, that in the Mysteries of Attis the officiating priest shouted to the initiates, in the course of the ceremony, the encouraging words: θαρρεῖτε μύσται τοῦ θεοῦ σεσωσμένοι· ἔσται γὰρ ἐκ πόνων σωτηρία (Firm. Mat., *Err. Prof. Rel.* 22, 1).

[88] It is paradoxical that a concept like μυστήριον which juxtaposes the creaturliness of man over against the infinity of the gods, and at that in the sphere of intellectual comprehension should have been developed among a people who were notorious for their familiarity with the gods, for the manner in which they attributed to their divinities every weakness and vice of their own, and who generally created their gods after their own hero and heroine prototypes! Perhaps this is why some of the more liberated minds among them (see *supra*, 2, C, iv, d note 3) did not scruple to behave with ὕβρις — 'arrogantly' — towards the Mysteries. Cf. V. d. Lof, *ZNW*, 1962, 251: "In der literarischen Welt war der Einfluss der Mysterien an sich nicht gross, aber im Volksleben waren diese Kulte in Augustins Zeit noch verankert".

used of a teaching, or truth, or purpose which transcends the human mind and is, on that acount, characterized as mysterious or incomprehensible.

Such is the usage for the most part in the NT, but the context here is religious once again. The NT μυστήριον — to confine myself to Eph and Col as exx. — is the mysterious purpose (πρόθεσις) or counsel (βουλή) of God in His saving plan — a plan that embraces the whole universe (Eph 1: 9 f.). The μυστήριον acc. to Rm 16: 25 f. is revealed by means of the prophetic scriptures. Yet Eph 3: 5 ff. states and Col 1: 26 ff. implies, that it was hidded from the men of previous generations. Was this a concealment in openess? — perhaps of the kind we have in Mt: they hear, but they do not understand; they see, but they do not perceive? Something of this sort seems to be suggested by a new factor in connection with the revelation of the mystery that emerges in the stage of drama in the NT. This factor is the Holy Spirit. But the Holy Spirit is divine and this means that a divine factor is *necessary* for the comprehension of the μυστήριον. This seems to be confirmed by the nature of the Holy Spirit's activity in this connection, which is *not* that of declaring, or revealing μυστήρια in the sense of *secrets*, but rather that of supplying man with the *necessary ability to grasp what is being revealed*, viz., the mysterious, or, otherwise incomprehensible counsels of God. The NT had left Eleusis behind it in this respect, for we find there no such divine factor. It would almost be a corollary from this that the absence of this factor from the OT contexts is responsible for the μυστήριον ἀποκεκρυμμένον.

CHAPTER II

SOME PECULIAR FEATURES IN EPHESIANS

The Epistle to the Eph exhibits a number of peculiarities not shared by the other Epistles of the NT. The peculiarities with which I shall concern myself here relate primarily to the division of the subject-matter, the vocabulary, and some types of literary genre.[1]

1. SOME STATISTICAL OBSERVATIONS

Eph has 2427 words with a vocab. of 526 words (including 6 prop. names), i.e. 21.6 % of its total word number.[2] Of these words 310 occur only once.

A. Parentheses—Digressions

Eph has eight parentheses [3] with a total of 76 words.[4] But it also has two long parentheses, or better, digressions — 2: 2—5 a (=77 words), and 3: 2—14 a (=190 words) — which ammount to 267 words.[5] The total of parenthetical-digressional words in Eph becomes 343 words, i.e. 14.1 % or 1/7 of its total word number.[6] The first digression of 77 words has a vocab. of 42 words (i.e. 54.5 %) with 6 *hapax leg.* in the Epistle. The second digression has 190 words with a vocab. of 88 words (i.e. 46 %) and 17 *hapax leg.*

---

[1] Detailed analyses of these and other phenomena can be found in many of the studies quoted below and occur in more profusion in Percy, *PKE*; Mitton, *EE*; and V. Roon, *AE*. Here I shall concern myself only with the more general (and palpable) evidence based on personal calculations on the GNT text.

[2] The figures for Col are: 1576 words with a voc. of 426 words, i.e. 27.6 %.

Some comparisons with Col will be given, because this is the Epistle with which Eph has most in common, but no reference will be made to the discussion regarding interdependence. Such a discussion in not only beyond the scope of my investigation, it also requires a length that is prohibitive for the space available.

[3] 2: 5 c=3 words; 2: 11 b=11 words; 2: 14 b=2 words; 4: 9—10=31 words; 4: 21 b (poss.) =6 words; 4: 22 b (poss.) =7 words; 4: 25 b=4 words; and 5: 9=12 words.

[4] Col has six such parentheses: 1: 5—6=39 words; 1: 20 b=6 words; 2: 9—10 a=15 words; 2: 23=21 words; 3: 20 b=12 words; and 4: 3 d=4 words: in all 97 words.

[5] Col lacks such digressions.

[6] For Col the figures are 6.1 % or 1/16.

That 1/7 of this Epistle is paranthetico-digressional may not be without significance for the understanding of the nature of Eph. This probably testifies to the lack of a formalised pattern or to a spontaneity in the writing of it.

B. The Major Divisions

Eph falls naturally into two almost equal parts, chs. 1—3 and 4—6.[7] The first part, chs. 1—3, begins with a Eulogy (1: 3—14) and ends with a Doxology (3: 20—21). The second part, chs. 4—6, begins with exhortation and closes in the usual epistolary way. The contents of the two sections are also clearly marked. Ch. 1 consists of a Eulogy and a Prayer. Ch. 3 begins with a Prayer in which a long Digression is inserted and ends with a Doxology (a form kin to the Eulogy). Between these chs. stands ch. 2, which, as will be seen in ch. III, forms a development of the relation to God of Jews and Gentiles as well as a development of their mutual relationship. These facts are too solid to allow any other major division.

C. Eulogy, Doxology, Prayers

Apart from the above-mentioned division Eph is capable of another division. The chief peculiarity of this Epistle relates to the fact that large sections of it are Eulogy, Doxology, or Prayer.

Thus, if we exempt the address containing 30 words, we note that of the remaining 2398 words, 750 words are taken up by the Eulogy, Doxology and Prayer.[8]

The Prayer and Eulogy sections, accordingly, form almost 1/3 (exactly 31.317 %) of the bulk of this Epistle. With respect to the first part of

---

[7] This is the traditional division (cf. Barth, I, 53 n. 219), which there does not seem to be any reason to upset. Barth's division (I, 55 f.) into three parts: 1: 15—2: 22; 3: 1—4: 22; and 4: 23—6: 20 is untenable. The fact that the Eulogy has been lately seen as 'the key' to the whole Epistle (Maurer, *Ev. Th.*, 1951—2, 151 ff.); or as the 'Präludium' to it (Dahl, *TZ*, 1951, 262) or as 'eine Summa' (Schlier, 72, and Sanders, *ZNW*, 1965, 230) does not mean that the division of the Epistle into two parts must be given up.

[8] I.e.

Eulogy	1: 3—14	12 vv.	202 words
Prayer	1: 15—23	9 „	169 „
Prayer	3: 1, 14—19	7 „	97 „
Mysterion Digression	3: 2—13	12 „	189 „
Doxology	3: 20—21	2 „	37 „
Prayer	6: 18—20	3 „	56 „
		45 vv.	750 words

the Epistle, the Eulogy-Prayer sections are over 2/3 (exactly 71.320 %) of it! This in itself is significant for the character of the Epistle as a whole as well as indicative of the division of the Epistle into two parts.[9]

Another point of interest, in this connection, is the fact that μυστήριον, admittedly one of the most important term in this Epistle (at least in the first Part), occurs 5 × in the Prayer-Eulogy sections, but only 1 × in the rest, i.e. 4 × in part I and 2 × in part II.

Below are appended some tables showing the statistical relations of the Eulogy-Prayer sections to the rest of Eph.

Table I

	All Wor.	Voc.	%	Pec. Wor.	% All Wor.	% Voc.
Eulogy-Prayer	750	202	26.9	75	9.9	37.1
Rest of Eph	1676	451	26.9	324	19.3	71.3

This chart shows that there is absolutely no difference in the relation of vocabulary to the total no. of words between the Eulogy-Prayer sections and the rest of Eph. In the matter of peculiar words,[10] however, the rest of Eph evinces a much larger percentage.

Table II

On no. of words of low NT frequency.

NT occur	Eulogy-Prayer					Rest of Eph				
	Wor.	Voc.	%	All Wor.	%	Wor.	Voc.	%	All Wor.	%
1 × ...	10	202	4.9	750	1.3	28	451	6.2	1676	1.6
2—5 × ...	25	202	12.3	750	3.3	72	451	15.9	1676	4.2
6—10 × ...	21	202	10.3	750	2.7	54	451	11.9	1676	3.2
11—15 × ...	14	202	6.9	750	1.8	30	451	6.6	1676	1.7
16— × ...	132	202	65.3	750	17.5	267	451	59.2	1676	15.9
	202					451				

This chart too, does not show any considerable deviation, the two sections are fairly comparable.

---

[9] The prayer of 6: 18—20 is not characteristic of Eph; it occurs in Rom 15: 30 ff.; Col 4: 2 ff.; I Th 5: 25. It is thus without significance against the concentration of prayer and Eulogy passages in Part I.

[10] By "peculiar words" is meant words occurring only either in the Eulogy-Prayer sections or in the Paraenetic Sections.

Table III

Peculiar words compared against the no. of words in their own section.

NT Occur.	Eulogy-Prayer			Rest of Eph		
	Words	Pec. Words	%	Words	Pec. Words	%
1 ×	10	75	13.3	28	324	8.6
2—5 ×	21	75	28	70	324	21.6
6—10 ×	13	75	17.3	47	324	14.5
11—15 ×	6	75	8	25	324	7.7
16— ×	25	75	33.3	154	324	47.5
	75			324		

The Eulogy-Prayer sections here have a slight advantage over the chiefly paraenetic sections in that the great bulk of their peculiar words are of lower NT frequency than those of the paraenetic sections. But even this chart does not lead to any important conclusions concerning the composition of Eph.

Table IV

Eulogy-Prayer sections: All Words 750; Voc. 202; Pec. Words 75; Theologically Important Words 125; Theologically Important Peculiar Words 60.

Paraenetic Sections: All Words 1676; Voc. 451; Peculiar Words 324; Theologically Important Words 155; Theologically Important Peculiar Words 90.

Eul.-Pr.	750: 125	202: 125	750: 60	202: 60	75: 60
	16.6 %	61.9 %	7.9 %	29.7 %	80 %
Paraen. sections .	1676: 155	451: 155	1676: 90	451: 90	324: 90
	9.2 %	34.3 %	5.3 %	19.9 %	27.7 %

This chart shows clearly that the Eulogy-Prayer sections are more loaded than the paraenetic sections with theologically important words and theologically important peculiar words. The last comparison of theol. imp. pec. words against the no. of peculiar words is too conspicuous to remain unnoticed.[11]

Statistics of such limited material is not of much value, but if any conclusions are to be drawn from the tables given, they boil down to two results: a) the vocs. of both groups of sections are in exactly the same relation to their respective no. of words, b) the Eulogy-Prayer sections contain more theologically important words and even more theologically important peculiar words in relation to their comparison referent than do the paraenetic sections. This would imply that the Eulogy-Prayer sections ought to be considered as forming the core of the theological content of the Epistle,[12] and that the almost exclusive occurrence of μυστήριον in these sections indicates its centrality for Ephesians.

---

[11] Even if these figures are not absolutely correct (because of the difficulty of deciding sometimes which words are important and which not) the conclusion they lead to remains unimpaired.

[12] Percy, ZNW, 43, 1950—1, 187, Merklein, CK, 10 f. conceive of 2: 11—22 and

2. THE EULOGY

A. The Genre

Many scholars use the term *Doxology* as a general characterisation of certain types of literary forms irrespective of whether these have the εὐλογητός/-μένος form or the αὐτῷ ἡ δόξα form.[13] Deichgräber,[14] on the other hand recognises three related types: "Doxologie, Eulogie (Berakha in engerem Sinn) und Charis-Spruch".[15] The differentiation between the first two (which concerns us in Eph) is here endorsed, since we are formally dealing with two literary types, though in the final analysis they both resolve to ascription of praise to God.[16] The term *Eulogy* is thus applied to Eph 1: 3—14, while 3: 20—21 is designated as *Doxology*.

The Eulogy is deeply rooted in the OT where εὐλογεῖν occurs over 400 ×, εὐλογία some 70 × and εὐλογητός 77 ×. The large no. of OT and Apocryphal eulogies are very short, but some of them are more substantial, while a few, e.g. Dan 3: 26—45 and Tob 13: 1—18 are quite long.[17] Judaism carried on the tradition in its most usual prayer form, the *Berakha*.[18] This finds expression in the late great Jewish prayer, the Sh^{e}mone 'Esre (the *Eighteen Benedictions*,[19] as well as in e.g. the ordinary prayers before meals.

There are, nevertheless, certain formal differences between our Eulogy and the eulogies of the LXX and of Judaism. The LXX eulogies that are of analogous length (Dan 3: 26—45 and Tob 13: 1—18) are not strict

---

2: 11—18 respectively as forming the core of Eph, though the centrality of μυστήριον is recognised (e.g. Merklein, *CK*, 62).

[13] E.g. Stuiber, *RAC*. IV, 210—26; Robinson, 13; Gaugler, 25; Dibelius, 58; Percy, *PKE*, 201 ('Einleitungsdoxologie').

[14] *GC*, 24; The separation is made also by Werner, *DSC*, 319 ff. Schlier, 39; Guthrie, *NTI*, (*PE*), 136; Dahl, *TZ*, 1951, 250; Gnilka, 56 also have 'eulogy' for 1: 3—14.

[15] Acc. to Deichgräber, *GC*, 24 f. the Doxology consists of three parts: a) the person named, b) the doxological predicate, and c) the eternity formula. The Eulogy takes its name from the vbl. εὐλογητός and is followed by a ptc., rel., or caus. clauses (p. 41). 'Charis-Sprüche' are for Deichgräber, *GC*, 43, the very short thanksgivings which are occasionally found in Paul's letters. Cf. Champion, *BD*, 19 ff. who considers that the Benedictions and Doxologies have for the most part common features.

[16] The helpful distinction between "*berichtender Lobpreis*" (i.e. Eulogy) and "*beschreibendes Lob*" (i.e. Doxology) by Westermann, *LGP*, 17 is accepted by Deichgräber, *GC*, 41; Gnilka, 57, *et al.*

[17] See Schlier, 37 n. 1; Gnilka, 56; Beyer, *TDNT*, II, 755—59 on OT eulogies.

[18] Elbogen, *JG*, 4 ff. traces this to II Chr 20: 26, but finds the technical sense first in Neh 9: 5. On the influence of Synagogue forms on the NT see Rowley, *WAI*, 241 ff. and Dugmore, *ISDO*, 113.

[19] At first there were eighteen Benedictions: the nineteenth being added by R. Gamaliel at the Academy of Jabneh (Blackman, *Mishn.* 1, 50). Schürer, *HJP*, II, ii, 87 f. thinks that it attained its present form between 70—100 A.D. On this Prayer cf. *Str-B*, IV, 208 ff., and Dugmore, *ISDO*, 114 ff.

eulogies for though they start out as such they gradually go over to confession,[20] exhortation and prayer.[21] In fact, the Danielic one is characterised with the words προσηύξατο and ἐξωμολογεῖτο (3:24 f.) and the Tobitic one as προσευχή (13:1), though at its close we read ἐπαύσατο ἐξομολογούμενος Τωβίτ (14:1).[22] This means that we do not find in these eulogies a perfect counterpart to our Eulogy, which is both strictly speaking Eulogy and also of considerable length. Another point of formal difference is that in both of these cases we have the formula εὐλογητὸς ὁ Θεός ... ὅτι, whereas in Eph 1:3 ff. the ὅτι is replaced by a ptc. clause.

The short eulogies of III Kin 1:48; Ps 72:18; 143:1 f.; I Mac 4:30, on the other hand, agree with the Eph Eulogy in having εὐλογητὸς ὁ Θεός ... ὅ, but they are, on the other hand, of conspicuously unequal length. What they have in common with our Eulogy is that they praise God for His acts, though again the content is far different.

The Sh^emone 'Esre, on the other hand, is about 4 × the length of our Eulogy, but it is a prayer and has the conspicuous difference that it repeats the formula ברוך יהוה in each of the 18 (19) Benedictions.

The two eulogies that come closer to our Eulogy are those of Mary (Lk 1:46—55), though formally not beginning with the formula εὐλογητὸς ὁ Θεὸς ὁ / ὅτι, and of Zacharias (Lk 1:68—79).[23] In both of them God is praised for His deeds, though Mary's 'eulogy' is of a more personal character,[24] and concerns herself and her privileged position. Zacharias' eulogy, on the contrary, is wholly taken up with the saving Event, and compares more favorably with Eph.[25] Nevertheless, this, too, has its limitations. The saving Event relates to Israel, is in fulfillment of OT prophecy and the salvation refers (also) to a deliverance from their enemies.

Among the eulogies of the LXX, the NT and Judaism the Eph Eulogy is incomparable for its thought. God's blessings are described in superlatives; they are all-inclusive. They are decided upon from all eternity and encompass both groups of mankind. Behind them stands the good-pleasure of God as the moving factor and initiator for every step towards their

---

[20] On the ambiguous use of confession as 'praise' and 'confession of guilt', see Bornkamm, Apo, 46—63.

[21] For the relation among εὐλογία, εὐχαριστία, ἐξομολόγησις, etc., see Audet, SE, 1959, 643—62.

[22] Cf. Robinson, Apo., 202 ff. for the development from berachoth to hodayoth.

[23] Vv. 76—79 are not considered as being part of the eulogy.

[24] Another eulogy relating to personal deliverance is II Cor 1:3 ff. Cf. Schlier, 41 n. 1.

[25] Cf. Schlier, 41, n. 1.

realisation. Not only are all national boundaries pulled down, but even the very curtain separating earth from heaven is, as it were, lifted, even if only partially, and we are enabled to see the all-embracing purpose of God in reference to the ages.[26]

B. A Hymn?

Since the appearance of Innitzer's article[27] a number of scholars have treated Eph 1:3—14 as a hymn[28] and attempted to reconstruct it.[29] Innitzer himself saw three strophes, 3—6; 7—12; and 13—14, each treating of one of the Persons of the Trinity, even if of unequal length. He was, nontheless, hesitant about calling it 'direkt poetisch'[30] and contented himself with the description "einen verhüllten Hymnus, einen Lobgesang im schlichten Gewande der Kunstprosa".[31]

An attempt by Lohmeyer in 1926[32] to divide Eph 1:3—14 into 4 strophes on colometric grounds called down a damaging criticism by Debrunner,[33] while another attempt by Ochel[34] "met with little response".[35]

Schlier (40) speaks of "Benediktion" in vs. 3 and its "Entfaltung" in vv. 4—10, to which a "Doppelstrophe" (vv. 11—14) is appended. He then divides vv. 4—10 into three strophes: ἐξελέξατο 4—6 a; ἐχαρίτωσεν 6 b—7 and ἐπερίσσευσεν 8—10. Gnilka (59) takes as key-words ὁ εὐλογήσας, προορίσας-ἐν ᾧ ἔχομεν τὴν ἀπολύτρωσιν, γνωρίσας-ἐν ᾧ ἐκληρώθημεν but refrains from speaking about strophes. He calls it, instead, "hymnische Sprache" similar to the Qumran *Hodayoth*.

Among more recent investigations of Eph 1:3—14 may be mentioned

---

[26] The eulogy of I Pet 1:3 ff. also relates to the saving work of Christ, but even this one lacks the universalistic character of the Eph Eulogy. On the eulogy see also Jewett, *ATR*, 1969, 18—34; Lyonnet, *RD*, 341—52; Cambier, *ZNW*, 1963, 58—104; Trevijano, *SE*, 1973, 537—40.

[27] *ZKT*, 1904, 612—21.

[28] For literature see Rese, *VF*, 1970, 75; Deichgräber, *GC*, 65—76.

[29] For criteria in identifying formulae and hymns in the NT, see Rese, *VF*, 1970, 85—87; Stauffer, *NTT*, 338—39; Schille, *FH*, 16—20, 47—50; Barth, I, 6—7.

[30] Innitzer, *ZKT*, 1904, 619; ". . . eine vielleicht sogar etwas *poetische* Form . . ." (616).

[31] *ZKT*, 1904, 619. For criticism of Innitzer's reconstruction see V. Roon, *AE*, 158 ff.

[32] Lohmeyer, *TB*, 1926, 120—25.

[33] Debrunner, *TB*, 1926, 231—34.

[34] Ochel, *ABKE*.

[35] V. Roon, *AE*, 12. Ochel was criticised by Percy, *PKE*, 373 n. 18, and Deichgräber, *GC*, 68—70.

Schille's,[36] Schattenmann's,[37] Krämer's,[38] Fischer's,[39] V. Roon's,[40] Deich-gräber's[41] and Sanders'.[42]

Schille calls Eph 1: 3—14 an initiation song. These vv. are then divided into 3—4, an "Introit", and into two strophes vv. 5—8 and 9—12 a.[43]

Schattenmann bases his examination on the researches of the music scientist Thrasyboulos Georgiades.[44] He finds four strophes, 3—6 a; 6 b—10 a; 10 b—12, and 13—14, based on a count of syllables. He then divides the whole into two halves: 3 b—10 a ("Oben: das Tun Gottes") and 11—14 ("Unten: das Erlebnis der Gläubigen").[45]

Krämer considers the ἐν Χριστῷ phrase not only as "den einheitlichen Mittelpunkt des ganzen Segengeschehens",[46] but also "das durchgehende Ordnungsprinzip".[47] The decisive arguments for the division of the Eulogy are found at the end of the sentence. He notes that the predications are semitic, i.e. the verbs come at the beginning of the clauses. He divides the text into three parts: I, vs. 3; II is subdivided into 3 strophes: i, 4—6; ii, 7—10; iii, 11—12; and III, vv. 13—14.

Maurer[48] divides the Eulogy on the basis of its contents into four parts: vv. 3—4; vv. 5—8; vv. 9—10 and vv. 11—14.

Fischer begins his examination of Eph 1: 3—14 by conceding that "So wie der Text jetzt vorliegt, kann es kein Hymnus sein".[49] Nevertheless, he takes up the challenge to discover the original hymn, on which other attempts have not produced "eine überzeugende Lösung".[50] The actual hymn begins with vs. 4 (vs. 3 being the "Aufgesang"). He distinguishes three strophes: 4—6 a; 7—8 + εἰς ἔπαινον δόξης αὐτοῦ (vs. 12); and 13 b—14. Between the first and the second strophe Fischer leaves out τῆς χάριτος ἧς ἐχαρίτωσεν ἡμᾶς ἐν τῷ Ἠγαπημένῳ (i.e. 8 words), while between strophe 2

---

[36] Schille, *LG*, in 1953.

[37] Schattenmann, *SNP*, in 1965.

[38] Krämer, *WD*, 1967.

[39] Fischer, *TA*, in 1973.

[40] V. Roon, *AE*, 1974. (The orig. Dutch was published in 1969).

[41] Deichgräber: *GC*.

[42] Sanders, *ZNW*, 1965.

[43] For criticism of Schille, see Deichgräber, *GC*, 69 f. In his *FH*, 66—9 Schille treats vv 11—13 as a (Pauline) prose interpolation to a pre-Pauline hymn.

[44] I.e. on ancient Greek meter and music. A number of his works are mentioned in *IEE*, III: B, 627 f.

[45] For criticism of Schattenmann, see Krämer, *WD*, 1967, 36—7, and Deichgräber, *GC*, 71 f.

[46] Schlier, 40 n. 2.

[47] Krämer, *WD*, 1967, 38.

[48] Maurer, *Ev. Th.* 1951—2, 154.

[49] Fischer, *TA*, 112.

[50] *TA*, 111.

and 3 he leaves out vv. 9—13 a (i.e. 79 words). In addition, he makes a few more changes and transpositions of small words.[51] In his ensuing discussion[52] he feels the difficulties for his arrangement, but excuses himself on the plea that the 'hymn' has been extensively reworked.[53].

Fischer's analysis is a good example of the extremes to which an over-enthusiastic chase for the discovery of hymns may lead one.

The above-mentioned works, and Fischer's certainly included, show us that "eine überzeugende Lösung" has not yet been found concerning the 'original hymn'.[54] The multitude of reconstructions presents not only a bewildering picture, but is accompanied by the inevitable effect of weakening each particular scholar's *Aufgliederung*. Drastic attempts at solution, like that of Fischer which leave out 87 of the 202 words of the Eulogy, are the least convincing, for they suffer from the fact that the Eulogy presents a unified whole, as will be seen in chs. III and IV.[55] To say that the original hymn has been heavily reworked necessitates the acceptance of two assumptions: a) that all dividing lines between the original material and the additions have been carefully obliterated,[56] and b) that certain scholars, notwithstanding this, are capable of penetrating to this undifferentiated material to the point of dividing between ἁρμῶν τε καὶ μυελῶν.

Again, the scholars who have tried to separate a hymn have been led chiefly by considerations of Greek meter and quantity.[57] But as the material stubbornly refuses to lend itself to such reconstructions, they have been obliged to have recourse to transpositions, and omissions of words, phrases, and even verses.[58] In other words, in their eagerness to make the 'hymn' fit the pattern each conceived (e.g. the so-called refrain εἰς ἔπαινον δόξης or the trinitarian formula) they failed to pay sufficient attention to the contents of the Eulogy.

According to the analysis of ch. IV the Eulogy makes good sense as it is: it, in fact, evinces a progression of thought from the general to the

---

[51] *TA*, 114.

[52] *TA*, 114—18.

[53] *TA*, 113.

[54] Cf. Sanders, *ZNW*, 1965, 227, "Every attempt to provide a strophic structure for Eph 1:3—14 fails, and places in very grave doubt the thesis that we have to do here with the quotation of a hymn". Vielhauer, *GUL*, 47, similarly, expresses doubt as to the hymnic character of the eulogy.

[55] From the point of view of the analysis presented in ch. IV the above mentioned reconstructions are very improbable.

[56] How else can we explain the fact that no two scholars are agreed as to the limits of the strophes!

[57] Though without ever attaining these.

[58] A glaring instance of this is Fisher's analysis in which, what for me is the very peak of the Eulogy (i.e. vv. 9—10) is for him not a part of his 'hymn' at all!

particular till it reaches its climax in the *anakephalaiōsis* of all things in Christ. No substantial part could be removed without causing irreparable damage to the progression of thought.[59]

Several scholars have, however, shown a different approach to the Eulogy. Deichgräber holds that the Eulogy (for him 3—12)[60] far from being poetry, is a "Lobpreis in *reiner Prosa*"[61] and appeals to the Qumran *Hodayoth* for its clarification.[62] V. Roon considers that the Eulogy is comparable to the Psalms[63] and that its style cannot be compared with Greek prose;[64] it is "lyrical, poetic, intensive"[65] as well as "epideictic".[66] He finds the Epistle "a homogeneous unit"[67] and rejects Schille's thesis that the author used "eine hymnische Vorlage" for the Eulogy.[68] Sanders is even more unequivocal when he declares, "If there remain, however, some element of doubt as to whether Eph 1: 3—14 is a quotation, it is still possible to say with even greater certainty that it is not a quoted *hymn*; for all attempts at 'reconstructing' a hymn here, i.e. at bringing rhythmic formal order to the passage, fail".[69]

To conclude this section, Eph 1: 3—14 has been designated as a Eulogy, and that may be deemed sufficient. We have seen that it has much in common with the OT, Apocryphal, and NT eulogies. This does not mean that it has been patterned on these eulogies,[70] for as we have already had occasion to note, the author of Eph exhibits an independence in thought from the above-mentioned eulogies, which puts him in a place all of his own. What is common to them all is that they are all inspired by the common Israelite-Jewish background, which has left more than mere traces of religious devotion in the Psalms and in the eulogies of the OT and Judaism. That the Eulogy is not structured in accordance with the rules of grammar is evident,[71] but this is also natural for the language

---

[59] Cf. V. Roon, *AE*, 191.

[60] *GC*, 65.

[61] *GC*, 66. But cf. also his statement on p. 65, "Die Gattung von V. 3—12 ist sicher als Hymnus zu bestimmen".

[62] *GC*, 72—5. Similarly, Gnilka, 59.

[63] *AE*, 184, 187 f., 192 f.

[64] *AE*, 184.

[65] *AE*, 185.

[66] *AE*, 186.

[67] *AE*, 191.

[68] *AE*, 191.

[69] *ZNW*, 1965, 224 and 232.

[70] Cf. Dugmore, *ISDO*, 113 who says that there was no "wholesale borrowing".

[71] Cf. Norden, *AT*, 253 n. 1 "Das montröseste Satzkonglomerat . . .", V. Roon, *AE*, 112 "an unintelligible construction", though Krämer, *WD*, 1967, 46 objects "Von Satzkonglomerat oder Verworrenheit der grammatischen Beziehungen kann, alles in allem, wohl kaum die Rede sein".

of devotion[72] in which it may be claimed that the heart is allowed to run before the mind. The result is that we are given a sentense of 202 words.[73] This does not mean that the contents are in a state of confusion, for as a matter of fact, though the relations between the clauses are not always clearly marked grammatically, they do sustain an intelligible logical relation which yields itself to a semantic analysis, though only after some toil. We see both a progression and a purpose. The 'conglomerating' effect may be due to another circumstance. In eulogies of great length the term εὐλογητός is repeated several times. In the case of the *Eighteen Benedictions* the word ברוך is repeated in each Benediction. In Eph, on the other hand, the author declares God εὐλογητός and then tries in one sweep to enumerate all his reasons for eulogising Him. The result may be somewhat clumsy, but it is quite effective in another way, in presenting, in a torrential manner, all that constitutes God's blessings. Indeed, vv. 4 ff. do nothing else than explain what these blessings are.[74] There is no need for a repeated εὐλογητός.[75]

C. The Delimitation, Position and Function of the Eulogy

"It is a 'breakthrough' for the understanding of the letter in general to realise that Eph 1:3—14 'can be named a summa of the entire letter, if . . . only in a narrow sense'" writes Sanders [76] quoting Schlier.[77]

As a matter of fact 1951—52 saw the publication of two studies, by Dahl [78] and Maurer,[79] which treated the Eulogy as a kind of introduction to the whole epistle.[80]

---

[72] Cf. V. Roon, *AE*, 112 "a lack of formative education". Kuhn, *PQ*, 117, links it up with Qumran, esp. the *Hodayoth*.

[73] The longest sentence I have hitherto noted in ancient literature is the first sentence of Long, ΠΥ, consisting of 130 words. Col 1:9—20 numbers 218 words.

[74] So too. Dahl, *TZ*, 1951, 254.

[75] Nor should the Christian be given up to vain babbling, cf. Mt 6:7 and our Lord's prayer with its single mention of Πάτερ ἡμῶν.

[76] *ZNW*, 1965, 230.

[77] Schlier, 72. Cf. also Barth, I, 53 f.

[78] Dahl, *TZ*, 1951.

[79] Maurer, *Ev. Th.* 1951—2.

[80] Käsemann, *RGG*, II, 217—18, and Marxsen, *INT*, 194—95 consider ch 1 as an independent introductory part corresponding to the thanksgiving and introduction of the genuine Pauline Epistles. Kümmel, *FBK*, 247, regards the whole of chs. 1—3 as an extended epistolary introduction. To this the admonitions are immediately attached, with the result that the usual core of a Pauline epistle is omitted. Cf. Dibelius, 78 and Gaugler, 161. Similarly Barth, I, 55 "a prologue or the overture to the whole that follows".

Dahl, who gives Eph 1:3—14 the appelation 'Briefeingangs-Eulogie',[81] distinguishes between the Eulogy, which praises God for His acts, and the Thanksgiving, which praises Him for an experience and is thus of a more intimate nature.[82] He thinks that, as in the case of the introductions, there is a correlation between the Eulogy and the contents of the Epistle.[83]

Maurer decides that the contents of Eph 1:3—14 betray a relation with the "entscheidenden Anliegen" of the whole Epistle.[84] He claims that "die entscheidenden Aussagen des ganzen Briefes im Eingangshymnus *in nuce* enthalten sind" [85] and declares the 'Hymnus' the key to the whole Epistle.[86]

---

[81] Of which there are two more exx. in the NT; i.e. II Cor 1:3 ff., and I Pet 1:3 ff., and one more in Suron's letter in Eupolemus *apud* Eus., *Praep. Ev.* 9, 34.

[82] Following Schubert, *FF*, 183 f., Dahl sees Paul's use of a Eulogy instead of a Thanksgiving in II Cor as being motivated by the disturbance of his relations with that church.

[83] Dahl, *TZ*, 1951, 261. Dahl then puts forward the thesis that the Eulogy is a Baptismal Eulogy. "Tatsächlich spielen in Eph 1:3—14 Taufmotive eine grosse Rolle" (264). He mentions that Flemington, *NTDB*, 69—71; V. Stromberg, *STPT*, 61 n. 1, independently drew similar conclusions, and approves of Lüken's supposition (*SNT*,) that Eph is a 'Taufpredigt'. In *STK*, 1945, 85—103 Dahl sees baptism as the main theme of Eph. (esp. p. 103). Similarly Schlier, 69 f., 109 ff.; Schille, *FH*, 34, 43, 57, 103; Coutts, *NTS*, 1957—8, 115 ff.; Pokorny, *EG*, 17 ff.; Kirby, *EBP*, 150 ff.; Percy, *PKE*, 447; Wilson, *SE*, 1964, 676—80; V. Roon, *AE*, 55 n. 1; Merklein, *CK*, 63 ff. For further literature, see Beasley—Murray, *BNT*, who has his own distinctive understanding. Gnilka, 60 n. 2 comments, "Das muss jedoch Vermutung bleiben". and Dunn, *BHS*, 160, "Any identification of the seal of the Spirit with baptism or confirmation is to be rejected". See Barth, I, 135 n. 336 for literature in this discussion. Barth, (I, 138 ff.) himself rejects this understanding. See I, 135—44 for a discussion of the two interpretations.

In addition to Barth's objections, two very serious points may be urged against the baptismal theory: a) the curious and inexplicable fact that an Epistle devoted to baptism should make only a single bald mention of that term (i.e. 4:5), and at that, not for the sake of baptism itself, but merely as one of the points that constitute the Christian faith; (The 'points of contact' between the Eulogy and other NT sources dealing with baptism, enumerated by Coutts, *NTS*, 1957—8, 124 ff. are, to say the least, very questionable. Coutts moves all the time in the world of probabilities. On no occasion has he proved a point beyond doubt. Acc. too Deichgräber, *GC*, 70, Coutts' reconstruction is not only 'tentative' as he calls it himself, but 'falsch'), and b) the inappropriateness of the teaching of Eph for new converts. Writing to the Corinthians Paul remarks that they neither were nor are at present sufficiently mature to receive proper food (βρῶμα). Instead, they had to be given milk. Similarly Heb 5:12 ff. allots milk to the νήπιος but στερεά τροφή to the mature. Could it be rightly claimed that Eph is but spiritual milk? Is it not rather στερεά τροφή of the highest kind?

[84] Maurer, *Ev. Th.* 1951—2, 152.

[85] Maurer, *Ev. Th.* 1951—2, 168.

[86] Maurer considers the concept of Head and Body, as covering the whole Christology and Ecclesiology of Eph, in a gnostic light. His understanding of the Eulogy

The insight of Dahl, Maurer and others, that the Eulogy is to be understood as in a certain way prefiguring the contents of the entire Epistle, is certainly valuable and in line with my own findings. Before, however, attempting to offer some points of contact between the Eulogy and the rest of Eph, another question has to be decided, i.e. the limits of the Eulogy.

It was hinted, above, that scholars are not agreed as to where the 'Hymn' ends,[87] nor do two scholars divide the Eulogy in the same way. This is the result of different criteria applied to the text, criteria aimed at discovering a hymn.[88]

The criteria applied to it in this study are, in the first place, considerations of content, and in the second place syntactical considerations, with the semantic method of analysis and its consequences always kept in the back of the mind. A comparison with other eulogies too, plays its part.

In what is said here there is a certain anticipation of chs. III and IV. Vv. 3—14 are taken to constitute the larger Eulogy. Within these 12 vv. we have what may be called the Eulogy proper, or Eulogy in narrower sense, which consists of vv. 3—10[89] and deals with transcendental questions regarding God, His purposes and His acts. To this are joined three applications dealing with the partial fulfillment of God's purpose in time: a) ἐν αὐτῷ (vs. 10) + vv. 11—12 in reference to the Jews; b) vs. 13, in reference to the Gentiles, and in this case, in reference to the recipients of the Epistle; and c) vs. 14, the common participation of Jews and Gentiles in the redemption. The reasons for this division may be set forth as follows;

---

is also interwoven along gnostic lines with OT (esp. Isa.) language about the 'Ebed-Yahweh.

[87] Innitzer, *ZKT*, 1904, 619, regards vv. 3—14 as "einen verhüllten Hymnus"; Ochel, *ABKE*, 3—14 "ein kultisches Lied"; Schattenmann, *SNP*, 1—10 vv. 3—14 "Hymnus"; Gaugler, 25 ff. vv. 3—14 "Hymnisches Prooemium"; Coutts, *NTS*, 1957—8, vv. 3—14 (actually only 126 words of the 202 words of the Eulogy, enriched by Coutts' own creations: roughly vv. 7 b—10 and 11 b—12 being omitted) "Homily based on Prayer"; Lohmeyer, *TB*, 1926, 120—25, vv. 3—12, with vv. 13—14 as an application; Schille, *LG*, 16 ff. vv. 3—12 a "Hymnus"; Schlier, 39 f. v. 3 "Benediktionsformel", vv. 4—10 "Eulogie", vv. 11—14 "eine Doppelstrophe"; Deichgräber, *GC*, 65, vv. 3—12 "Hymnus"; Barth, I, 98 n. 148, vv. 4—10 "More rythmic part"; Fischer, *TA*, vv. 4—6 a, 7—8 + εἰς ἔπαινον δόξης αὐτοῦ; vv. 13 b—14 "Hymnus".

Dahl, *TZ*, 1951, 262 f. and Sanders, *ZNW*, 1965, 230 and *passim*, accept vv. 3—14 since they do not consider them a hymn.

[88] Cf. Barth, I, 100. Stauffer, *NTT*, 338 f.; Schille, *FH*, 16 ff., 47 ff. for criteria.

[89] I am in total agreement with the editor's colon after ἐπὶ τῆς γῆς, but my division is not because of it!

i. Comparison with Eulogies in OT and Judaism

An examination of the longer eulogies of the OT, NT, Apocrypha, and Judaism shows that they normaly fail to sustain their eulogistic character to the end,[90] and pass on instead to prayer, confession, admonition, etc. Thus, the 'eulogy' in Dan (LXX) 3: 26—45 is eulogy, properly called, only in vv. 26—33, thereafter becoming prayer (petition) with final vs. 45 reverting to eulogy. The case of Tob (LXX) 13: 2—18 is a mixture of blessing, prayer and exhortation, containing no pure eulogistic part. Vs. 1 characterises it as προσευχή εἰς ἀγαλλίασιν and at the close (14: 1) we read ἐπαύσατο ἐξομολογούμενος ὁ Τωβίτ. Of interest is also the fact that εὐλογητός etc. is addressed to God no less than 6 ×, and ἐξομολογοῦμαι 5 ×. Blessing and petition are all the time closely interwoven.[91] The situation with I En 84: 2—6 is not any different. Vv. 5—6 form a petition, while vs. 4 is an observation on God's judgement.[92]

The significance of these observations is that no one can claim *a priori* that the eulogy of Eph 1 must necessarily end at vs. 14.

ii. Focus (semantic)

Syntactically, the gramm. subj. of all the Event clauses till vs. 10 is God, with the only exception of vs. 7 (ἔχομεν).[93] But suddenly in vs. 11 the gramm. subj. is changed to 'we', though the constructions become pass. Semantically, this does not imply a change of subj., since God is still the logical or semantic subj. of the Event words κληρῶ, προορίζω, etc. But it does imply something else which is of considerable significance

---

[90] By Eulogy is understood only the ascription of blessing to God on account of what He has done.

[91] Similarly, Tob 3: 11—15, has eulogy in vs. 11 and prayer in vv. 12—15. Even Tob 8: 5—7 goes over into petition in vs. 7, as does also Tob 8: 15—17 in vs. 17 b.

[92] The *Sh(e)mone 'Esre* is to some extent similar to the Tob. 'eulogy' in that God is eulogised at the end of each of the eighteen petitions. II Cor starts out as a eulogy like Eph 1: 3, but in vs. 4 b the enumeration of God's acts terminates and the author goes on to speak about the comfort he gives others. In other words, the whole passage is not pure eulgy. The paragraph of I Pet 1: 3—9 is eulogy only till vs. 5, after which the author takes up the situation of the addressees. The 'eulogy' of Zacharias (Lk 1: 68—79) is no exception. The eulogy terminates with vs. 73, the following vv. being taken up with a prophecy about the future ministry of John. A notable exception to this is Mary's *Magnificat* (Lk 1: 46—55) which is, in its entirety, an enumeration of God's acts, though formally it neither uses the formula εὐλογητὸς ὁ Θεός nor is it described as a eulogy. Another case but of more limited extent is Simeon's *Nunc Dimittis* (Lk 2: 29—32).

[93] This exception is, however, only apparent, since the real subj. behind ἀπολύτρωσις is Christ and behind ἄφεσις is God. Ἔχομεν does not predicate an Event of 'us'.

in a semantic consideration. The surface form [94] is determinative of the focus of attention in a given text.[95] Up to vs. 10 God was the gramm. subj. of every event. He was in the center of focus. It was an enumeration, in direct form, of what God had done. With vs. 11, however, God is backgrounded and 'we' is pushed into the foreground. God is, to be sure, still the logical subj. of almost all clauses of vv. 11—14, but there is a shift in focus. Vv. 11—14 are no longer concerned with what God has done, but with what 'we'/'you' have experienced! [1]

iii. Climax

The structure of a eulogy is simple. It consists of the statement that God is εὐλογητός and of a series of statements enumerating God's acts which serve as the grounds for eulogising Him. Vv. 4—10 are concerned with what God has done. Though one cannot say that one act of God is more important than another, esp. since they are, for the most part, causally chained to one another, it is, on the other hand, possible to say that there is a climactic progression in the Eulogy. Firstly, each succeeding statement is more definite and specific than the previous one.[2] Secondly, the enumerated acts take us through a circle: we start in heaven with election, we come down to earth with the shedding of blood and redemption and we are again taken to heaven with the *anakephalaiōsis*. Thirdly, the closing part of the Eulogy (vv. 8 b—10) is replete with theologically important terms. Fourthly, there is a dwelling on χάρις which leads to two semantic statements (ἐχαρίτωσεν and ἐπερίσσευσεν), the second of which implies a preparation for something else which is of momentous importance, i.e. the revelation of the μυστήριον. There is moreover a lingering on this weighty term whose content is not disclosed till words like θέλημα, εὐδοκία, προτίθημι, οἰκονομία, πλήρωμα καιρῶν adequately have described its setting.[3] And fifthly, the final inf. ἀνακεφαλαιώσασθαι disclosing the essence of the μυστήριον as it does, forms a very apt climax to the passage.[4] Being

---

[94] For an elucidation of semantic categories see ch. III.

[95] The phrase εὐλογητὸς ὁ Θεός would, in deep structure mean 'we bless God' since it is 'we' who utter these words. Yet the form εὐλογοῦμεν τὸν Θεόν, though meaning 'we bless God', directs attention to what 'we' do, whereas the Eulogy formula focuses on God and His character, i.e., that He is praiseworthy.

[1] It is such a refined form that I call 'Eulogy proper', for otherwise, in a broad and tolerant sense, the whole passage (3—14) may be termed a eulogy.

[2] Cf. analysis in ch. IV.

[3] Cf. Merklein, *CK*, 62 "... für den Eph im Zentrum stehende Begriff 'Mysterium'."

[4] Cf. Schubert, *FF*, 4 ff. and Sanders, *JBL*, 1962, 357, who speak of an 'eschatological climax' with regards to Thanksgivings.

an item of eschatology and not yet an event, it very fittingly rounds up the enumeration of the acts which constitute God's purpose. As soon as this climax has been reached,[5] the structure changes and the focus is shifted.[6]

iv. Contents prefiguring the entire Epistle

The division advocated here, namely 3—10 and 11—14, receives striking confirmation from the contents of the two parts *vis à vis* the contents of the two parts of the Epistle. Vv. 11—14 have been divided into three semantic statements dealing with the Jews (11—12) and designated by a phrase borrowed from Rom 1: 16 'to the Jew first', the Gentiles (13) and designated 'and also to the Greek', and the common participation of the two in redemption (14).

The claim that the Eulogy anticipates the discussion of the Epistle must be understood in rather broad but sufficiently clear lines. One must neither expect to find in the ensuing chs. a detailed examination of each topic in the Eulogy as if the Eulogy were merely the announcement of a sermon's contents (since it has instructive function itself), nor must one think, on the other hand, that the points of contact between the Eulogy and the rest of the Epistle are rather hazy and undefined.

Below are appended all the words of vv. 3—10 and of vv. 11—14 which occur in the rest of the Epistle. To the right of the list are given the references in chs. 1—3 and to the extreme right the references to chs. 4—6. The references that really correspond in meaning to the Eulogy occurrences are left unbracketed. These are the only references that matter. The bracketed ones are of no significance since the terms are used with a different sense, but are, nevertheless, given to make the comparison objective and ascertainable. The terms ἀνακεφαλαιῶ and φρόνησις do not have formal parallels, but they do have synonymous expressions in ὑπέταξεν (1: 23) and σύνεσις (3: 4) respectively. In the second list πιστεύω does not occur elsewhere, but πίστις, taken as equivalent, does.

---

[5] *Contra* Dunn, *BHS*, 159, who sees the climax in vv. 13 f.

[6] Another difference — stylistic — is that whereas the ptcs. προορίσας, γνωρίσας of the Eulogy proper are used loosely carrying on the argument (see ch. IV), those of vv. 11—14 — προορισθέντες, ἀκούσαντες, πιστεύσαντες — are used in the usual way as temporal circumstantial ptcs. in close relation to their finite vb. From the point of view of the information flow (cf. on this K. Callow, *DCTWG*, 69 ff.), there is very little that is new in vv. 11—14, the main items being κληρῶ, σωτηρία, σφραγίζω, προελπίζω, ἀρραβών, περιποίησις. On the contrary, vv. 3—10 steadily pour forth new elements.

Vv. 3—10	Chs. 1—3	Chs. 4—6
ἅγιοι κ. ἄμωμοι		5: 27
αἷμα	2: 13	(6: 12)
ἀνακεφαλαιῶ	1: 23 (ὑπέταξεν)	
ἀπολύτρωσις		(4: 30)
γνωρίζω	3: 3, 5	6: 19
μυστήριον	3: 3, 5, 9	6: 19
θελήματος		
δόξα	(3: 16)	
ἐν τοῖς ἐπουρανίοις	1: 20; 2: 6; 3: 10	6: 12
εὐλογία πνευματική		(5: 19; 6: 12 πνευματικ.)
θέλημα	(2: 3)	(5: 17; 6: 6)
κόσμος	(2: 12)	
οἰκονομία	3: 2	
παράπτωμα (ἄφεσις)	2: 5—8	
πλήρωμα	(3: 19)	(4: 13)
καιρῶν	(2: 12)	(5: 16; 6: 18)
πλοῦτος χάριτος	2: 7—8	
σοφία	1: 17; 3—10	
φρόνησις	3: 4 (σύνεσις)	
τὰ πάντα	1: 22; 3: 9; 3: 15	? 4—10
τὰ ἐπὶ τοῖς οὐρανοῖς	3: 15	(4: 10; 6: 9)
τὰ ἐπὶ τῆς γῆς	3: 15	(4: 9)
χάρις	6 × in chs. 1—3	(3 × in chs. 4, 6)

Vv. 11—14	Chs. 1—3	Chs. 4—6
ἀκούω	(3: 2)	4: 21
ἀπολύτρωσις		4: 30
κληρονομία		5: 5
θέλημα (βουλή)	(2: 3)	5: 17 (6: 6)
ἐνεργῶ	(2: 2) 3: 20	
δόξα (ἔπαινος)	(3: 13, 16, 21)	
εὐαγγέλιον	3: 16	6: 19 (6: 15)
σωτηρίας		? 6: 17 (σωτηρίου)
λόγος		6: 19 (4: 29; 5: 6) ? 6—17 (ῥῆμα)
ἀληθείας		4: 17—25 (4: 15; 5: 6—9; 6: 14)
πιστεύω	2: 8 (πίστις)	(4: 5, 13—4; 6: 16 πίστις)
πνεῦμα ἅγιον	(3: 16)	4: 30
ἐπαγγελίας	(2: 12; 3: 6)	(6: 2)
πρόθεσις	3: 11	
σφραγίζω		4: 30
τὰ πάντα	(3: 9)	? 4: 6

These comparisons speak quite eloquently. Vv. 3—10 have most of their points of contact with chs. 1—3, while vv. 11—14 have them with chs. 4—6! One detail must not pass unnoticed: four of the eight words of vv. 11—12 ('to the Jews first') do not occur again; the discussion centers instead on the Gentiles. This leads to another observation. The main discussion of the relation between Jews and Gentiles does not take place in chs. 4—6 but in ch. 2. In 1: 14 Jews and Gentiles are common participants in the redemption, but no indication is given there about their unification. If any anticipation of this theme at all is to be sought in the Eulogy, it will have to be sought in the anakephalaiōsis of τὰ πάντα . . . ἐπὶ τῆς γῆς (which, manifestly, includes both). Nevertheless, vv. 11—13 may also imply such a unification (cf. καὶ ὑμεῖς vs. 13).[7]

The above comparisons have, I hope, demonstrated, beyond serious doubt, not only the correctness of my division of the Eulogy into vv. 3—10 and vv. 11—14, but also established the division of the Epistle into two parts, chs. 1—3 and chs. 4—6 which are correspondingly prefigured in the two parts of the Eulogy.

3. THE PRAYERS

Eph has two prayers (1: 15 ff.; 3: 1, 14 ff.) and one exhortation to prayer (6: 18 ff.). The first prayer which is characterised as a Thanksgiving is the one that has received the greatest deal of scholarly attention.[8]

The interest of this study does not lie in the Thanksgiving except indirectly, and at that, owing to the peculiarity that Eph is the only NT Epistle that has both a Eulogy and a Thanksgiving prayer.[9] My interest is directed more to the prayer of 3: 1, 14 ff., but once again, not in the prayer as such, but in the peculiarity that that prayer containes a digression with the fullest treatment of μυστήριον in this Epistle.

Schubert's statement that the Thanksgiving of Eph 1: 15 ff. is "superfluous" after the Eulogy [10] is based on the assumptiom that the Eulogy

[7] Wilson, SE, 1964, 676—80 claims that whereas 'you' always refers to the Gentiles, 'we' refers not to the Jews alone, but to all Christians, Jews and Gentiles.

[8] Schubert, FF, 1 claims (indirectly) to be the first one to carry out a "detailed and comprehensive study" of the Pauline Thanksgivings. Other studies on the subject are: Flowers, ET, 1926—7; Boobyer, TGG; Harder, PG; Sanders, JBL, 1962; O'Brien, NTS, 1974; Robinson, Apo.

[9] Cf. Dahl, TZ, 1951, 253. Schubert, FF, 44 in rather sweeping manner brands the Thanksgiving as "a conscious immitation of the genuine Pauline Thanksgivings particularly influenced (as is everything else in Eph) by Col", and as superfluous after the liturgical proemium (1: 3—14)". See V. Roon, AE, 65 for criticism of Schubert, and Barth, I, 161 n. 80.

[10] FF, 44.

and the Thanksgiving have an identical function.[11] Dahl, who also thinks that the function of both Eulogy and Thanksgiving is "dieselbe",[12] differentiates "Die Eulogien haben deshalb ein Handeln Gottes zum Gegenstand, während sich die Danksagungen zunächst auf ein Erlebnis oder ein Sich-Verhalten der Briefempfänger beziehen".[13] But in this case the function of the one must be differentiated from that of the other.[14]

Dahl's distinction, may be accepted as a basis. God is eulogized for His acts. A Thanksgiving is offered to God on the occasion of receiving good news. Of the two the first one is more elative, it is more centered on God, whereas the second is focused on the believers. But there are more differences. Whereas the Eulogy is expressed on the occasion of the writing of an Epistle, the Thanksgiving is refered to as being offered πάντοτε, ἀδειαλείπτως, ἐπὶ τῶν προσευχῶν μου. Furthermore the Eulogy gives an indication of the subjects occupying the mind of the author, but this, despite Schubert, cannot be said with equal reason and to the same extent of the Thanksgivings.[15] Sweeping generalisations must be avoided.[16]

---

[11] The Thanksgivings are for Schubert a "formal introduction to the body of the letter" (24); "an essential functional element within each letter" (25); while in the case of I Th "the Thanksgiving *is* the letter" (26). With respect to the Eph Thanksgiving Schubert notes that it follows "the real introduction to the letter (1:3—14)" (33). The presence of both in Eph (somewhat puzzling to him, cf. p. 3) is explained as "a highly conscious effort on the part of the author to omit nothing which he considered formally essential in Pauline epistolography" (44). For criticism of this explanation, see V. Roon, *AE*, 65.

[12] *TZ*, 1951, 251.

[13] *TZ*, 1951, 251 f. Cf. Schubert, *FF*, 183 f.

[14] The difference which Schubert draws between them is that the "less intimate εὐλογητός — proemium of II Cor (1:3—11) characterises a letter which is directed to a church with which Paul is in open battle over personal matters" (183—84) over against the more intimate forms (Schubert speaks of two forms) of Thanksgiving. According to Schubert then an author eulogises God only when he is in open hostility with the congregation he addresses, while he thanks God when he is on right terms with it (to the same effect are Dahl's remarks, *TZ*, 1951, 253). But such an understanding leads to total confusion in the case of Eph where we have both the 'hostility' or 'bad relations' formula as well as the 'intimate' one. No doubt we need another distinction, and in this case too, the function must be differentiated properly.

[15] Schuberth, *FF* regards the three Thanksgivings of I Th 1:2—5; 2:13—14; 3:9—13 not as three Thanksgivings with two digressions in between, but as one Thanksgiving made up of the whole of 1:2—3:13 (17—27), containing "all the primary information that Paul wishes to convey" (26). See also Barth, I, 160; Boers, *NTS*, 22, 1975—6, 140—58. Thus in this case he has been able 'to show', not only that the Thanksgiving announces the contents of the epistle, but that it "*is* the letter" (26). In the case of Phil 1:3 ff. (71—82) he applies a causal interpretation on ἐπὶ πάσῃ τῇ μνείᾳ ὑμῶν and plausibly shows that the reasons for the writing of this epistle are indicated in the Thanksgiving. His following conclusion is, however, too sweeping: "Thus we have here a most convincing and instructive example of the fact which holds true in every

54

Schubert is right in pointing out that the Thanksgiving is sparked off by a causal-logical antecedent.[17] This is the case also in Eph 1:15 f. The author gives thanks because he has received a good report about the addressees. As we shall see in ch. IV the exclamation εὐλογητὸς ὁ Θεός is also depended upon a causal-logical antecedent, i.e. ὁ εὐλογήσας. Thus the author of Eph blesses God *because* God has done this or that and he thanks God *because* the addressees have done this or that (i.e. πίστιν, ἀγάπην!).[18] Each of the periods has its own peculiar function, so Schubert is quite wrong in saying that after the Eulogy the Thanksgiving is 'superfluous'. He fails to distinguish sufficiently between them.

The Eulogy is taken up wholly with the divine counsel, its conception outside time and its outworking in time, and in a fairly clear manner announces the chief burden of the Epistle. Vv. 15 ff.[19] do not strictly constitute a Thanksgiving! The author mentions that he has received a report about the readers' faith and love and that he, on that account, thanks God on their behalf wherever he prays. The present passage is

case, that each Thanksgiving not only announces clearly the subject matter of the letter, but also foreshadows unmistakably its stylistic qualities, the degree of intimacy and other important characteristics" (77). However this statement may relate to I Th and Phil it may not be rightly claimed that the Thanksgiving of, e.g., Rom 1:8 ff. foreshadows the contents of that epistle. Again, the Thanksgiving in Phlm is chiefly concerned with Philemon's love and good works, but it does not touch upon the main subject and purpose of the letter, i.e. the Onesimus problem. Cf. Beekman—Callow, *TWG*, 319—42 for a semantic analysis of Phlm.

On the other hand, the Eulogy in II Cor 1:3 ff. is chiefly concerned with θλίψεις and παράκλησις, and these subjects actually occupy the major part of that epistle. The same may be claimed for I Pet 1:3 ff.

[16] Schubert seems to be prone to such generalizations; e.g. he divides all the epistolary Thanksgivings into two types only: I a and I b (Robinson, *Apo*, 202, relates Type I b with the pre-Christian Jewish prayers), but in order to make this division he is obliged to label several Thanksgivings as of a "mixed type" and to take great pains to explain why the rest of the Thankgivings exhibit variations in their formula parts; for if strict criteria were employed the result would be that almost each Thanksgiving would represent a type of its own! (see table in *FF*, 54—5).

[17] It makes no substantial difference that Type I a has a causal ptc. or adv. phrase, while Type I b has a causal ὅτι — clause (the chief criterion for the two types). Both causal types function in the same way as far as the εὐχαριστῶ is concerned.

[18] Hence V. Roon's claim (*AE*, 48 f.) that for the Jewish-Hellenistic mind "there is no distinction between this eulogy and the eucharistia-formulation that was native to hellenic culture" cannot be accepted. I Cor 14:16—19, Ps 71:19 *vis a vis* Rom 1:21, and II Cor 4:15 (quoted by V. Roon, *AE*, 49 n. 1) do not prove that no distinction is drawn between the two terms, nor is this proved from *OGIS*, 234, 11, 20 ff. (quoted by Schubert, *FF*, 147).

[19] Schubert, *FF*, 8 thinks the Thanksgiving continues to "at least" vs. 19 (his criterion is the "eschatological climax"). Sanders, *TOB*, 356 challenges this holding that it continues to "at least as far as 2:10".

not a Thanksgiving as is usually assumed, but a prayer, or more correctly, an abstract of a prayer, in which reference is made to a giving of thanks. Beginning with the final ἵνα the author delineates for his readers the chief points that usually highlight his prayers for them. Where this abstract of prayer or prayer sample ends is more difficult to say. There are three alternatives: at 1:19 (Schubert's view); at 1:23 (the usual view); and at 2:10 (Sander's view).[20] Whichever view is accepted, the prayer ties up with the Eulogy in that it forms the burden that the author has for the readers as well as indicates the teaching content which he wishes the readers should acquire. This burden is none other than the content of the Eulogy. It may then be said that the function of both Eulogy and prayer is ultimately instructive. The Eulogy and the prayer are used as vehicles for instruction each with its own peculiar overtones. The prayer, for example, entails an author involvement which is absent from the Eulogy.

4. THE DIGRESSION OF 3:2—13

The question now is, How does the digression relate to the prayer of 3:14—19? Is it causally related or not? And if not, what is its function? Furthermore, is τούτου χάριν in vs. 14 merely resumptive or does it posess a new force in view of the foregoing?

Part of the prayer opening (i.e. who prays and for whom) actually comes already in vs. 1. The term τούτου χάριν shows that it has a causative antecedent. Since ch. 1 is taken up with the Eulogy and the prayer, this antecedent must be sought in the contents of ch. 2, and esp. in the last semantic paragraph which forms the conclusion to that ch. (vv. 19—22).

The second τούτου χάριν (vs. 14) must be either purely resumptive after a long parenthesis, or with a view to the contents of vv. 2—13. In the second case, the digression must be considered as necessary for the setting of the prayer, and in a certain sense as causally related to it, i.e., the prayer being somehow deepened by it. A comparison between the contents of the prayer and the contents of the digression, shows, however, that there are no particularly strong ties between the two passages. On the contrary, the contents of the prayer may be found in ch. 2, and there are, besides, some points of contact with the prayer of 1:17 ff. There remains, therefore, the other option, namely, that τούτου χάριν is merely resumptive.

But if the digression does not function as a basis for the prayer, what then is its function? A prayer consists of four or five moments: a) the

---

[20] See III, 4.

person who prays; b) the verb of praying; c) the person addressed; d) the content of prayer; and (when not a personal prayer) e) the persons for which one prays. Our prayer has five moments. Moments a and e come in vs. 1. Moments b and c come in vs. 14 and moment d comes in vv. 16 ff. Moments a—c and e may be amplified in various ways. Thus, b has, instead of a simple προσεύχομαι, the dramatic circumlocution κάμπτω τὰ γόνατά μου and c has the whole of vs. 15 as a further definition. By the same token moments a (ἐγὼ Παῦλος ὁ δέσμιος τοῦ Χριστοῦ Ἰησοῦ) and e (ὑμῶν τῶν ἐθνῶν) receive their amplification in the ensuing digression. Such a long digression is, of course, neither necessary nor usual, but in line with the character of Eph. Its occurrence is an express sign that the author considers it important to enlarge upon these two points — himself and the addressees. The digression and esp. vs. 13 confirms and explains ὁ δέσμιος (vs. 1), as well as adds intensity to the form the verbal phrase predicating the praying activity (vs. 14) takes. In this sense, but only in this, and not contentwise, the second τούτου χάριν is strengthened afresh by the digression. He who bows his knees and utters the following words is the one who has been appointed to enlighten them and who, as a result, undergoes tribulation on their behalf. The digression is occasioned by the triangle of relationship: a) ἐγὼ Παῦλος ὁ δέσμιος, b) τοῦ Χριστοῦ Ἰησοῦ, c) ὑπὲρ ὑμῶν τῶν ἐθνῶν — I Paul am a prisoner *because* I serve Christ which I do *for the benefit* of you, Gentiles.

---

[21] Harder, *PG*, 200 thinks the Thanksgivings are genuine and are no mere "Eingangsformel".

CHAPTER III

AN ANALYSIS OF THE LARGER SEMANTIC
UNITS OF EPH 1—3

A. SEMANTIC CONSIDERATIONS

In this and the following chapter I address myself to part of the text of Eph. My ultimate intention is to discover the place and significance of the term μυστήριον in the argument of chs. 1—3.

To this end I apply some of the insights of semantics concerning the structure of a text and attempt to go below the verbal communication, i.e. the surface structure, to a level in which the author's meaning is more readily perceived, i.e. the semantic structure.

Though the fundamental laws operating in semantics seem to be generally accepted, there are different interpretations and applications of them, and consequently various approaches.[1] Even within one general approach there are several theories[2] and, what is sometimes a little confusing, a diversity of terminology.[3] This is due to some extent to the comparative youth of the discipline which has not yet made feasible a crystalisation of terminology[4] and approach.[5]

Not being a linguist myself I have had to depend rather heavily on others with respect to the analytic model I followed. Nida applied his

---

[1] Olsson, *SMFG*, 8—14 mentions French structuralism, German "Textlinguistik" and American discourse Analysis.

[2] E.g. within the American discourse analysis Olsson, *SMFG*, 13 mentions a structuralist (e.g. Z. S. Harris), a tagmemic (e.g. Pike—Pike, *Ling*, 94, 1972, 43—52), a stratificational (e.g. Lamb) and a generative-transformational grammar (e.g. Nida, *TST*; *ESS*; Nida—Taber, *TPT*).

[3] Thus, while Nida e.g. speaks about "nuclear structures", "kernels" and "primary and secondary configurations", Beekman—Callow speak generally of "components of meaning", "concepts" and "propositions". No set-matching is hereby implied.

[4] Fluctuations of terminology occur even within the same author. Nida, for example, in an earlier draft of *ESS* had equated "nuclear structures" with "primary and secondary configurations" (cf. Olsson, *SMFG*, 14), but this is avoided in the published form of *ESS*.

[5] Olsson, *SMFG*, 14—17, combined some of the insights of the three schools, above, with heavier dependence on Nida, but supplemented the method with a "hermeneutic interpretation model" making possible the inclusion of philological, cultural and historical material by which to bridge the gulf between the N.T. and our time.

method to an article in the *Time* magazine[6] but this seems to be too removed from the N.T. milieu, and Louw applied a similar method on Lk. 9: 57—62 and Rom 5: 12—21.[7] These studies deal also with smaller semantic components — not of primary interest for my task. The method which I found best suited for my purpose is that set forth by Beekman and Callow.[8]

For Beekman and Callow the discourse is constituted in the following way: two or more *components of meaning* combine to form *concepts* which in turn combine into *propositions*.[9] Propositions make up *statements* and these compose *paragraphs*. Paragraphs form *sections* and these constitute *larger semantic units* which make up the total *discourse*.[10] Each of these categories has one such unit nuclear or central to itself. Propositions are of two kinds: those that represent an event are called *Event Propositions* while those that signal a relation are called *State Propositions*. Naturally, events are represented by vbs. but often they are communicated by abstract nouns as well.[11] The central proposition (hence P, pl. Pp) in a statement is called *Main P*, while the central P in a paragraph or section is called *Theme P*. The Main and Theme Pp carry on the discourse and are termed *developmental*, while those that support the developmental Pp are named *support Pp*. The developmental relation is one of addition (i.e. it implies equal semantic rank) and this may take the form of a *sequence*, a *simultaneity*, an *alternative*, a *conversational exchange*, or a *matched support*.[12] The supporting relation, on the other hand, is one of *association* (i.e. of unequal semantic rank) and includes by far the larger ammount of P relations. When the support which a P gives is of classificatory nature with information distinct from that of the P being clarified, it may be a case of *manner, comparison,* or *contrast*. When, however, the classificatory support carries information similar to that of the P being clarified, the relation is one of *equivalence, generic-*

---

[6] *ESS*, 54—9 in which he indicates the semantic relations between the secondary configurations. In Nida—Taber, *TPT*, 154—6 the authors analysed briefly and with different criteria Eph 1: 3—10, but this analysis has proved of no help to me.

[7] *BT*, 24, 1973, 101—18.

[8] *TWG*, esp. 267—367. Two other supplementary books on this method are K. Callow, *DC* and Larson, *MPS*. I owe Olsson a debt of gratitude for calling my attention to these books.

[9] B—C's definition of a proposition is: "A proposition is the minimal semantic unit consisting of a concept or a combination of concepts which communicates an Event or a Relation".

[10] Occasionally "a larger semantic unit may consist of anyone and only one of the smaller units" B—C, *TWG*, 273.

[11] B—C, *TWG*, 273 f., 281, 327 ff.

[12] B—C, *TWG*, 275; 291 ff.

specific, or *amplification-contraction/summary*. Pp which support by arguing evince a variety of logical relations and are the most frequent type in a text like Eph. These are essentially *cause-effect* relations and exhibit the following relations: *reason-result, means-result, means-purpose, condition-consequense, concession-contraexpectation*, and *grounds-con-clusion*. Some support Pp describe the temporal or spatial setting and are called *orienting Pp*. They give *time, location*, and *circumstance*. Three supporting Pp relate not to full Pp, as do all other types mentioned so far, but only to a part of another P. These are concerned with the relations of *identification, comment* and *content*.[13]

The relations between Pp are set forth in this and in the next ch. in two ways: by labeling them with one of the above labels and by indenta-tion. The point of indenting Pp is to show their semantic rank. Thus a Main P is indented to the extreme left in a display, while support Pp assume various grades of indentation to the right in accordance with their semantic focus. The Main or Theme Pp are not labeled since they develope the discourse.[14]

The rest of this ch. will be occupied with an analysis of the larger semantic units such as sections and paragraphs (hence pgr., pgrs.) in chs. 1—3 and the next ch. with a propositional analysis of 1:3—10 and 3:1—13.

The purpose of this ch. is to discover the content structure of Eph 1—3 in which to fit the μυστήριον pgrs. (ch. IV) in order to determine more satisfactorily the position, function and importance which the concept μυστήριον has in the Epistle to the Ephesians (ch. VI).[15]

B. AN ANALYSIS OF THE SECTIONS AND PARAGRAPHS OF EPH 1—3

1. 1:1—2. These two vv. form the *praescript*[16] and so constitute the most formal section of the Epistle.[17] This section is made up of two pgrs.,

---

[13] For full discussion of developmental and support Pp see B—C, *TWG*, 287—312.

[14] On the indentation method see B—C, *TWG*, 313—17.

[15] The exclusion from the discussion of 5:32 and 6:19 does not seriously impair the claim that chs. 1—3 give the definitive use of μυστήριον for Eph. The instance in 6:19 is no more than a back reference to 3:3, 4, 9 while 5:32 is a special use of the term verging more on the incomprehensibility of the union of the Church with Christ (and of the husband with the wife) rather than on the salvation-historical significance of the term in chs. 1 and 3. (On 5:32 see Cambier, *Bib*, 47, 1966, 43—90; Sampley, *OF*, esp. 86—102).

[16] Deissmann, *LAE*, 151 n. 3 objects to the term *address*.

[17] Deissmann, *LAE*, 228—245 differentiates between the literary Epistles and the non-

in the first of which the author presents himself and names the recipients, while in the second expresses greetings, in accordance with ancient usage.[18] The division into two pgrs. is made on the basis of the content,[19] vs. 1 describing the author and the recipients with appropriate characterizations with vs. 2 taking up a conflation of the Greek and Jewish greetings.

The absence of finite vbs. is not detrimental to the relations among the various parts as these are signalled by means of the case relations, the nom. indicating the subj. while the dat. the recipients. By the same token the dat. of the second pgr. signals the recipients of 'grace and peace'. Each of the pgrs. contains an implicit event. For the first one the vb. 'to write' is the most appropriate,[20] while for the second the form εἴη is definitely the right one. The opt. expresses a wish on the part of the author to the end that the recipients should experience God's grace and peace, a wish expressed as his greeting. The vb. 'to be' represents not an event but a state. However, the collocation of it with 'grace' and 'peace' implies a giving of these to the recipients, i.e. broadly the event 'to bless'.

The Theme props. of the pgrs. may be stated as: vs. 1. *I Paul, write to you* . . . vs. 2. *May God bless you* . . .

2. 1:3—14. This unit is well-defined from the foregoing and ensuing ones. Firstly, in content and form 1:1—2 is the introduction and 1:15 ff. is a prayer, while the present unit is a eulogy. Secondly in 1:1—2 God is mentioned obliquely while here He is brought to the fore. At the close of this unit the enumeration of what the believer experiences is brought to a close by the ascription of praise to God, and a new Theme is began in 1:15 ff. by the words διὰ τοῦτο (vs. 15). Thirdly this unit constitutes but one sentence in Gk.

The view that 1:3—14 is a unit distinct from 1:1—2 and 1:15 ff. is universal as is seen from the division of the various *VV*. Here, however, I want to suggest that semantically 1:3—14 is not one pgr. but two pgrs.

---

literary letters among which he classifies Eph as all the Pauline letters. Käsemann, *RGG*, II, 518 describes Eph as "ein brieflich nur eingekleideter Traktat", while V. Roon, *AE*, 55 more or less sides with Deissmann. Since Eph cannot be compared with the non-literary letters which Deissmann cites, it is better to regard it as being somewhere between a non-literary letter and a literary Epistle, perhaps nearer the second. Cf. Demosthenes' epistles to the Athenian council which come near Eph. See also Robertson, *Gr*, 86; Milligan, *GP*, xxxi.

[18] On the ancient ἐπιστολή see Roller, *FPB*; Koskenniemi, *IPGB*; V. Roon, *AE*, 46 ff.; Doty, *LPC*; White, *BGL*; Andressen, *ZNW*, 1965, 232—59.

[19] This agrees with the Jewish usage in writing two sentences in place of one in Gk. circles, A to B χαίρειν, cf. V. Roon, *AE*, 46.

[20] B—C, *TWG*, 326 in the similar instance of Phlm choose "I Paul, greet you". This seems to me less plausible since the greeting is expressed by the second pgr.

which form a well-knit section.[21] The reasons for this claim have been set forth in II. 2. C. i—iv. The first pgr. (vv. 3—10) [22] making up the eulogy proper is divided into six semantic statements (or 30 Pp) and the second (vv. 11—14) composing a conjoined application is divided into three semantic statements.[23]

The eulogy pronounces God praiseworthy on the ground that He has lavished on 'us' manifold blessings and then in a series of five statements exemplifies the various acts which make up God's blessings: election, predestination, redemption, the giving of wisdom and the revelation of His *mysterion* to gather together all things in Christ.

This pgr. is constructed in the following way. The first P, which gives the pgr. its genre, is the Theme P. By it God is declared εὐλογητός. The ptc. construction ὁ εὐλογήσας ἡμᾶς stands in a logical relationship to the first P giving the reason for 'our' eulogizing God. Beginning with καθὼς ἐξελέξατο the following five statements disclose the nature of God's blessing to 'us'. These are related to His eternal decision (ἐξελέξατο, προορίσας), to His redemption through the Christ event (ἐχαρίτωσεν, ἀπολύτρωσιν), to His bestowal of qualities that characterise Him (e.g. σοφία) and to His disclosure of the *mysterion* (γνωρίσας . . .). Thus these five statements are specific instances of the claim that God has blessed 'us'. The last two statements, however, have a closer relation between themselves in that the impartation of wisdom and prudence is a prerequisite and preparation for the revelation and comprehension of the *mysterion*. The content of the *mysterion* is disclosed in the clause of the inf. ἀνακεφαλαιώσασθαι where the climax of the eulogy also lies.

Thus within these five statements the eulogy has spanned the great temporal gap from eternity past to eternity future and has portrayed the *mysterion* as God's great end in view embracing the destiny of all creation in relation to His exaltation. This is the purpose, the intention. The rest of chs. 1—3 describes in broad lines the mechanism set in motion to achieve that end.

The following pgr. (vv. 11—14) comes slowly down from the soaring heights of the divine counsel to the temporal and spatial by centering the realization of God's purpose for both Jews and Gentiles on the Christ event, and in particular, on the declaration of the Gospel. It is characteristic that the term προηλπικότας describes the Jews as preceding whereas to the Gentiles is ascribed a 'hearing' (ἀκούσαντες) and a 'believing'

---

[21] For the possibility that a gramm. pgr. may include more than one semantic pgr. see B—C, *TWG*, 273.

[22] This division is made also by *RSV*, *NEB*, *TEV*, and *Luth.*! (while *TEV* and *Luth.* also divide between vv. 6 and 7).

[23] a) vv. 11—12; b) vs. 13; c) vs. 14.

(πιστεύσαντες). The two descriptions form an apt summary statement of the connection of each group to God's saving event, which receives elucidation in chs. 2 and 3.

The role of the Spirit [24] is also brought to the fore and the pgr. is wound up by relating the full redemption to the *eschaton* (cf. the final εἰς ἀπολύτρωσιν).[25] The unity of the section (1: 3—14) is sustained by the triple repetition of God's ultimate aim to glorify Himself (i.e. vv. 6, 12, 14) [26] as also by the fact that this section is but one grammatical sentence. The P for the first Pgr. may take the form *We bless God because He blessed us*, and for the second *Both we (Jews) and you (Gentiles) are redeemed in order to glorify God*.

3. 1: 15—23. The markings of this section are as clear as those of 1: 3—14. Firstly, the opening words διὰ τοῦτο mark out the beginning of a new unit. Secondly, the subject of vv. 15 ff. may be initially stated to be that of prayer. Thirdly, καὶ ὑμᾶς (2: 1) introducing a discussion of the readers' previous state contrasts well with κἀγώ of vs. 15 and indicates that a change of participant involves also a change of subject.[27]

What is not so obvious is where this prayer ends.[28] The suggestion put forward here is that the prayer ends with vs. 19 and that vv. 20—23 form a second pgr. in this section,[29] which, as in the case of 11—14 in relation to 3—10, ties up closely with the prayer being a kind of expansion on its third item. The chief motivation for this division is that vv. 20—23 do not constitute any new item appropriate in an enumeration of petitions, but an expansion of the thought on God's power which operated in Christ. This will become more clear in the following discussion of the content of this unit.

There are 8 event words in the prayer: ἀκούσας, παύομαι, εὐχαριστῶν, ποιούμενος, δῴη, πεφωτισμένους, εἰδέναι, πιστεύοντας. As the finite vbs. are superior to ptcs. and infs. for the development of the Theme,[30] the choice lies between παύομαι and δῴη and hence the ind. παύομαι expresses the one unambiguously main clause. (But see below).

The vs. that presents the greatest problem is vs. 16. How are the ptcs. to be understood? Vs. 15 has 3 (expl. and impl.) event words, ἀκούσας,

---

[24] On the Spirit as ἀρραβών, see Hamilton, *HSEP*, 19 ff.

[25] These two pgrs. are discussed only summarily because their content and structure are touched upon elsewhere, notably in chs. II and IV.

[26] See ch. VI. 2.

[27] Though ὑμῶν, ὑμῖν occur in 15—23 the readers are only 'patients' not 'actors' as in 2: 1 ff.

[28] Cf. II. 3.

[29] Of ten VV. consulted only the *ModGk* has this division.

[30] The ptcs. and infs. depend on the finite forms for their reference. B—C, *TWG*, 319.

πίστιν, ἀγάπην.[31] Semantically these are resolved into: 'I heard', 'you believe', 'you love'. Since the relation of πίστις and ἀγάπη to ἀκούσας is that of content, 'that' is supplied, i.e. 'I heard that you believe . . . that you love . . .' and since both Pp stand in the same relation to ἀκούσας, they are joined by 'and'.

The surface structure form ἀκούσας is a circumstantial ptc. of cause which brings about another action as a result (effect). This action is the Theme P of the pgr. (vs. 16). However, διὰ τοῦτο is generally taken by commentators [32] as referring to the preceding (gramm.) paragraph, though some [33] refer it only or especially to vs. 13. This means that what is done in vs. 16 is only in part the result of ἀκούσας. The report received actually elicits the reaction represented by εὐχαριστῶν, but this seems to be almost incidental in comparison with the other event(s) of this vs., μνείαν ποιούμενος ἐπὶ τῶν προσευχῶν μου. Though the report did give an extra drive to the prayer, it would be gratuitous to say that the author prayed for them only whenever he heard some news. Moreover, contentwise, the prayer is shaped in a manner that suits the contents of the eulogy. In other words, he prays in order that they may comprehend the things he has set forth in the eulogy.

The question now is what is the relation between εὐχαριστῶν and μνείαν ποιούμενος? Are both of them or only the first one to be connected to the finite παύομαι? That εὐχαριστῶν is a complementary ptc. is obvious.[34] If ποιούμενος also is made dependent on παύομαι we get two coordinated ptcs. forming the main clause and hence the Theme P. They then correspond to the two causes for the result of prayer: a) διὰ τοῦτο and b) ἀκούσας. Furthermore, since εὐχαριστῶν is related to the second cause and μνείαν ποιούμενος to the first, we are presented with a case of a chiasmus. This further implies that here we have "ein wirkliches Asyndeton . . . wo . . . das letztere (sc. Partizip) als eine Steigerung zu betrachten ist".[35]

The question is further complicated. Beeckman-Callow [36] refer to

---

[31] Events are not represented only by vbs., but also by abstract nouns. See B—C, *TWG*, 274, 281, 327 ff.

[32] E.g. Abbott, 24; Schlier, 75; Robinson, 149; Simpson, 37; Hendriksen, 95; Gnilka, 88; Zerwick, 44; Foulkes, 58; Gaugler, 56.

[33] Barth, I, 145; Alford, 81.

[34] Cf. Robertson, *Gr.* 1119; *BDR*, § 414.

[35] Kühner—Gerth, *AG* II, 2, § 492. Rudberg, *CN*, 1948, 1—38 quotes this vs. along with other corresponding vv. in the corp. Paul. and classifies them as ". . . Asyndeton eigentlich, aufzählend, anreichend" (14), and again "Das in den Briefen . . . begegnende Asyndeton, das anreichende, wirkliche Asyndeton, das präsentierende, characterisierende, ermahnende und warnende, ist anderer Art als das erzählende . . ." (37).

[36] *TWG*, 330.

Burton [37] who says "such phrases as κάμπτω τὰ γόνατά μου (Eph 3:14) and μνείαν ποιοῦμαι ἐπὶ τῶν προσευχῶν μου (Eph 1:16; Phlm 4; cf. Col 4:12) . . . are paraphrases for προσεύχομαι". Beeckman-Callow then proceed to turn the gist of Burton's statement into the P 'I pray for you'. This can be challenged. The phrases μνείαν ποιούμενος and ἐπὶ τῶν προσευχῶν μου describe two events — 'I mention' and 'I pray' — and cannot be equated since they are not identical as to the extent of their meaning. 'Mentioning you' is only one item along with others that are taken up in the author's prayers since it cannot be supposed that the author's praying is limited to the recipients of this letter. The coalescing of the two events into one is, accordingly, out of the question. [38] The prep. ἐπί with gen. naturally indicates time, [39] so the construction means 'when I pray'. We thus get: 'I cease not to thank (God) for you and to mention (you) whenever I pray.' [40]

On the other hand, an independent use of the ptc. building its own clause and sentence is established with the grammarians. [41] In this case even if ποιούμενος is not related to παύομαι in the same way as εὐχαριστῶν is, it can still be considered as forming its own independent clause.

Vs. 16 needs further modification. Παύομαι 'I stop', is an antonym of 'I continue'. Taken together with the neg. it becomes a synonym of it. Since εὐχαριστῶν is a complementary ptc. we do not have to do with two events — 'I do not stop' and 'I thank' — but with one event, namely 'I thank continually /unceasingly/ always'. [42] Vs. 16 takes now its final form: 'Because I heard . . . I always give thanks for you and mention you when I pray'.

The following vs. (17) is a subordinate clause beginning with ἵνα. This conj. in late Gk. tends to lose its 'telic' force and becomes instead an 'ecbatic ἵνα'. [43] In ModGk it has further been thinned down to νά c. subj. in various dependent clauses and in imper. use. This vs. constitutes the content of vs. 16.

---

[37] MT, 86.

[38] Naturally, it may be pointed out that when the author mentions the recipients in his prayers, he "prays" for them; but this collocation cannot replace the surface str. which is manifestly wider and more inclusively than that.

[39] So BAG, s. v. ἐπί I, 2.

[40] The other alt. 'I do not cease to thank (God) for you when I mention (you) (ποιούμενος=circumstantial, temp. ptc.) in my prayers' would require ἐν ταῖς προσευχαῖς μου.

[41] Cf. Robertson, Gr. 1132 ff.; Moulton, Prol. 222 "That the ptc. can be used for ind. or imp. seems to be fairly established now by the papyri".

[42] Cf. πάντοτε in Col 1:3; I Th 1:3; Phil 1:3 f; Phlm 4.

[43] Cf. Moulton, Prol. 206 f.; Turner, Synt. 102; Robertson, Gr. 997 ff.; Jannaris, HGG, § 1951.

The form δώη (sic) can be either a late opt. (in lieu of δοίη) or an Ionic subj.[44] Simpson[45] takes it as opt.; Schlier[46] leaves it open. Abbott[47] would seem to prefer a subj. while Barth[48] takes it as subj. along with a 'telic' ἵνα. I prefer the subj. with a weakened ἵνα.[49]

Whether we understand an implied form of αἰτεῖν or προσεύχεσθαι or not the fact remains that μνείαν ποιούμενος and ἐπὶ τῶν προσευχῶν μου are predications of prayer, the first more specific and the second more general. Hence what follows the ἵνα can only be the content — not the purpose — of that prayer.[50] The thought of ἵνα δώη is continued on by εἰς τὸ εἰδέναι (vs. 18).

The collocation πεφωτισμένους τοὺς ὀφθαλμούς[51] etc. has been explained variously: a) "in apposition with πνεῦμα as the immediate effect, and so dependent upon δώη";[52] b) as an anacolouthon from the dat. ὑμῖν,[53] τοὺς ὀφθαλμούς being an acc. of respect or specification; c) as being an instance of the acc. abs.[54] d) as "eine freie Partizipialverbindung".[55]

The relation of vv. 16—18 among themselves may be set forth as follows: vs. 16 characterises the following vv. as a prayer; the prayer has as content vv. 17—19. Vs. 17 indicates that the prayer is to the effect that God may give them something. This something is defined as πνεῦμα σοφίας καὶ ἀποκαλύψεως. This is at once the content of the prayer and the means for the P behind ἐν ἐπιγνώσει αὐτοῦ, i.e. 'you know Him.' (αὐτοῦ being obj.

---

[44] Moulton, *Prol.* 55, 293 f., 296 prefers subj. (i.e. δώη); so Turner, *Synt*, 100, 128 f. Robertson, *Gr.* 326 f. reads it as opt. (i.e. δώη). *BDF* and *BDR* §§ 95, 1 and 369, 1, take it as subj.

[45] In a footnote the ed. says that F.F. Bruce has added notes to Simpson's comm. so it is not clear what ammount, if any, of the notes is Simpson's own.

[46] *Eph.* 77.

[47] *Eph.* 27.

[48] *Eph.* I, 148.

[49] Abbott, 26 directs attention to Col 1: 9 αἰτούμενοι, and comments "A vb. of asking must be followed by words expressing the content of the request. And there is an abundance of examples to show that in this and similar cases ἵνα has almost lost or rather entirely lost its final sense".

[50] Cf. C. F. D. Moule, *IB*, 145.

[51] See V. Roon, *AE*, 122 on this.

[52] Abbott, 28.

[53] Robinson, 149 f.

[54] Bengel, *Gn.*, ad. loc. Simpson, 38 remarks "This acc. abs. apparently breaks the symmetrical construction of the sentence and is usually regarded as modified by the subsequent inf. (εἰδέναι, 'to know') but really dependent on the preceeding ὑμῖν . . . Thucidides indulges a good deal in acc. abs. irregularly introduced. They lend additional saliency to a proposition". Moulton, *Prol*, 74 allows only one instance of acc. abs. (I Cor 16: 6), so *BDR*, § 424. Robertson, *Gr.* 490 f. says it "is rare in the NT" and quotes a few instances, but not this vs.

[55] Schlier, 79.

gen.). Vs. 18, πεφωτισμένους τοὺς ὀφθαλμοὺς τῆς καρδίας [ὑμῶν], is the result of the giving of πνεῦμα σοφίας καὶ ἀποκαλύψεως,[56] and at the same time the means for the next P, εἰς τὸ εἰδέναι ὑμᾶς 'that you may know'. Now, how are the words πεφωτισμένους τοὺς ὀφθαλμούς etc. to be related to the foregoing? The second view (Robinson's), above, is out of the question since our text has the acc. and we must reckon with it. Of the other two, if the acc. abs., whose presence in the NT is almost non-existent, is to be ruled out, the first view, which makes this phrase appositional and the immediate effect (result) of δώῃ πνεῦμα σοφίας καὶ ἀποκαλύψεως, yields tolerable sense. The inf. clause εἰς τὸ εἰδέναι is, in that case, the result of δώῃ. We thus have '(I pray God) that He may give you the wise and revealing spirit so that you may get to know Him and enlighten your spiritual eyes so that you may know . . .'.

The inf. εἰδέναι has as its content three items: a) the hope to which they have been called; b) the very glorious inheritance among the saints,[57] and

---

[56] Cf. Dahl's remarks, JP, 70 f. On Qumran paralls. see Flusser, ADSS, 249 f.

[57] The words τίς ὁ πλοῦτος τῆς δόξης τῆς κληρονομίας αὐτοῦ ἐν τοῖς ἁγίοις present difficulties. One of the issues to be decided is whether αὐτοῦ is subj. or not. This is further complicated by ἐν τοῖς ἁγίοις. Stier; Robinson, 40; and Simpson, 39 take it as subj., i.e., 'God's inheritance in the saints', while De Wette, EH; Meyer; Alford, 83 f.; Abbott, 30; Gnilka, 91; Gaugler, 68 f.; Schlier, 84; Allan, 66 (apparently); Zerwick, 51 f.; Foulkes, 61 f.; Hendriksen, 99; Barth, I, 151 take it of the believer's inheritance. Ἐν τοῖς ἁγίοις has been referred variously to Israel (cf. Barth, I, 151 and refs. there), to 'the perfected saints' in contrast to 'militant' saints (Alford, 84), and to angels (e.g. Schlier, 84; Gnilka, 91). This last finds support in 1QS 11:7—8; 1QSa I, 9:12 f.; 1QSb 4:23; 1QH 11:11 f.; etc.

For my part I find the reference to angels as too obscure to communicate sense, particularly, since the recipients have been designated as ἅγιοι (1:1), and κληρονομία is discussed in connection with the Jews and Gentiles (cf. 1:14; 2:19 with 3:6 and 5:5). Nor need we differentiate too sharply between Jewish and Gentile Christians. The Epistle itself describes their unification as their definitive state (cf. Hammer, JBL, 1960, 267—72 on the future conception of κληρονομία in Eph). With Gaugler, 69; Percy, PKE, 377 f.; Abbott, 30; Barth, I, 151 f.; et al. it is better to refer it to the saints, both Jews and Gentiles.

The surface structure gives the impression that the author speaks of God's inheritance in the saints. This has an OT parall. in Israel's being Yahweh's inheritance (so V. Hofmann, 45), though Israel's inheriting Yahweh's promise is even more pronounced. Further consideration, however, gives a different picture. The prayer consists of three petitions the first and the third of which are analysed as 'He called us to hope' and 'He exercises a very great power toward us', in other words, the Actor is God and the addressees are the experiencers or beneficiaries of that action. It would certainly be incongruous if in the second petition God suddenly became the beneficiary of κληρονομία. Besides, the context indicates that the author has in mind what God has in store for and is already giving to His people. Moreover, the prayer reflects the contents of the eulogy, i.e. God's blessings to 'us', see supra II, 3. And finally, κληρονομία, συγκληρονόμος in Eph is predicated of the believers (i.e. 1:14; 3:6; 5:5).

c) His overwhelmingly great power which operates in those who believe. The following adv. phrase is understood in conjunction with πιστεύοντας or with the whole of the third point, and serves as resumptive after πιστεύοντας for the characterization of God's power (i.e. vs. 20).

At this point the prayer reaches its end, but as in the case of the section 1: 3—14, that end is not abrupt, but is followed by a smooth transition by means of a rel. clause to a further elucidation of the third petition which forms the ensuing pgr.

The structure of this pgr. is as follows: The vb. ἐνήργησεν has as its antecedent the subst. ἐνέργειαν (vs. 19, cogn. acc.). This ἐνέργεια was exercised upon Christ. The aor. ptc. ἐγείρας is circumstantial modal/temporal[58] and gives simultaneous action with the fin. ἐνήργησεν. The ptc. καθίσας, also aor., expresses an addition (note καί) to ἐγείρας and thus has the same relation to ἐνήργησεν. The two ptcs. specify and exemplify the mode in which the event predicated by ἐνήργησεν took place. Vs. 21, ὑπεράνω πάσης ἀρχῆς etc. supplies the local setting for the event of καθίσας.

Vs. 22 has a different constr. with inds.[59] The obj. which experiences God's activity, is, in the first place, not Christ, but τὰ πάντα. Yet in the next clause Christ is again the direct obj. of the vb. δίδωμι. Nevertheless, here we have a double acc. constr. where the 'patient' is not Christ, as in ἐγείρας and καθίσας, but the church.

Vs. 23 is a comment on the last item of vs. 22 (ἐκκλησία). Here we have the weighty term πλήρωμα[60] with the bold explanation that Christ, who

A further question is whether ἐν τοῖς ἁγίοις belongs with πλοῦτος or κληρονομίας. Most comm. connect it with the latter; Abbott, 30, objects and connects it with πλοῦτος: "The community of believers is the sphere in which alone this πλοῦτος κ.τ.λ. is found".

In the constr. δόξα τῆς κληρονομίας the abstract δόξα is understood attributively as 'glorious inheritance' (see Beekman—Callow, TWG, 253; Nida, TST, 64 f.). Ὁ πλοῦτος τῆς δόξης is a gen. constr. indicating degree (cf. B—C, TWG, 253) and is rendered with 'very . . .'. The whole phrase becomes 'very glorious inheritance'. And since the subst. κληρονομία represents the event 'to inherit', the P is turned to 'How very glorious among the saints is that which we shall inherit from God'.

[58] Turner, Synt. 154; BDR, § 418.

[59] It is tempting here to suppose that ὑπέταξεν and ἔδωκεν really ought to have been ptcs., additions to ἐγείρας and καθίσας, and that the change to finites was facilitated partly by the distance from καθίσας by the intervening vs. 21 — as anocolouthic (cf. Robertson, Gr, 440) — and partly by the quotation (presumably) of Ps. 8 (ὑπέταξας). Vs. 22, however, is best understood as a specification of the import of καθίσας, and hence subordinate to vs. 20.

[60] See the detailed study by Ernst, PPC., Further Schlier, 96 ff.; Abbott, 34—8; Barth, I, 200—10; Delling, TDNT, VI, 298—305. For the possibility of OT rather than Gnostic influence on this term, see Münderlein, NTS, 8, 1962, 264—76 and Barth, I, 203 ff.

fills everything and so the Church, is in a certain sense Himself filled by the Church [61] as His body.[62]

The structure of this section may now be set forth diagramaratically:

Because of this (i.e. foregoing)
Because I heard
I give thanks for you
I pray for you
May God give you the wise spirit which reveals
    To know Him
(and) enlighten your eyes

  To know:

    The hope to which He called you
    The very glorious inheritance you will receive from
        Him among the saints
    The overwhelming power (exemplified in:)
    God raised up Christ
    God seated Christ above all
    God subjected everything under Him
    God made Him Head over the Church
      She fills Him
      He fills everything

The Theme P for the Prayer must reflect not only the praying but also some of the content of praying: *May you grasp the full magnitude of the riches you have in Christ.* The Theme P for the second pgr. is abstracted as *God exalted Christ above every being.*[63]

4. 2: 1—10. This pgr. begins with a new subj., καὶ ὑμᾶς, in contradistinction to διὰ τοῦτο κἀγώ, of the previous section. Following the eulogy and the prayer, the author concentrates on his readers in a special way.

The pgr. is made up of 3 sentences: a) vv. 1—7; b) vv. 8—9; c) vs. 10. It contains 6 main clauses: a) the first five vv. with συνεζωοποίησεν as the

---

[61] The active sense (the church filling Christ is advocated by Chrysostom; Calvin; v. Hofmann; B. Weiss; Robinson, 255—9; 42 ff; Abbott, 34—7; Hendriksen, 103 ff; Simpson, 42 f; v. Soden, 111 f. The passive (i.e. the church is filled by Christ) has the support of Lightfoot, *Col*, 257—73; Percy, *PKE*, 384; Delling, *TDNT*, VI, 304; Gaugler, 80; Barth, I, 205 ff; while Warnach, (*KE*, 13 f.); Benoit, *ET*, 277 f.; Ernst, *PPC*, 120 accept "ein ambivalentes Verständnis", i.e. active-passive with the meaning of "Fülle und Vollendung".

[62] For a similar pre-christian use of σῶμα see Manson, *JTS*, 37, 1936, 385.

[63] This section was treated in more detail owing to its close connection with the eulogy, its difficult structure, and in order to exemplify the method of section and paragraph analysis as greater length. Chs. 2 and 3 will be treated more briefly.

main vb. (1—5); b) ἔστε σεσωσμένοι (5 b); c) συνήγειρεν (6); d) συνεκάθισεν (6); e) ἔστε σεσωσμένοι (8); f) ἔσμεν ποίημα (10).

Apart from these explicit clauses there are 3 clauses in which the vb. is implicit: a) καὶ τοῦτο οὐκ (ἐστιν) ἐξ ὑμῶν (8); b) Θεοῦ (ἐστιν) τὸ δῶρον (8); c) οὐκ (ἐστιν) ἐξ ἔργων (9).

The structure of the pgr. is simple. The first sentence is drawn out by means of a tortuous elocution on the past state of the readers with the result that its main vb. is not expressed until vs. 5, where 3 vbs. follow almost upon one another: συνεζωοποίησεν, συνήγειρεν, συνεκάθισεν (vv. 5—6).

Not only do the καί interconnections of these vbs. indicate that they are additions (i.e. coordinate), their very form with συν- by means of which they bring the readers into fellowship with Christ, shows that they are used very closely. All of them relate back to the same obj. (ὑμᾶς vs. 1), and their content is analysed as developmental of the Theme: συνεζωοποίη-σεν, συνήγειρεν, συνεκάθισεν are progressional. These events relate to the previous pgr.: συνεζωοποίησεν corresponding to ἣν ἐνήργησεν; συνήγειρεν to ἐγείρας and συνεκάθισεν to καθίσας (all in 1: 20). In 1: 20 these events were predicated of Christ. Here, however, the focus is on the sharing of believers in the exaltation of Christ. Vs. 7 expresses the purpose of the three events and connects back to the reiterated εἰς ἔπαινον in the section 1: 3—14.[64]

Between the first two events comes the parenthetical event χάριτί ἐστε σεσωσμένοι. This parenthesis is taken up for further discussion in vs. 8 as soon as the author has ended the discussion of his main Theme: the resuscitation, resurrection and exalted seating of believers with Christ as a concrete manifestation of God's supreme goodness. The two explicit events in χάριτί ἐστε σεσωσμένοι (8) and αὐτοῦ ἐσμεν ποίημα (10),[65] as well as the three implicit events — vv. 8—9 a mentioned above — are a devel-opment of the parenthetical χάριτί ἐστε σεσωσμένοι of vs. 5.[66]

These considerations show that vv. 1—10 are a well defined pgr. The Theme P will have to be abstracted from the three main Pp συνεζωοποίησεν, συνήγειρεν, συνεκάθισεν: *In spite of your spiritual deadness God by His grace revived, raised, and seated you with Christ*. Or more briefly: *God gave you new life in Christ*.

5. 2: 11—13. The limits of this pgr. are almost as obvious as those of 2: 1—10. With the conjs. διό (11) and γάρ (14), indicating the start of

---

[64] Cf. ch. VI. 2 (the supreme end in view). The connection to 1: 3—14 rather than to 1: 15—23 is in this regard, very apt, since the purpose of God is treated in the eulogy and its sequel and not in the prayer or its sequel. On the other hand, the three events, representing the outworking of that purpose, refer not to the eulogy but aptly again, to the sequel of the prayer.

[65] On this whole vs. see Crowther, *ET*, 1970, 170 f.

[66] This is an example of a backgrounded unit of communication which gradually comes into focus (cf. B—C, *TWG*, 314).

new pgrs. as well as the difference of Theme as compared with the foregoing and following pgrs., the limits are well established.

There are three fin. vbs.: μνημονεύετε (11), ἦτε (12) and ἐγενήθητε (13). The second vb. builds a subordinate clause and is the content of the first vb. (cf. ὅτι). The editions put a period at the end of vs. 12 [67] and many *VV* regard the pgr. as consisting of two sentences,[68] though some *VV* divide it into more than two.[69] The question whether there are one,[70] two or more statements is significant for the relation of ἐγενήθητε either to ἦτε or to μνημονεύετε. In the first case ἐγενήθητε is an addition to ἦτε and the two together form the content of μνημονεύετε. In the second case ἐγενήθητε is of equal semantic value to μνημονεύετε. None of these alts. is satisfactory.[71] The recipients are called upon to remember only what they were, since it is unlikely they would forget what they now are. Moreover, vs. 13 makes up a complete sentence without being dependent on the ὅτι. On the other hand the main content of this pgr. is a contrast between the past and present state of Gentile Christians. And this contrast has its two poles in vv. 12 and 13.[72] The νυνί and ἐγγύς of vs. 13 are contrasted both to the τῷ καιρῷ ἐκείνῳ and to the substance of vs. 12 respectively, as well as to the ποτε and μακράν — a summary of vs. 12 — in vs. 13.

This means that the main clause of ἐγενήθητε is in contrast to the sub. clause of ἦτε. There is, in other words, a skewing between grammar and semantics.[73]

The focal point in vv. 11—12 is not the main vb. — a mere summons to remember something — but the content of 'remember', i.e. what they were (vs. 12).[74] This is taken over in vs. 12 in summary form (οἳ ποτε ὄντες μακράν) and is sharpened up by contrast to their present state. The two contrasted elements are thus brought together in vs. 13 and hence that vs. may be considered as the most pointed one. Since the event ἐγενήθητε ἐγγύς implies a different past state, the final seven words with νυνί may be considered as the Theme P of this pgr.: *You have now come near through the blood of Christ.*[75]

---

[67] T.e. *GNT*, *Nest.*, ΚΔ.
[68] So e.g. *RV*; *RSV*; *JB*; *ModGk*; *BKÖ*.
[69] E.g. *NEB* has three, *JBPh* and *UW* four, while *TEV* six sentences.
[70] *AV* notably understands the pgr. as one sentence.
[71] Merklein, *CK*, 13 f. ranks all three as equal.
[72] The content of vs. 11 is a characterization of the Gentiles from the Jewish standpoint and a characterization of the Jews from the Christian viewpoint.
[73] On this see B—C, *TWG*, 273.
[74] Rese compares this with Rm 9: 4 f. (*TZ*, 31, 1975, 219 ff).
[75] This understanding fits excellently the pattern usually followed in Eph where each main point in the discussion develops into another point. The following pgr. is

6. 2: 14—18. The beginning of this pgr. is clearly marked, but its end is less obvious. There seem to be three semantic statements corresponding to the three sentences in the *GNT*. The first statement has as its main P the principal clause 'He is our peace' [76] which is elucidated in various ways by the five ptcs. and the two subjunctives which follow. The art. ptc. ὁ ποιήσας, equivalent to a rel. clause, is a characterization of αὐτός and at the same time provides a justification for the claim that 'He is our peace', i.e. He has made the two elements of humanity into one. The clause τὸ μεσότοιχον τοῦ φραγμοῦ λύσας [77] is understood as a means for ποιήσας, while the ptc. καταργήσας is either a means to λύσας or an addition to it and with it a means to ποιήσας [78] The ἵνα κτίσῃ is final and so is the ἀποκαταλλάξῃ clause joined to the first one by καί. The two clauses give the purpose for the events represented by the ptcs. Each of these has a ptc. construction, the first, ποιῶν εἰρήνην (pres.), expressing the abiding result of κτίσῃ εἰς ἕνα καινὸν ἄνθρωπον, while the second, ἀποκτείνας τήν ἔχθραν, (aor.) giving the prerequisite for ἀποκαταλλάξῃ, etc.[79]

The second statement, as the conj. 'and' shows, is an addition to the acts of Christ in vv. 14—16.[80] Nevertheless, this, unlike the previous acts which were preoccupied with the salvific event, is concerned with the declaration of the consequences of those acts. It is thus a further statement with additional information.

The final statement rounds up the pgr. by pointing to the abiding result (pres. ἔχομεν) of the salvation work and uses it as an additional ground (cf. the causal ὅτι) for the initial claim 'He is our peace'.

The gist of the pgr. may accordingly be expressed by the Theme P *It is through Him that both Jews and Gentiles have peace with God.*[81]

7. 2: 19—22. This pgr. has two coordinate clauses and several dependent clauses expressed by finites and ptcs. It is, accordingly, one sentence. The first of the coordinate clauses, οὐκέτι ἐστὲ ξένοι καὶ πάροικοι, puts the

---

developed out of vs. 13. For detailed exegesis, besides the Comm., see Merklein, *CK*, 16—27.

[76] On this see esp. Gnilka's article in *ZJ*, 190—207.

[77] The "middle wall" is variously understood: of the balustrade and prohibiting inscription at the Jer. temple (Robinson, 59 ff.); gnostically (Schlier, *CK*, 18—26); against the Jewish apocalyptic background (Gnilka, *ZJ*, 196 f.; id., *BZ*, 15, 1971, 170); as metaphor for the law (Mussner, *CAK*, 84). For various interpretations, see Mussner, *CAK*, 81—5; Barth, I, 283—7.

[78] The various possibilities for taking vv. 14—15 cannot be discussed here; see Abbott, 60—5; Robinson, 58—64; Schlier, 122—35; Barth, I, 260—5; 283—91.

[79] For the view that 2: 14—16 is a hymn, cf. Sanders, *CH*, 88—92.

[80] Merklein, *CK*, 14 ranks all three statements as equivalent.

[81] For an exegesis of this pgr. see Merklein, *CK*, 28—61.

matter in the negative, while the second, ἐστὲ συμπολῖται . . . καὶ οἰκεῖοι, expresses it positively. The relation between the events represented by these clauses, signaled by ἀλλά, is one of contrast. The inferential particle ἄρα, introducing the pgr., indicates that it is in a conclusion relation to the foregoing. It is noted, furthermore, that the first clause with ξένοι etc. refers back to 2: 11—13 while the second with συμπολῖται etc. is an abstraction of 2: 14—18. This pgr. is thus a conclusion with respect to the two previous pgrs. This means, in turn, that 2: 11—22 forms another block almost as closely connected as (sections) 1: 3—14 and 1: 15—23.

Vv. 20—22 are of some interest. They use 8 terms concerned with building: ἐποικοδομηθέντες, θεμελίῳ, ἀκρογωνιαίου, οἰκοδομή, συναρμολογουμένη, ναόν, συνοικοδομεῖσθε and κατοικητήριον. The accumulation of such words seems to be occasioned by the mention of οἰκεῖοι (vs. 19). This last term, however, has nothing to do with building, but refers to the members of a household. Still, the mere thought of a household suggests to the author the metaphor of a house and so the Gentiles are compared to building material. There is a transition here from a personal characterization to one of material objects. And yet, he eventually shows that he is thinking of a spiritual building, a ναός, in which God dwells through the Spirit. In this process, the ground is also shifted: whereas in vs. 19 the believers are the ones who live in God's House, here they constitute the House in which God dwells.[82]

Vv. 20—22 may thus be understood as a certain development of οἰκεῖοι, yet one that is not central. Hence, the Theme is extracted from the two Pp of vs. 19: *Therefore, you are no longer outcasts, but members of God's family.*

8. 3: 1—13. This pgr. is marked out as clearly as those in 1: 3—14 and 1: 15—23. A characteristic of this pgr. is that it is a Digression occasioned by the word ἐθνῶν (3: 1). The thought of 3: 1 is taken up again in vs. 14. Vv. 1, 14 ff. constitute another Prayer. Thus the immediate context of this pgr. is that it is a digression within a Prayer. There is, however, another connection too. The pgr. is, (as I said above) occasioned by the term ἐθνῶν. That vs. starts with τούτου χάριν. This is most probably a neut. gen. referring to some foregoing point. A reading of the previous three pgrs. (2. 11—13; 14—18 and 19—22) leads to the conclusion that τούτου χάριν refers to the main clauses of the last pgr.: ἄρα οὖν οὐκέτι ἐστὲ ξένοι καὶ πάροικοι, ἀλλὰ ἐστὲ συμπολῖται τῶν ἁγίων καὶ οἰκεῖοι τοῦ Θεοῦ. The Prayer then takes its occasion from this statement, and inasmuch as this statement summarises the previous two pgrs. τούτου χάριν can be said to be

---

[82] On the spiritual temple and its possible background in Qumran, see Coppens, *SE*, 1973, 53—66.

occasioned by all three, or by the section which they build. Thus once again a Prayer is started by occasion of some exposition or relation of God's acts.

The pgr. consists of three sentences: a) vv. 2—7; b) vv. 8—12 and c) vs. 13 (or 41 Pp). The first sentence is the longest, albeit it contains no principal clause. The reason for this may be that this sentence — call it this string of subordinate clauses, if you like — is started off as an aside, and has, to some extent, a seeming dependence on vs. 1, which was intended as a main clause, but which, in view of the digression, has remained lame of its principal verb. This, as a matter of fact, is not added till vs. 14, and then only with a resumptive mention of τούτου χάριν — the causal element.

This sentence contains 21 Pp. Finding a Main P in this sentence is no straightforward task. Since it lacks a principal verb and hence an explicit Main P, the Theme P will have to be abstracted from the various subordinate clauses. The central concept here is the *mysterion*. This was kept hidden from mankind in the past, but has now been revealed to the apostles and prophets. The *mysterion* entails the inclusion of the Gentiles in the salvation scheme of Christ. The mention of συγκληρονόμα, σύσσωμα, συμμέτοχα recalls certain Pp from the previous Pgrs. (i.e. 1: 11, 14, 18; 2: 12—19). Even the συν- in the above three words recalls the three συν-verbs in 2: 5, 6: συνεζωοποίησεν, συνήγειρεν, συνεκάθισεν, as well as the rare συμπολῖται (2: 19).[83] With respect to the first sentence vs. 2 gives the circumstantial setting; vs. 3a is the Main P while vs. 3b is parenthetical. Vs. 4 is a comment in parenthetical form; vs. 5 is a comment on the Main P in vs. 3a. Vs. 6 is the content of *mysterion* in vs. 3a, and vs. 7 is a comment on εὐαγγελίου in vs. 6. We are thus left with the Main P in vs. 3a and the specification of its content in vs. 6. A P may be attempted: 'God revealed to me His *mysterion* to make the Gentiles also partakers (representing the συν in all three terms) of His promised salvation by Christ'.

The second sentence has 16 Pp. The main clause hangs upon ἐδόθη (vs. 8), though the passive construction keeps the Agent (sc. God) in the background and brings forward the Patient (sc. Paul). The final inf. εὐαγγελίσασθαι is in focus just as the other final inf. φωτίσαι, which is joined to it by καί (i.e. an addition). The ἵνα clause is certainly final and has the two infs. as means to itself. Vs. 11 specifies that the statement in vs. 10 is in accordance with an eternal plan which was conceived in Christ. Vs. 12 is a comment on part of vs. 11, sc. Christ. With regards to the development of the theme, it may be remarked that though the

---

[83] Συναρμολογουμένη is a special case belonging to the building terminology.

principal verb is ἐδόθη, this can hardly be taken as adding new information since it occurred before (i.e. δοθείσης, vs. 2), and hence cannot be considered the Main P in this vs. This is rather done by the infs. εὐαγγελίσασθαι and (its addition) φωτίσαι. Ἐδόθη is a mere means to these infs. Vs. 10 has a final clause which has a relation of purpose with the infs. as means. The Theme P is accordingly to be structured from these three Pp. I suggest: 'God gave me the privilege of evangelising and enlightening the Gentiles in order to exhibit His many-sided wisdom to angelic beings'.

The relation between sentence one and sentence two is a logical one: sentence two is the means for the realisation of sentence one. A coalescence of the two statements may now be assayed as a summary of the contents of the two sentences: *God revealed to me His m y s t e r i o n concerning the Gentiles' part in salvation and gave me the privilege of enlightening them about it with the ultimate purpose in view to demonstrate His wisdom before all.*

The third sentence (vs. 13) has its main verb in αἰτοῦμαι. The sentence is started off with the inferential particle διό which indicates that it stands as a conclusion to the foregoing sentences. The mention of θλίψεσιν recalls the opening words of the chapter — ὁ δέσμιος τοῦ Χριστοῦ — and serves to round up the period neatly. We are again where we started. The contents of the pgr. (vv. 2—12) account for and explain the conduct of Paul in the first vs. of ch. 3 τούτου χάριν . . . ὁ δέσμιος τοῦ Χριστοῦ . . . ὑπὲρ ὑμῶν τῶν ἐθνῶν (κάμπτω). Thus vs. 13 seems to be an integral part of Paul's commission. It was one of the items of the οἰκονομία τῆς χάριτος which was given to him (cf. Phil. 1: 29). Cf. further Col. 1: 24.

9. 3: 14—19. The words τούτου χάριν recall 3: 1 where the same words introduce what turned out to be a digression, but which had been intended to be a prayer. Here, at last, at the conclusion of the digression on the *mysterion*, comes the belated prayer introduced afresh by the same phrase. Nevertheless, the intervening digression has perhaps contributed to the twist which the prayer takes.[84]

---

[84] The formal structure of this prayer is different from the prayer of 1: 15 ff. Burton (see III, B, 3) considers the clause κάμπτω τὰ γόνατά μου as a periphrasis for προσεύχομαι. As a general rule this may be conceded. However, a closer look at it brings to the surface certain differences. The Greek habit in prayer was γόνυ κλίνειν, while the barbarian one γονυπετεῖν. (see Stanton, *Glot*, 1968, 1—6). The most common subst. in the Fathers was γονυκλισία (cf. Schlier, *TDNT*, I, 739 and *PL*, s. v.). The form we have here would seem to be half-way between the two, though κάμπτειν τὰ γόνατα is used in class. lit. of the taking of rest (e.g. Hom, *Il*, 8, 116; *Od*, 5, 453; Aes, *Pr*, 398; Eur, *Hec*, 1150). The oriental manner in prayer was more expressive than the Greek one of the feeling of abasement and prostration. The combination κάμπτειν γόνυ / γόνατα is occasionally collocated with ἐξομολογεῖσθαι (e.g.

Vv. 14—19 is but one sentence: vs. 14 contains the principal vb. κάμπτω, while vs. 15 is a comment on πατέρα (14). Vv. 16—17 set forth the basic request and vv. 18—19 describe the contemplated result of the prayer.[85]

As in 1: 17, the basic request is ἵνα δῷ ὑμῖν. This vb. has as obj. the infs. κραταιωθῆναι and κατοικῆσαι and the ptcs. ἐρριζωμένοι and τεθεμελιωμένοι.[86] The contemplated result behind the prayer is expressed by the clause ἵνα ἐξισχύσητε καταλαβέσθαι the obj. of which are the four dimensions.[87]

What these dimensions are cannot be understood properly if vs. 18 is, as it is sometimes the case, lifted out of its context. Logically, vv. 16 b—19 are a unit.[88] The prayer is that these Gentile converts shall be inwardly strengthened by the Spirit and that Christ shall dwell in them by faith. The result of these conditions will be that they will have been rooted deeply and grounded firmly upon love.[89] The ἵνα ἐξισχύσητε clause is dependent on the two requests κραταιωθῆναι and κατοικῆσαι as well as on their result ἐν ἀγάπῃ ἐρριζωμένοι καὶ τεθεμελιωμένοι. The fact that ἐν ἀγάπῃ occurs in the last clause, where it also occupies emphatic position, indicates that the contemplated result for the prayer — the ἵνα ἐξισχύσητε clause —

Rm 14: 11; Phil 2: 10) which denotes an utterance of thanksgiving and praise to God (cf. Lightfoot, *Phil*, 114 f.).

The implication of these observations is that the way prayer is described here is more intense than that in 1: 16. In Col 4: 12 the term ἀγωνιζόμενος gives an inkling as to the intensity with which Epaphras prays. Similarly, in Eph 3: 14 κάμπτω τὰ γόνατά μου communicates more emotive meaning than μνείαν ποιοῦμαι ἐπὶ τῶν προσευχῶν μου. And this is not without significance for semantics (cf. Nida, *ESS*, 18 f.).

[85] On the various moments of this prayer, see II, 4.

[86] On the closer relation of the ptc. (as against the inf.) to the subj. rather than the vb. idea, cf. Robertson. *Gr*, 1101 f. and Goodwin, *SMT*, 357.

[87] For a lengthy treatment, of these see Feuillet, *CS*, 292—317. Schlier, 172 ff. thinks alternatively of a heavenly building and city conceived of as a cube and refers to Herm, *Vis*, 3, 2, 5; Rev 21: 16 and the great mag. Paris pap. (=*PGM*, IV, 968—72); on this cf. Deissmann, *LAE*, 254—63), or of the old conception of the four arms of Christ's cross.

In an interesting study Dahl (*JP*, 57—75) follows the use of the terms in Greek, Jewish and gnostic lit. and decides that they are cosmological terms. He draws a distinction between rational and revealed knowledge, the latter of which is the concern of the present passage (pp. 69 ff.). Thus, he concludes that the Eph author "wants his readers to understand everything worth understanding, all mysteries, even the dimensions of the universe. But the one thing that matters is to know the love of Christ" (p. 75).

For my part I am unable to see that 3: 14—19 takes an interest in cosmic mysteries and cosmological dimensions as we find in apoc. lit. In ch. V the Eph *mysterion* and the cosmic, etc. *mysteria* of *I En*, for example, have been shown to be widely apart.

[88] There is an *asyndeton* between vv. 16 and 17.

[89] By 'love' we need not understand specifically God's or Christ's love, but "the 'fundamental' principle of the Christian character" (Abbott, 98).

is also and primarily connected with it. In other words, the rooting and grounding in love is a condition or the means for the comprehension of the four dimensions. Vs. 18 is obviously elliptical. The author intended to speak of the breadth etc., of something. In actual fact, however, in the following words we get a synonym of καταλαβέσθαι in γνῶναι, with the paratactic conj. τε closely connecting the thought of the two vbs.[90] and a synonym of the superlative thought expressed by the four dimensions in ὑπερβάλλουσαν τῆς γνώσεως. Γνῶναι is a definite advance on καταλαβέσθαι[91] and ὑπερβάλλουσα τῆς γνώσεως is more pungent than the point made by the four dimensions. Moreover, the *oxymoron* in γνῶναι τὴν ὑπερβάλλουσαν τῆς γνώσεως brings the whole thought to a climax. My suggestion, therefore, is that the terms 'breadth', 'length', 'hight' and 'depth', rather than constituting a description of cosmological dimensions, describe the love of Christ as all-encompassing.[92] This is in turn described in vs. 19 as surpassing knowledge. The point of comprehending (καταλαβέσθαι) such a love is now underlined by the substitution of γνῶναι which is stronger than καταλαβέσθαι and is of the same root as γνῶσις with which it is contrasted. Thus it is more suitable in accentuating an intentional surface contradiction. This seeming contradiction underlines the idea that the impossible becomes possible.[93] Accordingly, the meaning suggested is 'That you may be able to grasp the breadth, the length, the hight and the depth (of the love of Christ) and (more than that) to get intimately acquainted[94] with the love of Christ which surpasses (rational) knowledge'.[95]

The ἵνα clause of vs. 19 is paral. with the ἵνα clause of vs. 18. In a concise way this clause summarises vv. 18 and 19 a. Indeed this clause may stand as an apt summary for the whole prayer. The Theme P then would be *May you be filled with all of God's fullness.*

10. 3: 20—21. That these two vv. form a separate pgr. is obvious from the terminal features, i.e. δέ and ἀμήν. In form this pgr. is a doxology.[96]

---

[90] So also Robertson, *Gr*, 1178.

[91] So also Abbott, 100.

[92] Similarly V. Roon, *AE*, 262—6.

[93] It is a question of revealed knowledge, as Dahl says (*JP*, 64 ff.).

[94] Cf. Phil 3: 10 γνῶναι αὐτόν.

[95] The statement is admittedly incomplete, so some explanatory words are included in parentheses to make the meaning clear. The advantage of this understanding is that it does not tear the four words out of their context. Furthermore, the ἐν ἀγάπῃ etc. of vs. 17 is seen to have a meaningful function and ὑπερβάλλουσαν τῆς γνώσεως is motivated by the four words.

[96] Cf. II, 2, A.

There are two finite vbs., αἰτούμεθα and νοοῦμεν. In vs. 21 after αὐτῷ we must understand an implicit ἔστω. This vb. is actually the principal vb. of the sentence (i.e. the pgr.). Vs. 20 is a characterization of the semantic goal (i.e. God) of vs. 21. The subj. of this sentence is an implied 'we'. The Theme P can be abstracted from the two vv. as *Glory be to Him whose acts transcend our conceptions.*

CHAPTER IV

A PROPOSITIONAL ANALYSIS OF
1:3—10 AND 3:1—13

A. SOME PRELIMINARY REMARKS

This ch. aims at elucidating the semantic structure of the Eulogy and the Prayer Digression. This is done by analysing the text into semantic units of such length as communicate an idea complete in itself. Most of these units or Propositions are Event communications though some of them are State communications. This means that occasionally a word (usually an Event word) has been supplied because it was sensed as being implicitly present. Nevertheless, the interest of this study being practical rather than theoretical the extent of analysis has been determined by this objective. Hence, some collocations of words which might have been analysed into implicit Pp (as e.g. 1:3 κυρίου ἡμῶν would be turned into the state P 'Jesus Christ is our Lord') have been left unanalysed. No P of significance has, however, been left untouched. And in this sense the analysis may be considered as complete. Apart from the logical relations between Pp full notice has been taken of philological works and commentaries. Indeed the semantic analysis and the 'dive' into the deep structure have been undertaken after careful consideration of the surface structure of the main terms and their usage in lit. This circumstance calls attention to the circular character of the procedure: we start with the surface structure (the meaning of words and their syntax), then dive into the deep structure in order to understand the surface communication and finally return to the surface structure with the insights won from the 'dive'. It is these insights that are set forth in the following pages.

B. ANALYSIS OF 1:3—10

1. Εὐλογητὸς ὁ Θεὸς καὶ Πατὴρ τοῦ Κυρίου ἡμῶν Ἰησοῦ Χριστοῦ. The gen. constrs. τοῦ and ἡμῶν may be taken here in the usual way as 'of' and 'our' respectively.[1] The first five words represent an implicit P. VV and

---

[1] E.g. *RSV*, *NEB*, *TEV*, Abbott, Robinson, Schlier, Gnilka, Barth. Nothing would be gained in the present context by presenting the gen. constrs. as implicit Pp. To save space they are left in their surface structure.

comm. are agreed that some form of εἰμί is to be understood after the vbl. adj.[2] If such a form is to be supplied my choice lies with the ind. ἐστίν.[3] The P becomes 'God . . . is worthy of being blessed'. The semantic

---

[2] Of some 77 instances of εὐλογητός in the LXX, quoted by *HR*, it occurs 57 × without any copula, 16× with εἶ, 3× with ἔσῃ, and 1× with ἔστι τῷ Κυρίῳ. Of these, 10× have the *v.l.* εὐλογημένος as well (i.e. 7× in one of א A B and 3× in the Sixtine Ed.). Apart from a negligible number these instances form rudimentary eulogies. Several of them, e.g. Gen 14: 19 f.; Ps 71 (72): 18 f.; 143 (144): 1 f.; III Kin 1: 48; I Mac 4: 30, are more substantial, while Dan 3: 26—45 and Tob 13: 1—18 are very long (the last-named being intermingled with prayer and exhortation). Though not one single instance has the copula ἐστίν — presumably through Heb. influence — it is evident that ἐστίν, ἔστω or εἴη is to be supplied.

[3] This question is somehow tied up with the meaning of εὐλογητός. *LSJ* and *BAG* render it with 'blessed', as if it were εὐλογημένος, and Schlier, 42, n. 5 says, "Doch können beide Formulierungen miteinander wechseln, wie Ps 71: 17; Judt 13: 18; Dan 3: 51 ff. zeigen". To the same effect Barth, I, 77 claims that "While in classic Gr. the verbal adj. denotes a being that is to be blessed, or is praiseworthy, in the vern. (koine) Gr. of the Hell. time and of the NT the same form of the verb is fully identified with the meaning of the passive form. It describes one (being) praised or blessed". The passages quoted by Schlier do not prove conclusively that εὐλογητός and εὐλογημένος are used identically, and Barth, unfortunately, does not offer any proofs for his claim.

The vbl. adjs. in -τέος and -τός are "closely allied" (Robertson, *Gr*, 373; Brugmann, *ECG*, IV, 605. The -τέος form is later (occuring first in Hes.): "It is peculiar to A [i.e. 500—300 B.C.] and has hardly outlived that period" (Jannaris, *HGG*, § 1051). The -τος form as an ordinary adj. has been in use at all times, but as a vbl. adj. it is much more rare in P—B compositions [i.e. 300 B.C.—A.D. 1000] than in A (Jannaris, *HGG*, § 1052). Both Moulton, *Prol*, 221 f., and Robertson, *Gr*, 372 and 1096, accept its vbl. character in the NT despite Blass, *GrNT*, p. 37. The two forms, do not, however, have the same significance. While the -τέος form denotes 'necessity', the -τός form denotes for Kühner—Blass, *AG*, I, ii, 288 f., "abgeschlossene Thätigkeit wie das Ptc. Pf. Pass." and "Möglichkeit" with a great variety of resultant ideas in translation; and for Jannaris, *HGG*, § 1052, "possibility or susceptibility". Robertson, *Gr*, 372, concludes, "With forms in -τος therefore two points have to be watched: first if they are vbl. at all, and then, if they are act., mid. or pass.".

Against the equation of εὐλογητός with εὐλογημένος the following points may be made: a) The vbl. adjs. μεμπτός, ὁρατός, πιστός (quoted by Abbott) mean 'that can be blamed' or 'blameworthy'; 'that can be seen' or 'visible'; 'that can be trusted' or 'trustworthy'. Similarly, εὐλογητός means 'deserving praise/blessing' or 'praiseworthy'. (So ΔΔ, s.v.). (See Robertson, *Gr*, 1096, for more vbl. adjs.); b) In the LXX εὐλογητός is predominantly used of God and εὐλογημένος of man; c) I Esd 8: 25 εὐλογητὸς μόνος ὁ Κύριος may have exerted some influence on later writers in applying this form alone to God; d) The NT uses εὐλογητός exclusively of God and εὐλογημένος of man; e) Ph., *Migr. Abr.* 107 f., draws a difference between εὐλογητός and εὐλογημένος; f) Theod. Mops. says "ἐπαινεῖσθαι καὶ θαυμάζεσθαι ἄξιος",

Beyer, *TDNT*, II, 764, notes that "εὐλογητός is a fixed term in rendering ברוך. It is used with εὐλογημένος as ברוך is with מבורך". Abbott, 3; Robinson, 142; Foulkes, 45, also draw the difference.

subj. of the implied event of blessing is 'we', and since the constr. is pass. it is rendered with 'by us'.

It must not be overlooked that semantically the vbl. adj. is not equivalent to a finite vb. The form εὐλογοῦμεν, for example, would direct attention to the act as performed and would be rendered 'we bless God'.[4] The vbl. adj. instead discloses the content of what is said when God is blessed. The content is that God is praiseworthy because of certain things He has done. The event of blessing is thus only implicit here — the collocation centering more on the content of the blessing. Hence the focus is not on something 'we' do, but on God's character and deeds which deserve our praise. In the surface form there is an implicit element of paraenesis[5] which is of consequence for the understanding of the genre of the eulogy. A eulogy expresses a delicate prompting to ponder what God has done and to ascribe to Him the glory which is His due.[6] To render the orig. emphasis the P may be expressed as *'Blessworthy' is the God and Father of our Lord Jesus Christ.*[7]

This P has a key significance in the Eulogy: firstly, it gives the name

---

NT usage: The term occurs in Mk 14: 16 of God absolutely; in Lk 1: 68 (Zechariah's eulogy); in the three introductory eulogies (II Cor 1: 3; Eph 1: 3; I Pt 1: 3); in Rm 1: 25 and 9: 5; and in II Cor 11: 31. In Rm 1: 25 the point being made is that men worshipped the creation rather than the Creator who alone is *worthy of praise!* Rm 9: 5 and II Cor 11: 31 do not speak of an act performed in the past, but of an act called forth ever and anon by the character of Christ's worthiness. In none of these cases could εὐλογητός be substituted by εὐλογημένος.

Of the three forms of the copula ἔστω occurs in II Chr 9: 8 and εἴη in Jb 1: 21, but both of these instances use εὐλογημένος. "Here", says Salmond, 245, "as generally where εὐλογητός is the word used and not εὐλογημένος, the sentence is best taken as an affirmation, ἐστίν being supplied", and Beyer, *TDNT*, II, 764, "In the NT εὐλογητός has an exclusively indicative signification", cf. *BDF*, § 128, 5.

[4] Or 'We thank God' as Nida—Taber, *TPT*, 154.

[5] The *NEB* gives evidence of sensing this when it translates 'Praise be to God', and the *TEV* hits upon it with its rendering 'Let us give thanks to the God . . .' I think, nonetheless, that *TEV*'s explicitness on the paraenetical element is not warranted by the form εὐλογητός which only implicitly and indirectly urges the believers to praise God, its primary function being to state what God deserves of men.

[6] The collocation of 'being worthy of' and 'blessing' actually occurs in Rv 5: 12 ἄξιον ἔστιν τὸ ἀρνίον . . . λαβεῖν . . . δόξαν καὶ εὐλογίαν.

[7] The constr. is full of significance. He who deserves 'our' praise is related to Jesus Christ in a twofold manner: as God and as Father, and Jesus Christ is, in turn, related to 'us' as Lord.

The constr. ὁ Θεὸς καὶ πατὴρ τοῦ Κυρίου ἡμῶν needs some attention. Some *VV* place a comma after Θεός and refer only πατήρ to Christ, appositionally to Θεός, as if it were ὁ Θεὸς ὁ καὶ πατήρ. So did the *Peshitto* and Theodoret, and lately Barth, I, 76; Dibelius, 58; Conzelmann, 59. The *RSV*, *NEB*, and *TEV*, on the other hand, in agreement with older *VV* have 'the God and Father of our Lord'. (See Robertson, *Gr*, 785). To this it is objected that we ought to have τε after Θεός, but this objection is not serious, cf. 4: 6 εἷς Θεὸς καὶ πατὴρ πάντων. That God can be described not only as the

and substance to the whole paragraph as to its literary genre (i.e. a Eulogy), and secondly, by its position in the sentence, it constitutes the only main, if verbless, clause of the entire Eulogy. All subsequent matter is both logically and syntactically subordinate to it and supplies the grounds for the claim made in 'Worthy of our praise is the God . . .'.[8] It is, therefore, indented to the far left on the Display.

2. ὁ εὐλογήσας ἡμᾶς ἐν πάσῃ εὐλογίᾳ πνευματικῇ ἐν τοῖς ἐπουρανίοις ἐν Χριστῷ. The phrase ἐν πάσῃ εὐλογίᾳ does not signal an event distinct from that denoted by the ptc. The adj. πνευματικῇ can be construed in two ways: a) as opposed to material blessings, and b) as proceeding from the Spirit. The close proximity of ἐν τοῖς ἐπουρανίοις would seem to point to the first alt. However, the phrase ἐν Χριστῷ may be an indication that here all three Persons of the Trinity figure in the blessings bestowed on the believers.[9] Actually, the two renderings need not be considered as mutually exclusive, since the one term is derived from the other.

Father of Jesus Christ, but also as His God, is seen clearly in vs. 17: ὁ Θεὸς τοῦ Κυρίου ἡμῶν Ἰησοῦ Χριστοῦ, ὁ πατὴρ τῆς δόξης (cf. also Jn 20:17). Similarly, Theophylact; Chrysostom; Abbott, 4; Robinson, 142; Schlier, 43; Simpson, 24; Hodge, 27 f.; Salmond, 244 f. (whom see for further arguments).

There is a further problem here. If 'God' were collocated with 'us' the relation would be analysed as 'He whom we worship'. But when God is related to Christ, is this analysis a correct one? In which sense is God the God of Jesus Christ, in particular in this context? Is it the God whom Jesus presumably worshipped during His earthly life, as when He made His prayers to Him (e.g. Mk 6:46), or uttered the cry of derelliction (Mt 27:46), or even when after His resurrection called Him 'my God' (Jn 20:17), though later than Eph), or is it the God whom Jesus revealed to His followers? The collocation πατὴρ τοῦ Κυρίου ἡμῶν would be analysed as 'He who begot Jesus Christ'. Analogically, the same gen. constr. should express the same meaning in the relation of God to Christ, i.e. 'He whom Jesus Christ has as his God/He whom Jesus Christ worships'. This would seem to be the most natural way to take it. On the other hand, the context is not really concerned with the relation of God to Jesus Christ but with the relation between God and 'us'. The gen. constr. seems to be a further specification and description of the God who deserves and claims 'our' praise. This consideration would have the effect of taking away the emphasis from the thought of worship on the part of Christ and place it instead upon God as the One who stood behind the saving work of Christ.

Another alt. is possible still. As Schlier, 43, remarks, the phrase Θεὸς καὶ πατήρ "Ist fast *ein* Begriff. Gott wird dadurch als der väterliche Gott und der göttliche Vater des Jesus Christus charakterisiert". In 3:14 f. God is the Father of every family in heaven and on earth. In keeping with the universal character of Eph God is probably presented here in a cosmic way in which He is God and Father of all including Jesus Christ, and that the intended meaning was not the specific relation of God to Jesus as His God.

[8] Similarly Schlier, 39, "Die Benediktionsformel ist die Basis der ganzen Eulogie".

[9] Abbott, 4; Robinson, 19 f., prefer the first while rejecting the second. Schlier, 44; Barth, I, 78; Dibelius, 59; Conzelmann, 60; Gaugler, 26, also have 'spiritual'.

The phrase ἐν τοῖς ἐπουρανίοις defines the *locus* [10] and the phrase ἐν Χριστῷ either gives the instrument or supplies a further specification of locality — i.e. not merely 'in the heavenlies', but more particularly, 'in Christ'.[11]

The event is denoted by the ptc. and the art. shows that the Agent is God (P 1). Though the ptc. constr. is equivalent to a rel. clause (i.e. 'who has blessed us'), logically this P is not a mere characterisation of God (i.e. a *comment*). It rather has a cause-effect relation.[12] God is declared praiseworthy on account of something He has done.[13] This P is accordingly related as *reason* to P 1 (*result*) and as *generic* to all subsequent Pp which are *specific* to it. It takes the form (*Because*) *He blessed us with every spiritual blessing in the heavenlies in Christ.*

3. καθὼς ἐξελέξατο ἡμᾶς ἐν αὐτῷ. The Agent of the event word is God (P 1) and its semantic goal is 'us'. The phrase ἐν αὐτῷ refers to Christ.[14] Καθώς serves as a link between this and the previous P. But what is its meaning? Its usual sense is comparative, but *BDR*,[15] Robertson[16] and *BAG* (s.v.) recognise also a causal sense which, as a matter of fact, they apply to this passage.

The contents of this and the last Pp seem to require a different relation. P 2 states, in general terms, the fact that God has blessed 'us' with all (kinds of) spiritual blessings, but no indication is given as to their nature. Only the fact is stated and at that in a most general way. Then, in P 3 we are given a specimen (to be followed by more) of these blessings, i.e. election. 'To bless' is *generic*; 'to elect' is *specific*. Thus, the semantic relation which is sensed here is that P 3 is *specific* to P 2 which is *generic*. P 3 illustrates, amplifies and reinforces the generic statement of P 2. It forms a particular instance of it.[17]

In view of this conclusion it is difficult to give καθώς a causal sense.[18]

---

[10] So too Abbott, 5; Gnilka, 62 f.; Barth, I, 78 f. (with some hesitation). Robinson, 20 ff., takes it of the supra-sensual world and renders it with 'in the heavenly sphere'. For a discussion of this phrase, see the relevant excursus in ch. VI.

[11] See the excursus in VI.

[12] See III, A and B—C, *TWG*, 300.

[13] The Christian blesses God because God blessed him first, cf. I Jn 4: 19.

[14] The phrase ἐν Χριστῷ, ἐν αὐτῷ etc. occurs some 11× in 1: 3—14. Of these only the occurrence in vs. 9 may admit a reflexive reference to God, and even this is rather questionable. On the understanding of this phrase, see VI, 1 and the relevant excursus.

[15] § 453, 2.

[16] *Gr*, 968, 1382.

[17] So Alford, 70.

[18] Rm 1: 28; 1 Cor 1: 6; 5: 7; Eph 4: 32 (quoted by *BDR* and *BAG*) can be construed in a causal sense, but our passage is rather different.

The comparative meaning is not much more appropriate.[19] Nevertheless, the word does have an argumentative function in that it supports the claim made in P 2.[20] This function is, however, only secondary in comparison with the one advocated above. The relation of *generic—specific* is eminently suitable in a eulogy which does not *argue* for what God has done, but simply *enumerates* His acts. The P takes the form (*That is to say*) *He chose us in Him*.

4. πρὸ καταβολῆς κόσμου. The term καταβολή when collocated with κόσμος represents the event 'to create'.[21] In post-class. Gk. it generally denotes the foundation of a building. It makes actually little difference, if any, whether we render 'before the world was created' or '. . . founded'. The constr. focuses attention on καταβολή. The semantic subj., nevertheless, is God, so the P becomes *Before He created the world*. Its semantic relation to the previous P is that it gives the *time* for the event of ἐξελέξατο.

5—6. εἶναι ἡμᾶς ἁγίους καὶ ἀμώμους κατενώπιον αὐτοῦ. The constr. is the so-called inf. c. acc. Both the gramm. as well as the semantic subj. is the acc. ἡμᾶς. The inf. does not predicate existence; it is used as a copula with the adjs. ἁγίους and ἀμώμους. Thus, two things are predicated of 'us': 'to be holy' and 'to be blameless'. Consequently, here we have not one but two Pp combined by the inf. and the additive conj. καί. Since the ensuing phrase applies to both adjs. equally, it is regarded as more appropriate not to split ἁγίους from ἀμώμους but to retain them together. These collocations do not express events, but relations, hence these are State Pp denoting the intended state of 'us' which God had in view when He elected 'us'. The phrase κατενώπιον αὐτοῦ gives the locality,[22] viz. the presence of God, for the exhibition of 'our' holiness [23] and blamelessness.

---

[19] Schlier, 49; Gnilka, 69, n. 3, combine the two "vergleichenden und begründeten" and render it with "demgemäss dass".

[20] Similarly Abbott, 6, "It has a certain argumentative force, but does not mean (as the word sometimes does) 'because'". Older interpreters as Hodge, Salmond, Lenski make election the ground for the subsequent blessings of P 2. This interpretation requires the sense of 'because' for καθώς. In my view the election is not exclusive and antecedent to the blessings of P 2, but one of them. Cf. Schlier, 48, "V. 4 beginnt die nähere inhaltlich Bestimmung des Segens".

[21] This phrase occurs, acc. to Simpson, 25, n. 5, only in an astrological work outside the NT, though καταβολή is used by Arist. 129, and Plut., *Mor.* 956, in the sense of 'creation'. Cf. *MM*, s.v. κόσμος and *BAG*, s.v. καταβολή.

[22] Cf. Schlier, 51 f., "Der Ausdruck . . . auf das immerwährende Sein von Gottes Augen zu beziehen (ist)".

[23] The word ἅγιος is usually explained as 'one set apart'. This significance is the one that comes to the fore more than any other in e.g. the epistolary addresses, as in vs. 1. The meaning wanted here is much more loaded: to be holy and blameless means

These Pp are related to the previous ones by the final inf. The Pp are stated as *That we should be holy and (that we should be) blameless in His sight*, and are labeled as *purpose* of P 3 (which is *means*).

7. ἐν ἀγάπῃ. The word ἀγάπη being an abstract noun represents the event 'to love'. Its surface form and position, however, make it notoriously difficult to decide who the semantic subj. is and with which part of the context it should be connected.

Nest. and the ΚΔ connect it with προορίσας; *WH* and the *GNT* with the foregoing. Of the *VV* the *RSV* and the *TEV* join it with προορίσας, while *NEB, JB* and *BKÖ* to ἁγίους καὶ ἀμώμους.[24]

---

to exhibit those qualities which mark one out as belonging to God and distinguish one from those who do not belong to Him. The term is no longer used in a so to speak 'neutral' sense, but in a positive one connoting holiness, purity, etc.

[24] There are three possible ways of construing it: a) with ἐξελέξατο (championed by Ephraim, Pelagius, Calvin, Westcott, Dibelius, Trinidad, Gaugler, 32 f., Krämer, *SFE*, 40); b) with the preceding clause (Ambrosiaster, Erasmus, Luther, Beza, Calvin, Alford, 71 f.; Robinson, 27, 143; Lightfoot, *NEP*; Salmond, 250 f.; Hodge, 34 f.; Lenski, 359; Schrenk, *TDNT*, IV, 175; Zerwick, 30 f.; Foulkes, 47); c) with προορίσας (*Peshitto*, Theodore, Chrysostom, Theophylact, Bengel, v. Soden, H. A. W. Meyer, 38; Percy, *PKE*, 268; Dahl, *TZ*, 1951, 255; Maurer, *EvTh*, 155; Abbott, 8; Schlier, 52; Gnilka, 72; Bruce, 28). Barth, I, 79 f., wavers between the last two alts.

Of the three alts. the first seems to be the least probable, chiefly on the grounds of remoteness, cf. Alford, 71 and Salmond, 250. The second alt. implies that the 'love' is man's love, whereas in the third alt. it must be God's love. In Eph ἀγάπη occurs 10× of which 3× it is the love of God/Christ and 6× the love of the believers (the tenth is our instance). Five times out of six of the Christians' love it occurs in the phrase ἐν ἀγάπῃ: 3:17 ἐν ἀγάπῃ ἐρριζωμένοι καὶ τεθεμελιωμένοι; 4:)2 ἀνεχόμενοι ἀλλήλων ἐν ἀγάπῃ; 15 ἀληθεύοντες δὲ ἐν ἀγάπῃ; 16 τὴν αὔξησιν τοῦ σώματος ποιεῖται εἰς οἰκοδομὴν ἑαυτοῦ ἐν ἀγάπῃ; 5:2 περιπατεῖτε ἐν ἀγάπῃ. In all these instances love is connected with the behaviour of Christians, as is also 1:15 (though without the ἐν). Conversely, the divine love is nowhere connected with predestination or election. This circumstance is in favour of alt. b. Again, as Alford, 71 points out, "In the whole construction of this long sentence, the vbs. and ptcs. as natural in a solemn emphatic enumeration of God's *dealings* with His people, *precede* their qualifying clauses . . . In no one case, except the necessary one of a *relative* qualification (ἧς vs. 6 and again vs. 8), does the vb. *follow* its qualifying clause . . ." Cf. Krämer, *WD*, 1967, 38 ff. Furthermore, there is some parallel evidence. Though ἄμωμος in Col 1:22, as in most of its occurrences in the NT, is not followed by an ἐν-phrase (as is also the case with its near equivalent ἄμεμπτος), in the three instances where ἄμωμος (Jd 24) ἀμώμητος (II Pt 3:14) and ἄμεμπτος (I Th 3:13) *are* followed by an ἐν-phrase, the prep. phrase clearly modifies these terms.

The chief objection against this interpretation is that ἐν ἀγάπῃ comes after κατενώπιον αὐτοῦ. Gaugler, 32 objects that ἅγιοι and ἄμωμοι are nowhere else collocated with a 'Tugend'.

The third alt. is also possible, though it lacks the more weighty arguments in favour of the second. Nevertheless, the mention of κατὰ τὴν εὐδοκίαν τοῦ θελήματος αὐτοῦ

Semantically the event 'to love' can be predicated either of God or of 'us'. In the first case ἐν ἀγάπῃ is to be joined either with ἐξελέξατο or with προορίσας. In the second case it will either be an *addition* to ἁγίους καὶ ἀμώμους, i.e. 'That we be holy and blameless before Him and love Him', or ἁγίους καὶ ἀμώμους will be *abstractions* modifying the event to love, i.e. 'That we love Him purely and blamelessly'.[25]

Joining ἐν ἀγάπῃ with ἁγίους καὶ ἀμώμους, which on other grounds, seemed to be preferable (cf. note 24), appears less plausible under semantic scrutiny. The greatest objection to taking it as an *addition* to ἁγίους καὶ ἀμώμους is the following: the Eulogy is made up of an enumeration of God's acts. Throughout the Eulogy the semantic Agent is God and 'we' are the Patients (see II, 2, C, ii). It would mean shattering this pattern here if an event of such momentous importance had as its Agent 'us' rather than God. This very important consideration renders every form of connection of ἐν ἀγάπῃ with ἁγίους καὶ ἀμώμους most improbable. Furthermore, making ἀγάπη a Christian virtue would imply that the ἐξελέξατο clause would be more specific than the clause on adoption and this would be against the recognition that the direction of the Eulogy is from the more general to the specific.[26]

There remains the other possibility of predicating the ἀγάπη of God either with ἐξελέξατο or with προορίσας. The first alt. has the advantage that it coincides with an OT tenet where the election of Israel is ascribed to Yahweh's love.[27] Nevertheless, the separation of the two terms by the intervening four phrases make the connection of ἐν ἀγάπῃ with ἐξελέξατο very difficult. In favour of the connection may be said that ἐν ἀγάπῃ has

constitutes an obstacle since it is rather awkward to start with ἐν ἀγάπῃ as the driving force of the predestination and then to round it up with the almost tautological κατά clause.

Though it is not possible to arrive at a firm conclusion on this point, on the whole it seems that the second alt. has slightly better arguments in its favour. But see the semantic considerations below.

[25] This, however, is shattered by κατενώπιον αὐτοῦ.

[26] P 2 has been analysed as *generic* with all the succeding Pp as *specific* to it. The various items are unfolded in logical sequence as well as deductively. Thus, ἐξελέξατο seems to be prior to προορίσας (see next P), ἐχαρίτωσεν is subsequent to προορίσας while ἐπερίσσευσεν is one more step after ἐχαρίτωσεν. This is moreover amplified in the clause on ἀπολύτρωσις which is in turn amplified by the ἄφεσις clause; and finally the clause on God's rich grace leads to the more specific act of endowment with wisdom and prudence as prerequisites for the revelation of the *mysterion*. These events describe the steps by which 'we' have been blessed. The event of προορίσας is related to adoption. If the event of ἐξελέξατο was related to the purpose of 'our' showing love, the προορίσας clause would become more *generic* than the ἐξελέξατο clause and this would cancel the deductive method obtaining in the Eulogy at large.

[27] See e.g. the *locus classicus* Deut 7: 6 ff. and cf. V. Rad, *OTT*, I, 178 f. and Quell, *TDNT*, IV, 163: "Love and faithfulness . . . determine the divine choice".

been edged away from proximity to ἐξελέξατο by the conj. καθώς, but even so the position it now occupies makes other connections possible. In the second alt. ἐν ἀγάπῃ ill-fits the ptc. προορίσας, but fits admirably the concept of υἱοθεσία. The difficulties mentioned in note 24 are real, but if ἀγάπη is to be predicated of God this is perhaps a somewhat more natural connection. In this case ἐν ἀγάπῃ gives the *reason* for the event of προορίσας, and the P takes the form *Because He loved us*.

8. προορίσας ἡμᾶς. Προορίζειν seems to have come in vogue with early Christianity. In the NT it occurs 6×.[28] The question facing us is how this ptc. relates to the finite ἐξελέξατο? There are at least three ways of construing it: a) as antecedent to it[29] giving the grounds for the election, i.e. 'Because He predestined us . . . He chose us'; b) as coincident with it, giving the mode for the election;[30] and c) as subsequent to it.[31]

In the first case the circumstantial ptc. must be taken as temporal-causal, but would the ptc., in this case, be so remote from the main vb.? Is it not very awkward to transfer the ptc. logically some 16 words backwards in order to give the sense desired?[32] Besides, is a temporal or a causal relation a correct semantic analysis of the relations between these Pp?

The second alt. in which the ptc. gives the mode of election can be hardly maintained. Προορίσας cannot possibly give the mode of ἐξελέξατο since it is itself a loaded term and belongs with ἐξελέξατο to the group of terms used with reference to God's primordial decisions. Furthermore, purely by way of content it cannot modify ἐξελέξατο.[33]

---

[28] The only pre-Christian instance quoted by *BAG* is Dem., 31, 4. The term is a strengthened form of ὁρίζειν, which occurs quite frequently in class. lit. Schmidt, *TDNT*, V, 452, cites four instances (Soph., *Ant.* 452; Eur., *Frg.* 218; Epict., *Diss.* I, 12, 25 and Meleager in *Anth. Pal.* 12, 158) in which the gods ὁρίζουν. In the NT the idea that everything is foreknown and prearranged in the counsels of God is accentuated; hence προορίζειν is more emphatic than ὁρίζειν. On the other hand, the prep. πρό is sometimes so weakened as to refer only to "the future realisation" (Abbott, 8).

[29] *BDR*, § 339, 1; Moulton, *Prol*, 130—4; Robertson, *Gr*, 861 ff., 1113 f.; Turner, *Synt*, 79, recognise antecedent and coincident action for the aor. ptc., but deny subsequent action.

[30] So Salmond, 251, who renders 'In that He foreordained us'.

[31] Burton, *MT*, 65; Ramsey, *PTRC*, 212; Rackham, Acts, 183 f., think that there are instances in the NT where the aor. ptc. is used of subsequent action, and Moulton himself (*Prol*, 132) concedes that in Pind., *Pyth.* IV, 189, λέξατο ἐπαινήσαις ("mustered and thanked") "The exact order of proceedings" does place the ptc. as subsequent to the finite vb.

[32] In the exx. quoted by Robertson, *Gr*, 1126—28, the ptc. and the main vb. are very contiguous, often next to each other.

[33] Nor would Pp 8—9 very fittingly be described as giving either the *means* or the *manner* for Pp 5—6.

The third alt. is the most probable one. Here we are not so much concerned with the grammatical debate on whether the aor. ptc. can be used for subsequent action to that expressed by the main vb. It is recognised by grammarians [34] that the ptc. is sometimes used loosely, just carrying on the argument. Analysing the contents of Pp 3—7 and Pp 8—9 we note that this is precisely what this ptc. does.[35] The information conveyed by Pp 8—9 is over and above the information conveyed by Pp 3—6. At the same time προορίζειν and ἐκλέγειν are two aspects of divine activity with reference to God's pre-temporal plans, and as such are linked together by the relation of *addition*.[36] This relation is eminently fitting, particularly in view of the weakening of πρό in προορίσας with the consequent meaning 'to destine', the πρό being simply in reference to "the future realization".[37]

The P becomes *He (pre)destined us*. This P is of equal semantic rank as P3 (i.e. *addition*, and together with P3 *specific* to P2).

9. εἰς υἱοθεσίαν διὰ ᾿Ιησοῦ Χριστοῦ εἰς αὐτόν. The abstr. nown υἱοθεσία is resolved to the event 'to adopt'.[38] The phrase διὰ ᾿Ιησοῦ Χριστοῦ is instrumental, and the pron. αὐτόν is probably reflexive, referring to God Himself.[39] This is more consonantly taken with κατενώπιον αὐτοῦ which refers to God, rather than with ἐν αὐτῷ. which, in the Eulogy, is predominantly applied to Christ. Υἱοθεσίαν can be construed either actively of God, i.e. 'He adopts', or passively of 'us', i.e. 'we are adopted'. The structure of P 8 requires the pass. alt., i.e. (And He (pre)destined us) *to become His adopted children by means of Christ*.[40]

This P is related to P 8. The final significance of the prep. εἰς fits this case well, and the relation is accordingly analysed as one of *purpose* to P 8 precisely as Pp 5—6 were related to P 3.

---

[34] E.g. Robertson, *Gr*, 431.

[35] The use of the ptc. needs greater attention than it has received in Grammars. As a rule Grammars treat the simpler exx. of circumstantial ptcs. in the Gospels. But the real problems of the student are in connection with the shifting use of the ptcs. in argumentative discourse, as in the Epistles.

[36] Or, as Nida would say, 'Additive-different'.

[37] Abbott, 8; Salmond, 251.

[38] This term is late but sufficiently old (occurring in II B.C. inscriptions) for Deissmann, *BS*, 239, to say that "Paul (Rm 8:15; Gal 4:5 al.) was availing himself of a generally intelligible figure when he utilized the term υἱοθεσία in the language of religion" (*MM*, s. v.). The class. term was εἰσποίησις. For the Roman custom of adoption, see Salmond, 251 f. See further Martitz and E. Schweizer in *TDNT*, VIII, 397 ff.

[39] V. Soden; Gnilka, 73; Schlier, 54 (hesitantly), refer it to Christ. Abbott, 9; Robinson, 27; Salmond, 252; Gaugler, 34; Simpson, 26 f.; Barth, I, 80; Alford, 72; Moule, *ES*, 29; Hodge, 36, refer it to God.

[40] The vb. 'become' rather than 'be' is chosen, because the reference is, in the first place, not to 'our' state as children, but to the (legal) procedure of 'our' becoming His children (i.e. through Christ).

10—11. κατὰ τὴν εὐδοκίαν τοῦ θελήματος αὐτοῦ. The last two words represent the event 'He willed'. The abstract εὐδοκία [41] may represent a State P, i.e. 'He is well-pleased' (i.e. with some one) or an Event P which comes close to 'He purposed'.[42] Here, the absence of a person toward whom the εὐδοκία is felt and the combination with θέλημα indicate that it must be taken as an event, i.e. 'It seemed good to Him'.

The gen. constr. may certainly be explained by the predilection of Eph to use cumulations of synonymous gens. for emphasis.[43] Nevertheless, a real distinction is being made between the two terms. Θέλημα refers to the will or decision of God as carried out in the previous events, εὐδοκία indicates that the θέλημα is not to be understood as arbitrary or blind; it was shaped under the constraint of εὐδοκία, that which seemed good to God. The good pleasure thus guides the decision. Hence, the gen. constr. may be resolved to 'He considered good and willed/decided', the 'and' signaling not only *sequence* [44] but logical priority and *cause* as well. The will is not merely what God wished, but that which took effect in the acts of God enumerated in the Eulogy.

The prep. κατά indicates the norm,[45] i.e. the previous events are in keeping with what God considered good and decided (to put into effect). In logical terms, this means that the predestination to adoption etc., did not just happen to be in line with God's εὐδοκία and θέλημα, it was rather determined by them. Hence, the proper relation is that Pp 10—11 give the *reason* for the previous events. These Pp, constituting no events that relate to the blessings of the Eulogy, are regarded as out of focus and relative to both Pp 3 and 8. They are stated as *This was in accordance with what He considered good and willed/decided upon.*[46]

---

[41] For εὐδοκέω see Schrenk, *TDNT*, II, 738 ff.

[42] Cf. Abbott, 9, "It means either 'good pleasure, purpose', εὖ δοκεῖν, 'as it seems good to'; or 'good will', according as the satisfaction is conceived in action, or as felt towards a person".

[43] Cf. CD 3:15 חפצי רצונו and Kuhn, *PQ*, 118, and see further Vogt, *SNT*, 114—7. Εὐδοκία and θέλημα have been understood as synonymous terms (cf. Schrenk, *TDNT*, II, 747, "To give a fuller characterisation of what is said Eph often uses cumulative, synonymous genitives (cf. 1:19; 2:14, 15; 3:7). It is thus that the divine will is described as εὐδοκία in vs. 5") though a difference is also perceived (e.g. Schrenk, *TDNT*, II, 747, "It is the content of this counsel as the free good pleasure which, grounded in God alone and influenced by none else, is His gracious resolution to save").

[44] See B—C, *TWG*, 264.

[45] Cf. *BAG*, s. v., II, 5, a.

[46] The rendering ". . . *what* He considered good . . ." is borne out by the fact that εὐδοκέω may be used with a dat. of pers. or thing. What God ηὐδόκησε ἐν here is not the 'adopted children', but the act of predestination. So, the ellipsis may be filled by 'what' or 'that which'.

12. εἰς ἔπαινον δόξης τῆς χάριτος αὐτοῦ. Older commentators connected δόξα with χάριτος.[47] More recently Schlier[48] and Gnilka[49] incline to the view that ἔπαινος δόξης is one concept — 'Herrlichkeitslob'.[50] An argument against Schlier and Gnilka's understanding is that in vv. 12 and 14 the δόξα is definitely the goal of the praise.[51] The constr. is identical with δόξα κληρονομίας in 1: 18.[52] It was decided there that δόξα functioned as an attributive on κληρονομία in lieu of the adj. The meaning really is that God's grace has a glory, it reflects glory, in other words, it is glorious. The collocation may be attributed to semitic influence, but more probably it is owing to the emphasis intended. Ἔνδοξος χάρις lays the emphasis on the grace, whereas δόξα χάριτος lays the emphasis on the glory which characterizes it.[53] With these considerations in mind and in view of the rel. ἧς (P 13) it is perhaps more convenient to render it 'His glorious grace'.[54]

The abstract ἔπαινος represents the event 'to praise' and since it is directed towards God's grace the Agent is 'we'. The prep. εἰς signals purpose and indicates that this P expresses the *purpose* of the events of election and (pre)destination. The P becomes *That we might praise His glorious grace* and is labeled *purpose* of Pp 3 and 8 and ultimately also of Pp 10—11.

13. ἧς ἐχαρίτωσεν ἡμᾶς ἐν τῷ Ἠγαπημένῳ. The event word means 'to endue with grace'.[55] This has been understood both in a semitic way, 'to grant favour',[56] and in a Gk. way, 'to endue with beauty or grace-

---

[47] E.g. Alford, 73; Abbott, 10; Robinson, 28; Salmond, 253.

[48] Schlier, 57.

[49] Gnilka, 74, n. 1.

[50] The same view is shared by *BDR*, § 168, 2, and Turner, *Syn*, 218, n. 3. The fact that D E read τῆς δόξης, which would consequently be 'praise of the glory of His grace', would seem to support this view since the minority reading could be explained as an attempt to refer δόξα to χάριτος. For concatenations of gens. see Percy, *PKE*, 26 f., 61 ff., 188 ff., 197 ff. See also V. Roon, *AE*, 121—8.

[51] The omission of the def. art. before δόξης here cannot rule out this view since vs. 12 reads ἔπαινον δόξης and vs. 14 ἔπαινον τῆς δόξης which are, evidently, meant identically. Nor is it justified to argue that in vs. 12 the goal of the praise is God, whereas in vs. 14 it is His glory.

[52] See III, B, 3, n. 57.

[53] See Percy, *PKE*, 189 and V. Roon, *AE*, 122.

[54] Alford, 73, objects to this, "Beware of the miserable *hendiadys*, 'His glorious grace'"; similarly Abbott, 10; Salmond, 253. Their view comes out in Chrysostom's explanation ἵνα ἡ τῆς χάριτος αὐτοῦ δόξα δειχθῇ.

[55] Robinson, 227.

[56] Robinson, 227 f.; Abbott, 10 f.; Schlier, 56; Barth, I, 81 f.; Salmond, 253; Gaugler, 37. Conzelmann, *TDNT*, IX, 397, has the colourless rendering 'to bless'.

fulness'.[57] The statement that this proceeding took place in connection with the Ἠγαπημένος together with its explication in vs. 7 shows that the intended meaning is the semitic one.[58]

The Agent of the event is, of course, God, while the goal is 'us'. The form of the rel. ἧς is owing to attraction to the gen. χάριτος. The form generally favoured is the acc. ἥν.[59] The P becomes 'Which (sc. grace) He bestowed on us in the Beloved'.[60]

The term Ἠγαπημένος is considered to be a messianic title,[61] just as the more frequent ἀγαπητός in the Gospels, where we have a fuller description with υἱός. That the ptc. conceals an event is made evident by a look at Col 1:13, τοῦ υἱοῦ τῆς ἀγάπης αὐτοῦ. — 'The son whom He (sc. God) loves'. This is precisely the meaning of the ptc. here. The pass. ptc. yields the pass. constr. 'In the Son who is loved by God/by the Father'. Nevertheless, since this word is used as a title, it is better that it be left unanalysed, i.e. 'Beloved'.

This P is connected by the rel. to the foregoing P, but semantically this connection serves only to carry on the discourse, there being no content relation between the two Pp otherwise. The mention of χάρις in P 12 opens up another semantic statement to be developed in Pp 13—18. P 13, being the main P of this statement, is left unlabeled. Otherwise, it is of equal semantic rank as Pp 3 and 8 and so *specific* to P 2. The P becomes *He bestowed His grace freely on us in the Beloved*.

14. ἐν ᾧ ἔχομεν τὴν ἀπολύτρωσιν. The abstract ἀπολύτρωσις represents the event 'to redeem'. It would seem at first sight that there are two Pp represented by ἔχομεν and ἀπολύτρωσις. On further thought, however, it is seen that ἔχομεν combines with ἀπολύτρωσις to form one event, i.e. 'to be redeemed'. The dat. of the rel. refers to Ἠγαπημένῳ, so the Agent of the event, when stated actively, is the Ἠγαπημένος and 'we' are the goal of redemption. The reason why the Agent of redemption is spoken of only indirectly is that the Eulogy is concerned with what God (not Christ) has done. Hence, the focus in this statement is on God's part in redemption, that is, His grace as the ultimate cause (i.e. P 13). The surface structure is equivalent to the restatement *Who redeems us*.[62]

---

[57] E.g. Chrysostom, ἐπεράστους ἐποίησε; and a number of R.C. expositors.

[58] For more details, see the excursus in Robinson, 226—8.

[59] Salmond, 253; Schlier, 56, n. 1; Gnilka, 74, n. 2; Gaugler, 36, though Robinson, who prefers an orig. ἥ (p. 144), says "There appears to be no warrant for a cognate acc." (p. 228). For more cognate constructions, see 1:19 f.; 2:4; 4:1.

[60] The play between χάριτος and ἐχαρίτωσεν cannot be transferred into English.

[61] E.g. Robinson, whose excursus (pp. 229—33) provides ample proof. See also Schlier, 56 f., and Barth, I, 82 f.

[62] On the OT background of ἀπολύτρωσις see Abbott, 11 ff.; Salmond, 253 ff. On its

The relation to the previous P is, as indicated by the rel. ᾧ, one of *comment* (on Ἠγαπημένῳ) as well as *specific* of P 13.

15. διὰ τοῦ αἵματος αὐτοῦ. The poss. pron. indicates that the author speaks of Christ's blood. This word belongs to the semantic class of Things, rather than Events. However, the collocation here is an elliptic way of describing an event, the event word being left implicit. This is the vb. 'to shed'.[63] The meaning is 'He shed His blood', and in order to lay the emphasis on 'blood' as in the Gk., 'The blood which He shed'.[64]

The relation to the foregoing is signalled by the prep. διά. So the final form becomes *By means of the blood which He shed*, and is labeled as *means* with P 15 as *result*.

16. τὴν ἄφεσιν. Ἄφεσις represents the event 'to forgive'. The word is in the same case relation to ἔχομεν as ἀπολύτρωσιν, i.e. 'we have redemption . . . forgiveness'. The vb. ἔχομεν denotes the recipient, so the constr. is equivalent to a pass. one, 'we are forgiven'. Both of these events are related in some way to Christ (ἐν ᾧ), yet the two events must be construed with a different semantic subj. The ἀπολύτρωσις is brought about by Christ's shed blood, so the Agent of redemption is Christ. The forgiveness, on the other hand, is either in line with or the result of God's rich grace (P 18).[65] Therefore, the semantic subj. of the event represented by ἄφεσις must be God. The structure of vs. 7 shows that the forgiveness is closely related to and dependent upon the Son (ἐν ᾧ), and specifically on the blood which He shed, and which issued in redemption.

The form this P takes is (*And in connection with whom God*) *forgives us* and the P is an *addition* to P 14.

17. τῶν παραπτωμάτων. Παράπτωμα signals the event 'to sin/trespass'.[66] Though a word indicating the subj. is absent, the 1st pers. pl. ἔχομεν

NT usage, Büchsel, *TDNT*, IV, 351 ff. For a detailed study on ἀπολύτρωσις and related terms in the OT, rabbinism, etc. see Morris, *APC*, 11—62. See also Gaugler, 37—43.

[63] The word αἷμα is collocated with προσφέρω in Heb 9: 7, but the context speaks of the high priestly function. A nearer equivalent to the idea here is Heb 9: 22, the compound subst. αἱματεκχυσία, which is actually collocated with ἄφεσις as here. Cf. also Heb 11: 28 πρόσχυσιν τοῦ αἵματος.

[64] Cf. Behm, *TDNT*, I, 174," The interest of the NT is not in the material blood of Christ, but in His shed blood as the life violently taken from Him. Like the cross . . . the 'blood of Christ' is simply another and even more graphic phrase for the death of Christ in its soteriological significance". See further Morris, *APC*, 112—28; Stibbs, *MWB*; Robinson, 29; Abbott, 13; Salmond, 254 f.; Gnilka, 75, "Das interesse haftet an dem gewaltsam genommenen Leben und der diesem Tod anhaftenden Sühnkraft".

[65] Ἄφεσις is related to ἀπολύτρωσις as 'included' (Robinson, 30); as a 'further definition' (Abbott, 13); as 'Apposition' (Schlier, 58).

[66] *BAG*, s. v.

indicates that the forgiveness of God is directed toward 'our' trespasses. The def. art. τῶν indicates not only definite acts of trespassing,[67] but comprehends them all as well. To render the force of the structure we may choose (All) the sins we commited. This P is the content of P 16.

18. κατὰ τὸ πλοῦτος τῆς χάριτος αὐτοῦ. The pron. is subj. and refers to God. This is seen from Pp 12 and 13. The second instance (P 13) refers forward to P 14—17, while this one refers backward to the same Pp. In other words the events expressed by Pp 14—17 are encompassed by two Pp stating the grace which God has shown. Significantly, these are precisely the events that relate to man's sin and to God's forgiveness and redemption! In the second occurrence the statement about God's grace is intensified by means of the subst. πλοῦτος. The abstraction πλοῦτος indicates degree and is rendered with 'rich grace'.[68]

The prep. κατά shows that all this (Pp 13—17) is in keeping with God's gracious character. The relation might even be conceived as one of reason. As in the case of Pp 10—11 and in view of the indirectness of the act of Christ in redemption (P 14), it is better to relate this P as reason to Pp 13—17 (result). It is stated as In accordance with the rich grace He possesses.

19. ἧς ἐπερίσσευσεν εἰς ἡμᾶς. The constr. is identical with that of vs. 6, ἧς ἐχαρίτωσεν, so the subj. is God. The rel. ἧς is very probably an attraction to the gen. χάριτος for the acc. ἥν,[69] as the direct object of the trans. περισσεύειν.[70] BAG gives as the meaning of this vb. here 'to cause to abound', etc.

The P may be stated as (And) which He lavished on us.[71] Since it begins a new statement it is left unlabeled, like P 13.

20—21. ἐν πάσῃ σοφίᾳ καὶ φρονήσει. This prep. phrase poses a double problem: a) Is it to be connected with ἐπερίσσευσεν or with γνωρίσας? and b) Does it refer to God or to 'us'? With regards to the first question RSV, TEV and UW join it with γνωρίσας, while NEB, JBPh, JB and ModGk

---

[67] The morpheme -μα denotes a particular act of the kind of action denoted by the root.

[68] See III, B, 3, n. 57.

[69] So BAG, s. v.; Robinson, 144; Abbott, 14; Gnilka, 77; Gaugler, 45. See Abbott, 14, for other alts.

[70] Cf. II Cor 9: 8.

[71] 'Lavished' has been preferred because 'to cause to abound' gives the impression that there are two events. On the vb. see Hauck, TDNT, VI, 58—61; and Salmond, 256 f.

connect it with ἐπερίσσευσεν. The majority of interpreters, too, join it to ἐπερίσσευσεν [72] and refer it to 'us'.[73] The σοφία and the φρόνησις [74] are thus the result of God's lavishing of grace on the believers rather than a modifying clause on God's action of lavishing grace. The sense is that through the lavishing of grace God has endued 'us' with a super-abundance [75] of wisdom and prudence. This phrase, accordingly, involves two implicit events related as *additions* in which God is the Agent and 'we' are the goal, i.e. (*And so He made us*) *very wise and very prudent*. It is *result* with P 19 as *means*.

22—23. γνωρίσας ἡμῖν τὸ μυστήριον τοῦ θελήματος αὐτοῦ. The semantic subj. of γνωρίσας is God.[76] This ptc., like προορίσας (P 8), is taken as in-dependent of rather than dependent on ἐπερίσσευσεν, carrying on the argument. Thus, the ptc. has the same semantic rank as e.g. ἐξελέξατο and προορίσας and begins the fifth and last semantic statement on the acts of God which have already transpired. The remaining event about the *anakephalaiōsis* is eschatological.

The last two words represent the event 'God willed'. The gen. constr. μυστήριον τοῦ θελήματος may be rendered with a) 'the *mysterion*, namely, what He willed' in which case θέλημα is an *identification* of μυστήριον; b) 'the *mysterion* about what He willed', i.e. μυστήριον is in *reference* to θέλημα,[77] or c) 'the *mysterion* which He willed'. The relation of the last alt. is ambiguous. Either the μυστήριον is the *content* of the event repre-sented by θέλημα, or the θέλημα is a *comment* on μυστήριον. The resultant renderings imply essentially no change of meaning albeit they involve a different semantic relation within the gen. constr.[78] Of the 3 alts. (b) lays the emphasis on θέλημα which ill-fits the context. Of the other two (c) clearly stresses the μυστήριον and puts θέλημα in the background. Of the two options of (c) that of *comment* allows more emphasis on μυστήριον.

---

[72] E.g. Alford, 75; Meyer, 44; Abbott, 15; Robinson, 30; Salmond, 256 f.; Dibelius, 60; Schlier, 59; Gaugler, 45; Bertram, *TDNT*, IX, 233; Barth, I, 84; Bruce, 31, hold that neither φρόνησις nor πάσῃ etc. could be predicated of God. A few, e.g., Chrysostom, Theodoret, Percy, *PKE*, 309; Gnilka, 77, join it to γνωρίσας while Hodge, 43, to ἧς.

[73] Abbott, 15; Robinson, 30; Salmond, 257; Gaugler, 45; Schlier, 59 f. Barth, I, 84, is undecided. Alford, 74, refers it to God.

[74] On σοφία see Wilckens and Fohrer, *TDNT*, VII, 465—528; on φρόνησις see Bertram, *TDNT*, IX, 220 ff. and for a comparison between the two, Abbott, 14 f., and Trench, *SNT*, 263—66. Cf. Dan 2:23.

[75] Πᾶς is often elative rather than literal, cf. Reicke, *TDNT*, V, 888, 896.

[76] Γνωρίζειν — one of the terms used about revelation — is in Eph the only predicate with μυστήριον (1:9; 3:3, 5; 6:19).

[77] Cf. B—C, *TWG*, 256.

[78] Cf. 3:4 'the *mysterion* which is about Christ', and 6:19 'the *mysterion* which we preach/of the gospel'.

Alt. (a), on the other hand, foregrounds equally both concepts which fits the context well.

Θέλημα represents not merely the event of willing but more especially, the content of that which is willed. This fits admirably with μυστήριον as a designation of the divine will, purpose, or plan. The characterisation of the divine resolve as a μυστήριον is an apt designation of God's will which was decided and shaped by factors hidden in God's εὐδοκία; a will, moreover which without revelation and a special endowment with σοφία and φρόνησις would have remained unknown. The constr. is taken as appos.-expl. and is rendered with *He made known to us the mysterion, namely, what He willed/ the will He resolved upon.* Being the Main P of this statement it is left unlabeled.

24. κατὰ τὴν εὐδοκίαν αὐτοῦ. This P is identical with P 10. Its function is to state that the momentous event of the revelation of the *mysterion* was, like the events of election, etc., in complete accordance with, in fact, determined by, God's good-pleasure. It may be rendered with *In accordance with what He considered good* and be labeled as *reason* for 22 (*result*).

25. ἣν προέθετο ἐν αὐτῷ. The pers. pron. must refer to Christ.[79] The event word προέθετο when used of God's counsels means 'to resolve, to purpose'.[80] The force of προ- is absent from the Eng. words. In line with certain earlier Pp it refers to a time before the realization.

The correl. ἣν shows that this P is a *comment* on εὐδοκία of the previous P. It takes the restatement *Which He purposed in Him* (sc. Christ).

26. εἰς οἰκονομίαν. The abstr. noun represents the event 'to administer/ manage'. It is the office and function of an οἰκονόμος.[81] Though no subj. is indicated, the fact that this administration is related to the final act of God (ἀνακεφαλαιώσασθαι) leaves no doubt that God is the Agent, i.e. 'God administers'.

The semantic relation is indicated by εἰς. Among the many uses of this prep. is a final one denoting purpose. This is precisely the relation that

---

[79] The reading ἑαυτῷ is supported only by P Tert, Hil. The rest (and also best) MSS have αυτω. The refl. pron. may have been facilitated by the mid. προέθετο i.e. 'to purpose in oneself'.

The pers. pron. is more consonant with the previous Pp in which God's acts are bound up in and with Christ, and in Which He never stands alone: i.e. εὐλογήσας — ἐν Χριστῷ; ἐξελέξατο — ἐν αὐτῷ; προορίσας — διὰ Ἰησοῦ Χριστοῦ; ἐχαρίτωσεν —ἐν τῷ Ἠγαπημένῳ.

[80] Cf. Maurer, *TDNT*, VIII, 165 ff.

[81] See Reumann, op. cit. in IV, B, ii, 2.

fits the context best. The meaning is that God laid up His good pleasure in Christ in order to administer it at the time indicated by the following P.

The P takes the form *In order to administer* (*it*) and is labeled as *purpose* of P 25.

27. τοῦ πληρώματος τῶν καιρῶν. This collocation may be resolved either passively to 'The times are completed' or actively to 'God completes the times'.

The gen. constr. is usually understood as the content of the previous P.[82] Another alt., however, is to regard an implicit repetition of εὐδοκία as the content of the event of οἰκονομία, and relate the event of οἰκονομία temporally to the πλήρωμα τῶν καιρῶν.[83] This will underline the backgrounded or parenthetical character of Pp 24—27 and render smoother the connection of the inf. ἀνακεφαλαιώσασθαι with the μυστήριον.

In this understanding the present P is turned to (*When*) *the times are completed/mature*, the 'when' expressing simply the temporal aspect sensed in the constr. Its label is *time* for P 26.

28. ἀνακεφαλαιώσασθαι τὰ πάντα ἐν τῷ Χριστῷ. This inf.[84] is to be understood as the content of μυστήριον τοῦ θελήματος of Pp 22—23.[85] Τὰ πάντα is the semantic goal of the event, while ἐν Χριστῷ is, so to speak, the *locus* in which the *anakephalaiōsis* is to take place.[86]

The position of this P is climactic. Not only is it the last of the acts of God (though not yet transpired) enumerated in the Eulogy, it is moreover the event to which all the previous acts of God look forward to, and in relation to which they may be regarded as preparatory. In particular, statement five of God's acts leads to statement six, while within that statement the ground is carefully prepared for P 28. Instead of letting P 28 follow directly upon Pp 22—23, the author tells us that the *mysterion* was in line with God's good-pleasure, this was in turn bound up with Christ and would be administered at the proper time. And when he has described the setting adequately from the standpoint of *reason, purpose* and *time*, he takes up the *content* of the μυστήριον τοῦ θελήματος αὐτοῦ.

---

[82] E.g. Lindemann, *AZ*, 79, who makes τοῦ πληρώματος τῶν καιρῶν object of οἰκονομία. Mussner, *GE*, 61, comes nearer "nicht . . . von einer 'Ökonomie der Fülle der Zeiten'. Die Ökonomie Gottes bezieht sich also offensichtlich auf die *Anakephalaiōsis* der Schöpfung in Christus, die 'die Fülle der Zeiten' arrangieren wird".

[83] Cf. Rev 10: 6 f. in which the end of time is collocated with the carrying out of God's *mysterion*. Similarly Michel, *TDNT*, V, 152; *JB*, *BKÖ*.

[84] Schlier, 62 ff., and *id.*, *TDNT*, III, 682.

[85] So lately *BKÖ*.

[86] See esp. ch. VI.

There the climax is reached and there ends the Eulogy proper. The following two Pp are but *amplifications* of τὰ πάντα. The P takes the form (*Namely*) *to sum up all things in Christ* and is *content* of Pp 22—23.

29. τὰ ἐπὶ τοῖς οὐρανοῖς. These words represent a State P i.e. *The things which are in the heavens.* Semantically, it is an *amplification* of τὰ πάντα of P 28.

30. καὶ τὰ ἐπὶ τῆς γῆς. This phrase too, represents a State P i.e. *The things which are on earth.* Semantically, it is both an *amplification* of τὰ πάντα of P 28 and a *contrast* to P 29.

C. ANALYSIS OF 3: 1—13

i. The Context: the Prayer of 3: 1, 14—19

a. Τούτου χάριν ἐγὼ Παῦλος. As was shown in II, 4 and III, B, 8 these words were meant to introduce a Prayer. The vb. of praying is the circumlocution κάμπτω τὰ γόνατά μου (vs. 14) which was 'displaced' by the intervening Digression, vv. 2—13 (see II, 4). Therefore, the above words constitute the implicit P *On account of this I, Paul, (pray for you)* (but see III, B, 9, n. 84).

b—c. ὁ δέσμιος τοῦ Χριστοῦ ['Ιησοῦ]. The word δέσμιος represents an implicit P, i.e. 'I am bound/prisoner'. The gen. τοῦ Χριστοῦ also represents a P, namely, 'I belong to Christ' or 'I serve Christ'. The two Pp are related together causally, and so the Pp take the form *Who am a prisoner because I serve Christ.* P c is *reason* for P b and the two together are a *comment* on Παῦλος of P a.

d. ὑπὲρ ἡμῶν τῶν ἐθνῶν. The prep. ὑπέρ implies that something happens for the sake of someone. This is the event behind δέσμιος τοῦ Χριστοῦ. The P may take the form (*I suffer*) *on account of you, Gentiles.* Like P c it constitutes a (second) *reason* for the event signaled by δέσμιος (P b). Furthermore, it may be regarded as *amplification* of P c, i.e. 'because I serve Christ, that is, because I serve you'.

ii. The *Mysterion* Digression of 3: 2—13

1. εἴ γε ἠκούσατε. The collocation εἴ γε [1] is understood with most comm. in a affirmative sense. The surface structure is thus a delicate form for the P *Surely you have heard.*

---

[1] The particle γε normally intensifies the word to which it is appended (ΔΔ, s. v.; *BAG*, s. v.). The combination εἴ γε occurs only 5 (6) times in the NT: here, in

2—3. τὴν οἰκονομίαν τῆς χάριτος τοῦ Θεοῦ τῆς δοθείσης μοι εἰς ὑμᾶς. The term οἰκονομία,[2] representing the event 'to administer', occurred in the Eulogy with God as the semantic subj. This was quite natural in a passage concerned with a series of events whose Agent was God. Here, however, the situation is different. The Digression is concerned primarily with the author's role in the carrying out of God's purpose and not with God's purposes or acts as such. This means that to render οἰκονομία in the same way as in 1:10 — i.e. 'Surely you have heard that God administers . . .' — would be devoid of any point in this context. The sense needed is one that brings forward the connection of the author with the οἰκονομία . . . The οἰκονομία is of course God's οἰκονομία, but this relation is secondary here, where the author focuses on the οἰκονομία τῆς χάριτος as given to him.[3] The gen. τῆς χάριτος is taken with most comm. as obj.[4] The term χάρις at this instance does not seem to have the usual sense of 'grace' or 'unmerited favour', but a technical one relating to the commission the

---

ch. 4:21; Gal 3:4; Col 1:23; II Cor 5:3 and Rm 5:6 (in B, cop sa.). The meaning depends largely on the context. Comm. are divided as to whether the sense is 'if, indeed, you have heard' (e.g. Abbott, 77 f.; Lightfoot, *Gal*, 135 f.), and a form implying certainty, as 'since/ for surely you have heard' (e.g. Robinson, 75; Scott, 182, 167; Hodge, 158, who says: "It may properly be rendered 'since', 'inasmuch as'. It is only a more refined or delicate form of assertion"; Barth, I, 328). Others again see an irony (e.g. H. G. C. Moule, *ES*, 110 n. 1), or a rhetorical point (e.g. Bruce, 59). Schlier, 147 n. 1, says "Es heisst *siquidem* und deutet eine grosse Bestimmtheit der Annahme an". So BDR, § 454, 2 and Gnilka, 163.

The *RSV* translates 'assuming that you have heard', the *NEB* 'for surely you have heard', the *TEV* 'surely you have heard' and *ModGk* ἀφοῦ ἀκούσατε (since/ inasmuch as you have heard). *BAG* has both 'if indeed' and 'inasmuch as', as also does Kühner—Gerth, *AG*, II, 177 c.

Though a decision here is no straightforward matter, it seems better, on the whole, to take it with the *VV* and the Comm. as a mild way of affirmation and perhaps not unmixed with some touch of irony. A similar point is being made in 4:21. The point being made in Gal 3:4 is, I think, affirmative: 'Have you suffered so much in vain?' εἴ γε καὶ εἰκῇ = 'it is certainly in vain' (if this is how things are with you) — the sentence being elliptical. Cf. also Sampley, *OF*, 13 and V. Roon, 84.

[2] See *LSJ* s. v. and Michel, *TDNT*, V, 151—3. It occurs 9× in the NT of which 3× in Eph and 1× in Col. In Lk 16 (3×) it has the meaning of mundane stewardship. In Eph and Col (apart from Eph 1:10) it is used in connection with God's grace shown to the Gentiles as also in I Cor 9:17. It is a moot question whether it denotes God's plan (Abbott, 79), or has a more dynamic meaning as 'administration' (so e.g. Schlier, 148; Barth, I, 328). The latter seems more preferable. For an extended discussion of the term see Reumann, *NovT*, 1959, 282—92; esp. *id.*, *NTS*, 1966—67, 147—67; the same author's dissertation *UOGS* (on microfilm); and his articles in *SE*, 1968, 86—115; and *JBL*, 1958, 339—49; Tooley, *ScJT*, 1916, 74—86, and Prestige, *GPT*, 57 ff.

[3] Robinson, 167, says with regard to 1:10; 3:2, 9; Col 1:25 "In all these passages God is ὁ οἰκονομῶν: so that they are not parallel to I Cor 9:17".

[4] E.g. Alford, 103; Abbott, 79; Salmond, 303; Schlier, 148 (or 'expliz.'); Barth, I, 328.

author claims to have received.[5] The gen. case of the ptc. agrees with χάριτος. However, since attraction is not a rare phenomenon in the Epistles, some have ventured to relate δοθείσης with the acc. οἰκονομίαν.[6] Nevertheless, most comm. are of the opinion that what was given to the author is the χάρις rather than the οἰκονομία.[7] The prep. εἰς in the collocation εἰς ὑμᾶς shows that what the author received was intended for the addressees.[8]

The above collocations of words are considered together for two reasons: because they all constitute the content of ἠκούσατε (P 1) and because they are very closely related to one another. The addressees are presumed to have heard not only of the οἰκονομία, but more specifically of the οἰκονομία τῆς χάριτος. The χάρις is of course God's own, but here the focus is particularly on its having been given to the author for the express purpose that he serve the addressees. The οἰκονομία, therefore, does not describe God's administration of His grace or purpose (as in 1: 10) but is in close conjunction with the χάρις which was given to the author. Hence both the grace and its administration were given to him. The whole collocation may be turned into '(Surely you have heard) that I was given God's grace in order to serve you'. It may now be broken down into P 2 as *I was given God's grace* and P 3 as *in order to administer it to you*. P 3 is the *purpose* of P 2 and both are the *content* of P 1. The reason why οἰκονομία comes first is that it belongs closely with χάρις and that in Gk. it would have been impossible to reverse the order between the ptc. δοθείσης and χάρις. Despite the fact that P 1 is the first P and includes the only finite vb. in this statement (Pp 1—3), it is analysed as sub-thematic with P 2 giving the gist of the statement and the pgr. P 2 (and P 3) state quite generally that God has commissioned the author to minister to the Gentiles. The following statements take up this matter of commission and service in greater detail. Therefore, P 2 is related as *generic* to the succeeding Main Pp.

4—5. [ὅτι] κατὰ ἀποκάλυψιν ἐγνωρίσθη μοι τὸ μυστήριον. The pass. ἐγνωρίσθη signals God as the Agent of the event. The abstract ἀποκάλυψις represents the event 'to reveal' and since this is intimately connected with ἐγνωρίσθη God must be understood as its Agent. Nevertheless, the pass. constr. tends to remove the focus from the Agent (who is only implicit) and place it instead on the event itself as well as on the experiencer.

---

[5] Cf. Rm 1: 5; 12: 3; 15: 15 ff.; Gal 2: 7—9.

[6] See Abbott, 79.

[7] Mitton, *EE*, 91 ff. sees a tension between this passage and Col 1: 25 where the οἰκονομία is actually said to be given to Paul. Barth, I, 328, 358 f. thinks "there cannot be an absolute contrast between the two affirmations", and concludes that both are functionally given to Paul.

[8] The same is the import in vv. 7 and 8. So too, e.g. Abbott, 79; Robinson, 167, 221—28.

The relation between these two Pp is signaled by the prep. κατά. The uses of this prep. are numerous. When construed with an acc., one of them is that of 'Norm' or 'Standard' by which the action is measured or compared and is then translated by some form of 'in accordance with'. This is the sense given by *BAG*.[9] But this sense is inappropriate here. ΔΔ says that when κατά is construed with an abstract subst. it functions as a modal adv.[10] This is precisely the sense needed here. As Schlier [11] says "Das κατὰ ἀποκάλυψιν gibt den Modus des γνωρισθῆναι an".

The Pp thus become: 'That it was by way of a revelation which God granted me that the *mysterion* was made known to me/that I became acquainted with the *mysterion*'. Essentially, there is here but one event, i.e. 'God revealed to me His mysterion! But had the author written ὅτι ἀπεκαλύφθη . . . the focus would center on the event of revelation, and its result, i.e. 'it was revealed to me and now I know it'. The intention of the writer was, however, to draw attention to the manner in which his acquaintance with the *mysterion* came about. To preserve that emphasis it is better to render the collocation as two Pp.

The relation of these Pp to their context may be indicated by the ὅτι. In terms of semantic relations this word introduces either the reason for or the content of an event. There is no event in the foregoing Pp that requires a reason, but there is one that requires a content, i.e. ἠκούσατε. These two Pp may therefore be analysed as *content* [12] of P 1 with P 4 signaling the *manner* for P 5. Since Pp 2—3 were also analysed as content of P 1 the two groups will have to be considered as additional.

But another and more preferable way of construing it is possible. P 5 is analysed as more specific than P 2 since it gives a more detailed description of what was given to the author and with its support Pp (i.e. 4, 6—21) constitutes a more specific statement than the first statement of the pgr. Hence P 5 is regarded as the main P of statement two and is accordingly left unlabeled. Pp 4 and 5 take their final form as *It was with a revelation which God granted me* and as *that the mysterion was made known to me/that I became acquainted with the mysterion* respectively.

6. καθὼς προέγραψα ἐν ὀλίγῳ. The term προγράφω has three main senses: a) 'to write before' (in another document); b) 'to write before' (in the same document, hence, 'to write above') and c) 'to write publicly'/'to placard'. The third sense is clearly that in Gal 3: 1. The first one is found

---

[9] *BAG*, s. v. quote this vs. under "The Norm is at the same time the reason, so that 'in accordance with' and 'because of' are merged". But there is no 'Norm' here. Nor is it possible to assign to it the meaning "Because of revelation the *mysterion* was made known to me".

[10] See ΔΔ, s. v., 15 for exx; also *LSJ*, s. v.

[11] Schlier, 148. Similarly Abbott, 79, who relates it to Gal 1: 12 δι' ἀποκαλύψεως.

[12] Similarly V. Roon, 184, n. 4.

in Rm 15: 4. For our passage both the first and the second senses have their advocates.[13] My own choice lies with the second meaning because the contents of chs. 1—2 are such as suffice to justify this reference to them, whereas no other writing is known to which such a reference might have been made, and because the whole *Corpus Paulinum* (Goodspeed's theory, shared by Mitton with modifications) could not be described as ἐν ὀλίγῳ.[14] Most comm. also agree that the reference is specifically to 1: 9 f.[15] The phrase ἐν ὀλίγῳ is adverbial and is taken as meaning 'briefly'.[16]

The relation of this P to the foregoing is clarified by the adv. καθώς. The chief function of this adv. is to introduce comparison (*BAG* s.v.). The comparison is between Pp 4—5 and what he has written above more specifically between κατὰ ἀποκάλυψιν ἐγνωρίσθη and γνωρίσας (in 1: 9). The P becomes *As I briefly wrote above* and is labeled *comparison* of 6 (i.e. 1: 9 etc.) with 4—5. This together with Pp 7—9 is parenthetical.

7. πρὸς ὅ . . . ἀναγινώσκοντες. The ptc. is dependent for its personal reference on the finite δύνασθε (P 8) which implies that it represents the event 'you read'. The collocation πρὸς ὅ is "unusual",[17] but there is a parallel in II Cor 5: 10. The sense is nonetheless clear, i.e. 'according to which'[18] referring to the account written above. For the sake of a smoother rendering the collocation is rendered as a simple rel., i.e. *Which when you read.* It is a *comment* on P 6 and the *condition* for P 8.

---

[13] Goodspeed, *ME*; Mitton, *EE*, 234 f. (with variations in details) hold that it refers to the previous letters of Paul (or at least some of them — Mitton). Most scholars, however, see in it a reference to chs. 1—2 (e.g. Alford, 103; Robinson, 167; Abbott, 79; Salmond, 303; Schlier, 149; Simpson, 69; Barth, I, 329; Gnilka, 164; Merklein, *CK*, 10 f; Percy, *PKE*, 350; Gaugler, 130; V. Roon, 84).

[14] The phrase is applied to the five chs. of I Pet (5: 12) as well as to the thirteen chs. of Heb (13: 22), but could not very well be applied, as Mitton claims, to a body of writings as large as the *Corpus Paulinum*. In antiquity books were generally short, so that the phrase ἐν ὀλίγῳ used by one of the ancients could not be compared with a similar phrase used in modern times when books often are massive.

[15] All the comm. mentioned in note 13 as favouring the reference to the present letter, except for Percy, *PKE*, 350 (partly); Gaugler, 130; Merklein, *KAE*, 216, who prefer a reference to 2: 11 ff. There is some corroboration for this from a papyrus of the II A.D. (*BGU*, 780, 2) where the term προγραφή is a 'heading' or 'preliminary form'. The word occurs also in Men. Prot. 16 D (IV A.D. as προσχέδιον (ΔΔ)); while in Gal. 13.777 it is the 'title' of a prescription. It is not impossible that προγράφω is in reference to the προγραφή of the Epistle, i.e. the Introduction (1: 3—14). Lindemann's (*ZNW*, 1976, 244 f.) 'psychological suggestion' explanation sounds incredible.

[16] Elsewhere in the NT this phrase occurs only in Acts 26: 28, 29, but the sense required there is different. Here the phrase is equivalent to δι' ὀλίγου (I Pt 5: 12) and διὰ βραχέων (Heb 13: 22). So too, most comm.

[17] Robinson, 167.

[18] Abbott, 80. Similarly *BAG*, s. v. πρός III, 5, d.

8. δύνασθε . . . νοῆσαι. At first sight it looks as if there are two events here. However, δύνασθε being a vb. of incomplete predication, forms one event with the inf., i.e. *You can understand*. The P is related to P 7 as *consequence*.

9. τὴν σύνεσίν μου ἐν τῷ μυστηρίῳ τοῦ Χριστοῦ. The abstract σύνεσιν represents the event 'to understand' (cf. συνίημι). The pers. pron. μου indicates that the gen. is subj., so the event is 'I understand'. The gen. τοῦ Χριστοῦ may be either poss. or obj. Abbott favours the obj.[19] The prep. ἐν has a local sense indicating that in which the σύνεσις lies, the full phrase being τὴν σύνεσίν μου τὴν ἐν τῷ μυστηρίῳ. Kuhn draws attention to Hebrew usage where vbs. of revealing, including הודיע are normally constructed with ב and illustrates from Qumran (1QH 2: 13 דעת ברזי פלא) what to him is a parallel usage.[20] When σύνεσιν is transformed into an event the prep. phrase becomes the obj.: *That I have insight into the mysterion concerning Christ*. This P is related to P 8 as *content* (of νοῆσαι) and as such is parenthetical to Pp 4—5.

10. ὃ ἑτέραις γενεαῖς οὐκ ἐγνωρίσθη τοῖς υἱοῖς τῶν ἀνθρώπων. The collocation τοῖς υἱοῖς τῶν ἀνθρώπων is a Heb. idiom (common in the OT) which means simply 'men'.[21] The combination ἑτέραις γενεαῖς serves to point out a contrast to the following P. Which part of the following P does it contrast, ἀποστόλοις καὶ προφήταις perhaps? This is unlikely, since this collocation is contrasted to the circumlocution υἱοῖς τῶν ἀνθρώπων. The only other contrastive element in P 11 is the temporal adv. νῦν. This is the answer. Accordingly, ἑτέραις γενεαῖς is a way of indicating the past[22] and contrasting it with the present.[23] The rel. pron. ὅ is correl. with the word *mysterion*. Now, since this term has occurred already twice (in Pp 5 and 9), it is important to decide to which of the two occurrences it relates, because such a decision is also determinative of the relation of this P to the foregoing. The event word ἐγνωρίσθη is in pass. form. It was noted that the terms dealing with the author's reception of God's revelation were both in the pass. (i.e. δοθείσης P 2; ἐγνωρίσθη P 5) and that the vb. relating to his impartation of the revelation to others was in active form (προέγραψα P 6). Moreover, the event in the following P (ἀπεκαλύφθη

---

[19] Abbott, 80. Barth, I, 331, thinks the mystery regarding the admission of the Gentiles is not different to the mystery which "consists of the Messiah", his relation to the Father and his salvation accomplishment. It is all one mystery and this goes for Col 1: 27, which Mitton, 89 and Abbott, 80, see as different.

[20] Kuhn, *PQ*, 118 f.

[21] So Abbott, 81. For Schlier, 149, the expression is "ein feierlicher Ausdruck für τοῖς ἀνθρώποις . . . auch ein 'biblisches' Wort, . . . vielleicht auch ein liturgischer Ausdruck".

[22] So too, Robertson, *Gr.*, 523; Barth, I, 331.

[23] So Schlier, 149; Barth, I, 333.

τοῖς ἀποστόλοις) is also in the pass. form. The change of voice is indicative not only of the limits of the parenthesis, of which I spoke earlier, but also of the relation between these Pp. I conclude that this P is related to P 5 and that the relation is one of *comment* on the term *mysterion*. The P is presented as *Which in the past was not made known to men/ mankind*. The absolute statement of this P will be modified by the adv. ὡς in the next P.

11—12. ὡς νῦν ἀπεκαλύφθη τοῖς ἁγίοις ἀποστόλοις αὐτοῦ καὶ προφήταις ἐν πνεύματι. In the phrase ἁγίοις ἀποστόλοις . . . προφήταις there is a covert P: 'The apostles . . . the prophets are holy'. This is no event P, but a State P which has a Relation rather than an Event as its nucleus. The abstraction 'holy' is in an attributive relation to the 'Things' apostles and prophets. The dat. ἐν πνεύματι is instrumental and is to be related not to ἁγίοις (i.e. holy by means of the Spirit), but to the event word ἀπεκαλύφθη as specifying the Agent of revelation. The adv. νῦν has already been dealt with above. The adv. ὡς has a host of uses. One of its chief uses is to introduce a comparison. This meaning has two nuances: a) an absolute comparison, and b) a comparison of degree. Of these the second one seems to be more appropriate here.[24] The Pp become (11) *In the same degree as it has now*

[24] Schlier, 150, chooses the first sense: "als Anzeige eines absoluten Gegensatzes verstehen müssen". He is followed by Barth, I, 333 f. But this is to hide one's head in the sand. The writer of Eph was certainly acquainted with the OT promises about the eventual place of the Gentiles in God's salvation. Rm 16: 25 f. also, states that the *mysterion* is made known through the προφητικαὶ γραφαί. It rather needs to be inquired here whether ὡς does not bear the sense of degree. Grammatically it can have it. Contextually, it would seem that it is demanded. This understanding is perhaps reflected in Col 1: 26, where the *mysterion* ἐφανερώθη to the saints. In Col 4: 4 he who φανερεῖ the *mysterion* is the apostle. I suggest that the φανεροῦν to the saints in Col is in reference to the commission of the apostle whereas the revealing in Eph is entirely different, referring to God's revelation to the apostles. And in this latter case, it is the degree of knowledge that is contrasted with that possessed by the men of old. This explains why no comparison is made in Col between the men of the past and the NT saints. Accordingly, Mitton's 'discrepancy' between the revelation experiencers of the two epistles is unfounded. This is borne out also by the different terms used. Cf. Brown, *SB*, 58, n. 170.

The ancients interpreted it similarly: Theophylact has, οὕτως ἀκριβῶς οὐκ ᾔδεσαν οἱ παλαιοὶ τὸ μυστήριον, and Chrysostom, οὕτω δὲ ἀκριβῶς οὐκ ᾔδεσαν. So also Theodoret. It is understood in the same way by Alford, 104; Salmond, 304; Abbott, 82; Bruce, 61.

There is another point to be taken into consideration. Paul specifies that the *mysterion* was revealed through the agency of the Holy Spirit. In I Cor 2: 7—16 he speaks of the role of the Spirit in revelation. Since the Spirit was not widely given to 'the sons of men' in the OT a consequence would be ignorance of the *mysterion* (cf. *supra* I, 6). It follows that the revelation of the *mysterion* goes along with the allotting of the Spirit. There remain thus three possible ways to understand the words: a)ὡς denotes comparison in degree; b) No knowledge at all, with the reference limited to

been revealed by the Spirit to the apostles and prophets and (12) *Who
are holy.* P 11 is related as *contrast* to P 10, while P 12 is an attributive
comment on ἀποστόλοις and προφήταις of P 11.

13—18. εἶναι τὰ ἔθνη συγκληρονόμα καὶ σύσσωμα καὶ συμμέτοχα τῆς ἐπαγγελίας ἐν Χριστῷ Ἰησοῦ διὰ τοῦ εὐαγγελίου. The three συν- words taken together with the inf. constitute the three Pp 'The Gentiles are coinheritors
. . . concorporate . . . coparticipants'. These may be conceived of as State
Pp describing the Gentiles. On the other hand, it may be remarked that
the abstract words συγκληρονόμα and συμμέτοχα, and perhaps also σύσσωμα,[25]
conceal the events 'to inherit with',[26] 'to participate with' and 'to belong
to one body'. The abstract ἐπαγγελία represents the event 'to promise' and
the context makes it clear that it refers to the well-known promise of
God.[27] This was touched upon already in 2: 12. The Agent is naturally
God. The phrase ἐν Χριστῷ Ἰησοῦ gives primarily the means but is
distinguished from the instrumental phrase διὰ τοῦ εὐαγγελίου by the use

---

'sons of men', i.e. the ordinary people excepting the prophets, and that because the
Spirit was not given; c) the prophets here are OT prophets (favoured by Brown, *SB*, 58,
n. 170). Alt. c is shattered by νῦν. Of the other two (a) squares with the facts best.

[25] This is the earliest instance of σύσσωμα which occurs exclusively in Christian
authors (cf. *BAG*, s. v.). As indicated in III, B, 8, the three συν- words have their
antecedents in the previous pgs.: συγκληρονόμα and συμμέτοχα, synonymous in use
though different aspectually, are developed out of the explicit thought presented in
1: 11, 14, 18; and the implicit thought of 2: 12 f., 19. By the same token σύσσωμος
takes up the thought of 2: 14 (τὰ ἀμφότερα ἕν), 15 (ἕνα καινὸν ἄνθρωπον) and esp. 16
(ἐν ἑνὶ σώματι). It is possible that the term was created *ad hoc* to correspond with the
other two terms (cf. Robinson, 78). The meaning is 'united in one body', 'belonging
to one body' 'forming one body'. The 'body' is not distinct from those who constitute
it; it is identified with its constituents. Hence this collocation may be regarded as a
state P. Nevertheless, there is an active aspect as well in it, in that the constituents by
uniting 'make up' the body, i.e. bring it into being. Since the term occurs between two
words which ultimately represent events, it may be convenient to regard this also as
an Event P, and render it with 'Belong to one body'.

[26] Cf. Nida, *TST*, 64 ". . . the word *heir* identifies not only an object (the individual
in question) but states that something has happened or will happen, namely, that he
inherits property, rights, title, etc.".

[27] A question which naturally poses itself here is whether ἐπαγγελία is the object
of all three συν- words, of the first and third, or only of the third one. The relation of
σύσσωμα to ἐπαγγελίας is ruled out since these terms cannot collocate meaningfully.
Parallel usage endorses the collocation of συγκληρονόμα with ἐπαγγελία (with the latter
as object of the former; cf. Heb 6: 12, 17; 11: 9) and there are thus no *a priori* grounds
for excluding the possibility. The chief difficulty is that the intevening σύσσωμα de-
stroys the flow of thought and renders the connection very awkward. Another consideration is in order. The term (συν)κληρονόμος is much more definite in content by a
rich usage in tradition (i.e. OT and Judaism) than (συμ)μέτοχος which requires a more
explicit object to complete the idea. These considerations, among others, possibly
account sufficiently for referring only συμμέτοχα to ἐπαγγελίας as does Abbott, 83.

of preps. Ἐν Χριστῷ does not mean simply 'through Christ'[28] it rather conceals the event 'to be in Christ/united with Christ' as the condition for salvation. The word εὐαγγέλιον is really an event, i.e. 'to evangelise', but the partial non-matching of grammar with semantics occasionally makes it impossible to transform an abstraction to an event.[29] The use of the abstraction serves to objectivise an event[30] and in view of the following P it is necessary to retain the abstraction in its surface form, i.e. 'gospel'. The phrase διὰ τοῦ εὐαγγελίου is best understood with εἶναι giving the means by which the Gentiles attain equal status with the Jews: i.e. it is not by circumcision or proselytism, but by the Gospel. It is this equality of treatment of both sectors of humanity that is new, and not the fact that the Gentiles also are blessed. The latter *was* known to the men of old, but *not* the former! This consideration gives additional support to the view that ὡς in P 11 indicates comparision in degree. The inf. εἶναι is generally understood as epexegetical[31] giving the content of the *mysterion*. The relation may be to P 5, P 9, P 10 (correl. ὃ), or P 11 (implicit correl.). Since P 9 was analysed as parenthetical, it is ruled out. Of the other options the relation to P 5 bringing the content of the *mysterion* into direct connection with the *mysterion* as revealed to the author, rather than connecting it to the *mysterion* as revealed to the apostles and prophets (P 11) is more appropriate with the whole tenor of the Digression. After all, to whichever P these Pp relate, they are still the *content* of the *mysterion*. The Pp are stated as (P 13) *That the Gentiles inherit together (with the Jews)*; (P 14) *And belong to the same body together (with the Jews)*; (P 15) *And partake together (with the Jews)*; (P 16) *Of that which God promised*; (P 17) *By being incorporated into Christ Jesus/united with Christ Jesus*; (P 18) *Through the preaching of the Gospel.*

19. οὗ ἐγενήθην διάκονος. This collocation actually represents the event 'to serve'. Again, the pass. constr. focuses attention on the event. The P becomes *Whose servant I was made (by God)* and, as the rel. pron. shows, it is a *comment* on εὐαγγέλιον (P 18).

20. κατὰ τὴν δωρεὰν τῆς χάριτος τοῦ Θεοῦ τῆς δοθείσης μοι. The abstract δωρεὰν is really a surface representation for the event 'to give freely'. The

---

[28] So also Abbott, 83. See *infra* VI, 1 and relevant excursus.

[29] Cf. B—C, *TWG*, 222 n. 9.

[30] See Nida, *TST*, 64 and B—C, *TWG*, 219 f.

[31] Chrysostom; Alford, 104; Abbott, 83; Hodge, 164; Salmond, 305; Schlier, 151; Bruce, 62; Simpson, 72. Barth, I, 336, disagrees: "Rather the inf. fulfills the function of a sentence that begins with 'that' and describes a perception, a belief, an utterance, or a piece of information" and endorses *JBPh*'s translation, "(the secret that was hidden . . .) 'is simply this: that the Gentiles . . . are'". It is difficult to see wherein Barth's rendering differs from that of others who explain it as epexegetical.

gen. τῆς χάριτος is obj. and the gen. τοῦ Θεοῦ is subj. The first six words (apart from κατά) thus mean, 'God gives freely of His grace'. The ptc. indicates also the event 'to give', and since both δωρεάν and δοθείσης refer to the same word, they are considered as one event in which δωρεάν adds the modifying component 'freely'. This P is related to P 19 by the prep. κατά.[32] The relation that is required here is a causal one.[33] But the reason-result relation established for 1:5 is not the most appropriate one here. Nor is the relation of manner posited for 3:3 better. The most suitable sense here would be one of means with P 19 as result, since the author's becoming a servant was dependent upon God's grace, but if we must chose from the two established senses, that of *reason* would come closer. The P takes the restatement *'Because God gave me His grace freely'*.

21. κατὰ τὴν ἐνέργειαν τῆς δυνάμεως αὐτοῦ. The abstract ἐνέργειαν represents the event 'to be active/to operate/to work'. The ultimate Agent is naturally God. The gen. τῆς δυνάμεως either gives the immediate agent of the event 'to be active' or the means for it. This P is parallel with P 20 as is indicated by the κατά introducing them both, and by the parallelism δωρεάν//ἐνέργειαν and χάριτος//δυνάμεως. It is an *addition* to P 20 and with it bears the same relation to P 19. It is rendered *(And) because He worked mightily (in me)*.[34]

22. ἐμοὶ . . . ἐδόθη ἡ χάρις αὕτη. This P begins the third semantic statement of the Digression. In each of the three statements something is given to the author, but the order of the parts of each statement is different. If we represent what was given by A, the vb. of giving by B, and the author by C, we note that P 2 has A B C; P 5 B C A; and P 22 C B A. The focus has definitely shifted from the commission and the giving, to the person of the author. This is underlined by the descriptive adj. ἐλαχιστότερος, which shows that the author dwells upon his own person.

It was noted above that statement one was generic in respect to statements two and three. Statement two was primarily concerned with the revelation of the *mysterion* to the author and its content relative to the Gentiles. Statement three places the accent on the actual administration of it and some of its results relative to the principalities and powers. The ἐμοὶ τῷ ἐλαχιστοτέρῳ is to be understood in light of this. Statement three may then be considered, broadly speaking, as the means for statement two.

All this implies that this P looks forward to what is coming. It is stated

---

[32] For a discussion of this word see *supra* IV, B, 10, 18, and C, 4.

[33] It would seem that the κατά phrases need further investigation at least in Eph in order to define precisely their range of meaning.

[34] 'In me' is supplied as being implicit. In Col 1:29 the ἐνέργεια is actually said to be ἐνεργουμένην ἐν ἐμοί.

as *To me (God) gave this grace/commission* and being a main P is left unlabeled.

23. τῷ ἐλαχιστοτέρῳ πάντων ἁγίων. The form ἐλαχιστότερος is a comparative of a superlative, but is most probably used to intensify the superlative idea.[35] It appears that this P relates to P 22 as a comment (on ἐμοί), yet on further reflection it becomes evident that the author expresses amazement that of all men he should have been singled out for this grace. Hence, it is better to analyse the relation as one of *concession-contraexpectation* to P 22, and give it the form *Though I was the least of all the saints*.

24. τοῖς ἔθνεσιν εὐαγγελίσασθαι τὸ . . . πλοῦτος τοῦ Χριστοῦ. The gen. τοῦ Χριστοῦ is either poss., i.e. 'the riches Christ has' or obj., 'the riches (we) have in Christ'. Since this 'riches' is meant for mankind (cf. εὐαγγελίσασθαι) either of the two renderings 'the riches Christ has for us' and 'the riches we have in Christ' is permissible. The subj. of the inf. is ἐμοί of P 22. The inf. is final and signals the *purpose* of the giving of grace (P 22). The P takes the restatement *In order that to the Gentiles I might proclaim the riches Christ has for them*.

25. ἀνεξιχνίαστον. This abstract represents the event *(Which) cannot be explored* and being in an attributive relation to P 24 it is a *comment* on πλοῦτος.

26. καὶ φωτίσαι (πάντας). The event of φωτίσαι has, the ἐμοί of P 22 as its subj. The reading πάντας does not enjoy undisputed MSS support,[36] but if accepted it becomes the object of the inf.

The relation to the previous P is signaled by the conj. καί. This conj. normally marks an addition, in which case P 26 and P 24 are of equal semantic rank and bear the relation of *purpose* to P 22 (*means*). Another relation is, however, possible, namely, to read καί as 'and so', i.e. as a *result* of the proclamation of P 24.[37] In this view P 24, which is the *purpose* of P 22, is itself the *means* for P 26. The relation of addition is

---

[35] Cf. Robertson, *Gr.*, 278, 670; *BDR*, § 61, 2; Jannaris, *HGG*, § 506. Moulton, *Prol.*, 236, "whether as comp. or true superl. the sentence leaves uncertain". Cf. also *MM*, s. v.

[36] If πάντας is not original, the object of φωτίσαι becomes the οἰκονομία τοῦ μυστηρίου (Abbott, 87, seems to favour this alt. as also does Schlier, 152). In that case φωτίσαι would mean 'to bring to light', i.e. the administration of the *mysterion*. But this rendering founders upon the pron. τίς and the nom. case of οἰκονομία. The other alt. is here favoured because it is more consonant with 1:18 where it is not the message that is brought to light, but the Gentiles who become enlightened. This view is accepted by Barth, I, 342, but rejected by Robinson, 170.

[37] So taken by Schlier, 152.

favoured both syntactically and semantically, and thus the P is regarded as giving a more remote *purpose* (in relation to that in P 24) of P 22 and takes the form *And to enlighten all men.*

27. τίς ἡ οἰκονομία τοῦ μυστηρίου. The constr. is similar to that in 3:2 where χάριτος corresponds to μυστήριον here. Once again the agent of the event 'to administer' is the author. The *mysterion* is God's purpose or plan as such, the οἰκονομία is the administration of the *mysterion* while the χάρις is the gracious commission given to the author which involves both the *mysterion* and the οἰκονομία. All three are given to the author.

The inter.-indef. pron. τίς is used idiomatically. It expresses the indescribability of the subj. following it.[38] Here it is equivalent to the adj. ἀνεξιχνίαστος. Pp 26 and 27 are equivalent to Pp 24 and 26. In each case the author is the agent of the event (εὐαγγελίσασθαι and φωτίσαι), the experiencers are τὰ ἔθνη and πάντας, the contents of the two parallel Pp are ὁ πλοῦτος τοῦ Χριστοῦ and ἡ οἰκονομία τοῦ μυστηρίου, while the indiscribability of the πλοῦτος and the οἰκονομία is brought out by ἀνεξιχνίαστον and τίς respectively.

Owing to the skewing of grammar and semantics, certain changes will have to be made to present the P in a semantic display. It may take the form *On the (wonderful) administration of the mysterion (which I have been entrusted and carry out).* It is the *content* of P 26.

28. τοῦ ἀποκεκρυμμένου ἀπὸ τῶν αἰώνων ἐν τῷ Θεῷ. The pass. ptc. represents the event 'to hide'. The phrase ἀπὸ τῶν αἰώνων marks the temporal setting while ἐν τῷ Θεῷ marks the location for the concealment of the *mysterion.* The implied Agent is God. The ptc., being a vbl. adj., stands in attributive relation to μυστήριον (P 27) and this implies that P 28 is a *comment* on P 27. It is stated as *Which (God) hid eternally in Himself.*

29. τῷ τὰ πάντα κτίσαντι. The dat. τῷ agrees in case with τῷ Θεῷ (P 28) indicating that this P bears the same relation to part of P 28 as P 28 bore to part of P 27, i.e. the relation of *comment*. The P may be stated as *Who created all things.*

30. ἵνα γνωρισθῇ νῦν ταῖς ἀρχαῖς καὶ ταῖς ἐξουσίαις . . . ἡ . . . σοφία τοῦ Θεοῦ. The event γνωρισθῇ is here overtly stated. Its content (sc. σοφία τοῦ Θεοῦ) is reserved for purposes of emphasis till the end of this long clause after the various adjuncts have adequately described the context in which God's wisdom will be revealed.[39] The temp. νῦν contrasts with ἀπὸ τῶν

---

[38] So V. Roon, 185 "Evenals in 1:18, 19 brengt het pronomen indefinitum interrogativum tot uiting dat het om een onbeschrijfelijke zaak gaat".

[39] A similar example was noted in 1:9 f. with respect to ἀνακεφαλαιώσασθαι.

αἰώνων (P 28) and this shows that in essence the πολυποίκιλος σοφία and the μυστήριον come extremly close. The *mysterion* is shaped by God's wisdom, it is a product of it. At the same time God's wisdom is reflected and revealed in the *mysterion*.[40] There is an interblending of conceptual components between these two terms (cf. I Cor 2: 7 σοφία ἐν μυστηρίῳ).

The relation of this P is indicated by the ἵνα. This conj. may be either consecutive or final.[41] If the consecutive sense is chosen, the meaning cannot be other than 'contemplated result',[42] but this is not far from purpose. On the whole it is preferable to take ἵνα as final and construe this P as the ultimate object in view of Pp 22—28, but in a special way dependent on P 22 (ἐμοὶ . . . ἐδόθη). Abbott protests that "This would make St. Paul ascribe to his own preaching a result in which the other apostles had their share".[43] But this objection is beside the point, since the author's theme is his own part in the realization of God's purpose. The P becomes *In order that at this time (God) might make known His . . . wisdom to the principalities and powers.* Though the P is stated as the *purpose* of the previous Pp, it is also in a way the content of the *mysterion* with respect to the powers.

31. ἐν τοῖς ἐπουρανίοις. This collocation represents the implicit P (*The principalities . . . the powers) are in the heavenlies* [44] and signals *location*. At the same time it is a way of *identification* by location of which ἀρχαί and ἐξουσίαι he is speaking of, i.e. they are not earthly but heavenly.

[40] Cf. Dahl, *ALC*, 65.

[41] That ἵνα has from Greco-Roman times on a consecutive sense along with its ancient telic sense is now generally accepted, cf. Jannaris, *HGG*, § 1756 ff.; Sophocles, *Lex*, 600; Moulton, *Prol.*, 206—9; Robertson, *Gr.*, 997 ff.; *BAG*, s. v. ἵνα II, 2; Turner, *Synt.*, 100 ff. Chrysostom explained the ἵνα of Rm 5: 20 as ecbatic. It is also agreed, that occasionally it is difficult to decide with certainty between the two (e.g. Turner, *Synt.*, 102; *BAG* as above: "in many cases purpose and result cannot be clearly differentiated, and hence ἵνα is used for the result which follows according to the purpose of the subj. or of God. As in Jewish thought purpose and result are identical in declarations of the divine will". Robertson, *Gr.*, 999, concludes that there are three uses of ἵνα: "final, sub-final, consecutive", and Moulton, *Prol.*, 208 f., advocates the freedom of comm. to interpret ἵνα as the sense may be. As a matter of fact comm. interpret it as a rule as final, e.g. Alford, 106 (actually before Moulton), who refers it to ἐδόθη; Robinson, 170; Abbott, 88; Salmond, 308; Hodge, 172; Lenski, 481; Schlier, 153; Bruce, 64; Simpson, 75; Gnilka, 173. Dibelius, 75 and Barth, I, 345 do not indicate.

[42] The term is applied by Sunday—Hedlam, *Rm*, 320, on Rm 11: 11. See further Moule's remarks in *IB*, 142—6, on final and consecutive clauses.

[43] Abbott, 88, This objection is not serious since Paul here speaks of his own part and does not exclude the role of the other apostles. Besides, he was in a particular way the apostle to the Gentiles.

[44] See relevant excursus in VI.

32. διὰ τῆς ἐκκλησίας. This collocation shows that the Church plays an instrumental role in the exhibition of God's wisdom to the powers. The question may be asked, in which way does the Church become instrumental in the revelation of God's wisdom to the powers? The answer is to be found in the contents of this Digression, and in particular in vs. 6: the formation of the Church of Jews and Gentiles as the effective result of the Christ Event. The author himself plays a prominent part in the establishment of the Church and is thus instrumental in the exhibition of God's wisdom to the powers.[45] The P may take the form *By means of (the calling into being of) the Church* and is labeled as *means* for P 30.

33. πολυποίκιλος. This adj. conceals the implicit P (*The wisdom of God) is extremely varied*. The word πολυποίκιλος is simply a strengthened form of ποικίλος and means 'very varied', 'many-sided', 'extremely diversified' and the like.[46] The P is an attributive *comment* on σοφία of P 30.

34. κατὰ πρόθεσιν τῶν αἰώνων ἣν ἐποίησεν ἐν τῷ Χριστῷ Ἰησοῦ τῷ Κυρίῳ ἡμῶν. The abstract πρόθεσιν represents the event 'to purpose'. The gen. τῶν αἰώνων has been understood variously, e.g. a) poss. of 'the purpose that runs through the ages';[47] b) obj. of the purpose concerning the ages;[48] and c) periphrastically, for 'eternal purpose'. Most comm. decide for the last interpretation.[49] The unexpressed Agent of the event is God, so the P becomes 'God purposes eternally'. The vb. ἐποίησεν may represent a new P signaling the realisation of God's purpose through the Christ

---

[45] See further ch. VI.

[46] In an excursus in his Comm. Schlier, (159—66) argues that πολυποίκιλος is equivalent to πολύμορφος and draws, for example, on material like Ap., *Met*, 11, 5, 762, where Isis is described as *multiformis Isis*. Although one, Isis takes many forms and presents herself as an 'All-Göttin'. Dahl, *ALC*, 67 ff., objects to the equation of πολυποίκιλος with πολύμορφος, pointing out, with Seesemann, *TDNT*, VI, 485, that πολυ- in πολυποίκιλος only strengthens the idea in ποικίλος and does not add the idea of 'many' as it does in πολύμορφος. "Wenn die Weisheit Gottes in Eph 3: 10 πολυποίκιλος gennant wird, liegt darin, dass sie sehr bunt, mannigfaltig, kompliziert, reich und prächtig ist, keineswegs aber, dass sie in verschiedenen Gestalten nacheinander in Erscheinung tritt".

[47] Abbott, 89. So also Salmond, 309 f.; Lenski, 483.

[48] Schlier, 157, "τῶν αἰώνων bezeichnet das Objekt dieser Vorbestimmung".

[49] Alford, 107; Hodge, 174; Dibelius, 75; Bruce, 65; Simpson, 76, See Barth, I, 347 f., for more possibilities of taking it. But even this rendering 'eternal purpose' needs some explanation, for this too can be one of the above two. Is it a purpose that was conceived of eternally, a purpose that runs through the ages? or a purpose concerning the ages? The phrase is related not only to ἵνα γνωρισθῇ (as Schlier, 157), but also to μυστήριον ἀποκεκρυμμένον ἀπὸ τῶν αἰώνων. So, both the time of the hiddenness and the time of the revelation are included in πρόθεσιν τῶν αἰώνων (as Barth, I, 346).

Event. It is more probable, however, that πρόθεσιν ἐποίησεν is a resolution for προέθετο (cf. 1: 9) referring to the original formation of the purpose in Christ.[50] The P probably relates to P 30 or perhaps also to Pp 27—28 and gives the reason both for the hiddeness and for the revelation of the *mysterion*. Nevertheless, since it occurs at the end of the main body of the Digression, it is probably better to regard it as a terminal feature supplying the *reason* for it all. The P takes the form *Because (so) He purposed eternally in Christ Jesus our Lord.*[51]

35—36. ἐν ᾧ ἔχομεν τὴν παρρησίαν καὶ προσαγωγὴν ἐν πεποιθήσει. This constr. is similar to that in 1: 7. The abstract nouns παρρησία and προσαγωγή combine with ἔχομεν to form the events 'to be bold' and 'to have access / approach'.[52] The words ἐν πεποιθήσει are to be connected only with προσαγωγήν.[53] The whole expression has been understood as a possible *hendiadys*, i.e. 'courage of confident access',[54] while the phrase in question has been taken adjectivally as 'full of confidence'.[55] This phrase was no doubt meant as a modifier of προσαγωγήν, i.e. 'we approach God with confidence'. Since the παρρησία and the πρασαγωγή are grounded in Christ, the restatement may take the form *Who gives us boldness and the right to approach (God) confidently / a confident access (to God)*, or, laying the emphasis on the personal exercise of what is given in Christ, *In Whom we have boldness and confident access (to God)*.[56] The Pp are a comment on Χριστῷ Ἰησοῦ of P 34.

---

[50] Some exx. of such resolutions are: Hdt., VI, 101, βουλὴν ποιέεσθαι; *id.*, V, 30, σκῆψιν ποιεύμενος; Din. II, 1, ἀπόφασιν ποιῆσθαι. These exx. are, however, construed with the mid. It is precisely this difficulty (as also the mention of 'Jesus') that has led some comm. to consider ἐποίησεν as referring to the carrying out of the purpose in Christ rather than to its formation. This interpretation, however, raises more difficulties than it solves. Ποιεῖν is too weak to express fulfillment (cf. Abbott, 90 and Robinson, 172). On the difficulty the name Jesus presents, see Robinson, 172. On the other hand, in Late Gk. the mid. recedes before the act. in such constrs.; cf. *BDR*, § 310, 1; Jannaris, *HGG*, § 1484 and Robinson, 172. Two exx. are LXX Isa. 29: 15; and 30: 1 βουλὴν ποιοῦντες. Schlier, 157 and Gnilka, 177, along with Abbott, Robinson, *et al.* refer it to the formation of the purpose, while Barth, I, 346 f., takes the other view.

[51] τῷ Κυρίῳ ἡμῶν is left in its surface structure. See IV, B, 1.

[52] Their respective vbs. occur e.g. in Eph. 4: 20 (παρρησιάζομαι) and I Pt 3: 18 (προσάγω).

[53] So e.g. Abbott, 91 (alternatively); Gaugler, 148; Gnilka, 178.

[54] Hendriksen, 161, "courage of confident access".

[55] Bultmann, *TDNT*, VI, 8, who adds "προσαγωγὴ ἐν πεποιθήσει and παρρησία are synonymous expressions, in keeping with the tendency in Eph to heap up synonymous words or phrases".

[56] Another alt. would be to consider all three abstract nouns as events: 'We are bold', 'we have access', 'we have confidence' (as we enter God's presence). Still another

37. διὰ τῆς πίστεως αὐτοῦ. The gen. αὐτοῦ is surely obj.[57] and this gives the event 'we believe in Him'. The prep. διά c. gen. denotes, among other things, the "efficient cause" [58] so the P may be stated so as to give the *reason* for Pp 35—36, i.e. *Because we believe in Him.*

38. διὸ αἰτοῦμαι. The inferential particle indicates that this P is a conclusion from the foregoing Pp and as such it is the main P of the last statement of the Digression. The question now is whether this conclusion is related to Pp 35—37 or to Pp 1—37. We have seen that vs. 1 is the introduction to a prayer. In that vs. the author characterised himself as a prisoner on account of Christ and because he served the Gentiles. As it shall be seen from Pp 39—41 this P is in reference to the same theme of suffering for the Gentiles' sake. This means that the body of the Digression is encompassed by vv. 1 and 13. Vs. 1 gives the Digression its *raison d' être* while vs. 13 returns to that *raison* and in light of the contents of the Digression claims that those sufferings instead of being regarded as a cause for dispondency ought to be regarded as a source of joy. The P is stated as *Therefore, I request (you)* and though it is left unlabeled in the Display, it is actually a *conclusion* with Pp 1—37 as its *grounds*.

39. μὴ ἐγκακεῖν. The inf. stands for the event 'to be discouraged'. The agent of the event is an implied ὑμᾶς, obj. of the previous P.[59] With the neg. particle the P becomes 'do not you be discouraged'. Since its relation to the last P is one of *content* after a vb. of 'saying', we must supply the declarative 'that', and thus the P takes the final form *That you do not be discouraged.*

40. ἐν ταῖς θλίψεσίν μου ὑπὲρ ὑμῶν. The gen. μου shows that the sufferer is the author. But what is the meaning of ἐν ταῖς? Abbott says "ἐν denotes the circumstances in which, etc".[60] The chief uses of this prep. are: Loca-

---

possibility might be: 'In whom we are confident that we have boldness and access to God. Whichever of all the alts. suggested is' chosen the sense remains the same.

[57] With Robinson, 173; Abbott, 91; Schlier, 158; Gaugler, 148, against Barth, I, 347.

[58] *BAG*, s. v. III, d.

[59] The absence of the pron. ὑμᾶς gives the possibility for two interpretations of the passage: a) the subj. of ἐγκακεῖν is the same as that of αἰτοῦμαι. i.e. the author prays to God (unexpressed) in order not to lose heart through his sufferings; b) the subj. is an unexpressed ὑμᾶς, i.e. the readers. All comm. prefer the second interpretation, mainly, because it is unlikely that the author in this context makes a prayer for himself. Robinson, 173, thinks that an original ὑμᾶς may have been "lost by homoeoteleuton" after αἰτοῦμαι and refers to Gal 4: 11 "where ὑμᾶς has been dropped after φοβοῦμαι".

[60] Abbott, 92.

tion, Time and Cause. Now the author expresses his fears that some of the faithful on hearing of his persecutions may lose heart and turn away from the faith. Ἐν ταῖς θλίψεσιν is, therefore, causally related to ἐγκακεῖν. The θλίψεις may cause the ἐγκακεῖν. Although *BAG* do not quote this vs. under any one of the senses they give for the general meaning of cause, ἐν ταῖς ought to be rendered by a form such as 'because'. The P takes the form *Because I suffer for your sake* and is labeled as *reason* for P 39 (*result*).

41. ἥτις ἐστὶν δόξα ὑμῶν. The gen. ὑμῶν is understood as poss., i.e. 'your glory'. The rel. ἥτις, though sg. refers to θλίψεσιν, which is in the pl., yet not distributively to each several θλίψις (act of persecution or defamation), but to the whole process of θλίβεσθαι. The meaning is 'my undergoing suffering for you means your glory (glorification?)'.[61] Acc. to Abbott "ἥτις introduces a reason; it is not simply equivalent to ἥ, but implies that what is predicated belongs to the nature of things, *quippe qui*, inasmuch as this'".[62] If this be accepted the P becomes *Since this* (sc. *my suffering for you) is your glory / will lead to your being glorified.* The P is no longer a comment on θλίψεσιν but the *reason* for the request μὴ ἐγκακεῖν (P 39).

D. CONCLUDING REMARKS

The Eulogy and the Digression were shown to be preoccupied with the concept of *mysterion*. This does not mean, however, that the second is but a mere repetition of the contents of the first. The theme may be the same but the angles of treatment are different.

In the Eulogy the *mysterion* is God's inscrutable plan conceived by Him before the creation of the world. It is an act of God both in conception and in revelation, though all those other acts predicated of God in the Eulogy are essentially parts of it. The *mysterion* has an aim, namely, the *anakephalaiōsis* of the whole *cosmos* in Christ. Things are now moving toward that end.

In the Digression the *mysterion* is still the central concept, but the actor

---

[61] The meaning of 'glory' has puzzled all interpreters. Chrysostom (*ad loc.*) comments: πῶς ἐστι δόξα αὐτῶν; ὅτι οὕτως αὐτοὺς ἠγάπησεν ὁ Θεὸς, ὥστε καὶ τὸν υἱὸν ὑπὲρ αὐτῶν δοῦναι, καὶ τοὺς δούλους κακοῦν. Ἵνα γὰρ οὗτοι τύχωσι τοσούτων ἀγαθῶν, Παῦλος ἐδεσμεῖτο. This interpretation is accepted by Alford, 108, and Abbott, 92, and is one of the interpretations contemplated by Barth, I, 361. Robinson, 80, calls this "a logic which we can hardly analyse".

[62] Abbott, 92.

is no longer God but the author. The οἰκονομία τοῦ μυστηρίου is exercised by an earthly administrator. Here we are not so much concerned with the *mysterion* as God's plan as with its realisation through the mission work of the author, the faith of the Gentiles and their incorporation into the Body as well as with the consequences of all this in respect to God and the believer's arch-enemies. This last point takes us back to the *anakephalaiōsis* and to 1:21 f., and underscores the unity of the concept in the two passages.

E. A PROPOSITIONAL DISPLAY OF EPH 1:3—10

LABELS

1.	Εὐλογητὸς ὁ Θεὸς καὶ Πατὴρ τοῦ Κυρίου ἡμῶν Ἰησοῦ Χριστοῦ	Blessworthy is the God and Father of our Lord Jesus Christ	
2.	ὁ εὐλογήσας ἡμᾶς ἐν πάσῃ εὐλογίᾳ πνευματικῇ ἐν τοῖς ἐπουρανίοις ἐν Χριστῷ	(because) He blessed us with every spiritual blessing in the heavenlies in Christ	*Reason* for 1 and *Generic* with 3—30 as *Specific*
3.	καθὼς ἐξελέξατο ἡμᾶς ἐν αὐτῷ	(that is to say) He chose us in Him	
4.	πρὸ καταβολῆς κόσμου	before He created the world	*Time* for 3
5.	εἶναι ἡμᾶς ἁγίους	that we should be holy	*Purpose* of 3
6.	καὶ ἀμώμους κατενώπιον αὐτοῦ	and (that we should be) blameless in His sight	*Addition* to 5; *Purpose* of 3
7.	ἐν ἀγάπῃ	(because) He loved us	*Reason* for 8
8.	προορίσας ἡμᾶς	He (pre)destined us	
9.	εἰς υἱοθεσίαν διὰ Ἰησοῦ Χριστοῦ εἰς αὐτόν	to become His adopted children by means of Christ	*Purpose* of 8
10.	κατὰ τὴν εὐδοκίαν	this was in accordance with what He considered good	*Reason* for 3 and 8
11.	τοῦ θελήματος αὐτοῦ	and willed	*Sequence* of 10 *Reason* for 3, 8
12.	εἰς ἔπαινον δόξης τῆς χάριτος αὐτοῦ	that we might praise His glorious grace	*Purpose* of 3 and 8
13.	ἧς ἐχαρίτωσεν ἡμᾶς ἐν τῷ Ἠγαπημένῳ	He bestowed His grace freely on us in the Beloved	
14.	ἐν ᾧ ἔχομεν τὴν ἀπολύτρωσιν	who redeems us	*Specific* of 13 and *Comment* on Ἠγαπημένῳ (13)
15.	διὰ τοῦ αἵματος αὐτοῦ	by means of the blood which He shed	*Means* for 14
16.	τὴν ἄφεσιν	(and in connection with whom God) forgives us	*Addition* to 14
17.	τῶν παραπτωμάτων	the sins we committed	*Content* of 16

114

18.	κατὰ τὸ πλοῦτος τῆς χάριτος αὐτοῦ	in accordance with the rich grace which He possesses	Reason for 13—17
19.	ἧς ἐπερίσσευσεν εἰς ἡμᾶς	He lavished (His grace) on us	
20.	ἐν πάσῃ σοφίᾳ	(and so He made us) very wise	Result of 19
21.	καὶ φρονήσει	and very prudent	Addition to 20
22.	γνωρίσας ἡμῖν τὸ μυστήριον	He made known to us the mysterion,	Identification of 22
23.	τοῦ θελήματος αὐτοῦ	namely, what He willed/ the will He resolved upon	
24.	κατὰ τὴν εὐδοκίαν αὐτοῦ	in accordance with what He considered good	Reason for 22
25.	ἣν προέθετο ἐν αὐτῷ	which He purposed in Him	Comment on εὐδοκία (24)
26.	εἰς οἰκονομίαν	in order to administer (it)	Purpose of 25
27.	τοῦ πληρώματος τῶν καιρῶν	(when) the times are fulfilled/ripe	Time for 26
28.	ἀνακεφαλαιώσασθαι τὰ πάντα ἐν τῷ Χριστῷ	(namely), to sum up all things in Christ	Content of 22—23
29.	τὰ ἐπὶ τοῖς οὐρανοῖς	the things which are in the heavens	Amplification of τὰ πάντα (28)
30.	καὶ τὰ ἐπὶ τῆς γῆς	and the things which are on the earth	Amplification of τὰ πάντα (28) and Contrast to 29

F. A PROPOSITIONAL DISPLAY OF EPH 3:1—13

a.	Τούτου χάριν ἐγὼ Παῦλος	On account of this I, Paul (pray for you)	
b.	ὁ δέσμιος	who am a prisoner	Comment on a
c.	τοῦ Χριστοῦ (Ἰησοῦ)	because I serve Christ	Reason for b, Comment for a
d.	ὑπὲρ ὑμῶν τῶν ἐθνῶν	(I suffer) on account of you, Gentiles	Reason for b
1.	εἴ γε ἠκούσατε	Surely you have heard	
2.	τῆς χάριτος τῆς δοθείσης μοι	I was given God's grace	(Content of 1)
3.	τὴν οἰκονομίαν . . . εἰς ὑμᾶς	in order to administer it to you	Purpose of 2
4.	κατὰ ἀποκάλυψιν	it was with a revelation which God granted me	Manner for 5
5.	ὅτι . . . ἐγνωρίσθη μοι τὸ μυστήριον	that the mysterion was made known to me	

6.	καθὼς προέγραψα ἐν ὀλίγῳ	as I briefly wrote above	*Comparison* of 6 (i.e. 1 : 9 f.) with 4—5
7.	πρὸς ὃ . . . ἀναγινώσκοντες	which when you read	*Comment* on 6 *Condition* for 8
8.	δύνασθε . . . νοῆσαι	you can understand	*Consequence* of 7
9.	τὴν σύνεσίν μου ἐν τῷ μυστηρίῳ τοῦ Χριστοῦ	that I have insight into the *mysterion* concerning Christ	*Content* of 8
10.	ὃ ἑτέραις γενεαῖς οὐκ ἀπεκαλύφθη τοῖς υἱοῖς τῶν ἀνθρώπων	which in the past was not made known to men	*Comment* on 5
11.	ὡς νῦν ἀπεκαλύφθη τοῖς . . . ἀποστόλοις αὐτοῦ καὶ προφήταις ἐν πνεύματι	in the same degree as it has now been revealed by the Spirit to the apostles and prophets	*Contrast* to 10
12.	ἁγίοις	who are holy	*Comment* on 11
13.	εἶναι τὰ ἔθνη συγκληρονόμα	that the Gentiles inherit together (with the Jews)	*Content* with 14—18 of *mysterion* (5)
14.	καὶ σύσσωμα	and belong to the same body together (with the Jews)	Addition to 13
15.	καὶ συμμέτοχα	and partake together (with the Jews)	*Addition* to 14
16.	τῆς ἐπαγγελίας	of that which God promised	*Content* of 15
17.	ἐν Χριστῷ	by being united with Christ Jesus	*Means* for 13—14
18.	διὰ τοῦ εὐαγγελίου	through the preaching of the gospel	*Means* for 13—16
19.	οὗ ἐγενήθην διάκονος	whose servant I was made (by God)	*Comment* on 18
20.	κατὰ τὴν δωρεὰν τῆς χάριτος τοῦ Θεοῦ τῆς δοθείσης μοι	because God gave me His grace freely	*Reason* for 19
21.	κατὰ τὴν ἐνέργειαν τῆς δυνάμεως αὐτοῦ	(and) because He worked mightily (in me)	*Addition* to 20, *Reason* for 19
22.	ἐμοὶ . . . ἐδόθη ἡ χάρις αὕτη	To me (God) gave this grace/ commission	
23.	τῷ ἐλαχιστοτέρῳ πάντων ἁγίων	though I was least of all the saints	*Consession-contra-expectation* to 22
24.	τοῖς ἔθνεσιν εὐαγγελίσασθαι τὸ . . . πλοῦτος τοῦ Χριστοῦ	in order that to the Gentiles I might proclaim the riches Christ has for them	*Purpose* of 22
25.	ἀνεξιχνίαστον	(which) cannot be explored	*Comment* on 24
26.	καὶ φωτίσαι (πάντας)	and to enlighten all men	*Purpose* of 22

116

27.	τίς ἡ οἰκονομία τοῦ μυστηρίου	On the (wonderful) administration of the *mysterion* (which I have been entrusted and carry out)
28.	τοῦ ἀποκεκρυμμένου ἀπὸ τῶν αἰώνων ἐν τῷ Θεῷ	which (God) hid eternally in Himself
29.	τῷ τὰ πάντα κτίσαντι	who created all things
30.	ἵνα γνωρισθῇ νῦν ταῖς ἀρχαῖς καὶ ταῖς ἐξουσίαις . . . ἡ . . . σοφία τοῦ Θεοῦ	in order that at this time (God) might make known His . . . wisdom to the principalities and powers
31.	ἐν τοῖς ἐπουρανίοις	(the principalities . . . the powers) are in the heavenlies
32.	διὰ τῆς ἐκκλησίας	by means of (the being established) of the Church
33.	πολυποίκιλος	(the wisdom of God) is extremely varied
34.	κατὰ πρόθεσιν τῶν αἰώνων ἣν ἐποίησεν ἐν τῷ Χριστῷ Ἰησοῦ τῷ Κυρίῳ ἡμῶν	because (so) He purposed eternally in Christ Jesus our Lord
35.	ἐν ᾧ ἔχομεν τὴν παρρησίαν	who gives us boldness/in whom we have boldness
36.	καὶ προσαγωγὴν ἐν πεποιθήσει	and the right to approach (God) confidently / and a confident access (to God)
37.	διὰ τῆς πίστεως αὐτοῦ	because we believe in Him
38.	διὸ αἰτοῦμαι	therefore, I request (you)
39.	μὴ ἐγκακεῖν	That you do not be discouraged
40.	ἐν ταῖς θλίψεσίν μου ὑπὲρ ὑμῶν	because I suffer for your sake
41.	ἥτις ἐστὶν δόξα ὑμῶν	since this (sc. my suffering for you) is your glory / will lead to your being glorified

Labels column:

Content of 26

Comment on 27

Comment on 28

Purpose and *Content* of *mysterion* (22—28)

Location and *Identification* of powers (30)
Means for 30

Comment on 30

Reason for 22—33 or even 1—33

Comment on 34

Addition to 35 and *Comment* on 34

Reason for 35—36

Conclusion 1—37 (grounds)
Content of 38

Reason for 39 (ἐγκακεῖν)
Reason for 38 and 39 (μὴ ἐγκακεῖν)

CHAPTER V

THE EPHESIAN *MYSTERION* AND ITS BACKGROUND USAGE

1. SUMMARISING CH. IV

Ch. III and especially IV showed that the term *mysterion* has a central place in Eph 1—3. In ch. IV it was noted that the position of our term in the Eulogy is climactic,[1] and that together with its amplification in the *anakephalaiōsis* it constitutes the final purpose to which God's acts, enumerated in the Eulogy, lead. Put briefly, the *mysterion* entails the gathering together of human and angelic beings and their subjection to Christ as the exalted Lord and Head of all. The theme of the Eulogy is thus a cosmic Christ who embraces the entire cosmos which in Him is brought to allegiance to God.[2] This involves the exaltation of Christ and the consequent subjugation of τὰ πάντα under Him, as is made plainer in the ensuing prayer (1: 15 ff.). The term ὑπέταξεν indicates the unwilling subjection of τὰ πάντα and is carefully contrasted with the phrase αὐτὸν ἔδωκεν κεφαλὴν . . . τῇ ἐκκλησία, which reflects a willing subordination, while the interjected phrase ὑπὲρ πάντα, taken as equivalent to ὑπεράνω πάσης (vs. 21), is understood locally of the exalted position of the Church.[3] The relation between her and Christ is on a higher level than that between Christ and the powers, i.e. above the powers. This point is further strengthened by the qualification in vs. 23 in which the Church is "the body" and so "the fulness of Him . . .".

The *mysterion* of Eph 1, therefore, is concerned with the final restoration[4] of order in the universe when all revolting elements, together with those which maintained their allegiance, shall be reconstituted under Christ though with a different relation to Him.

---

[1] So also Hanson, *UC*, 121.

[2] Not restricting the *anakephalaiōsis* to humanity as is done by Davies, *PRJ*, 57: "the reconstitution of the essential oneness of mankind in Christ as a spiritual community, as it was one in Adam in a physical sence".

[3] Similarly Chrysostom *ad loc.*, and Robinson, 152. Hanson, *UC*, 127 and Mussner, *CAK*, 30 f. understand ὑπὲρ πάντα as an attributive expression, i.e. "absolute Head" (Hanson) and "caput excellentissimum" (Mussner quoting Vosté). But as Schlier, *CK*, 55, points out the πάντα refers back to 22 a and that one refers to πάσης ἀρχῆς καὶ ἐξουσίας (vs. 21).

[4] So Hanson, *UC*, 125 f.

In ch. 3 we seem to have a more limited aspect of the concept of *mysterion* than in ch. 1. In line with the principle of arguing from the general to the particular [5] the *mysterion* of ch. 3 is a more particular facet of the general, programmatic use of the concept in ch. 1.[6] Here it refers to the acceptance of the Gentiles on the same basis as the Jews. The old distinction between Jews and Gentiles is removed: the distinction now is rather between the Church and the powers. There is a συγχώνευσις of Jews and Gentiles, which is precisely what had eluded the men of the past. Here the emphasis is laid more on the gospel content, the message itself, viewed from the angle of its proclamation by the author as well as from the angle of its conception by God and of its hiddeness in Him till the present time. The *mysterion* further entails a final purpose, as it does in 1:10. Here (in 3:10) the final purpose is the exhibition of God's many-sided wisdom before the powers. The instrument for this exhibition is the Church. Here, as in 1:22 f. the Church is ascribed greater intimacy with Christ than the powers, but the idea of subordination is not explicit. A conspicuous difference between the use of *mysterion* in ch. 1 and its use in ch. 3 is that whereas in ch. 1 the *mysterion* is that which God reveals to the author (among others), in ch. 3 it is what the author strives to make known to the Gentiles.[7] The reference is clearly, and understandably so, of a more limited nature.

In conclusion, it may be said that the *mysterion* of Eph 1—3 has two main usages: a) a general all-inclusive plan of God running through the ages and having as its ultimate goal, at the *eschaton*, the reconstitution of everything under Christ, with differences in the relations of the various entities; and b) a more limited aspect of (a), which is a prerequisite for the *anakephalaiōsis*, bringing into focus the author's missionary activity and his consequent contribution for the fulfillment of (b) which forms a part of and is a prerequisite for (a).

In light of this the ensuing discussion cannot develop into an extended examination of all *mysterion* occurrences in Greek and Jewish lit. but will focus only on such instances as have at least a seeming relevance for the Eph *mysterion*. The chief criteria applied for the selection of instances are: a) The *mysterion* must be God's purpose; b) it must be eschatological; c) it must have very wide dimensions (if possible, cosmic); d) it must be a unified plan (hence, the sg. is a decisive factor). These criteria at once dispose of all non-Jewish material, nevertheless, for the sake of fairness, a word or two will be said about the Mystery Religions and Gnosticism, to show that they are pronounced as irrelevant also on other grounds.

---

[5] Cf. IV. B. 7.

[6] Cf. V. Roon, *NovT*, 1974, 216 and *id.*, *AE*, 377 ff.

[7] Cf. IV. C. 11—12, n. 24.

2 THE MYSTERY RELIGIONS

In older times it was regarded as axiomatic that the NT use of *mysterion* reflected the influence of the Mystery Religions on Christianity.[8] This view has been subjected to scrutiny by various scholars and from different viewpoints with the result that scholars have become more hesitant nowadays in speaking of such influence on the NT.[9]

A number of other factors too have contributed to this negative turn. Research in the Apocrypha and Pseudepigrapha, which present material that is more congenial to NT ideas than that of any Mystery Cults, and in which the term *mysterion/ia* is used in conjunction with religious elements of an Israelite-Jewish ring, has played its role in the reorientation.[10] An even stronger impetus has been given by the more recent finds at Qumran in which the Pers. רז, translated in Dan with μυστήριον, occurs not infrequently.[11]

In view of these considerations it has become increasingly more usual to sever the ties of contact between the NT *mysterion* and the Mystery Religions, and establish them, instead, with the Jewish background. And this not without good reason either. In the NT the term is used 5 × in the pl.: thrice to refer to what God has in store for His own, and twice in a non-colored sense of things mysterious. Of the remaining 23 ×, in the sg., the term is used most conspicuously of God's plan or purpose. Such a meaning is simply widely removed from the use of the word in the Mystery Religions, in which the term occurs invariably in the pl. and is a designation of the whole rite of initiation. When therefore, Dan speaks of the revelation of a *mysterion* which God intends to carry through, or when Enoch says he knows the fate of the righteous and the unrighteous because he has read it in the heavenly tablets, or when the psalmist of Qumran praises God for the revelation of wonderful רזין, occasionally related to the end-time, it is natural for scholars to see in this literature

---

[8] E.g. Bousset, *KC*; Reitzenstein, *HM*; Bultmann, *TNT*. Cf. Wood, *ET*, 1967, 308; Maas, *TL*, 1913, 125. Anrich, *AMEC* and Clemen, *EMÄC* hold a limited influence, not on the *mysterion* terminology, indeed, but on Baptism and the Eucharist. More recently Mylonas, *EEM*, *passim*, sees many points of contact between Eleusis and Christianity. The most ardent advocate of Religionsgeschichte today is Pokorny, *EG* and *ZNW*, 1962, 160—94.

[9] Cf. e.g. M.-J. Lagrange in *RB*, 1919, 157—217 and 419—80; Prümm, (in Brown); Kennedy, *PMR*; Wagner, *PBPM*; Bornkamm, *TDNT*, IV, 842; Davies, *PRJ*, 86 ff; Colpe, *RS*; Fuller, *NTC*, 89 ff. Ellis, *PRI*, 24—34; Adler, *MThZ*, 1955, 286—301.

[10] Cf. Robinson's excursus in his Comm. on Eph, 234—40.

[11] Cf. Brown's three articles published in booklet form in *SB*; *id*. *ET*, 1966, 19—23 Wood, *ET*, 1967, 308—11. Also Kuhn, *PQ*, 115—31; Coppens, *PQ*, 132—58; Mussner, *PQ*, 159—78; Cerfaux, *SacPag* II, 378; Merklein, *KAE*, 210.

a more than likely sourch of *mysterion* thinking, e.g. such as meets us in the Epistle to the Ephesians.

3. GNOSTICISM

Gnosticism used our term in great profusion.[12] Its use oscillates between that of the Mystery Religions and the Jewish-Christian usage. There are thus some instances of apparent relevance. An insurmountable difficulty here is that most of these works evidence acquaintance with the NT and are generally dated in the II A.D. or later.[13] To be sure, a distinction is nowadays usually drawn between Gnosticism and *gnosis*, the latter term being broader in meaning though ill-defined. In this wider sense of *gnosis* as "knowledge of the divine mysteries reserved for an elect",[14] *gnosis* is usually accepted as being pre-Christian. The problem, however arises when this term, as a designation of certain trends which exerted an influence on the NT, takes its flesh and bones from the second and third century A.D. phenomenon![15]

There thus appears to exist no incontrovertible evidence for speaking

---

[12] The term occurs among the Nag Hammadi treatises e.g. in the *Gospel of Thomas* and the *Gospel of Truth*. Of the *CH* tractates the term occurs among others in *Poem* (1 ×) and in *CH* XIII. In the *Naasene Tract.* (=Hipp., *Phil*, V. 7—9 in ΒΕΠ, V=Wendland, *HROH*) it is found some 21 ×. The first book of *Jeu* containts it 9 × while the second one 140 ×. An *Unbekanntes altgnostisches Werk* (in Schmidt, *KGS*, 335—67) has the word 15 ×, (esp. in the form πανμυστήριον) while in the *Pistis Sophia* I have counted no less than 1054 instances!

[13] The gnostic question is still extremely complicated. The divergence of scholary opinion was underscored in the *Messina Colloquium* in 1966 where the distinction between pre-gnosticism and proto-gnosticism was also drawn. The Nag Hammadi discoveries in 1945—46 have added to the intricacies of the problem while the presence of some hermetic works in that library have brought the question of the relation between the *CH* and the rest of the gnostic lit. into focus. From the pace of publication work and the scholarly discussions on material so far published, it appears that several decades will elapse before any definite conclusions (if any) with regards to the origin of gnosticism will be drawn.

[14] The definition given at the *Messina Colloquium*; see McL. Wilson, *GnNT*, 17.

[15] Acc. to McL. Wilson, *GnNT*, 35 Bultmann in his *NTT*, I, 164—83, *Gnostic Motifs* consistently uses the term 'die Gnosis' in a wider sense and not as the equivalent of 'Gnosticism' as his Eng. translators do. This explanation, however, does not free Bultmann from the charge of Richardson, *INTT*, 41 f; that "The objection to speaking of Gnosticism in the first century A.D. is that we are in danger of hypostatising certain rather ill-defined tendencies of thought and then speaking as if there were a religion or religious philosophy, called Gnosticism, which could be contrasted with Judaism and Christianity. There was of course no such thing", and again "When scholars like Bultmann discribe a Gnostic doctrine they take their first-century 'evidence' from the NT itself".

of gnostic influence on the NT.[16] The similarities can be and have been interpreted in the opposite direction of dependence.[17]

4. THE OT

It is generally assumed that the OT uses two terms as equivalent of the Gk. μυστήριον, i.e. סוד and רז.[18] Though the word סוד occurs no less than 22 × and is translated by no less than 15 different words,[19] it is never translated by μυστήριον in the LXX! On the other hand, רז, which occurs 9 × in Dan, is always rendered by μυστήριον.[20] Brown (SB) in his search for a possible background in the OT took up both terms and laid under tribute a number of other books in which a picture of Yahweh in council is given, but such a procedure obviously does not coincide with my purpose. Hence, I shall confine myself to Dan since it is the only OT book that uses the term μυστήριον.

Daniel

i. General Considerations

The book of Dan is made up of certain dreams, events and visions involving various monarchs and different dates, but is held together by certain similar features, primary among which are their purpose and function.[21] Thus the interpretation of each dream is first attempted by the Babylonian soothsayers who invariably fail to measure up to the task, while Daniel always succeeds in elucidating it. In the case of the two test-events (the fiery furnace and the den of lions) Daniel and his friends' God overpowers the flame and shuts the lions' mouth, while the heathen

---

[16] Cf. Quispel, GW, (in Neil, INT, 180), "The view that it (sc. gnosis) was pre-Christian still awaits demonstration". Bultmann's position (NTT, I, 173 ff.; 179 f.; II, 134 ff., 151 ff.) that Eph for example is replete with gnostic concepts is very precarious.

[17] E.g. Neil, INT, 161 f.; 173—81; Grant, Gnost, 17 f.

[18] E.g. Brown, SB, 2; Schlier, 60 f.; Kuhn, PQ, 118; Gnilka, 78;

[19] I.e. σύνταγμα (Jb 15:8), ἰδόντες με (Jb 19:19), ἐπισκοπή (29:4); κραταίωμα (Ps 25:14); ἔδεσμα (Ps 55:15); συστροφή (Ps 64:2); γνώμη (Ps 83:3); βουλή (Ps 89:7; 111:1; Prov 11:13); συνέδριον (Prov 15:22, Jer 15:17); συνεδριάζει (Prov 3:32); ἀναχώρει (Prov 25:9); συναγωγή (Jer 6:11); ὑπόστημα (Jer 23:18); ὑπόστασις (Jer 23:22); and παιδεία (Ez 13:9; Am 3:7). The rest of the instances are missing in the LXX.

[20] Sym and Th render רזי (from רזה 'to diminish') in Isa 24:16 with μυστήριον. On this cf. Willi—Plein, VT, 1977, 71 ff.

[21] I am not here concerned with the question of the single or composite authorship of the book. For the unity of authorship, see Rowley, DM, 176 ff., Porteous, Dan, 16 ff. For other views see Mertens, DLTTM, 14 ff.

gods prove impotent before them. The superiority of Israel's God is thus set forth. In fact, the book takes us further. Not only is Daniel's God able to deliver from danger, to reveal dreams and to foretell the future; He is, in addition, the Lord of history, the Dispenser of the kingdoms of men, Who puts down one and sets up another.[22] Indeed, the primary purpose of the book seems to be to impress on men the idea that the real Lord of the kingdoms of men is the Most High [23] and that He is making known what will transpire at the *eschaton* (2: 28).

ii. The Image

The Image in Nebuchadrezzar's dream (ch. 2) has a human form and it consists of various metals each representing a world empire. The choice of form is quite appropriate [24] in signalling the human element in these kingdoms. The four kingdoms may represent a complete man, i.e. in their totality they give expression to what man can do. The various metals exhibit a difference in quality, the first (gold) being the most precious while the last (iron) being the cheapest. Whether what is being set forth by these metals is the extent of dominion alone, or whether there is a philosophy of history as well, namely, that each succeeding kingdom will be worse than its predecessor, is difficult to say, for while this could be said with certainty of the last kingdom, yet a Jewish author could hardly have characterised the Persian empire as worse than the Babylonian. However it may be with particulars, the author of Daniel is a pessimist concerning human history,[25] and has focused his hopes only on God's eschatological intervention.[26] Indeed, he sees no other way out but the destruction of these kingdoms of men by "a stone cut without hands" and their replacement by God's everlasting kingdom.[27]

iii. The Visions of Chs. 7 and 8

In ch. 7 we are presented with a vision of four beasts which must be considered as equivalent to the four metals of Nebuchadrezzar's image, and in ch. 8 with two animals which must be identified with two of the metals and two of the beasts. Nebuchadrezzar's dream is thus doubled

---

[22] E.g. 2: 21; 4: 22, 28; 5: 21 (*Th*).

[23] E.g. 4: 17, 25, 32, 35 (*Th*)

[24] Though not of much significance, since in ch. 7 these kingdoms are represented by beasts and in ch. 8 by a ram and a he-goat.

[25] This is the gist of the dream of ch. 2 and the visions of chs. 7 ff. cf. in particular 7: 23 ff.; 8: 23 ff.; 11: 36; 12: 10.

[26] E.g. 2: 44 f.; 7: 13 f., 22, 27.

[27] E.g. 2: 34 f., 44 f.; 7: 14, 22.

and partly tripled. This identification [28] has its value from our point of view in that the term רז, used of the dream in ch. 2, could as well have been applied to the vision of the beasts of ch. 7 and to the vision of the ram and the he-goat of ch. 8.[29] This means that the role of the Son of Man is easily brought into connection with God's *basileia* in ch. 2. Indeed, a NT author might easily pass from ch. 2 on to chs. 7 and 8, not to speak of chs. 9 and 11. Since these chs. deal with the same theme [30] an important detail of one ch. might easily be associated with the data of another ch. The point I am driving at is that the Danielic רז, is not to be associated solely with the image, but that rather all those passages dealing with the same theme of world history may be said to be considered as a רז by the author, although not called so expressly.

iv. A Comparison between the Dan רז and the Eph *mysterion*

It is of interest that the term רז is applied in Dan 2 both to the dream itself, i.e. its contents, as well as to its interpretation, i.e. its inner or

---

[28] There is wide diversity of opinion as to the identity of the various metals and beasts with the world empires, but hardly anyone doubts that the image of ch. 2 and the beasts of ch. 7 symbolise the same kingdoms. Cf. Rowley, *DM*, 63 ff.; Montgomery, *Dan*, 283; Plöger, *Dan*, 118 f.; Porteous, *Dan*, 103 f.; Walvoord, *Dan*, 151 ff. For a few exceptions see Rowley, *DM*, 67.

[29] That it is not, is perhaps owing to the absence of the attendant circumstances following Nebuchadrezzar's announcement of his dream and his decree; the feeling of bewilderment was intensified by fear of death, cf. ch. 2:18 (LXX): περὶ τοῦ μυστηρίου τούτου (the first occurrence!) — a phrase connoting bewilderment.

[30] Notice may be taken of the following parallels in key words and associations: 2:21; αὐτὸς ἀλλοιοῖ καιροὺς καὶ χρόνους with 7:25; 2:23, ἐγνώρισάς μοι ἃ ἠξιώσαμεν with 7:16; 2:28, ἃ δεῖ γενέσθαι ἐπ' ἐσχάτων τῶν ἡμερῶν implied in 7:9, 18, 22; 2:34, ἀπεσχίσθη λίθος ἐξ ὄρους ἄνευ χειρῶν with a possible equivalent in the Son of Man, 7:13; 2:44, ἐν ταῖς ἡμέραις τῶν βασιλέων ἐκείνων ἀναστήσει ὁ Θεὸς τοῦ οὐρανοῦ βασιλείαν with 7:14, 18, 22. Hartman, *PI*, 167—74 has illustrated well this point between Dan and Mk 13:9—13 and Mt 24:9—14.

The identification of the 'One like a Son of Man' is a matter of debate. The majority of scholars treat it as a symbolic figure for the redeemed Israel (= the saints of the Most High, e.g. Montgomery, *Dan*, 317—24; Rowley, *DM*; Porteous, *Dan*, 111; Plöger, *Dan*, 112 f.) though they also admit that the earliest interpretation of this figure was messianic (e.g. *I En* and *IV Ez*). Müller, *MM*, 33 ff. takes the figure "alene som symbol for Guds eskatologiske herredømme". For a messianic interpretation see Young, *PD*, 155 f.; Walvoord, *Dan*, 167 f. and the *JB*'s comment on Dan 7:13 (p. 1437). The arguments for the corporate interpretation are not compelling. The strongest card of this theory is that when the interpretation of the vision is given (vv. 17 f., 23—7) no mention is made of the Son of Man but only of the saints. On the other hand there are dissimilar elements in the description of the Son of Man and the saints which may indicate that we have to do with two distinct entities. In my excursus on the Ἀρχαί, Ἐξουσίαι etc. (ch. VI) I have put forward an alternative interpretation taking the Son of Man as an individual.

124

symbolic meaning.[31] It should be noted, moreover, that the term does not merely designate the uninterpreted dream, for the dream continues to be a רז even after its full import is known (2: 27 f.). Being a divine *mysterion*, it continues to retain its character after its disclosure.

The point of this dream is that God is making known to Nebuchadrezzar ἃ δεῖ γενέσθαι ἐπ' ἐσχάτων τῶν ἡμερῶν (2: 28). With the unfolding of the dream we see that there will be four world empires (incl. that of Nebuch.) and that at the end God shall establish His own kingdom. In the more detailed description of ch. 7 the kingdom is given to One like a Son of Man: καὶ αὐτῷ ἐδόθη ἡ ἀρχὴ καὶ ἡ τιμὴ καὶ ἡ βασιλεία, καὶ πάντες οἱ λαοί, φυλαί, γλῶσσαι δουλεύσουσιν αὐτῷ· ἡ ἐξουσία αὐτοῦ ἐξουσία αἰώνιος, ἥτις οὐ παρελεύσεται, καὶ ἡ βασιλεία αὐτοῦ οὐ διαφθαρήσεται (7: 14, *Th*). Since the climax of both the dream (ch. 2) and the vision (ch. 7) is the establishment of God's kingdom with its universal and abiding rule, the רז or *mysterion* in Dan contains what remains of human history and is particularly focused on God's eschatological act of subjecting all under His dominion. Moreover, even that part of human history that will yet unfold, with all that it may entail for God's people, is part of God's purpose. For the author of Dan historical events do not happen by any necessity other than that God Himself has so decreed. But there is a goal in history: at the end righteousness shall triumph and all evil shall be swept away.

Turning to Eph we note that there too the author ascribes to God a sovereign role in history.[32] Everything that happens is κατὰ τὴν εὐδοκίαν αὐτοῦ or κατὰ πρόθεσιν αὐτοῦ. The Eph *mysterion* too reaches its climax at the *ankephalaiōsis* of all beings in Christ. This too, will transpire at the proper time, or when the times are completed. The *anakephalaiōsis* thus must wait for its fixed time just like the kingdom of God does in Dan. But as surely as everything is subjected to God's kingdom in Dan, so too the *anakephalaiōsis* implies the subjection of everything under Christ.

These broad similarities between the Dan רז and the Eph *mysterion* may now be treated in more detail in the following parallels:

Dan 2   Eph 1 and 3

1). The revelation of the *mysterion* leads both authors to eulogise God:

19 f. (*Th*) εὐλόγησε τὸν Θεὸν   3 εὐλογητὸς ὁ Θεὸς
20 (*Th*) εἴη τὸ ὄνομα τοῦ Θεοῦ
εὐλογημένον

2). Dan ascribes to God wisdom and understanding, while this is implicit in Eph in the giving of these to the author:

---

[31] Cf. Brown, *SB*, 7.
[32] Cf. Eph. 1: 11 τοῦ τὰ πάντα ἐνεργοῦντος κατὰ τὴν βουλὴν τοῦ θελήματος αὐτοῦ.

125

20 (*Th*) σοφία καὶ σύνεσις [33]   8 σοφίαν 3: 4 σύνεσιν

3). In both authors the revelation of the *mysterion* is attended by an endowment in wisdom and prudence:

21 (*Th*) διδοὺς σοφίαν ... καὶ φρόνησιν   8 ἐπερίσσευσεν ἐν πάσῃ σοφίᾳ καὶ
                                              φρονήσει

23 (*Th*) σοφίαν καὶ σύνεσιν ἔδοκάς
μοι [34]
(LXX: σοφίαν καὶ φρόνησιν ἔδοκάς
μοι)

4). The *mysterion* is hidden in God:

22 (*Th*) ἀποκαλύπτει βαθέα καὶ ἀπό-   3: 9 ἀποκεκρυμμένον ἐν τῷ Θεῷ
κρυφα

5). For both authors the Revealer is God Himself:

28 (*Th*) Θεὸς . . . ἀποκαλύπτων   9 γνωρίσας ἡμῖν τὸ μυστήριον
μυστήρια καὶ ἐγνώρισε τῷ βασιλεῖ   3: 3 κατὰ ἀποκάλυψιν ἐγνωρίσθη . . .
                                    3: 5 ἀπεκαλύφθη τοῖς . . . ἀποστόλοις

6). For both authors the future events are divinely decreed: Dan stresses the decree, while Eph the will:

28 (*Th*) ἃ δεῖ γενέσθαι   9 τὸ μυστήριον τοῦ θελήματος αὐτοῦ

7). For both authors the events are to transpire at the *eschaton*:

28 (*Th*) γενέσθαι ἐπ᾽ ἐσχάτων τῶν   9—10 οἰκονομίαν πληρώματος καιρῶν
ἡμερῶν   ἀνακεφαλαιώσασθαι

8). For both authors God's final act has universal dimensions, subjecting everything:

35 (*Th*) ὁ λίθος ... ἐγενήθη ὄρος μέγα   10 ἀνακεφαλαιώσασθαι πάντα ἐν αὐτῷ
καὶ ἐπλήρωσε πᾶσαν τὴν γῆν   22 ὑπέταξεν τὰ πάντα

9). In both authors a number of identical and related words are grouped together:

37—8 (*Th*) βασιλείαν, ἰσχυράν, κρα-   18—22 δόξα, δύναμις, ἐνέργεια, κράτος
ταιάν ἔντιμον, κύριον, κεφαλή   ἰσχύς, ἀρχή, ἐξουσία, κυριότης,
(LXX): ἀρχήν, βασιλείαν, ἰσχύν,   κεφαλή
τιμήν, δόξαν, κυριεύειν, κεφαλή

10). There is a parallel in the idea of subordination under the 'head of gold' and under Christ:

---

[33] Σύνεσις with B O 88 C pl. and Rahlf, Ziegler prefers δύναμις with Q=M.
[34] Σύνεσις with L Aeth. Ziegler prefers δύναμις.

38 κατέστησέ σε κύριον πάντων   22 πάντα ὑπέταξεν ὑπὸ τοὺς πόδας
                                           αὐτοῦ

            Dan 7   *Eph 1*

There is a parallel in concepts between the dominion of the Son of Man
in Dan 7, and the dominion which Christ is given in Eph 1.

14 καὶ αὐτῷ ἐδόθη ἡ ἀρχὴ καὶ ἡ τιμὴ   20—22 καθίσας ἐν δεξιᾷ . . . ὑπεράνω
   καὶ ἡ βασιλεία, καὶ πάντες οἱ λαοί,   πάσης ἀρχῆς καὶ ἐξουσίας . . .
   φυλαί, γλῶσσαι δουλεύσουσιν αὐτῷ·   πάντα ὑπέταξεν ὑπὸ τοὺς πόδας
   ἡ ἐξουσία αὐτοῦ ἐξουσία αἰώνιος,   αὐτοῦ
   ἥτις οὐ παρελεύσεται, καὶ ἡ βασιλεία
   αὐτοῦ οὐ διαφθαρήσεται

This list showed that many important components belonging to the
concept of *mysterion*, chiefly in the Eulogy, are identical with those of
the Danielic רז. The Son of Man in Dan has his counterpart in Christ,
who is characterised also in the NT by that name.

The word κεφαλή is applied to Nebuchadrezzar as being the golden head
of the image (i.e. the perfect man). But Nebuchadrezzar has not learned
that the real Ruler in the kingdoms of men is the Most High Himself,
and takes all the credit to himself. Hence, too, his humiliation (ch. 4).
Now it has been recognised by many comm.[35] that although ἀνακεφαλαιώσασθαι in Eph 1: 10 is derived from κεφάλαιον rather than κεφαλή, the
author, nevertheless, uses it in reference to the headship of Christ. If the
association of the Eph *mysterion* with the Danielic one is at all main-
tainable,[36] in this vb. as well as in the noun κεφαλή (1: 22), we might have
an allusion to Dan 2.[37]

5. THE PSEUDEPIGRAPHA [38]

The books that contain the term *mysterion* are: *Ahik, III Bar, II En,
Sib Or, Test. XII Pat, Vit Ad et Ev, II Bar, I En, IV Ez*. Of these only the

---

[35] E.g. Chrysostom, *ad loc.*; Schlier, 64 f.; Gnilka, 80; Hanson, *UC*, 124 f.

[36] Cf. V. Soden, *ZNW*, 12, 1911, 198 "Es unterliegt wohl keinem Zweifel, dass die
Danielstellen den Ursprung des neutestamentlichen Sprachgebrauchs von μυστήριον
angeben".

[37] Riesenfeld, *BNT*, 447 f., thinks that the Pauline presentation of Christ and the
Church as Head and Body, stems from Dan 7 where Paul transfered the symbols of
head and body from the fourth beast to the figure of the Son of Man. This view
instead of weakening my thesis actually supports my overall view that the concepts
concerned with the *mysterion* and the powers in Eph are very probably to be understood in light of Dan, esp. 2 and 7. See also Colpe, *JUK*, 172—87.

[38] For the apocryphal references which are all non-eschatological, see *supra* I, 3,
C, i, and cf. Lebram, *AUV*, 320—4.

last three appear to use the term in a somewhat analogical way for Eph, i.e. of a more or less eschatological *mysterion*, but once again, of these three *I En* seems to be the most relevant.[39]

I Enoch

The earlier occurences of *mysterion* in chs. 9, 10, 16, of the secrets the Watchers revealed to women, are set aside as irrelevant. In the *Parables* (chs. 37—71)[40] the term 'secret' occurs some 31 × and the term 'hidden' some 17 ×.[41] Dan 7 is clearly laid under tribute from ch. 46 on, where we meet both the Head of Days as well as the Son of Man. The latter, also called the Elect one,[42] is seated on a throne of glory (45:3; 51:3; 69:29), judges (45:3; 49:4), reveals secrets (46:3; 51:3), puts down kings who fail to glorify God (46:4 f.), is a light to the Gentiles (48:4), is mighty and wise (49:2 ff.), judges the kings of the earth (62:1 ff.)

---

[39] *II Bar* 81:4 speaks of "the mystery of the times" (Charles), and *IV Ez* 14:5 of "the secret of the times" (Box). *IV Ez* makes express reference to Daniel's vision of the four kingdoms (7:7 f.) which he reinterprets (12:11 ff.). These two facts, the occurence of *mysterion* and *secret* and the assumption of Daniel's vision, would render the book *a priori* particularly relevant for consideration along with Dan. The fatal objection, however, is, as it is the case with *II Bar*, its date. For while it may be legitimate to consider these books for the latter development of the concept of *mysterion* in Judaism, as Brown, *SB*, 19, does, this from my own standpoint, which demands a text definitely antedating Eph, will not do. The final reduction of *IV Ez* is put by Box (*AP*, II, 553) around A.D. 120, with the *Eagle Vision* source, in which the reference to Dan occurs, between A.D. 81—96 or between A.D. 69—79 (see also Oesterley, *II Esd*, xliv and *IBA*, 155, and Violet, *AEB*, II, xlix. Kaminka, *BEEA*, argues for a VI B.C. date for the Heb. Urtext). Weiser, *IOT*, 437, sets the date in the last decade of the first century and Russel, *MMJA*, 37 f., dates it c. A.D. 90. *II Bar* written "as an apology for Judaism and in part an implicit polemic against Christianity" (Charles, *AP*, II, 470) is dated by Charles between A.D. 50—90. This date is currenty considered as too early. Violet, *AEB*, II, xci, places it in A.D. 100—120 while more recently Weiser, *IOT*, 440, Russel, *MMJA*, 38 and Bingham—Kolenkow, *II Bar*, recognise a dependence on *IV Ez* and consequently date it after A.D. 90. Most of *I En*, on the other hand, is considered as definitely pre-Christian, the various parts being dated between 170—64 B.C. (Charles, *AP*, II, 170 f.).

[40] Charles, (*AP*, II, 171) dated the *Parables* either between 94—79 or between 70—64 B.C.; similarly Weiser, *IOT*, 427. In recent years, however, a pre-Christian date for the *Parables* has been seriously questioned. Milik, *BE*, 91—8, impressed by the absence of any frgs. of this composition in Qumran and finding a dependence on the *Sib Or*, dates the *Parables* around A.D. 270, so already in his article in *HTR*, 1971, 375—8. Apart from this consideration it is interesting to note that the use of 'secret' and 'hidden' in the *Parables* differs markedly from the Eph μυστήριον.

[41] I.e. in Charles' translation (*AP*, II), since no Gk. text is extant.

[42] I.e. 45:3 f.; 46:3; 49:2 ff.; 51:5, etc.

whose repentance comes too late to avail (63: 1 ff.), will become a comfort to the just (48: 4 ff.; 58: 1 ff.; 62: 13 ff.), etc. etc.

The section is clearly eschatological setting forth the tribulation of the saints under the ungodly powers (47: 1 ff.) and the revelation of the Son of Man who assumes unlimited power and sets the stage for the great judgement.[43] Not only ordinary men, but the mighty as well, and even angels are to be judged.[44] Mention is also made of the resurrection of the dead (51: 1 ff.). Throughout these chs. 'secret' and 'hidden' are constantly used of the secret or hidden character of the Son of Man (48: 6; 62: 6—7), of the secrets which He reveals (49: 2; 51: 3), of the secrets of sinners which shall be brought to light in judgement (49: 4; 61: 9), and there are some back-flashes to the secrets of the Watchers (64: 2; 65: 6, 11; 68: 2; 69: 8, 15). What seems to be so conspicuously absent from this section of I En is the sense of a plan or purpose characterised as a 'secret' (i.e. *mysterion*) and covering the contents delineated briefly above. To be sure, at one place, but only at one place (68: 5), we get near the idea of a hidden purpose: "Therefore all that is hidden shall come upon them for ever and ever". Nevertheless, this statement is applied not to a general plan regarding the end-times, but merely to the punishment of the Watchers. Significant is also the fact that although the terms 'secret' and 'hidden' occur in this section some 48 ×, the author, it seems, never once thought of describing what he had to say by that term.[45] Another important observation is that although this section shows so much dependence on Dan, it appears never to have occurred to our author to apply to his description of future events the term *mysterion* as Dan did in ch. 2.[46]

On account of these considerations, therefore, no connection can be established between the Eph *mysterion* and the *Parables* of I En. And this conclusion is quite independent of the ascription of a late date e.g. by Milik.

---

[43] I.e. 48: 2 ff.; 55: 4; 62: 1 ff.; 63: 11 f.; 68: 2 ff.

[44] I.e. 53: 3 ff.; 55: 4; 62: 1 ff.; 63: 1 ff.; 65: 11; 67: 4 ff.; 68: 2.

[45] Nor do the *Dream visions* (chs. 83—90) which treat of world history from the fall of the angels and the deluge down to Alexander the Great — partly parallel with Daniel's vision — ever designate these events as a *mysterion*. In 83: 7 'secrets' is applied to human sin before the deluge.

[46] It could hardly have escaped our author's attention that the descriptions in Dan 2 and 7 by their similarity in interpretation ought to be seen as descriptions of the same entities and events. In 52: 1—9 there is a description of mountains of metal: iron, copper, silver, gold which might recall Dan 2, but the list here is longer, including two mountains one of 'soft metal' (whatever that may be) and one of lead. If this could be definely related to Dan 2, as Charles, *AP*, II, 219 apparently thinks, then the use of 'secret' in 52: 2 "mine eyes saw all the secret things of heaven that shall be, a mountain of . . ." might be an echo of Dan 2. The imagery is, however, obscure and there are serious omissions from the Danielic description.

In the final chs. *mysterion* occurs 3 ✕.[47] The word occurs in connection with a claim Enoch is making (103: 2),[48] namely, that he has read the heavenly tablets, and that from them he knows what is in store for the just and for the unjust respectively. The tone of the passage dealing with what is in store for the righteous (103: 3) is perhaps reminiscent of I Cor 2: 9, but can hardly evoke associations with Eph. The second occurrence of *mysterion* which Enoch knows is that sinners will pervert truth and righteousness (104: 10) and the third refers to his own writings (104: 12),[49] which shall be given to the just to strengthen and encourage them.

There is thus no comprehensive use of *mysterion* in *I En* designating the sum-total of his dreams or visions or descriptions of future events. Despite the great number of occurrences of *mysterion* 'secret', 'hidden', it is never used of a general plan of God with respect to the future, and needless to say, never in connection with blessings to be apportioned to the Gentiles.

6. THE QUMRAN WRITINGS

Among the parallel passages between Qumran and Eph to which K. G. Kuhn[50] has drawn attention there figures also the Eulogy, a circumstance first observed by Schille (*LG*). Coppens,[51] Mussner,[52] and Brown[53] also discuss the parallels between the Qumran רז and the Eph *mysterion*. Gnilka (59) and Deichgräber,[54] as mentioned earlier,[55] resort to 1QH for the elucidation of the Eulogy. All this might imply that Qumran and in particular the *Hodayoth* is the key to the Eph *mysterion*, at any rate to that as found in the Eulogy. A detailed comparison between this Qumran material and the *mysterion* in Eph 1 and 3, proves, however, somewhat disappointing.

The term רז occurs in the Qumran lit. in manifold contexts and in various senses. The most frequent use is that of God's רזין as revealed

---

[47] I.e. 103: 2; 104: 10, 12. The Gk. is here preserved. At 104: 10 two lines are missing, but the occurrence of μυστήριον is established by the Eth. *mestir*. In 106: 19 (Gk lost) the Eth. again has *mestir* but this ch. is part of the book of Noah. The reference is, nevertheless, similar to those in 103—04.

[48] See also 81: 1 f.; 93: 2; 106: 19.

[49] So, e.g. Charles, *AP*, II, 277, Milik, *BE*, 208.

[50] *PQ* 117 ff.

[51] *PQ*, 146 ff.

[52] *PQ*, 159—63.

[53] *SB*, 61—6.

[54] *GC*, 72—75.

[55] Pp. 41 and 44.

to and treasured by the community.[56] The revealer is God Himself[57] while the direct recipients are the TR (Teacher of Righteousness)[58] and the Master (1QS 11:5). The Master is in turn to instruct the community members[59] who are obliged to keep the knowledge secret (1QS 4:6). The author of the commentary on Hab states that God has revealed the רזי (=inner meaning) of the prophetic word to the TR (1QpH 7:5), and the TR himself[60] claims that God has hidden His רז in him (1QH 5:25). The nature of the רז is for the most part the general sense of divine things of a wonderful, deep and unfathomable nature,[61] of God's inscrutable ways[62] manifested sometimes in His rebukes,[63] and His severe and misunderstood providence.[64] God is further praised for His wisdom manifested in creation with all its רזיהם (1QH 1:11, 13, 29). The term is applied four times to the workings of evil,[65] and once it is part of the name inscribed on the trumpets of ambush (1QM 3:9). Three other instances are of obscure character.[66]

None of all these instances, however, has any particular relevance for the Eph *mysterion*, where the term does not primarily relate to wonderful things that God has revealed, but has a specific reference to God's eschatological purpose.[67] Among the many applications of רז in Qumran, there seem to be certain instances in which the term is used or appears to be

---

[56] The term רז occurs 44× in the pl. and 11× in the sg. acc. to Kuhn's *KQT*.

[57] 1QH 7:27; 1QH 13:3.

[58] 1QpH 7:5. Bruce, *TRQT*, 15 and *STDSS*, 94 f. thinks the TR is the author of *Hodayoth*, at least in part. Similarly, Mertens, *DLTTM*, 127, Lohse, *TQ*, 109, Benoit, *PQ*, 22; Grundmann, *PQ*, 86 ff. G. Jeremias, *LG*, 171—3 attributes to the TR the following: 1QH 2:1—19, 31—39; 4:5—5:4; 5:5—19; 5:20—7:5; 7:6—25; 8:4—40.

[59] 1QS 9:18; In 1QH 2:13 this is probably said of the TR.

[60] On the understanding that the *Hodayoth* or these passages are by him.

[61] 1QH 1:21; 1QH 13:2; 1QS 11:19; 1QS 11:5; 1QH 2:13; 1QS 9:18; 1QH 7:27; 1QH 4:27; 1QH 11:10.

[62] 1QS 11:19; 1QM 14:14; CD 3:18.

[63] 1QH 9:23; 1QH 12:20.

[64] Cf., e.g. the necessity for the fall of some of the footsoldiers in 1QM 16:11; 16; 17:9. The sense here is difficult. The רז seems to be the direct instrument for the fall of the soldiers, (so rendered by Vermes, *DSSE*, 145 and Lohse, *TQ*, 217) and therefore it is difficult to know what was meant by it (see Brown, *SB*, 23).

[65] 1QM 14:9; 1QH 5:36; 1Q27 1:1, 2; 1QH f. 50:5. Coppens, *PQ*, 136, wrongly includes 1QM 3:9; 16:11; 1QS 3:23; 4:18 under this heading.

[66] 1QH 8:6, 11 (bis). On these see Brown, *SB*, 26 f.

[67] This conclusion is maintained in the face of the statement by Mertens, *DLTTM*, 128, "Im Ganzen betrachtet ist das 'Geheimnis' nach der Hymnenrolle der verborgene, nur der Sekte geoffenbarte Plan Gottes über die Phasen des geschichtlichen Geschehens und vor allem über das Ende der Geschichte. Alle Stellen, die nur allgemein vom gerechten Wirken Gottes sprechen, lassen sich gut in diesem Zusammenhang einfügen".

used of God's purpose. It is with such instances that I am primarily concerned.

In the so-called dualistic section [68] in the *Serek hay-yahad* we are told that the Angel of Darkness succeeds in leading astray the righteous so long as his dominion lasts. But though this happens with divine permission and in accordance with God's רוי (1QS 3:23), it is not all; for "in the רוי of His understanding and in His glorious wisdom, God has ordained an end for falsehood".[69] The context does enunciate an eschatological intervention of God in judgement, a purification by the spirit of holiness, the establishment of truth and justice; but the description of this change is rather vague and may be explained by the widespread belief in the final triumph of good.

A certain purpose is discernible in 1QH 13:13 where the author in language reminiscent of Ps 8 and Isa 43 recounts God's creation: "Thou hast app[ointed] all these things in the רוֹ of Thy wisdom to make known Thy glory". But this purpose relates to creation, not to eschatology.

In his comm. on Hab the sectary quotes Hab 2:1—2 and comments that this applies to the time of the end but that God "did not make known to him (sc. Hab.) when the end would come about" (1QpH 7:2). In contradistinction to the ignorance of Hab stands the knowledge of the TR "to whom God made known all the רוי of the words of His servants the prophets".[70] The term רז is not specifically used of the time of the end, but of the meaning of what the prophets had said, and which they themselves had not understood. Our term also includes the knowledge about the end time, which had escaped the prophets, but is not primarily and specifically that, let alone the end itself with a content like the one we find in Eph.[71] The contradistinction between the ignorance of the prophets and the knowledge of the TR is set forth more clearly in the following comment on 2:3a: "the final age shall be prolonged, and shall exceed all that the

---

[68] Wilcox, *SC*, 86 ff., denies that we have to do here with a true dualism and rejects any connection with Iranian or gnostic thought. See further Davies, *SNT*, 159—71.

[69] 1QS 4:18, Vermes' rendering.

[70] 1QpH 7:4—5 in Vermes' trans. Bruce, *BEQT*, 7—11, 18 f., makes the interesting point that both in Dan 2 as well as in the Qumran comm. the terms רז and פשר occur together. "This principle, that the divine purpose cannot be properly understood until the *pesher* has been revealed as well as the *raz*, underlies the biblical exegesis in the Qumran comm. The *raz* was communicated by God to the prophet, but the meaning of that communication remained sealed until its *pesher* was made known by God to His chosen interpreter;" also, *id. TRQT*, 9 f.

[71] Hence I cannot agree with Bruce, *BEQT*, 19, when he says: "From the context it appears that these wonderful mysteries, like those revealed in Daniel, have to do with God's purpose which is to be realized in the end-time.

prophets save said, for the רזי of God are astounding".[72] Here, again, the רזין are not in the first place eschatological, but express the inscrutability of God's ways that eluded the prophets.[73] And finally interpreting Hab 2: 3b the sectary says: "all the ages of God reach their appointed end as He determines for them in the רזי of His wisdom" (1QpH 7: 13—4). Here, at last, it seems as if we have an instance of an eschatological רז. The concepts of רז and 'end-time' have come, indeed, very near, nevertheless, even here they have not become identified. In Eph 1: 9 f. the *mysterion* means that at the end-time God will gather together all under Christ. The component 'end-time' is part of the import of *mysterion*; the two are to a certain extent identical. In 1QpH 7: 13 f., on the other hand, the 'end-time' and the רז are two separate categories which do not merge. All that the commentator says is that in His רזי (=purpose, plan, inscrutable ways, etc.) God has *determined* that the times will be rounded up. Thus the concepts of רז and 'times' so far from becoming merged, stand over against one another; the one becoming the determinative factor for the other.

Thus, it cannot be proved that in 1QpH 7 we have an instance of eschatological רזין in the Eph sense.[74] This use of רז may not be any different from those other instances which spoke in general of God's wonderful thoughts, deeds, or ways.[75] In these inscrutable thoughts or plans God has also determined the delimiting of times but these times of the end and their content are not in 1QpH described as a רז.[76]

Finally, we come to what Milik[77] called *The Book of the Mysteries* because in a frg. of half a page רז occurs no less than 4 ×.[78] The beginning of the frg. is as follows: ". . . all . . . [t]ruth . . . רזי of iniquity . . . and they do not know the רז to come, and they do not comprehend the things of old, and do not know what will befall them, or how to deliver their life from the רז to come. This is for you the sign. It will come to pass when He hands over the descendants of iniquity for punishment. Then He will dispel wrong before justice as the darkness is driven away before

[72] 1QpH 7: 7—8 after Vermes.

[73] Bruce, *SC*, 72, thinks that it was the TR rather than the prophets which God's mysteries eluded.

[74] *Contra* Mertens, *DLTTM*, 129, who speaks of "den übergreifenden eschatologischen Aspekt" about the Qumran רז, as well as against Kuhn, *PQ*, 119.

[75] Cf. Pryke, *SC*, 53, "Of the many sectarian writings, the Habakkuk commentary is the most eschatological of them all, yet it has no direct reference to the Messianic hope".

[76] On the contrary, in Dan 2 רז is not the mysteries in which God has determined what shall transpire in the latter days, but the name given to all that shall take place at the *eschaton*.

[77] *DJD*, I, 102—7.

[78] Kuhn, *KQT*, 204 gives one more fragmentary instance of רז in 1Q27 13: 3.

light" etc.[79] The little we can make out of this context is that the passage speaks of those who practice the רז of iniquity and who do not know that they will be overtaken by a "רז to come".[80] Failing to receive a lesson from those who (presumably) were punished in the past, they are quite unprepared to save themselves from the רז to come, i.e. the coming judgment. Here in these two instances,[81] we finally have the sense of something that is future, that will come and that will, as surely, spell doom for the unjust. The context sets it at the end-time, for after this judgment, justice shall be revealed and knowledge shall fill the world.[82] Here we may assume that we have an eschatological רז.[83] What is not perfectly clear is what exactly are its contents. Is it the judgment aspect or also the ushering in of righteousness? From 1:1, 5 it seems that judgment of the descendants of iniquity[84] is only a preliminary to the רז and that its full coming shall coincide with a) the dispelling and anihilation of unrighteousness (negatively), and b) its replacement by righteousness ruling in the universe (positively). This change will have a double effect: ignorance of God shall become extinct while knowledge of God shall fill the earth.

It may then be conceded that in 1Q27 1:1, 3 ff. we have a use of רז, in the sg., that speaks of an eschatological plan[85] to put an end to the rule of sin and to usher in the rule of righteousness.[86]

---

[79] 1Q27 1:1, 2—4.

[80] See Rabinowitz, *JBL*, 1952, 22 f. and Milik, *DJD*, I, 104 for a future sense of רז נהיה.

[81] A third instance of "mystery to come" in 1QS 11:3—4, is unfortunately not clarified by the context. Lohse, *TQ*, 41, translates with "Geheim(nis) des Gewordenen". Vermes, *DSSE*, 209, Piper, *JR*, 1958, 95 ff. and Brown, *SB*, 28 take it as a future mystery. See also Mertens, *DLTTM*, 125 f.

[82] 1Q27 1:1, 3—4. Piper, *JR*, 1958, 96 ff., who defines the mystery as "a transcendental process which realises itself secretly", speaks of an "abstract" rather than a "dramatic eschatology" operating here: "no mention is made of a fight, a judgement, or a catastrophe. Rather the imagery points to a process in which, by the steady increase of light, darkness is made to disappear . . .".

[83] Note that all three instances so far mentioned as well as the two other instances [. . . רז נה]יה (1Q26 1:1 and 1:4) are all in the sg.! In 1Q27 1:1, 7 we have the pl. again, but that is not described as a 'mystery to come'.

[84] Presumably the Community's religious enemies.

[85] Over twenty years ago Starcky, *RB*, 1956, 66, (cf. Milik, *BE*, 91) announced that he has an eschatological work which uses the term very frequently, but, to my grief, this has not been made available to date.

[86] It is tempting to relate 1QM 3:23 and 4:18 to this context. Nevertheless, there may still be some relevance for Elliger's warning (*SHK*, 275) of more than two decades ago, that it is unsound at this stage of research to exegete one writing in the light of another.

7. CONCLUSION

This investigation has shown that the Eph *mysterion* belongs to the long jewish tradition of designating God's riches, truths and plans as a רז or μυστήριον. In this broad sense all of the pre-Ephesian lit. is relevant material for the postulation of a background to the concept as we meet it in Eph. And in this respect studies like those of Deden[87] and Brown[88] have done a real service in pointing us away from the wholly different material of the Mystery Religions to a more natural cradle of the NT *mysterion*, i.e. the OT and its continuation in the traditions of Judaism.

It is when we take up the specific usage of a particular NT book and look for definite, indeed palpable, connections with this pre-Ephesian material, that we can no longer be satisfied with the general connections with such a diffuse concept as the "semitic background", which, e.g. Brown has established. Without ignoring the possibility that a NT author might have made a more specific or a narrower use of a concept that was wider in his background material, I have directed my attention to such instances as are of analogous use. Only when the search for narrower parallels has failed to produce satisfactory results, are we justified in taking up the search after wider analogies.

My investigation has shown that, in the narrow sense of parallels as defined at the beginning of this ch., two bodies of lit. may be considered initially as relevant, i.e. Dan and Qumran.

The collocation of רז with the concept of the 'end-time' in 1QpH is significant, nevertheless, closer scrutiny revealed that it differed markedly from the Eph *mysterion* which in the Eulogy, at any rate, it includes both the *anakephalaiōsis* and the 'end-time' components. In the case of 1Q27 we come nearer Eph. The writer speaks of what is in store for the future which includes the anihilation of sin and the reign of righteousness. It may be that the brevity of the frg. gives a somewhat distorted picture of the meaning of the author. Nevertheless, the frg. we possess speaks of a future רז whose primary concern is the judgment of the wicked. God is not explicitly stated to be the Author of this רז, though this may be assumed, but its content is rather vague, at least when compared with the Eph *mysterion*. And besides all this, the connection between Qumran and Eph will have to be demonstrated, for it cannot be assumed as a matter of course.

The Danielic *mysterion*, on the other hand, meets all the requirements: it is God's purpose, it is eschatological, it has cosmic dimensions, and it

---

[87] Deden, *ETL*, 1936, 403—42.
[88] Brown, *SB*.

is a unified plan.[89] All of the important terms collocated with it in Dan are also evidenced in Eph. The concept of the principalities and powers and their subjugation to God as part of and as a prerequisite to God's eschatological purpose in Dan has an exact equivalence in Eph. The role of the Son of Man in Dan and the role of Christ in Eph may be considered as equivalent. And furthermore, what is not the case with the Qumran writings, the use of Dan by the Eph author is not only possible but probable, indeed, to be assumed.[90]

The similarities claimed between Dan and Eph need not imply a wholesale borrowing. There is adaptation, reinterpretation and new application of the concepts in question. But it does imply that the Eph author is conscious of standing in the Danielic tradition and carrying on what Dan has bequeathed, indeed, giving the final word on God's eschatological *mysterion* for the realisation of which he himself plays such an extraordinary role.

---

[89] This is, of course, not a new conclusion (so already V. Soden, *ZNW*, 1911, 188—230; cf. Brown, *SB*, 1, n. 1 and 34 n. 107), but it is still *the* conclusion after having considered the Mystery Religions, the Apocrypha, the Pseudepigrapha and the Qumran lit.!

[90] Ellis, *PUOT*, 150—4, assigns to Eph neither quotations nor allusions nor parallels with Dan, but in view of the evidence I presented above, V, 4, A, iv and in the excursus on Ἀρχαί καὶ Ἐξουσίαι, he is hardly justified in not doing so.

CHAPTER VI

ΜΥΣΤΗΡΙΟΝ IN EPHESIANS

1. THE EN-DIMENSION IN EPH AS A REFERENCE POINT

One of the most striking aspects of Eph is the frequency of the prep. ἐν in the phrases ἐν Χριστῷ, ἐν αὐτῷ, etc. In the greater Eulogy (1:3—14) for example, a passage of 202 words, this prep. occurs no less than 15 × describing the setting or sphere in which the Eulogy contents are to be understood. This setting or sphere may be called the ἐν-dimension of Eph.[1]

Thus God's blessings to 'us' (P 2), which give the *reason* why 'we' bless God (P 1) and which include all the specific blessings of Pp 3—30, are set in their proper dimensional perspective by being defined with the two pregnant ἐν-phrases, namely, ἐν τοῖς ἐπουρανίοις[2] and ἐν Χριστῷ.[3] These two phrases give expression to a new dimension. The occurrence of both in this key P also signals the fact that the ensuing blessings, and thus the *mysterion* also, must be understood in the light of this new dimension.

One of the features of this dimension is its timelessness. Accordingly, one of God's blessings to 'us' is His election of 'us' which transpired before the foundation of the world, and hence, before time and outside space. The author is able to speak of it as a blessing to 'us' who live within space and time, because he defines it as a blessing ἐν τοῖς ἐπουρανίοις, and ἐν Χριστῷ. The dimension, therefore, includes the components of timelessness or atemporality and of *beyond-world-ness* or the *hypercosmic*. The defining adj. πνευματικῇ, moreover, specifies this dimension as one belonging to the spiritual world, and hence, removed from the world of senses. This idea re-echoes again in the following chs. Thus, not only the powers have their sphere of work in this dimension, but 'we' too are said to be seated there despite the fact that 'we' are still in 'this body'. Thus the author can also say that through the being of the Church in this dimension, seated with Christ above the powers, God uses her to teach the powers His manifold wisdom.

It is thus obvious that the phrase ἐν Χριστῷ is not to be understood merely locally or simply instrumentally; this, as well as the phrase ἐν τοῖς

---

[1] It is not hereby implied that this dimension is peculiar to Eph; only that my interest lies in Eph.

[2] This occurs 5 × in Eph. See excursus, *infra*.

[3] This occurs 35 × in *Eph*. See excursus, n. 35, *infra*.

ἐπουρανίοις, is indicative of a new dimension that opens itself up for the Christian. It is a dimension in which the Christian, paradoxically enough, has always been, even before his existence in space and time; a dimension in which God makes available to him through Christ the realisation of His *mysterion* and its consequences, one of which is the assumption of his allotted place in the Body of Christ. It is there too, that he becomes aware of the spiritual world and consciously joins with God in His controversy with the evil powers.

The difference between the phrase ἐν τοῖς ἐπουρανίοις and the phrase ἐν Χριστῷ here is that whereas ἐν τοῖς ἐπουρανίοις has reference to that aggregate of ideas associated with the salvific process and pertaining to an other-wordly realm, the phrase ἐν Χριστῷ more directly brings into focus the personal element of this dimension, the ground of God's intention (i.e. that all He does is in indissoluble relation to Christ), the personal cause and the ultimate point of relationship which the Christian has in this dimension.

It is as much as claimed by the author that the Christian lives simultaneously in two spheres; the earthly and the ἐν-dimensional one. It is in this latter sphere that God is observed at work: His intentions and plans are conceived in connection with Christ, His atemporal *mysterion* is eternally laid up in Him to be executed at what, on the human level, is called τὸ πλήρωμα τῶν καιρῶν — there being no distinction drawn at the ἐν-dimensional level between its conception and its execution. The muddle which the difficult clauses of the Eulogy present when one attempts to fit them logically into one another is the result of the process of translating ἐν-dimensional 'events' into categories of human language. In that sphere, too, the sacrifice of Christ transpires (1:4—7); [4] there the powers can be seen unmasked, as real, potent, and yet defeated; there, too, the human finds his liberty, disowning his old masters — the powers — in order to place himself under a new Head.

The Eph *mysterion* therefore, is an ἐν-dimensional concept and can be apprehended to the extent to which it is related to this peculiar dimension. The concepts related to it, i.e. the *anakephalaiōsis* of all, the calling into being of the Church, the use of the Church as an object-lesson to the powers, all pertain to this complex of ideas which though expressing modality are not merely modal, though including locality are not simply local, but rather form that sphere where God acts with respect to everything from His fixed point of reference, namely, Christ, in Whom locality, instrumentality, and purpose meet (ἐν αὐτῷ, δι' αὐτοῦ, εἰς αὐτόν) and all things, be they powers, principalities, men or creation, become subservient to one great object in view — εἰς ἔπαινον τῆς δόξης αὐτοῦ.

---

[4] Cf. Rev 13:8 τοῦ ἀρνίου τοῦ ἐσφαγμένου ἀπὸ καταβολῆς κόσμου.

2. THE SUPREME END IN VIEW

In the greater Eulogy we meet three times with the phrase εἰς ἔπαινον (τῆς) δόξης (τῆς χάριτος) αὐτοῦ (vv. 6, 12, 14). Its repetition is significant since this is the only collocation of so many words that occurs more than once in this passage. Furthermore the 'final' prep. εἰς indicates that this phrase, far from being intended as a mere flourish in an already ornate style, supplies the purpose upon which all of God's undertakings, described in the Eulogy, hinge. It is the supreme end in view for the sake of which God does all that He does. This claim is signally confirmed by P 1 which, from the point of view of grammar, forms the only main clause of the entire passage, while from the semantic viewpoint it is analysed as the main P to which all the subsequent Pp of the Eulogy are subordinated.[5] This ultimate intention of God — to glorify Himself — comes to expression afresh at 2: 7: ἵνα ἐνδείξηται ἐν τοῖς αἰῶσιν τοῖς ἐπερχομένοις τὸ ὑπερβάλλον πλοῦτος τῆς χάριτος αὐτοῦ ἐν χρηστότητι ἐφ' ἡμᾶς ἐν Χριστῷ Ἰησοῦ, and again, at 3: 10: ἵνα γνωρισθῇ νῦν ταῖς ἀρχαῖς καὶ ταῖς ἐξουσίαις ἐν τοῖς ἐπουρανίοις διὰ τῆς ἐκκλησίας ἡ πολυποίκιλος σοφία τοῦ Θεοῦ; as well as rounding up the first part of Eph (1—3) at 3: 21: αὐτῷ ἡ δόξα . . . εἰς πάσας τὰς γενεὰς τοῦ αἰῶνος τῶν αἰώνων.

The fact that the phrase εὐλογητὸς ὁ Θεός and the doxology at 3: 21 are not cast in a form expressing purpose, but rather describe an act as taking place (i.e. the Christian praising his God), instead of detracting from their value as indications of God's intention add, in fact, depth to it.[6] The relation of P 2 to P 1 was analysed as one of *reason*, i.e. 'we bless God because He blessed us'. This may be reversed to 'He blessed us in order that we might bless Him'. This reversal is in itself not a deduction capable of general application and validity, but is quite legitimate in this particular context, which shows unmistakably that God's blessings have a certain aim in view.[7] The Eulogy formula, moreover, is anticipatory of the praise which 'we' have been called to ascribe to God; it is a first installment, so to speak, of something which shall endure throughout eternity (3: 21). It means that already here and now 'we' begin on a course of action and a mode of being — praising Him — which belongs properly to an eschatological time, i.e. to the *anakephalaiōsis* and beyond it.

I am here suggesting that for the author of Eph the election and re-

---

[5] See IV, B. 1.

[6] The fact that the surface structure of this P is different from that of the other three phrases, is no valid objection in this respect, since the deep structure of all four phrases have God's praise in view, cf. Nida—Taber, *TPT*, 155.

[7] Cf. B—C, *TWG*, 302, who actually make this reversal in the case of *means-result*, but who, however, admit that the relation of *reason-result* is closely connected with it. In the exx. they give it is the *means-result* that is in focus.

demption of man are not an end in themselves, but rather as means to an end.[8] Even the towering concept of a cosmic *anakephalaiōsis* is not the final purpose, but a prerequisite to God's glory. But the distinction between end and means occasionally becomes somewhat blurred since the two are made contiguous in Christ. It is in Christ, on the one hand, that God manifests His true nature (e.g. mercy, love, goodness, grace, (cf. 2: 4—8) which are the springboard and goal of 'our' praise), and it is through that manifestation, on the other, that He conditions 'us' so as to elicit from 'us' the praise due to Himself. The ἐν Χριστῷ concept, therefore, constitutes both the end and the means for God's praise. Hence, Christ and His event are the concretization of God's attributes (cf. Heb 1: 3), i.e. of that which God wants to exalt and glorify, and at the same time, the means for that exaltation as well as the sphere in which the exaltation is effected.

3. THE ΣΥΝ-STATE OF THE GENTILES

Eph recognises two obstacles for the fulfillment of God's purpose, the rebellion of the powers and the alienation of the Jews from the Gentiles (2: 12 ff.) as well as the estrangement of both from God (2: 16). The two incompatible elements of mankind must be unified and together, united into a new man in Christ, must be reconciled to God (2: 15 f.). Indeed, the unification of the two, i.e. the constitution of the two into an ἐκκλησία, will function as an eye-opener for the powers which through the establishment of the Church and her existence first come to the realisation that they have been outwitted by God (3: 10).[9]

In order to bring about this unification two conditions must be fulfilled: the unifying work of Christ on the cross (2: 16), and the declaration to the Gentiles of what Christ did for them (3: 2—9).

This, put briefly, is the content of the *mysterion* in ch. 3. But, once again, the weight of emphasis is on the Gentiles rather than on the Jews, since what is new in this connection is not the salvation of the Jews, but the participation of the Gentiles in redemption and in the Body of Christ.

The first use of *mysterion* in 3: 3 may be a reference to 1: 9 where the term is collocated with the same vb. as here, i.e. γνωρίζειν.[10] But neither

---

[8] For the close connection between creation and redemption in Pauline theology see Gibbs, *CR*, 139—45 and *id.*, *Bib*, 1975, 25 ff.

[9] I Cor 1: 25—8; 3: 19 and esp. 2: 8, though applied to different contexts, may serve as a commentary on this point.

[10] On καθὼς προέγραψα ἐν ὀλίγῳ see IV, C, ii, 6. Merklein, *CK*, 10 f. with Gaugler, 130 and Percy, *PKE*, 350, decides for 2: 11—18, or more narrowly, for 2: 14—18.

140

in the context of 1: 9 nor in 2: 11—8 [11] does the author say anything about ἀποκάλυψις as a means for making known the *mysterion*.[12] The possibility therefore exists that he is making a general reference to the *mysterion* and its revelation in the all-inclusive sense, intending to continue on from that point and treat one particular aspect of it, i.e. that which concerns the Gentiles.

The use in 3: 4, on the other hand, gives the σύν-state of the Gentiles as the content of *mysterion* in connection with the Jews. The three σύν-words correspond in substance to 2: 16—19; the Gentiles, having become συγκληρονόμα, σύσσωμα, συμμέτοχα of the promise, are no longer ξένοι καὶ πάροικοι but συμπολῖται τῶν ἁγίων καὶ οἰκεῖοι τοῦ Θεοῦ, or *vice versa*. Either way, the *mysterion* is brought into connection with the contents of 2: 11—22, as Schlier,[13] Merklein,[14] and others have noted. This means that the *mysterion* of chs. 1 and 3 does not cover only the contents of the immediate context in which the term occurs, but virtually the bulk of the contents of all three chs. The Eph *mysterion*, therefore, is not only the cosmic *anakephalaiōsis* and the unification of Jews and Gentiles, it is not only God's eternal plan, but also the outworking of that plan as well as its effective declaration by the author.

The *mysterion* is met at the level of plan or counsel of God. This plan is aimed at the final *anakephalaiōsis* of all things in Christ, which presupposes the bringing into being of the Church of Jews and Gentiles, and the subjection of the powers. It is, however, also met at the level of the mechanics or means to that end, which first of all relates to Christ's event and then to the declaration of that event and its consequences for the Gentiles by the author who is called thereunto. It is thus seen that the *mysterion* is a very comprehensive concept with the weight of emphasis placed on the aspect of the planning and the non-revealedness of it before the event of Christ, as well as on its openess at the present and its future consummation. However, we note once again that, among all these items of the *mysterion* concept, the author picks up just two for emphasis — the *anakephalaiōsis* and the inclusion of the Gentiles in the salvation scheme — and these two become the more emphasised aspects of the *mysterion* of Eph 1—3.

---

[11] As Merklein would have preferred.

[12] The context of 1: 8 f., however, implies a knowledge communicated by revelation, cf. σοφίᾳ καὶ φρονήσει γνωρίσας . . . τοῦ θελήματος αὐτοῦ. The conclusion that this context implies an ἀποκάλυψις is inevitable. In 2: 11—18, on the other hand, the concept of *mysterion* is absent, even if, in retrospect, when considering the content of 3: 5 f., it is found that 2: 11—18 is part of the mechanics of the *mysterion* of 3: 5.

[13] Schlier, 149, relates μυστήριον in 3: 3 b with 1: 3—14, 18—22 and ch. 2.

[14] *CK*, 10.

It was noted in another connection that the *mysterion* of 1:9 f. is the all-comprehending eschatological purpose of God as made known to the author (among others). In 3:4 it is that *mysterion* as proclaimed by the author to the Gentiles, applying to them in its limited aspect. Thus, in 1:8 f. it was through 'wisdom and prudence' that the *mysterion* was made known, while here the author claims 'understanding' in it. The thought of 3:9, as shall be seen, comes close to the thought of 1:9 which is a wider application of the term. But more on this below.

The *mysterion* of 3:4 ff. sets the present in contrast to the past. The differentiating line is the death of Christ. Before Christ there is but darkness, ignorance and hopelessness for the Gentiles. With Christ's event the picture changes completely. The three σύν-words are the death-blow to Jewish bigotry. The way is opened for full Gentile participation: they are made co-heirs on equal terms with the Jews; in the Body of Christ, the Church, they are made σύσσωμα, i.e. members of one and the same body, and they participate on the same conditions as the Jews in the promise of salvation by Christ. All the formal differences of the past are swept away so that in the newly-revealed *mysterion* of God's will it becomes evident that God's eschatological and definitive plan allows for no such differences between the various sectors of humanity. Here meet the past, present and future. These concepts are again relative to the human point of view. For God there is but present: He wills and acts eternally; He plans and performs outside the bounds of time. But from the human viewpoint the revelation of this eternal planning and execution comes bit by bit: first the Jews, then also the Gentiles; the result is the Church — that mighty weapon in God's hands in His controversy with the powers, the third group to be dealt with.

This brings us to the third instance of *mysterion* in ch. 3. This instance has the same general content as 3:4. But the direction of the point is different. Here it is no longer the inclusion of the Gentiles in God's salvation, but the ultimate purpose for bringing Jews and Gentiles together. If the use of *mysterion* in 3:4 ff. dealt the final blow to Jewish exclusivism and revealed its misunderstanding of God's purpose of her own election, its use in 3:9 ff. deals the decisive blow to the powers.[15] These, like the Jews, have been totally outwitted by God's counsel. The claim is thus made that the *mysterion* is new both for the Jews and for the heavenly

---

[15] The *v. l.* without πάντας at 3:9, supported by ℵ* A Orig., Jer., Aug., etc., is, from the present viewpoint, quite appropriate as it makes the lighting up of the οἰκονομία τοῦ μυστηρίου refer not to the preceding ἔθνεσιν but to the exhibition of God's wisdom in it (sc. the *mysterion*) to the powers. This is, nevertheless, not the only possible way of construing it, cf. *supra* IV, C, 26.

powers.[16] These two demonstrations of God bear their fruit: the first one, dealing with the Jews, issues in the coming into being of the Church, while the second one, dealing with the powers, leads to the defeat of the powers and their consequent *anakephalaiōsis*. Thus, the strain begun at 1: 9 f. is brought to its proper conclusion at 3: 1—13 in the context of Gentile participation in the Body of Christ.[17]

4. THE AUTHOR'S ROLE

In 3: 8 ff. the author contemplates the importance of his own mission work. Indeed, as we saw in ch. II, 4, the whole of vv. 2—13 is but an expansion in reverse order on two of the moments of prayer, namely, the person praying and the persons for whom he prayes. The role of the author (in which I am primarily interested here) is clearly indicated both in connection with the benefit that comes to the Gentiles as well as in connection with the lesson that is meted out to the powers.

The author's role in connection with the Gentiles is easily ascertained. He is a prisoner because he proclaims Christ to them (3: 1, 13; 6: 19 f.). God entrusted him with His grace for service among the Gentiles (3: 2); He made known to him His *mysterion* concerning them (3: 3 ff.), which was heretofore unnoticed (3: 5), that he might make it known to them (3: 4, 6, 8).

But along with this role the author becomes instrumental for another far-reaching consequence. The Church that comes into being through his labours becomes itself the instrument in God's hands to give the denizens of the heavenly regions a permanent instruction on His incomprehensible wisdom. The phrase διὰ τῆς ἐκκλησίας indicates that the role of the Church is purely instrumental, the One performing the instruction being God Himself. But the question is: In which way is the Church used by God to teach the angelic world His wisdom? The temporal adv. νῦν as well as the context of vv. 2—13 make it sufficiently plain that the author is thinking of the *mysterion* concerning the establishment of the Church, and in particular, of the composition of the Church. The powers failed to thwart God's plan. The establishment of the Church — the fruit of the cross and the seal of its success — is bad news for them. The Church's existence indicates that they have been fooled, they have been defeated and

---

[16] The ignorance of the Gentiles is taken for granted, and is, accordingly, not hinted at here.

[17] In this connection as also in general about the Eph *mysterion*, see the four studies by Scharlemann, *ConcTM*, 1969, 532—44; 1970, 155—64; 338—46 and 410—20. Further, Ryrie, *BS*, 1966, 24—31; Jones, *StEph*, 76—88; Gibbard, *StEph*, 97—120; Houlden, *SE*, 1973, 267—73 and Winklhoffer, *GCW*, *passim*.

have nothing else to look forward to but their subjugation by Christ as defeated foes.[18] Once again the author is back at the *anakephalaiōsis* of 1: 9 f., but with the added insight that the calling of the Church has been instrumental in the *anakephalaiōsis* of the 'things in heaven'. And not merely that, for in the establishment of the Church, he, the author, has played a most prominent part.

This would be particularly effective if the shorter *v.l.* were the original one. It would then mean that God's wisdom is made known when this long-hidden *mysterion* is lit up, and its contents — the establishment of the Church — emerge into full day-light.[19]

It is in such a context of universal and cosmic dimensions that the author places his own mission, and his claim, astounding as it is, is that he has a central place in the declaration of the eternally-hidden *mysterion* of eschatological import with consequences at once unversal, cosmic and all-enduring (e.g. 2: 7).

5. THE COSMIC ANAKEPHALAIŌSIS

The Eph *mysterion* is a comprehensive concept. It is met as a designation of God's supreme purpose, but it is also used of the mechanism set in motion for the fulfillment of that purpose. It may be conceived as a series of events leading to that end. The term is thus met at different levels, so that what at one level is *means*, at another level it becomes an *end*. This is signally illustrated by the use of the concept at 1: 9 f. and at, e.g., 3: 4. The latter occurrence is of more limited application than the former, nevertheless, they are not different *mysteria*, but wider or narrower aspects of one and the same *mysterion* — God's *mysterion* in Christ.[20]

It was noted in ch. IV that the various acts of God in the Eulogy such as election, (pre)destination, and redemption lead toward a general *anakephalaiōsis*. The phrase ἐν Χριστῷ is of the greatest significance here, for, as it was noted above, both God's aim to glorify Himself as well as God's nature which is to be glorified, are set forth in Christ. 'We' are called to praise His love, mercy, grace, etc. These aspects of God's charac-

---

[18] Col 2: 15 puts it more graphically: ἀπεκδυσάμενος τὰς ἀρχὰς καὶ τὰς ἐξουσίας ἐδειγμάτισεν ἐν παρρησίᾳ θριαμβεύσας αὐτοὺς ἐν αὐτῷ. The interpretation of ἀπεκδυσάμενος is debated. Its collocation with ἐδειγμάτισεν and θριαμβεύσας would seem to plead for a meaning in which the ἀρχαί and ἐξουσίαι are the experiencers of the activity, i.e. He stripped them off completely. Similarly, Schlier, *MG*, 43; cf. also Abbott, *Col*, 260 f.

[19] See *supra* VI, 4 *ad* n. 15.

[20] Cf. Schlier, 62. "nichts als drei Mysterien (including 5: 32), sondern als eines und dasselbe".

ter are revealed in the Christ event. At the same time this revelation becomes effective as redemption. Christ constitutes the ground on which revelation and redemption meet: hence the bringing of the creature into an awareness of its relation to its Creator takes place in Christ and is called *anakephalaiōsis*. This is essentially a future concept.[21] Therefore we do not yet see all things put under His feet. However, the Church which is already in Him, has begun fulfilling God's final purpose — *viz.* to praise Him (1:3).

The concept of *anakephalaiōsis* which is all inclusive refers to beings in heaven and to beings on earth. Our term is actually not very helpful in defining the relation that shall obtain,[22] however, one or two things become evident from it. Τὰ πάντα shall be reconstituted afresh[23] in Christ[24] and the relation is envisaged as one in which Christ is Lord or Head, i.e. they are subjected to Him. From this thematic presentation the author proceeds to treat the *anakephalaiōsis* in more detail by concentrating on the two chief representatives of 'things in heaven' and 'things on earth', i.e. the powers and the Church.

God is shown to be in controversy with the powers. These are presented not merely as rebellious toward God, but also as influencing mankind in the same direction (2:2 f.). There is thus a nexus between the revolting powers and the sin of man, and it is precisely this nexus that Christ comes to break by His death and resurrection (2:1, 5). The one must be forgiven (1:7; 2:5, 8), redeemed (1:7, 14), placed in Christ and with Christ ἐν τοῖς ἐπουρανίοις (e.g. 2:6), and made the Body of Christ (1:22 f.), while

---

[21] Lindemann's (*AZ*, 98 f.) understanding of the *anakephalaiōsis* as having already occurred is to be rejected. He says: "Gott hat uns kundgetan, was er vollbracht hat — nicht, was er erst noch tun will. Er *hat* das All in Christus zusammengefast, das πλήρωμα τῶν καιρῶν, die Aufhebung der Zeit, ist *jetzt* Gegenwart." He moreover, claims that grammatically it is absolutely impossible to construe the aor. inf. in a future sense, and speaks of an "'aoristisch-eschatologischem' Aspekt" of Christ's lordship over the powers, cf. also pp. 248 ff. Lindemann's claim that "Eine futurische Deutung ist grammatisch . . . auf keinen Fall möglich" (99) because ἀνακεφαλαιώσασθαι is an aor. inf. is 'falsch'. The inf. as well as the other moods of the aor. may be used of an act that lies in the future. I have argued this point at some lengt in an article (unpublished as yet) on ἔφθασεν ἡ βασιλεία τοῦ Θεοῦ. Lindemann's understanding of an already past *anakephalaiōsis* makes nonsense for example of the author's missionary work which is part of the mechanics for the realisation of the *anakephalaiōsis*. Cf. Mussner's view in *CAK*, 68 which coincides with mine. A proper understanding of the relation of present to future in Eph is attained when we take the ἐν-dimensional concept seriously into account.

[22] See Schlier, *TDNT*, III, 681 f., for its various senses, as well as Hanson, *UC*, 123 ff. and Mussner, *CAK*, 64 ff.

[23] This is the natural force of ἀνά even if the term does not bear this sense in Rm 13:9. Cf. Lee, *StEph*, 43 f.

[24] So e.g. Mussner, *CAK*, 66.

the other must be subdued (1: 21 f.). The *anakephalaiōsis* thus means one thing when referring to the Church, but quite another when applied to the powers.[25] Since God's base of operation is the earth, the work of Christ is primarily intended for mankind with the powers feeling only the repercussions of it. Thus, while the Church experiences the power of His resurrection in being made free and victorious (1: 19 f.), the powers are made to feel its opposite edge, in being defeated and made subject (1: 21 f.).

Although chs. 2 and 3 take up several of the strains of the Eulogy,[26] they mainly concentrate on the process leading to the *anakephalaiōsis*. This is consonant with the pattern of the Eph argumentation. Not only does the author focus on mankind and the powers, he even singles out the first for more detailed treatment. The *anakephalaiōsis* with respect to the powers implies their subjection as vanquished foes (1: 21 f.). This is already now a fact having followed on the resurrection. But this is not the whole truth, for Eph presents another picture in which the powers are both active and victorious, at least with regard to the υἱοῖς τοῖς ἀπειθείας (2: 2), and as holding at least their own in their fight against the Christian; they are, in fact, on the offensive (6: 12 f.). This tension (if it is to be called such) between the *already* and the *not yet* with regards to the powers is due to the very nature of the Eph duality in conceiving of events and existence, *viz.* on the ἐν-dimensional level and the earthly one.[27] Hence, the *anakephalaiōsis* of the powers is also, strictly speaking, an eschatological concept, which shall transpire when the Christian shall not only be seated ἐν τοῖς ἐπουρανίοις ἐν Χριστῷ (where he is already), but shall cease his fight against the powers and be effectively joined to his Head as a member of the Body.

In a certain sense, however, the process of the *anakephalaiōsis* of the powers has already begun. This is evident from the idea that the transference of believers from under their control and their being placed under the suzerainty of Christ (2: 1 ff.), and the powers' consequent awakening to the new situation brought about by God's inexplorable wisdom (3: 10), induce them to set all their diabolical machinery in motion against their former captives (6: 13—16).[28]

The final *anakephalaiōsis* of the powers envisages a subjugation of the most humiliating kind. Not only are they made subordinate to the exalted Christ, more than that, they are placed under His feet, i.e. they are reduced to a mere footstool (1: 22).[29] On the other hand, the *anakephalaiōsis* of

---

[25] Cf. Col 2: 10 where κεφαλή is used differently from Eph 1: 22.

[26] Cf. *supra* pp. 50—2 for parallels between the Eulogy and the rest of Eph.

[27] So also Mussner, *CAK*, 68.

[28] Cf. the similar idea in Rev 12: 12 b: εἰδὼς ὅτι ὀλίγον καιρὸν ἔχει.

[29] It is tempting to refer the 'feet' to the Church, and degrade the powers still more,

the Church implies a unique exaltation of the human to the realm of the divine.[30] To be sure, she is but a body and has a Head over her, but that Head is none else than the Son of God (1:3), and her being His Body means nothing short of being His fulness, i.e. that which fills or completes Him who fills all things (1:23).[31]

6. EXCURSUSES

A. Ἐν τοῖς ἐπουρανίοις

It would seem that ἐπουράνιος is not different from οὐράνιος in meaning.[1] The prep. does not have the force of 'upon', but merely that of 'at' or 'in'.[2] This term is attested as early as Homer. The following are its main uses: a) of the God/gods of heaven;[3] b) of those belonging to the divine heaven;[4] c) of the θεῖος Λόγος;[5] d) as equivalent to μετέωρα;[6] e) of the journey of the chaste after death;[7] f) of the divine ἐπιστήμη;[8] g) of heavenly things;[9] h) of things generally;[10] i) of God's/gods' dwelling;[11] j) of Christ;[12] k) of

since immediately following the Ps quotation Christ is described as the Head and the Church as the Body (to which the feet naturally belong). But such exegesis is untenable. The subjection of the powers is thought of in connection with the resurrected and exalted Christ, not in connection with the union of Christ with the Church. Cf. the similar point that is made in conjunction with the Danielic Son of Man in V, 4, iv and in VI, 6, C.

[30] This is not to be understood as implying *apotheosis*.

[31] Lindemann, *AZ*, 61, questions the derivation of the concept of πλήρωμα from Gnosticism, preferring a borrowing from the Jewish Wisdom teaching.

[1] So Traub, *TDNT*, V, 539; Schlier, 45.

[2] Traub, *TDNT*, V, 538 illustrates by ἐπιθαλάσσιος 'situated by the sea'.

[3] E.g. Hom., *Il.* VI, 129 οὐκ ἂν ἔγωγε θεοῖσιν ἐπουρανίοις μαχοίμην. Also line 131. Further, Hom., *Od.* XVII, 484; *Sib. Or.* 4.51, 135; III Mac 6:28; 7:6; *CH, Exc.* 12.1; 21.2; I Cl., 61:2; *P Flor.* 296.12 (VI A.D.); *SGUÄ*, 4166; synonymously with gods: Theocr., *Id.* 25.5; Mosh. 2.21; Luc., *D. Deor.* 4.3; and of heavenly beings: Ign., *Trall* 9:1; *Eph.* 13:2.

[4] Pind., *Frg.* 132.3 εὐσεβέων ἐπουράνιοι.

[5] *Orph. Frg.* 247. 33 ff. ἔστι δὲ πάντῃ αὐτὸς ἐπουράνιος.

[6] Pl., *Ap.* 19 b: τὰ τε ὑπὸ γῆς καὶ τὰ ἐπουράνια (*v. l.* οὐρανός). Also Ph., *Gig.* 62.

[7] Pl., *Phdr.* 256 d οὐ νόμος ἔστιν ἔτι ἐλθεῖν τοῖς κατηργημένοις ἤδη τῆς ἐπουρανίου πορείας (*v. l.* ὑπουρανίου).

[8] Ph., *Leg. All.* 3:168 f.

[9] Ph., *Gig.* 62; *Agr.* 10. Also Ign., *Trall.* 5:1—2; *Sm.* 6:1; Pol., *Ph.* 2:1.

[10] Cf. the striking example in *P Par.* 574.3042 καὶ σὺ λάλησον ὁποῖον ἐὰν ᾖς ἐπεουράνιον (*sic*) ἢ ἀέριον εἴτε ἐπίγειον εἴτε ὑπόγειον ἢ καταχθόνιον and cf. Deissmann, *LAE*, 261, n. 10. Also *CH, Ascl.* 3.32 b; *Frg.* 26.

[11] II Mac 3:39 κατοικίαν ἐπουράνιον; *EG*, 261, 9 f. δώματ' ἐπουράνια.

[12] *Mart. Pol.* 14.3; *Epil. Mosq.* 4.

food.[13] In *ModGk* it is used of God,[14] and in the pl. (vern.) of heaven,[15] as well as in the usual sense of 'heavenly'.[16]

The word occurs only 2 × in the OT: 1 × in Ps (LXX) 67: 15 of God Himself, and 1 × in Dan (*Th*) 4: 23 (*v.l.* οὐράνιος) of God's ἐξουσία.[17]

In the NT ἐπουράνιος occurs 14 × in various contexts,[18] and 5 × in Eph in the set phrase ἐν τοῖς ἐπουρανίοις.[19]

The applications of the term being many and varied, though always referring to that which is spatially distinct from the earth, it is not possible to ascertain the meaning of the phrase in Eph by pursuing further research into the use of the term in Greek lit. Even the rest of the NT occurrences are not of much help since in Eph we have to do with a formula [20] which is exclusive to it.

A difficult question to decide is whether τοῖς ἐπουρανίοις is masc. or neut. In the NT both forms occur.[21] "This much debated question", says Odeberg, ". . . cannot be decided with any certainty . . . the probability, however, rests with the opinion that the word is meant as a pl. neut.".[22] This view is favoured by most scholars.[23]

With regards to the reference of the phrase there is agreement in general but diversity of opinion in particulars. Alford long ago maintained that a phrase coined for use in this particular Epistle ought to have the same meaning in each one of its occurrences.[24] The meaning sensed is a local one, yet not in a literal but in a metaphorical sense. Robinson says "It is a region of ideas rather than a locality, which is suggested by the vague-

---

[13] Μηναῖον I, I 'Ωδ. 6 ἔθρεψας ψυχὰς πεινώσας τροφῇ τῇ ἐπουρανίῳ. For Patristic references, see *PL*, s. v.

[14] Κάλβος εἰς Πάργαν 16, 3 πάντοτε οἱ ἐπουράνιοι μεγαλόθυμον γένος ὑπερασπίζουν.

[15] Πολίτης, Ἐκλογὴ ἀπὸ Τραγούδια, 4, 1.

[16] No difference is perceived in *ModGk* between οὐράνιος and ἐπουράνιος, cf. also ΔΔ, s. v.

[17] It occurs 4 × more in II, III and IV Mac (noted above) and 1 × as a *v. l.* in IV Mac 11: 3. Of these 7 × in the OT and Apocrypha 3 × have the *v. l.* οὐράνιος.

[18] Jn 3: 12 (unspecified, possibly sc. πράγματα); I Cor 15: 40 (*bis*, σώματα); 48—9 (3 ×, ἄνθρωπος); Phil 2: 10 (πᾶν γόνυ); II Tim 4: 18 (βασιλεία); Heb 3: 1 (κλῆσις); 6: 4 (δωρεά); 8: 5 (unspecified); 9: 23 (unspec.); 11: 16 (πατρίς); 12: 22 (Ἰερουσαλήμ).

[19] I.e. 1: 3, 20; 2: 6; 3: 10; 6: 12.

[20] Mussner, *CAK*, 9, has "formelhaft".

[21] Masc.: I Cor 15: 48—49; Neut.: I Cor 15: 40; Jn 3: 12. The Fem. occurs too, e.g. II Tim 4: 18; Heb 3: 1.

[22] Odeberg, *VU*, 7. If understood as masc. then θεοί, ἄγγελοι, or τόποι should be supplied (Dibelius, 58). The consensus of opinion favours τόποι (e.g. Odeberg, *VU*, 7; Dibelius, 58; Schlier, 45; V. Roon, *AE*, 214; Gnilka, 62).

[23] E.g. Abbott, 5; Odeberg, *VU*, 7; Dibelius, 58; Schlier, 45; V. Roon, *AE*, 215; Gaugler, 27; Barth, I, 78; Bruce, 27; Mussner, *CAK*, 12.

[24] Alford, 70. Similarly Odeberg, *VU*, 7; Schlier, 45 f.; Dibelius, 58; V. Roon, *AE*, 215; Abbott, 5 objects to taking 6: 12 identically with the other occurrences.

ness of the expression" and renders it 'in the heavenly spheres'.[25] V. Roon regards ἐπουράνιοις as a "substantivised adj. (with art.) constituting a categorical indication of concrete phenomena".[26] He produces as parallels Phil 3: 19 (τὰ ἐπίγεια) and Col 1: 16 (τὰ ὁρατὰ καὶ τὰ ἀόρατα) and says that like these "τὰ ἐπουράνια may embrace not only things but also persons or beings".[27]

Of special interest are the studies of Schlier[28] and Odeberg.[29] Schlier, drawing upon apocalyptic material and gnostic cosmological theories, presents the ἐπουράνια as constituted of various heavens, seats of the various powers. The highest place is allocated to Christ and immediately under Him but also in Him is the Church. Outside Him but still in the ἐπουράνια is what the *Asc. Isa* calls the firmament, the seat of the satanic powers.[30] Thus "im Eph Christus, die Kirche, die Äonen, die feindlichen Mächte, ja selbst 'der Herrscher dieser Welt' und die Ungläubigen, die 'Söhne des Ungehorsams' . . . ihren Ort in den ἐπουράνια haben . . .".[31] Schlier then proceeds to offer his demythologised interpretation.[32] In his commentary he develops these views in even clearer existentialistic categories.[33]

Odeberg presents a different interpretation.[34] A basic tenet is that the phrase ἐν τοῖς ἐπουρανίοις is 'stereotypical',[35] and this involves the further

---

[25] P. 20. Similarly Abbott, 5 "as designating the heavenly region"; H. C. G. Moule, *ES*, 50 "heavenly regions". Lightfoot, "The heaven which lies with and about the true Christians". Salmond, 247 appears to endorse Chrysostom and Theodoret's view in taking the phrase as a further description of the spiritual blessing.

[26] *AE*, 215.

[27] *AE*, 215.

[28] *CK*, 1—18, esp. 5—6; and Comm. 45—8.

[29] *VU*, esp. 3—14.

[30] *CK*, 5.

[31] *CK*, 6; also Comm. 45 f.

[32] *CK*, 6, n. 1.

[33] Pp. 46—8. The ἐπουράνια is a transcendental space opening up an unlimited breadth and depth of possibilities for man. It offers man the 'heavens', the heavens of being. However, these heavens are a place of powers. "Die Himmel des Daseins gehen den Menschen als Dimension ihrer und seiner Mächte übermächtig an und fordern ihn durch ihren Geist, z. B. durch den Zeitgeist, zu sich heraus. Das geschieht nicht erst und eigentlich überhaupt nicht durch besondere Aktionen, sondern einfach schon durch ihr Dasein, d. h. durch die bewegende Kraft ihrer sich dem Menschen einräumend aufdrängenden Dimension". (47). Man is faced with an existential decision for the one or the other heaven of his being. In both of them man is ἐν τοῖς ἐπουρανίοις but in Christ Jesus man is also above the heavens and transcends the powers. This is because man is united with the Body of Christ. Etc. etc.

[34] He regards Schlier's thesis as unsatisfactory (*VU*, 14).

[35] *VU*, 7. Dibelius, 58 calls it 'Formel'.

corollary that the phrase has a constant meaning.[36] Like Schlier, he holds that God, Christ and the cosmic powers are situated in the ἐπουράνια. "The highest as well as the lowest regions are included".[37] He refrains, however, from identifying the phrase with ἐν (τοῖς) οὐρανοῖς because in the Eph phrase no contradistinction to ἐπίγεια is perceived, as in the other case.[38] On the contrary "ἐπουράνιος includes that which elsewhere is expressed by that term *and* the term signifying its opposite *viz.* ἐπίγειος".[39] From the point of view of the Church, this phrase, which in itself is not equivalent to ἐν Χριστῷ, is closely bound up with it.[40] He then states the position thus: "By being in Christ — the Body of Christ — the Church is brought in contact with, brought into, exactly the realm, in which Christ is and in which He works. Thus the Church participates in the Divine blessings, is placed together with Christ Jesus in God's presence, is in and with Christ the medium of revelation of the Divine Mystery to all the cosmical powers, and participates in the universal warfare waged by Christ against the cosmical and evil spiritual powers. The author designates this realm as a condition of the Church in Christ by the term ἐπουράνια".[41]

Interesting though Odeberg's interpretation may be, it is, nontheless, unsatisfactory in some respects. To include the ἐπίγεια in the ἐπουράνια, is, to my mind, misplaced. Nor is it possible to say with Odeberg that "spiritual blessing . . . (etc.) are the consequences of the Church's being ἐν τοῖς ἐπουρανίοις",[42] since some of these blessings relate to a time πρὸ καταβολῆς κόσμου (Eph 1:4 f.). Odeberg argues: "The seemingly absurd hypothesis that in Eph ἐπουράνιος includes that which elsewhere is expressed by that term *and* the term signifying its opposite *viz.* ἐπίγειος actually seems to find its support in the fact that earthly man, sc. the believer, whereas expressely not in 'heaven' (6:9), already in his earthly life is in the midst of τὰ ἐπουράνια: 2:2 . . . and 6:12 . . . The blessings conferred upon the believers are not something of the future to the exclusion of the present . . . Hence, we may conclude, the believer, acc. to Eph, is already now in

---

[36] The Eph view of the Universe is, nontheless, dynamic, not static, VU, 5.

[37] VU, 8. Acc. to Mussner, *CAK*, 17, "Er liegt zwischen der transzendenten Gottessphäre mit dem Christusthron als höchster Spitze oben und der Erde unten".

[38] VU, 8 f.

[39] VU, 9.

[40] VU, 13.

[41] VU, 13. For criticism of this see Mussner, *CAK*, 11. Gnilka, 64 ff. thinks the Eph 'Weltbild' is to be appreciated against the background of the development of such views in the Greek world.

[42] VU, 13.

his earthly life ἐν τοῖς ἐπουρανίοις".[43] Thus for Odeberg the ἐπουράνια is different from οὐρανοί and thus, too, the ἐπίγεια is part of it!

It must not escape our attention that we are here dealing with the paradox of Christian language. In ch. 2:1 living Christians who, for all we know, never went through Lazarus' experience, are said to have been 'dead', and in vs. 5 they are said to have been resuscitated. What is meant by the expression ὄντας νεκρούς is made plain by the qualification τοῖς παραπτώμασιν. They were 'dead' not in a sense apprehensible and verifiable in the natural world, but in an other-worldly, 'spiritual', sense. Man is considered on two planes: the earthly, the physical, where life is according to sight (cf. II Cor 5:7), and a higher, spiritual, plane.

The difference at this point between my interpretation and Odeberg's is that whereas Odeberg is obliged by the differentiation he makes between heaven and ἐπουράνιος, to transfer the ἐπίγεια into the ἐπουράνια, I consider man as living similtaneously on two planes, the ἐπίγειον and the ἐπουράνιον. The ἐπουράνια in this view, is, in accordance with lexical usage outside Eph, not different from οὐρανός, and makes up the space in which God, Christ, and the various hosts of cosmic powers dwell.[44]

Τὰ ἐπουράνια is meant locally and stands for that which is above the earth. In it is God's throne, and under this latter is the sphere in which the spiritual world lives and works. Eph 1:3 is understood of the blessings as appertaining to heaven: they have heaven as their source and as their goal, since the blessings, as later named, are to the intent and effect that man should attain his allotted position in heaven.[45] In 2:6 the believers are seated ἐν τοῖς ἐπουρανίοις not in any real sense as yet, but in anticipation by virtue of their being the Body of Christ, Who is Himself seated there, viz. above the principalities and the powers (1:20). In 3:10 the principalities and the powers inhabit the ἐπουράνια and from there exert their malignant influence upon this world. In 6:12 the evil powers are in the ἐπουράνια but 'we' are *not* there! The fight is going on not in the 'heavenlies',[46] but on earth,[47] yet in a 'spiritual' sense. What the author

---

[43] *VU*, 9.

[44] Cf. Rev 12:7—9: καὶ ἐγένετο πόλεμος ἐν τῷ οὐρανῷ . . . καὶ ἐβλήθη ὁ δράκων ὁ μέγας, . . . ὁ καλούμενος διάβολος . . . ὁ πλανῶν τὴν οἰκουμένην ὅλην . . . καὶ οἱ ἄγγελοι αὐτοῦ μετ' αὐτοῦ. This gives a clear picture that Satan and his agents dwell in heaven (=τὰ ἐπουράνια) and from there pursue their activities in leading the world astray. At the same time Satan has access to God and accusses the believers (Rev 12:10; cf. Jb 1:9 ff.). Then, suddenly, he and his emmissaries are hurled down and confined to earth (Rev 12:9—10, 12—3). Cf. also Lk 10:18.

[45] E.g. υἱοθεσία; εἰς ἔπαινον τῆς δόξης αὐτοῦ.

[46] As Schlier would have it.

[47] Cf. 3:1; 6:20. The author suspects that behind his earthly persecutors lie the πνευματικὰ τῆς πονηρίας with their malevolent designs.

means is that 'we' do not fight against 'flesh and blood', i.e. human enemies, but against foes of a higher realm — τὰ ἐπουράνια [48] — so this type of warfare demands not an earthly, physical, armour, but a spiritual one.[49]

One point needs clarification, viz. τὰ ἐπουράνια vis-à-vis οὐρανός. This term occurs in 1:10; 3:15; 4:10 and 6:9. Of these the last instance is theologically unimportant. The first and the second occurrences are important, but pose no problem for our understanding of ἐπουράνιος. The third case, is, nevertheless, difficult, or at least apparently so: ὁ καταβὰς αὐτὸς ἐστιν καὶ ὁ ἀναβὰς ὑπεράνω πάντων τῶν οὐρανῶν, ἵνα πληρώσῃ τὰ πάντα. How can the ἐπουράνια in which Christ is seated (1:20) be identified with οὐρανός, with regard to which Christ is said to be ὑπεράνω? It is a question of reconciling ὑπεράνω πάντων τῶν οὐρανῶν with ἐν τοῖς ἐπουρανίοις.

There is no doubt that Eph, as is the case with other NT books, thinks of several heavens. How many we are never told.[50] A look at a NT concordance makes it clear that οὐρανός is a very comprehensive term: we read of τὰ πετεινὰ τοῦ οὐρανοῦ (Mt 6:26); of antiquity's metereological bulletin (Mt 16:2 f.); of the nations being spread under the skyvault (Ac 2:5), as well as the more theological instances of Christ's ascent into heaven (Ac 1:11; Heb 9:24) of the believers' membership in the heavenly commonwealth (Phil 3:20), a.s.o. It is obvious that οὐρανός has many different senses. It is possible too, that several strata of Heaven are in mind, though not systematically distinguished, or that several heavens are in view. God's throne would be at the highest spot of the highest heaven, and this would go some way in explaining Eph 4:9.

We have, as a matter of fact, more than an analogy in the Epistle to the Hebrews. In 4:14 we have ἀρχιερέα μέγαν διεληλυθότα τοὺς οὐρανούς; in 7:26 Christ is ἀρχιερεύς, ὅσιος, ἄκακος, ἀμίαντος . . . καὶ ὑψηλότερος τῶν οὐρανῶν γενόμενος; and in 8:1 we have ἀρχιερέα, ὃς ἐκάθισεν ἐν δεξιᾷ τοῦ θρόνου τῆς μεγαλωσύνης ἐν τοῖς οὐρανοῖς (the phrase could easily have been ἐν τοῖς ἐπουρανίοις). The same Christ who went *through* the heavens, Who arrived *above* the heavens, is also seated *in* the heavens. I suggest that both Eph 4:9 and Heb 4:14 and 7:26 are merely superlative ways of emphasizing the extremely high position which Christ attained in His

---

[48] Ἐπουράνια is here used in contraposition to αἷμα καὶ σάρκα.

[49] Cf. II Cor 10:3 f. ἐν σαρκὶ γὰρ περιπατοῦντες οὐ κατὰ σάρκα στρατευόμεθα — τὰ γὰρ ὅπλα τῆς στρατείας ἡμῶν οὐ σαρκικὰ ἀλλὰ δυνατὰ τῷ Θεῷ.

[50] II Cor 12:2 speaks of three heavens without implying that there are no more; perhaps the opposite. A plurality of heavens is presupposed in the OT, the Apocrypha and the Pseudepigrapha. A number of the last group of writings give their number as seven: e.g. *Test L.*, 2:7—3:8; *Asc. Isa.*, 6—11; *Chag.* 12. *III Bar.* has five, while II En 3—21 speaks altogether of ten heavens.

exaltation,[51] and that they do not in any way constitute a contradiction to their respective statements that Christ is seated at the right hand of God ἐν τοῖς ἐπουρανίοις/οὐρανοῖς.[52]

In conclusion it may be said that τὰ ἐπουράνια although overlapping with οὐρανός is not completely identical with it. Οὐρανός stretches from the air space where the birds fly and the clouds pour down their rain all the way up to God's very throne, while the ἐπουράνια constitute only the higher layers of this space, from God's throne down to the sphere where the cosmic powers dwell and work. Τὰ ἐπουράνια is thus bound up with the salvation events, and has, in contradistinction to οὐρανός, a *heilsgeschichtlich* import.

B. Ἐν Χριστῷ κτλ.

According to Deissmann (*ICJ*, 75) the phrase ἐν Χριστῷ, ἐν Κυρίῳ κτλ. occurs 196 × in the NT of which 164 × it occurs in Paul.[1] Since the prep. ἐν construed with a pers.name does not figure in Gk. lit., Deissmann's observation is engaging: "Während in der gesamten Gräcität einschliesslich der urchristlichen Literatur ἐν mit persönlichem sing. ein sehr seltene Sprachgebrauch ist, finden wir es bei einem einzigen Autor in einer bestimmten Formel so überaus häufig, dass sich von selbst die Frage erhebt: Wie ist diese Vorliebe des Paulus für das ἐν und zwar gerade in dieser Formel zu erklären? Die Antwort steckt in der Frage: wir haben hier eben einen oder besser *den Lieblingsbegriff der religiösen Sprache des Apostels*" (p. 70). Deissmann thinks of Paul as the originator of what he calls 'Formel', not in the sense that Paul was the first author to couple the prep. ἐν with the sing. of a pers. name, but in the sense that he "*einen ganz neuen terminus technicus schuf*".[2]

Deissmann goes into some trouble to discover the meaning of ἐν, and concludes that its use is a local one, (p. 79) that the pers. name with which ἐν is connected must indicate a living person, (p. 79) and that the ἐν cannot be substituted by διά (p. 80). The phrase ἐν Χριστῷ characterises the relation of the Christian to the living Christ as a locality and must, therefore,

---

[51] I cannot accept Caird's view that this passage deals with Christ's descent at Pentecost (*SE*, 1964, 535—45.

[52] The claim that Christ διῆλθεν τοὺς οὐρανούς and ἀνέβη ὑπεράνω πάντων τῶν οὐρανῶν holds good at least in reference to the many heavens or layers of heaven (those of the birds, of the clouds, of the stars, of the cosmic powers), recognised in the NT, which Christ on His way to the Father must have passed.

[1] I.e. for Deissmann all except Col, Eph, and the Past.

[2] P. 70. Cf. also p. 79 "Der Totaleindruck dieser Stellen bestätigt die These von dem eigentümlich paulinischen Character der Formel: für *solche* Fügungen fehlt es in der vorpaulinischen Literatur durchaus an Analogien".

be rendered with 'in Christ'.[3] Accordingly, "Die Formel ist der technische Ausdruck für den paulinischen Centralgedanken der κοινωνία mit Christus" (p. 82).

The question for Deissmann now becomes: "Ist die Vorstellung des εἶναι ἐν Χριστῷ, im *eigentlichen oder uneigentlichen Sinne zu verstehen?*" (p. 84). Deissmann here avails himself of the phrase ἐν πνεύματι,[4] which he thinks is in "nahe Verwandschaft" (p. 88) with the ἐν Χριστῷ phrase. This gives him the clue. It is impossible to use ἐν in connection with either a living or a dead person, as e.g. 'in Abraham' or 'in Plato' or even of the synoptic Jesus, "Wohl aber 'in' dem pneumatischen lebendigen Christus des Paulus".[5] Thus he concludes that the phrase is to be understood as an "eigentlich räumlich Beziehung" (p. 95) as a "Lokal aufzufassendes Sichbefinden in dem pneumatischen Christus".[6]

This mystical interpretation of Deissmann's has been much criticised, among others, by Bang,[7] Hansen,[8] Büchsel,[9] and Neugebauer (*IC*).

Büchsel thinks the question has two sides: a gramm. one concerning the significance of ἐν, and a christological one pertaining to the view taken of the person of Christ (p. 142). According to him the prep. ἐν — occurring 269 × in the NT — has such a wide variety of uses,[10] that one is not warranted in taking it always locally:[11] "Bei den Verbindung mit ἐν ist gedacht an einen Bereich, in den etwas ist, geschieht usw. Der Bereich kann räumlich, zeitlich, eine Person, eine Gemeinschaft, aber auch ganz abstrakt sein. Ἐν ist ferner in NT vielfach instrumental gebraucht, aber auch kausal und endlich modal" (p. 142). Büchsel rejects Deissmann's claim[12] that ἐν Χριστῷ has always the same meaning.[13] He holds that the problem can be solved only by detailed exegesis of each particular instance.

Büchsel notes that the phrase is used both adjectivally and (mostly) adverbially, (pp. 143 f.) and after surveying 153 instances summarises: "überblickt man die behandelte 153 Stellen, so ergibt sich: ἐν ist in den

---

[3] P. 81. Cf. "Das ungewönliche 'ἐν' ist nur durch ein ungewönliches 'in' korrekt wiederzugeben".

[4] This phrase, acc. to Deissman, occurs in Paul 19 ×, in 15 × of which it is connected with the same specific and basic pauline concept.

[5] P. 88. In objection to this may be mentioned I Cor 15: 22 ἐν τῷ Ἀδάμ.

[6] P. 97. Cf. also p. 98.

[7] *TTs*, 1920, 35—88, 97—128.

[8] *TTs*, 1929, 135—59.

[9] *ZNW*, 1949, 141—58.

[10] Cf. *BAG* s. v. ἐν, "The uses of this prep. are so many-sided, and often so easily confused, that a strictly systematic treatment is impossible".

[11] Büchsel, 142.

[12] Deissmann, *ICJ*, 77.

[13] Büchsel, 143.

meisten instrumental, seltener modal, noch seltener kausal, einigemal lokal im übertragenen Sinne zu verstehen".[14] He then examines 12 more instances which he considers as modal (pp. 150 f.) rejecting their mystical interpretation (pp. 152 f.). The deepest reason for this he finds in the idea that for Paul Christ is and remains primarily Lord and Judge (p. 154). Though Christianity contains a mystical element, one should refrain from calling Paul a mystic, for he is a practical man (Leistungsmensch).[15]

Oepke,[16] writing before Büchsel, thinks along with Deissmann that Paul is probably the creator of this formula. The formula cannot be explained from the Heb. ‫ב‬ nor wholly "In terms of a mystically local conception of 'dwelling in a *pneuma* element comparable to the air' (i.e. the exalted Christ)" as Deissmann would have it.[17] "At root is the view of Christ as a universal personality".[18] This is understood by Oepke not in a mystical way in the current hellenistic sense, but cosmically and eschatologically.[19] He refers to the first and the second Adam (I Cor 15: 22; 45—49; Rm 5: 12—21) and says "Each includes his adherents in and under himself".[20] By baptism the believers are transferred from the sphere of the first Adam to that of the second, and "This underlying spatial concept gives us the true significance of the formula ἐν Χριστῷ Ἰησοῦ and its parallels. Yet here too there is both a local and an instrumental element".[21]

Allan concentrates his discussion[22] on the Eph occurrences of the phrase — a circumstance of particular relevance in this connection — but unfortunately mars his investigation by turning the subject into a pursuit for proofs against the pauline authorship of Eph instead of trying to discover the meaning and use of the phrase. Accordingly, he gives the phrase an instrumental force "predominantly, if not exclusively"[23] and states

---

[14] P. 149. In the course of his examination he too notes that I Cor 15: 22 is against Deissmann's mystical interpretation (p. 145). Nor is Christ a kind of fluid in which Paul is (p. 146).

[15] Pp. 154 ff. On the question as to whether the phrase is a formula Büchsel expresses himself thus: "Am ehesten kann man den Gebrauch des ἐν Χριστῷ usw. in manchem Partien des Eph formelhaft nennen, z. B. 1: 3—14 kehrt es auffalend häufig wieder; öfters für unser Empfinden überflüssig. Das hängt aber auch mit den tiefsten theologischen Absichten des Eph zusammen . . . so dass das ἐν Χριστῷ usw. auch hier nicht eigentlich formelhaft ist" (p. 157).

[16] *TDNT*, II, 541 f.

[17] Deissmann, *ICJ*, 98. J. Weiss *TSK*, 1896, 7—33) and H. Böhlig *NS*, 170—75 do not see any specifically mystical element in Paul and draw a sharper distinction.

[18] *TDNT*, II, 542.

[19] *TDNT*, II, 542.

[20] *TDNT*, II, 542.

[21] *TDNT*, II, 542.

[22] *NTS*, 1958—9.

[23] *NTS*, 1958—9, 59.

repeatedly that the Writer of Eph unable to grasp Paul's deep and rich meaning of the corporate personality uses it merely of God's activity in Christ, and at a popular level.[24] How much Allan has misunderstood the Eph phrase is readily perceived from his preposterus claim that "The Writer of Eph has no such cosmological interests (sc. as Col). He is interested in the unifying work of Christ in the Church, and this reference to 'all things' (in 1: 10) *is not much more than a rhetorical flourish . . . There is no indication that the Writer is thinking of Christ as an all-comprehensive cosmic being*" [25] (Italics mine).

Neugebauer's article,[26] followed by his dissertation,[27] is an examination of the pauline phrase (i.e. excluding from the main discussion Col and Eph). The multiformity of the phrase erects an obstacle to considering it a fast formula, so the term 'Formel' in Neugebauer means no more than 'formula-like'.[28] Neugebauer differentiates between the phrase ἐν Χριστῷ and variants which have *heilsgeschichtliche* associations, and belong to the so-called Indicative, and the ἐν Κυρίῳ phrase which is bound up with the Imperative.[29] Neugebauer thus rejects Deissmann's local, mystical sense of the phrase[30] maintaining that "'in Christus' bedeutet also: bestimmt sein durch das eschatologische Geschehen von Kreuz und Auferstehung, einbezogen sein in diese 'Geschichte'".[31] He appeals with some reservation, among others, to Heidegger (*Sein und Zeit*) in order to define the pauline ἐν in terms of a union of 'Zeitlichkeit und Räumlichkeit'. It is a geschichtlich ἐν "d.h. ein auf Geschehen bezogenes".[32]

With regards to Col and Eph Neugebauer maintains that Col corre-

---

[24] E.g. pp. 58 ff.

[25] P. 58. Cf. his concluding sentence on p. 62: "We may get nearer to the Writer's mind if instead of trying to find in these images profound and subtle theological speculations we are content to find simple and beautiful but rather vague images of the unity of the Church".

[26] *NTS*, 4, 1 (1957—8), 124—38.

[27] *IC*, 1961.

[28] *NTS*, 1957—8, 125 f.; *id. IC*, 20.

[29] Neugebauer is obliged to speak of some insignificant exceptions to this rule in Phlm! (i.e. *NTS*, 1957—8, 132 f.). The ἐν Χριστῷ phrase then is considered soteriologically, christologically, ecclesiologically and in reference to the apostle (*IC*, 65—130; *NTS*, 4 (1957—8), 128 ff.). It should be noted in this connection that Schmauch in his dissertation (*IC*, e.g. pp. 130 ff.) draws a difference between ἐν Χριστῷ and ἐν Χριστῷ Ἰησοῦ as well as between these and ἐν Κυρίῳ.

[30] *NTS*, 1957—8, 137, "Nach allem bisher Gesagten aber dürfte es keinen Zweifel daran geben, das es auf jeden Fall falsch ist, diesem ἐν ein lokales bzw. räumliches Verständnis zu unterschieben".

[31] *NTS*, 1957—8, 132. Cf. p. 138 "Auch der Sinn des ἐν ist also am Geschehen orientiert, so dass, man beinahe sagen möchte: dieses ἐν ist eher zeitlich als räumlich zu verstehen".

[32] *NTS*, 1957—8, 138.

sponds completely to the homologoumena,[33] while Eph, presenting as it does a wide variety of form of this phrase, conforms not wholly but to a great extent to the pauline usage.[34]

The phrase ἐν Χριστῷ and ten other variants occur in the Epistle to the Eph 35 ×,[35] of which 14 × occur in ch. 1, 8 × in ch. 2, and 4 × in ch. 3. With Neugebauer I am unable to regard it a set formula, nevertheless, it must be stated that the prep. is quite loaded in content. This implies that the above discussions, though interesting, are somewhat one-sided — at least if they would be applied to Eph. The favorite 'entweder . . . oder . . .' is not applicable here. The case is rather that Deissmann, Büchsel and Neugebauer are all encountered, and that not simply in different instances of the phrase, but often in one and the same occurrence.[36] The phrase so far from having been 'thinned down' (Allan), has actually 'swollen out'! Allan deprecates that "'in Christ' is no longer for this Writer the formula of incorporation into Christ, but has become the formula of God's activity through Christ".[37] As a matter of fact Eph goes further than what is usually considered the pauline concept of incorporation. So far from lacking this feature,[38] Eph even states that the Church is part of Christ, i.e. His body or His fulness.[39] And so far form

---

[33] *NTS*, 1957—8, 136.

[34] *IC*, 179 ff. The imperative is founded upon the Indicative.

[35] I.e. including 1: 9. These are: ἐν Χριστῷ 3 ×; ἐν τῷ Χριστῷ 3 ×; ἐν Χριστῷ Ἰησοῦ 6 ×; ἐν τῷ Χριστῷ Ἰησοῦ 1 ×; ἐν τῷ Ἰησοῦ 1 ×; ἐν αὐτῷ 4 ×; ἐν αὐτῷ 1 ×; ἐν ᾧ 7 ×; ἐν τῷ ἠγαπημένῳ 1 ×; ἐν Κυρίῳ 7 ×; ἐν τῷ Κυρίῳ Ἰησοῦ 1 ×.

[36] Though occasionally one aspect may be more outstanding than another. The local element, for example, is seen in 2: 13 where ἐν Χριστῷ is contrasted to χωρὶς Χριστοῦ ('outside Christ'). *BAG*, χωρίς, gives the sense of 'outside' only in connection with a thing, e.g. σῶμα in II Cor 12: 3. But this is the whole question. In II Cor 12: 3 χωρίς is contrasted to ἐν locally, precisely as in Eph 2: 11—13 where the Gentiles once were outside Christ, but now are in Christ. If χωρίς is understood as 'without' it cannot constitute a contrast to ἐν in the sense of 'in', and again if ἐν Χριστῷ is understood instrumentally, the point of ἦτε τῷ καιρῷ ἐκείνῳ χωρὶς Χριστοῦ is completely lost. The most straightforward sense is obtained with the rendering "You were at that time outside Christ . . . but now in Christ . . .".

[37] *NTS*, 1958—9, 59. Actually Eph knows to use διά c. gen. to express instrument (cf. 1: 5). 'God's activity i Christ' is for Allan a less exalted matter than incorporation into Christ: ". . . here is a writer who takes a pauline formula that in depth and intensity of religious meaning is beyond the experience of most, and so uses it that our attention is fixed steadily on Christ as the centre of Christianity, and having our attention so fixed we may begin to realise the possibility of an intimacy with Christ beyond our normal experience. Thus Paul's marvellous insight into the meaning of Christ for life is made more readily available at the level of the ordinary Christian, even if in the process something of Paul's intensity and power is lost" (pp. 59 f.).

[38] Cf. 2: 15 ἐν αὐτῷ (with *GNT*) εἰς ἕνα καινὸν ἄνθρωπον.

[39] πλήρωμα taken in the active sense. Cf. 5: 29 ff.

implying divine activity alone (if that were indeed to be disparaged as Allan implies), Eph takes us to the very *adytum* of the divine counsels, where 'we' are 'blessed', 'elected', and '(pre)destined' in indissoluble union with Christ before the creation of the world. Eph views the believer as being in Christ before his very existence. That is, Eph so far from failing to take up the in-being of the believer in Christ following the Christ event, actuall alleges that that was his position already in God's counsel, in God's μυστήριον.

The phrase ἐν Χριστῷ indicates at once the 'sphere' in which the believer was placed by election in God's counsel (e.g. 1:4) and is now positioned following the saving event (e.g. 1:1; 2:22), the 'sphere' in which all of God's decisions were made (e.g. 1:9; 3:11) and have now in the Christ event taken effect (e.g. 1:9 f.), and the 'sphere' in which the salvific event with its resultant blessings become realisable for the believer (e.g. 1:7). And finally, ἐν Χριστῷ indicates also the 'sphere' in which the believer shall have his future existence (e.g. 1:10).[40]

C. Ἀρχαί, ἐξουσίαι, κτλ.

In the ἀνακεφαλαιώσασθαι τὰ πάντα ἐν τῷ Χριστῷ which forms the climax of the Eulogy, are included not only the Church (as belonging to τὰ ἐπίγεια),[1] but also certain spiritual potentialities enumerated in the ensuing prayer.[2] The importance of the powers for the Eph *mysterion* is borne out also by the fact that Eph has relatively much to say about them and further from the observation that the real antithesis in Eph is not between the Jews and the Gentiles, but between the Church and the powers.

Naturally, the discussion has centered around the origin, nature, activity and Christ-inflicted defeat of these powers. The possibility for Babylonian, Persian, Greek and gnostic influence on this terminology has been explored.[3] It is not the purpose of this excursus to examine in detail these

[40] See also Reid, *TT*, 1960, 353—65.

[1] Acc. to Rm 8:19 ff. the natural creation shall also be redeemed. Τὰ πάντα here is to be understood, in light of 3:9, of the whole creation. So Mussner, *GE*, 61.

[2] I.e. 1:21 f. Also in 2:2; 3:10; 6:12. Col 1:16 substitutes θρόνοι for δυνάμεις. The designation παντὸς ὀνόματος ὀνομαζομένου (1:21) is most probably not a specific class of cosmic beings along with the ἀρχαί (as Schlier, *MG*, 11 supposes; Mussner, *CAK*, 18 rightly excludes it from his enumeration of the powers), but merely a way of saying "And any other order of beings that may be recognised". Bietenhard, *TDNT*, V, 242—83 does not discuss this use of ὄνομα. The phrase πνευματικὰ τῆς πονηρίας (6:12), despite the prep. πρός is probably not a separate class either, but a closer definition of the ἀρχάς, ἐξουσίας, κοσμοκράτορας, i.e. they are evil spiritual beings, being antithetical to αἷμα καὶ σάρκα.

[3] E.g. by Bultmann, *TNT*, I, 172—83; Macgregor, *PP*; Caird, *PP*, 1—15; Whiteley,

issues, but merely to draw attention to a possible source which has occupied only peripheral place in scholarly discussion.[4] This is the book of Dan, in particular ch. 7.[5] The Aram. text uses the term שׁלְטָן 7 ×. The LXX translates it always with ἐξουσία and has ἀρχή once in a phrase which is missing in the Aram. (sc. 7: 27). Th has 3 × ἐξουσία and 4 × ἀρχή. The relevant passages are:

Th	LXX
11 ἀνῃρέθη τὸ θηρίον . . .	
12 καὶ τῶν λοιπῶν θηρίων ἡ ἀρχὴ μετεστάθη, καὶ μακρότης ζωῆς ἐδόθη αὐτοῖς . . .	καὶ τοὺς κύκλῳ αὐτοῦ ἀπέστησε τῆς ἐξουσίας αὐτῶν . . .
13 ἐθεώρουν . . . καὶ ἰδοὺ . . . ὡς υἱὸς ἀνθρώπου ἐρχόμενος . . .	
14 καὶ αὐτῷ ἐδόθη ἡ ἀρχὴ καὶ ἡ τιμή, καὶ ἡ βασιλεία, καὶ πάντες οἱ λαοί, φυλαί, γλῶσσαι δουλεύσουσιν αὐτῷ· ἡ ἐξουσία αὐτοῦ ἐξουσία αἰώνιος, ἥτις οὐ παρελεύσεται, καὶ ἡ βασιλεία αὐτοῦ οὐ μὴ διαφθαρήσεται.	καὶ ἐδόθη αὐτῷ ἡ ἐξουσία, καὶ πάντα τὰ ἔθνη τῆς γῆς κατὰ γένη καὶ πᾶσα δόξα λατρεύουσα αὐτῷ· καὶ ἡ ἐξουσία αὐτοῦ ἐξουσία αἰώνιος, ἥτις οὐ μὴ ἀρθῇ, καὶ ἡ βασιλεία αὐτοῦ, ἥτις οὐ μὴ φθαρῇ.
26 καὶ τὸ κριτήριον ἐκάθησε καὶ τὴν ἀρχὴν μεταστήσουσι τοῦ ἀφανίσαι καὶ τοῦ ἀπολέσαι ἕως τέλους	καὶ τὴν ἐξουσίαν ἀπολοῦσι
27 καὶ ἡ βασιλεία καὶ ἡ ἐξουσία καὶ ἡ μεγαλωσύνη τῶν βασιλέων τῶν ὑποκάτω παντὸς τοῦ οὐρανοῦ ἐδόθη ἁγίοις ὑψίστου, καὶ ἡ βασιλεία αὐτοῦ βασιλεία αἰώνιος, καὶ πᾶσαι αἱ ἀρχαὶ αὐτῷ δουλεύσουσι καὶ ὑπακούσονται	καὶ τὴν βασιλείαν καὶ τὴν ἐξουσίαν καὶ τὴν μεγαλειότητα αὐτῶν καὶ τὴν ἀρχὴν πασῶν τῶν ὑπὸ τὸν οὐρανὸν βασιλειῶν ἔδωκε λαῷ ἁγίῳ ὑψίστου βασιλεύσαι βασιλείαν αἰώνιον, καὶ πᾶσαι (αἱ) ἐξουσίαι αὐτῷ ὑποταγήσονται καὶ πειθαρχήσουσιν αὐτῷ.

There are some apparent problems here. According to vv. 11—14 the ἀρχή/ἐξουσία of the wild-beasts is taken away from them and given to one like a Son of Man, but acc. to vv. 26—7 it is given to the saints of the Most High. The situation is further complicated by the different senses deduced from the LXX and Th respectively. Acc. to the LXX the ἐξουσία etc. are given to λαῷ ἁγίῳ ὑψίστου, whereas acc. to Th they are given to the ἁγίοις ὑψίστου. The significance of this difference is that whereas in Th

EP; Lee, DP; Foerster, TDNT, II, 571—74; V. Roon, AE, 216—27; M. Barth, I, 170—83; Schlier, MG; Mussner, CAK, 9—39. Galloway, CC, 24 ff.; Rupp, PP; Berkhof, CM.

[4] Cf. e.g. Whiteley, EP; Macgregor, PP; Caird, PP; M. Barth, I, 170 ff.

[5] My attention was drawn to it in connection with the investigation of the background of mysterion (cf. ch. V).

the ἀρχαί are made subject to the ὑψίστου (or to an understood Son of Man), in the LXX they are subjected to the λαῷ ἁγίῳ ὑψίστου.[6] But such an understanding ill-fits the special sense of ἀρχαί/ἐξουσίαι here, which is different from the sense obtaining in all of the previous occurrences. Previously it was used in the abstract sense of power, authority, rule; here it is a personification of spiritual potentates. This claim is corroborated from 10: 13, 20, 21 where Persia, Greece and the Jews are said to have an ἄρχων over them. The ἄρχων of the Jews is Michael and the presumption is that the ἄρχοντες of Persia and Greece are similarly invisible powers who are the real or ultimate rulers behind their earthly counterparts.[7] And since it is impossible that such invisible powers should be made subject to the λαῷ ἁγίῳ, the *Th* text is considered as more consistent with itself and as best fitting the sense demanded for ἀρχαί/ἐξουσίαι here.

This conclusion is moreover borne out by the exegesis of the passages in question. In vv. 11—14 the power of the wild-beasts is given to the Son of Man, whereas in vv. 26—27 it is the power of the kings τῶν ὑποκάτω παντὸς τοῦ οὐρανοῦ that is given to the saints. I am suggesting here that the power of the wild-beasts and the power of the kings under heaven are not precisely identical. The concept of wild-beast in Dan does not stand for any one king, but rather for the sum total of power as exercised by several earthly rulers who are inspired and directed by an invisible ἄρχων. The wild-beast thus coincides more nearly with the ἀρχαί/ἐξουσίαι of vs. 27 and the ἄρχων of 10: 13, 20, but is not merely this; it consists of the complex made up of the invisible guardian, the human delegate and the entire state mechanism that makes possible the execution of the ἄρχων's projects, in short, the *genius* of a nation. There are consequently three related concepts in Dan 7: the invisible ἄρχων or ἀρχαί/ἐξουσίαι of 2: 27b, the human ruler, and the two together when in collusion are described as a wild-beast. When this complex mechanism is in operation the wild-beast is active; when it breaks down the wild-beast is slain.[8]

Accordingly when it is said that the wild-beast is slain we are to understand that the ἄρχων has been robbed of his power, that his underling,

---

[6] This agrees with the Aram. which is followed by the *RSV* and *NEB*.

[7] Cf. Deut (LXX) 32: 8 f; Jud 15: 31 f.; Targum of Ps — Jon on Gen 11: 7 f. Further cf. Charles *Late Heb Test N* 8: 4 ff. This belief has its Greek counterpart in e.g. Pl., *Leg.*, 4, 713 Cff.; 5, 738 D, who calls the guardians of cities δαιμόνια. Cf. also Pl., *Symp.* 202 E and with this *Test D* 6: 2. See further Mertens, *DLTTM*, 100—2.

[8] Scholars have noted that in the NT the concept of ἀρχαί, ἐξουσίαι etc. also fluctuates in meaning between that of cosmic powers and earthly potentates, and sometimes a double reference is intended, cf. e.g. Macgregor, *PP*, 22 ff.; Cullmann, *CT*, 193; M. Barth, I, 174; Foerster, *TDNT*, II, 573; Caird, *PP*, 17, 23. etc. Delling, *TDNT*, I, 489.

the king, has become powerless and that the system has collapsed. The apocalyptic Daniel views the changes in world affairs on a plane far above the earthly, in the region where the fight is going on between the *genii*, the gardian spirits of nations.

This much we can deduce from vv. 11—14. Now as the power of these invisible ἄρχοντες was visibly exercised in a given nation, by the same token the power of the Son of Man has its visible manifestation in the rule of the ἁγίοις ὑψίστου (vs. 27).[9] The ἀρχή which the saints obtain in vs. 27 is, strictly speaking, not the ἀρχή/ἐξουσία of the wild-beasts or the invisible ἄρχοντες (this ἀρχή/ἐξουσία in a supreme sense is given only to the Son of Man), but the delegated ἀρχή/ἐξουσία of the kings ὑποκάτω παντὸς τοῦ οὐρανοῦ. Thus Persia and Greece are now succeeded by the ἁγίοις ὑψίστου and their ἄρχοντες by the Son of Man.

Vs. 27 changes its reference by the sing. αὐτοῦ and refers not to the λαῷ (as the LXX does) but to the ὑψίστου or to the Son of Man. It is to Him that the ἀρχαί (note, no longer wild-beasts, for the concept of wild-beast, consisting of the ἄρχων+king+nation, is now dissolved!), i.e. the invisible powers, are made subject and not to the saints.

The concepts interwoven with the idea of βασιλεία or rule bring to the surface certain similarities with the NT and Eph in particular. The saints rule by virtue of the assumption of unlimited power by the Son of Man. Their rule is a sharing in His victory (implied), power and dominion, after the persecution they endured, and this is made possible by the relation they bear to Him. But the evil powers who were deprived of their dominion are made subject to the Most High or to the Son of Man. The relevance of this for Eph is only too evident. Following His victory over the powers Christ is seated on His regal throne ὑπεράνω πάσης ἀρχῆς καὶ ἐξουσίας etc. All things are put in subjection (ὑπέταξεν, the same word as in Dan (LXX) 7:27) under His feet. The phrase τὰ πάντα is of more limited reference than in 1:10, where it includes all created things in heaven and on earth. Here it is a quotation of Ps 8 and is used as a comprehensive term for the various powers.[10] While the Church is part of τὰ πάντα at 1:10, it is expressly excluded at 1:22. This is proved by the careful terminology chosen. At 1:10 it is a question of *anakephalaiōsis*,[11] which can

---

[9] The equation of the Son of Man with the saints of the Most High is unnecessary and misses the point of delegated authority as well as the parallelism. See Montgomery, *Dan* 317—24 for the three main understandings of the Son of man figure. Cf. Delling, *TDNT*, I, 488 who differentiates between the One like a son of Man and the saints of the Highest.

[10] Cf. V. Roon, *AE*, 217 f.

[11] It has been observed that though ἀνακεφαλαιώσασθαι is derived from κεφάλαιον, the author uses the vb, with reference to Christ's being the κεφαλή of the Church. The

certainly apply to the Church too, whereas in 1:22 it is a question of subjugation, which while befitting enemy powers, is totally unfit to express the amiable relationship obtaining between Christ and the Church, i.e. κεφαλή — σῶμα. Now inasmuch as the Church is Christ's body she is seated with Him above the powers and shares in His victory and rule, yet the powers, as in Dan 7 are directly put under Him but not under the Church.

This deep-going similarity between Dan 7 and Eph concerning the powers becomes all the more striking when related to the affinities discovered with regards to the use of *mysterion* in the two works (in ch. V).

It is not claimed here that all the Eph terminology about the powers stems from Dan 7,[12] but that within its limits the terminology of Dan lies at the basis for the more extended terminology of Eph and the NT. Indeed, Dan seen in the light of other Jewish writings [13] some of which it probably influenced, and which illustrate the trend of development,[14] seems to provide a sufficiently sure basis for the NT teaching on the powers. Though certain details may have been filled in from extraneous sources,[15] the basics, nevertheless, as has been occasionally recognised,[16] appear to have sprung upon Jewish soil.[17]

---

term is general enough to be applicable to the Church as well as to the powers and the rest of creation. Cf. Schlier, *TDNT*, III, 681—82; Staerck, *RAC*, I, 411—14; Schlier, 62 ff.; Maurer, *HES*, 164 ff.; Hanson, *UC*, 125 f.

[12] Besides ἀρχαί, ἐξουσίαι and ἄρχων (cf. Eph 2:2), in *Th* and the *LXX* we have several other words, abstract as yet in Dan, which are personified in the NT, e.g. θρόνοι (7:9, cf. Col 1:16); κύριον/κυριεύειν (2:38, cf. κυριότης, Eph 1:21); δόξαν (2:37, cf. II Pt 2:10; Jd 8). See also ch. V, 4, iv and cf. Delling, *TDNT*, I, 483.

[13] E.g. *Asc. Isa.* 1:4; 2:2 "authorities and powers" (Flemming—Duensing in (Hennecke—Schneemelcher) *NTA*, II, 644 f.; *Test L* 3:8 θρόνοι καὶ ἐξουσίαι; *I En* 61:10 "all the angels of powers and all the angels of principalities" (Charles in *AP*, II, 227); *II En* (A) 20:1 "archangels, incorporeal forces, and dominions, orders and goverments, cherubim and seraphim, thrones . . ." (Forbes and Charles in *AP*, II, 441); *Apoc. Soph.* (*apud* Cl. Al., *Str.*, V, 11) ἀγγέλους καλουμένους κυρίους; *Test. Sol.* 20:15 ἀρχαὶ καὶ ἐξουσίαι καὶ δυνάμεις; 8:2 στοιχεῖα κοσμοκράτορες τοῦ σκότους. See also Michaelis, *TDNT*, III, 913 f. For rabbinic material see Foerster, *TDNT*, II, 572, and *Str-B*, II, 552.

[14] Part of this material is post-NT.

[15] See authors listed in Note 3.

[16] E.g. Foerster, *TDNT*, II, 572; Caird, *PP*, 5 ff.; M. Barth, I, 172.

[17] Cf. Caird, *PP*, esp. ch. 1, who traces these ideas back to various OT books.

BIBLIOGRAPHY

I. TEXTS

The abbreviated forms show how these works are met with in the text.

1. Biblical Texts and Translations

MT=*Biblia Hebraica*, ed. R. Kittel *et al.*, Stuttgart, [13]1962.

LXX=*Septuaginta*, ed. A. Rahlfs, 2 Vols., Stuttgart, 1935, rp. 1971.

LXX=*Vetus Testamentum Graecum auctoritate Societatis Litterarum Gottinensis editum*, Vol. XVI, 2 Susanna, Daniel, Bel et Draco ed. J. Ziegler, Göttingen, 1954.

GNT=*The Greek New Testament*, (UBS) ed. K. Aland, M. Black, C. M. Martini, B. M. Metzger, A. Wikgren, Stuttgart, [2]1968.

KΔ=Η ΚΑΙΝΗ ΔΙΑΘΗΚΗ, ed. E. Nestle, G. D. Kilpatrick, London, [2]1958.

Nest=*Novum Testamentum Graece*, ed. E. Nestle, K. Aland, Stuttgart, [25]1963.

WH=*The New Testament in the Original Greek*, ed. B. F. Westcott, F. J. A. Hort, London, 1896.

AV=*The Authorized Version*, 1611.

BKÖ=*Bibelkommissionens Bibelöversättning* (in progress): Ephesians, Uppsala, 1976.

JB=*The Jerusalem Bible*, N.Y. 1966.

JBPh=*The New Testament in Modern English*, Trans. J. B. Philips, London, 1960.

Luth=*Die Bibel oder die ganze Heilige Schrift des Alten und Neuen Testaments* nach der deutschen Übersetzung Martin Luthers, Stuttgart, 1960.

ModGk=A Modern Greek Translation of the NT: Η ΚΑΙΝΗ ΔΙΑΘΗΚΗ, Trans. by four Professors at the Univ. of Athens, Athens, 1967.

NEB=*The New English Bible*, Oxford, Cambridge, 1970.

RV=*The Holy Bible. The Revised Version*, Oxford, rp. of 1881 ed.

RSV=*The Holy Bible. The Revised Standard Version*, N.Y. 1952.

TEV=*Today's English Version*, N.Y. 1960.

UW=*Das Neue Testament*, übers. U. Wilckens, Hamburg, 1970.

2. Pseudepigrapha

AP=*The Apocrypha and Pseudepigrapha of the Old Testament* in English, 2 Vols., Vol. II, ed. R. H. Charles, Oxford, 1913.

Black, AHG=*Apocalypsis Henochi Graece* (PVTG, III, 1—44), Leiden, 1970.

Box, *IV Ez*=G. H. Box, *IV Ezra* in AP, II, pp. 542—624.

Charles, *II Bar*=R. H. Charles, *II Baruch*, in AP, II, 470—526.

— *I En*=*I Enoch* in AP, II, pp. 163—281.

— *Late Heb Tes N*=*Translation of a Late Heb. Test. of Naphtali, which contains fragments of the Original Testament*, in AP, II, 361—3.

— *TTP*=*The Greek Versions of the Testaments of the Twelve Patriarchs, etc.* ed. R. H. Charles, Oxford, 1908, rp. G. Olms, 1960.

Denis, *FP=Fragmenta Pseudepigraphorum quae supersunt Graeca.* Una cum Historicum et Auctorum Judaeorum Hellenistarum Fragmentis (PVTG, III, 46—246), collegit et ordinavit A.-M. Denis, Leiden, 1970.

Flemming, *BEÄT=Das Buch Henoch: Äthiopischer Text,* in TU, ed. J. Flemming, Leipzig, 1902.

— -Duensing, *Asc Isa=The Ascension of Isaiah* in *NTA,* II, 642—63, ed. J. Flemming, H. Duensing, Eng. Tr., London, 1965.

Forbes-Charles, *II En=Second Enoch, or the Book of the Secrets of Enoch* (=Slavonic Enoch), in *AP,* II, 425—69.

Kautzsch, *AP=Apokryphen und Pseudepigraphen des Alten Testaments,* Tübingen, 1900.

McCown, *Test S=The Testament of Solomon:* edited from MSS at Mt Athos, Bologna, Holkham Hall, Jerusalem, London, Milan, Paris and Vienna. With Intro., in UNT, 9, Leipzig, 1922.

Milik, *BE=The Books of Enoch:* Aramaic Fragments of Qumran Cave 4, ed. by J. T. Milik with the collaboration of M. Black, Oxford, 1976.

Morfill, *Retr.=Retranslation of the Second Recension* (S^2) *of the Slavonic Version* by Prof. Morfill, in Charles, *TTP,* 263—94.

NTA=New Testament Apocrypha, ed. E. Hennecke, W. Schneemelcher, Eng. Trans. ed. R. McL. Wilson, 2 Vols., London, 1965.

Oesterley, *II Es=*W.O.E. Oesterley, *II Esdras,* 1933.

Phoc.=(Pseudo-) *Phocilides,* in Denis, *FP,* above.

*Sent.=*Sententiae.

Violet, *AEB=Die Apocalypsen des Esra und des Baruch:* in Deutschen Gestalt (GCS), 2 Vols., ed. B. Violet, Leipzig, 1910—24.

3. Rabbinic, Josephus and Philo

Blackman, *Mishn=Mishnayoth,* ed. Ph. Blackman, 6 Vols., London, 1951—55.

Jos.=*Josephus,* ed. H. St. John Thackeray—R. Marcus, 9 Vols. (LCL), London, 1926—65.

*Ant.=*Antiquitates Judaicae.

*Ap.=*contra Apionem.

Ph.=*Philo Judaeus,* ed. F. H. Colson, G. H. Whitaker, *et al.,* 10 Vols. (LCL), London, 1929—53.

*Agr.=*De agricultura

*Cher.=*De Cherubim.

*De Imm.=*Deus immutabilis.

*Gig.=*De gigantibus.

Leg. All.=Legum Allegoriarum.

*Migr. Abr.=*De migratione Abrahami.

4. Qumran.

DJD=Discoveries in the Judaean Desert, 6 Vols., many eds., Vol. I: Qumran Cave 1, ed. D. Barthelemy, J. T. Milik, Oxford, 1955, Vols. 2—6, Oxford, 1961—66.

Lohse, *TQ=Die Texte aus Qumran:* Hebräisch und Deutsch, etc. Darmstadt, 1964.

Vermes, *DSSE=The Dead Sea Scrolls in English,* Tr. G. Vermes, 1968.

5. Hermetica, Gnosticism, etc.

CH = Corpus Hermeticum. Texte établi par A. D. Nock et traduit par A. J. Festugière, 4 Vols., Paris, 1926—54.

Ascl. = Asclepius.

Exc. = Excerpta.

Frg.Div. = Fragmenta Diversa.

Poem. = Poemandres.

Tract. XIII = Tractate XIII.

Lidzbarski, *JBM = Das Johannesbuch der Mandäer*, ed. M. Lidzbarski, 2 Vols., Giessen, 1905—15.

Naasene Tractate (Sermon) = Hipp., *Phil*, V, 7—9, in Refutatio omnium Haeresium, GCS (= ΒΕΠ, Vol. 5), ed. P. Wendland, Leipzig, 1916.

Reitzenstein, *Poem* = Poemandres. Studien zur griechisch-ägyptischen und früh-christlichen Literatur, Leipzig, 1904.

Schmidt, *KGS = Koptisch-gnostische Schriften*, Vol. 1: Die Pistis Sophia, Die beiden Bücher des Jeu, Unbekanntes Altgnostisches Work (GCS), ed. C. Schmidt, Leipzig, 1905.

6. Christian Authors

Ambrst. = *Ambrosiaster*, in *MPL*, Vol. 17, 45—508.

Ast. = *Asterius*, in *MPG*, Vol. 40, 324 ff.

Hom. = Homiliae.

Athenag. = *Athenagoras*, in *Die ältesten Apologeten*, ed. E. Goodspeed, Göttingen, 1914.

Chrysostom = Τοῦ ἐν ʽΑγίοις Πατρὸς ἡμῶν ΙΩΑΝΝΟΥ ἀρχιεπισκόπου Κωνσταντινουπόλεως τοῦ ΧΡΥΣΟΣΤΟΜΟΥ ʽΥπομνήματα εἰς τὰς πρὸς Γαλάτας καὶ ʼΕφεσίους ʼΕπιστολάς, Oxford, 1852.

Clem. Al. = *Clemens Alexandrinus*, On Protrepticus and Paedagogus ed. O. Stählin, U. Treu, Berlin, [3]1972 and on Stromateis, ed. O. Stählin, L. Früchtel (GCS), Berlin, 1960—70 (= ΒΕΠ, Vol. 7, 17—361 and Vol. 8, pp. 11—316).

Paed. = Paedagogus.

Protr. = Protrepticus.

Str. = Stromateis.

I Clem. = *I Clement* in *Apostolic Fathers*, 2 Vols., ed. K. Lake (LCL), London, 1970.

Did. = *Didache*, in *Apostolic Fathers*, 2 Vols., ed. K. Lake (LCL), London, 1970.

Diogn. = *Diognetus*, in *Apostolic Fathers*, 2 Vols., ed. K. Lake (LCL), London, 1970.

Ephr. = *Ephraim Syrus*, in *Ephraem Syri Opera*, ed. S. J. Mercati, Rome, 1915.

Epil. Mosq. = *Epilogus Mosquensis*, in *die apostolische Väter*, ed. F. X. Funk, K. Bihlmeyer, Tübingen, [2]1956.

Eus. = *Eusebius*, ed. K. Mras (GCS), 2 Vols., Berlin, 1954—56.

Praep. Ev. = Praeparatio Evangelica.

Greg. Naz. = *Gregorius Nazianzenus*, in *MGP*, Vol. 35, pp. 395—1252 and Vol. 36, pp. 11—664.

Herm. = *Hermas*, in *Apostolic Fathers* (LCL), ed. K. Lake, London, 1970.

Vis. = Visio.

Hipp = *Hippolytus*, on Philosophoumena, ed. P. Wendland, Refutatio omnium haeresium (GCS = ΒΕΠ Vol. 5) and on Ad Noetum in ΒΕΠ Vol. 6., Athens, 1956.

Ad Noet. = Ad Noetum.

Phil = Philosophoumena.

Ign.=*Ignatius*, in *Apostolic Fathers*, ed. K. Lake (LCL), London, 1970.

Eph.=Ephesians.

Magn.=Magnesians.

Sm.=Smyrnaeans.

Trall.=Trallians.

Iren.=*Irenaeus*, in *MPG*, Vol. 7, pp. 437—1224.

Ad. Haer.=Adversus Haereses.

Just.=*Justinus Martyrus*, in ΒΕΠ, Vol. 3, pp. 162—338 and Vol. 4, pp. 11—235.

Ap.=Apology.

EOO=Ἔκθεσις 'Ορθῆς 'Ομολογίας (Doubted).

Tr.=Dialogue with Trypho the Jew.

Lact.=*Lactantius*, in *MPL*, Vol. 6, pp. 1017—94.

Div. Inst. ep.=Divinarum Institutionum epitome.

Mart. Pol.=*Martyrdom of Polycarp*, in *Die apostolischen Väter*, ed. F. X. Funk, K. Bihlmeyer, Tübingen, ²1956.

Pel.=*Pelagius*, in *MPL*, Vol. 30, pp. 823—42.

Ad Eph.=In Epistolam ad Ephesios.

Pol.=*Polycarpus*, in *Apostolic Fathers*, ed. K. Lake (LCL), London, 1970.

Ph.=Philippians.

Sync.=*Syncellus* in M. Black, *AHG*, above.

Syn.=*Synesius*, in *MPG*, Vol. 66, pp. 1111—1164.

Dion.=Dionysus.

Tert.=*Tertullianus*, in *MPL*, Vol. 1, Ad Nationes, pp. 559—608.

Ad Nat.=Ad Nationes.

Theod.=*Theodorus*, *MPG*, Vol. 66, Ad Ephesios, pp. 911—22.

Ad Eph.=Ad Ephesios.

Theodt.=*Theodoretus*, in *SC*, Vol. 57, ed. P. Canivet, Paris, 1958.

Ther.=Therapeuticus.

Theoph.=*Theophylactus*, in *MPG*, Vol. 124, pp. 1031—1138.

Ad Eph.=Ad Ephesios.

7. Greek Inscriptions, Papyri. etc.

BGU=*Berliner griechische Urkunden* (Ägyptische Urkunden aus den Königlichen Museen zu Berlin), Berlin, 1895—.

CAF=*Comicorum Atticorum Fragmenta*, ed. T. Kock, 3 Vols., Leipzig, 1880—88.

Dieterich, *ML*=A. Dieterich, *Eine Mitrasliturgie*, Leipzig, ³1923.

DMG=*Documents in Mycenaean Greek*, by M. Ventris—J. Chadwick, Cambridge, 1956.

EG=*Epigrammata Graca*: ex Lapidibus Conlecta, ed. G. Kaibel, Berlin, 1878.

IG=*Inscriptiones Graeca*e, concilio et auctoritate Academiae litterarum Borussicae editae, ed. maior 15 Vols. (incomplete), Berlin, 1873—1939.

*IG*²=*Inscriptiones Graecae*, as above, ed. minor, Berlin, 1913—.

Jacoby, *MP*=F. Jacoby, *Das Marmor Parium*, 1904.

OF=*Orphicorum Fragmenta*, ed. O. Kern, Berlin, 1922.

OGIS=*Orientis Graeci Inscriptiones Selectae*, ed. W. Dittenberger, Leipzig, 1903—5.

OH=*Orphei Hymni*, ed. G. Quandt, Berlin 1955.

Oliver, *Hesp*, 1935=J. Oliver, "Greek Inscriptions", Hesp. 4, 1935, pp. 5—107.

P Flor=*Papyri Florentini*, documenti publici e privati dell eta romana e bizantina, 3 Vols.: I, ed. G. Vitelli, 1906; II, ed. D. Comparetti, 1908—11; III, ed. G. Vitelli, 1915, Milan.

PGM=Papyri Graecae Magicae. Die griechischer Zauberpapyri, ed. K. Preisendanz, Leipzig, 1928—31.

PML=Papyrus Magica musei Lugdunensis Batavi, ed. A. Dieterich (in JKPh, Suppl. 16), pp. 793—818, Leipzig, 1888.

P Par 574=The Paris Magical papyrus, ed. C. Wessely, in Denkschriften der philosophisch-historischen Classe der Kaiserlichen Akademie der Wissenschaften zu Wien, Bd. 36, Wien, 1888, pp. 27—208.

SGUÄ=Sammelbuch griechischer Urkunden aus Ägypten, 12 Vols., ed. F. Preisigke, *et al.*, Strassburg, etc. 1915—75.

SIG=Sylloge Inscriptionum Graecarum, ed. W. Dittenberger, Leipzig, ³1915—24.

8. Ancient Authors

Ach. Tat.=*Achilles Tatius*, ed. S. Gaselee (LCL), London, 1917, rp. 1961.

Ael.=*Aelianus*, ed. R. Herscher, 2 Vols., Leipzig, 1864—66, rp. 1917.

Aes.=*Aeschylus*, ed. G. Murray (OCT), Oxford, ²1966; H. J. Mette, Berlin, 1959.

　　Frg.=Fragmenta.

　　Pr.=Prometheus Vinctus.

　　Sept. Th.=Septem contra Thebes.

Alex. Tr.=*Alexander Trallianus*, ed. T. Puschmann, 2 Vols., Vienna, 1878, rp. 1963.

And.=*Andocides*, ed. D. MacDowell (On the Mysteries) Oxford, 1962.

　　Myst.=De Mysteriis.

Anecd. Gr.=Anecdoda Graeca, ed. I. Bekker, 3 Vols., Berlin, 1814—21.

Apolld.=*Apollodorus*, ed. J. G. Frazer, 2 Vols. (LCL), London, 1921.

　　Bib.=Bibliotheca.

　　Epit.=Epitome.

Apoll. Rh. =*Apollonius Rhodius*, ed. R. C. Seaton (OCT), Oxford, 1900.

　　Argon.=Argonautica.

Ap.=*Apuleius*, ed. (On Book XI) J. G. Griffiths, Apuleius of Madaurus: *The Isis Book*, Metamorphoses, Book XI (EPRO), Leiden, 1975.

　　Met.=Metamorphoses.

Ar.=*Aristophanes*, ed. F. W. Hall—W. M. Geldart, 2 Vols. (OCT), Oxford, 1906—7.

　　Av.=Aves.

　　Ec.=Ecclesiazusai.

　　Eq.=Equites.

　　Nu.=Nubes.

　　Pax=Pax.

　　Pl.=Plutos.

　　Ra.=Ranae.

　　Th.=Thesmophoriazusai.

　　Vez.=Vespae.

Aret.=*Aretaeus*, in *CMG*, ed. K. Hude, Vol. II, Leipzig, 1923.

　　CD=Χρονίων νούσων θεραπευτικόν.

Aristl.=*Aristoteles*, ed. (On *EN*) I. Bywater, 1913; (On *Rh*) D. Ross, 1959 (OCT), Oxford.

　　EN=Ethica Nicomachea.

　　Rh.=Rhetorica.

Ath.=*Athenaeus*, ed. G. Kaibel, 3 Vols. (BT), Leipzig, 1887—90.

Batr.=Batrachomyomachia, ed. H. G. Evelyn-White (LCL), London, 1914, rp. 1970.

Dem.=*Demosthenes*, ed. S. H. Butcher, 3 Vols. (OCT), Oxford, 1903—31.

Din=*Dinarchus*, ed. F. Blass (BT), Leipzig, 1888.

Diod. Sic.=*Diodorus Siculus*, ed. F. Vogel et C. T. Fischer, 5 Vols. (BT), Leipzig, 1888—1906, rp. 1964.

Diog. Laert.=*Diogenes Laertius*, ed. H. S. Long, 2 Vols. (OCT), Oxford, 1963.

Epict.=*Epictetus*, ed. W. A. Oldfather, 2 Vols. (LCL), London, 1925—28, rp. 1961—6.

   Diss.=Dissertation.

Et. Mag.=*Etymologicum Magnum*, ed. T. Gaisford, Oxford, 1848, rp. 1962.

Eun.=*Eunapius*, ed. I. Giangrande, 1956.

   Vit. Soph.=Vitae Sophistarum.

Eur.=*Euripides*, ed. G. Murray, 3 Vols. (OCT), Oxford, 1913.

   Ba.=Bacchae.

   Frg.=Fragmenta.

   Hec.=Hecuba.

   Hel.=Helena.

   IT=Iphegenia Taurica.

   Rh.=Rhesus.

   Supp.=Supplices.

Firm. Mat.=*Firmicus Maternus*, ed. A. Pastorino, Firenze, 1956.

   Err. Prof. Rel.=De errore profanarum religionum.

Gal.=*Galenus*, in *CMG* ed. C. G. Kühn, Leipzig, 1821—33.

Hdt.=*Herodotus*, ed. H. R. Dietsch—H. Kallenberg, 2 Vols. (BT), [2]1887.

Heracl.=*Heraclitus*, ed. W. H. S. Jones (in Vol. IV of Hippocrates, LCL), London, 1953.

Hdn.=*Herodianus*, ed. C. Stavenhagen (BT), Leipzig, 1922, re. 1967.

Hes.=*Hesiodus*, ed. R. Merkelbach—M. L. West (OCT), Oxford, 1970.

   Th.=Theogonia.

Hesych.=*Hesychius*, ed. M. Schmidt, 5 Vols., Jena, 1858—68; K. Latte, 3 Vols., Hauniae, 1953—66 (in Progress).

Hom.=*Homerus*, ed. D. B. Munro—T. W. Allen, 5 Vols. (OCT), Oxford, 1911—20.

   Il.=Iliad.

   Od.=Odyssey.

Hor.=*Horatius*, ed. E. C. Wickham—H. W. Garrod (OCT), Oxford, [2]1912.

   Od.=Odae.

Hymn=*The Homeric Hymn to Demeter*, ed. H. G. Evelyn-White (with Hesiod, LCL), London, 1970.

Hymn ad Pl.=*Orphic Hymn to Pluto*, in *OF*, ed. O. Kern, Berlin, 1922.

Iambl.=*Iamblichus*, ed. G. Parthey, Berlin, 1857; Pistelli (BT), Leipzig, 1888.

   Myst.=De Mysteriis.

   Protr.=Protrepticus.

Isocr.=*Isocrates*, ed. G. B. Norlin—Larue Van Hook (LCL), London, 1928—45 rp. 1961.

   De Big.=De Bigis.

   Pan.=Panegiricus.

Lib.=*Libanius*, ed. R. Foerster, 12 Vols. (BT), Leipzig, 1903—27.

   Plethr.=Plethrum.

Liv.=*Livius*, ed. B. O. Foster—E. T. Sage—F. G. More—A. C. Schlesinger, 14 Vols. (LCL), London, 1935—59.

Long.=*Longinus*, ed. A. O. Prickard (OCT), Oxford, 1947.

   ΠΥ=Περὶ Ὕψους.

Luc.=*Lucianus*, ed. A. M. Harmon—K. Kilburn—M. D. Macleod, 8 Vols. (LCL), London, 1913—61.

   D Deor.=Dialogi Deorum.

   Demon.=Demonax.

Herm.=Hermotimus.

Lex.=Lexiphanes.

Pseudol.=Pseudologista.

Salt.=De Saltatione.

Lys.=*Lysias*, ed. K. Hude (OCT), Oxford, 1912, rp. 1960.

Meleag.=*Meleager*, (in *Anthologia Palatina c. Planudea*) ed. H. Stadtmüller, 3 Vols. (BT), Leipzig, 1894—1906.

Men.=*Menander*, in *CAF*, Vol III, ed. T. Kock, Leipzig, 1880—8.

Inc.=Fabula incerta.

Men. Prot.=*Menander Protector*, in *Historici Graeci Minores*, ed. L. Dindorf (BT), Leipzig), 1870—1.

Mnes.=*Mnesimachus*, in *CAF*, Vol. II, ed. T. Kock, Leipzig, 1880—8.

Mosch.=*Moschus* (Bucolicus), in *Bucolici Graeci*, ed. A. S. F. Gow (OCT), Oxford, 1952.

Paus.=*Pausanias*, ed. W. H. S. Jones—H. A. Ormerod—R. E. Wycherley, 5 Vols. (LCL), London, 1918—35, and on *Attica* N. Παπαχατζη, ΠΕΠ, see main Bibliography for details.

Philst.=*Philostratus*, ed. F. C. Conybeare, 2 Vols. (LCL), London, 1912, rp. 1960.

Vit. Ap.=Vita Apollonii.

Pin.=*Pindarus*, ed. M. Bowra (OCT), Oxford, ²1947.

Ol.=Olympian Odes.

Pyth.=Pythian Odes.

Frg.=Fragmenta.

Pl.=*Plato*, ed. J. Burnet, 5 Vols (OCT), Oxford, ²1905—15.

Ap.=Apologia.

Euthd,=Euthydemus.

Gor.=Gorgias.

Leg.=Leges.

Men.=Meno.

Phd.=Phaedo.

Phdr.=Phaedrus.

Pol.=Politicus.

Res.=Respublica.

Soph.=Sophista.

Symp.=Symposium.

Tht.=Theaetetus.

Tim.=Timaeus.

Plut.=*Plutarchus*, ed. LCL (many eds.), London. Vols. IV, IX, 1916—20, rp. 1959.

Alc.=Alcibiades.

Demetr.=Demetrius.

Is-Os=Isis et Osiris.

Mor.=Moralia.

Vit.=Vitae Parallellae.

Frg.=Fragmenta.

Procl.=*Proclus, In Platonis Timaeum Commentarii*, ed. E. Diels, 3 Vols. (BT), Leipzig, 1899—1906.

Tim.=Timaeum Commentarii.

Ps-Hom.=*Pseudo-Homeric*, see *Batrochomyomachia*.

Ps-Lys.=*Pseudo-Lysias*, ed. same as for Lysias.

Sch.: Ar.=*Scholia in Aristophanem*, ed. W. J. W. Koster, Groningen, 1960 ff.

Sch.: Soph.=*Scholia in Sophoclis Tragoedias Vetera*, ed. P. N. Papageorgius (BT), Leipzig, 1888.

Sop.=*Sopater*, in *Rhetores Graeci*, ed. Ch. Waltz, Stuttgart, 1832—6.

Soph.=*Sophocles*, ed. A. C. Pearson (OCT), Oxford, 1928, rp. 1971.

Aj.=Ajax.

Ant.=Antigone.

OC=Oedipus Coloneus.

OT=Oedipus Tyrannus.

Tr.=Trachiniae.

Sor.=*Soranus* (Medicus), ed. V. Rose (BT), Leipzig, 1882.

Gyn.=Gynaeciorum.

Stob.=*Stobaeus, J.*, ed. C. Wachsmuth—O. Hense, 5 Vols., Berlin, 1884—1912, rp. 1958.

Ecl.=Eclogae.

Str.=*Strabo*, ed. H. L. Jones, 8 Vols (LCL), London, 1917—32, rp. 1959—60.

Suet.=*Suetonius*, ed. J. C. Rolfe, 2 Vols (LCL), London, 1914, rp. 1965.

Ne.=Nero.

Sui.=*Suidas*, in *Lexicographi Graeci*, ed. A. Adler, 5 Vols., 1967—71.

Them.=*Themistius*, ed. L. Spengel, 2 Vols., Leipzig, 1866.

Theocr.=*Theocritus*, ed. A. S. F. Gow, 2 Vols., Cambridge, ²1952.

Id.=Idyll.

Thuc.=*Thucidides*, ed. H. S. Jones, 2 Vols. (OCT), Oxford, ²1942, rp. 1966.

Xen.=*Xenophon*, ed. E. C. Marchant, 5 Vols. (OCT), Oxford, 1900—20, rp. 1961—70.

Cyrop.=Cyropaedia.

Hell.=Hellenica.

II. LITERATURE AND WORKS OF REFERENCE

The following abbreviations preceding the = mark show exactly how the various works are cited in the text. Commentaries on Eph are cited by the name of the author alone; for all other biblical commentaries an abbreviation of the biblical book is given. Books are cited by the main initials of their title, while articles are cited by an abbreviation of the journal and the year of publication.

Abbott=T. K. Abbott, *A Critical and Exegetical Commentary on the Epistles to the Ephesians* . . . (ICC), Edinburgh, ⁴1922.

— Col=*A Critical and Exegetical Commentary on the Epistles to the . . . Colossians* (ICC), Edinburgh, ⁴1922.

Alford=H. Alford, *The Greek Testament*: with a critically revised text: a digest of various readings: marginal references to verbal and idiomatic usage: prolegomena: and a Critical and Exegetical Commentary, 4 Vols., Cambridge, ⁴1865.

Allan=J. A. Allan, *The Epistle to the Ephesians*. Introduction and Commentary (TBC), London, 1959.

— *NTS*, 1958—9="The 'in Christ' Formula in Eph.", *NTS*, 5, 1958—9, pp. 54—62.

Althaus, *Rm*=P. Althaus, *Der Brief an die Römer* (NTD), Göttingen, 1965.

Anderson-Scott, *CAP*=C. A. Anderson-Scott, *Christianity according to St. Paul*, Cambridge, 1927, repr. 1966.

Andresen, *ZNW*, 1965=C. Andresen, "Zum Formular frühchristlicher Gemeindebriefe", *ZNW*, 56, 1965, pp. 233—59.

Anrich, *AM*=G. Anrich, *Das antike Mysterienwesen in seinem Einfluss auf das Christentum*, Göttingen, 1894.

170

Arvedson, *MC*=T. Arvedson, *Das Mysterium Christi*. Eine Studie zu Mt 11: 25—30, Uppsala, 1937.

Audet, *SE*, 1959=J. P. Audet, "Literary Forms and Contents of a Normal Εὐχαριστία in the First Century", *SE*, 1, 1959, pp. 643—62.

BAG=W. Bauer—W. F. Arndt—F. W. Gingrich, *A Greek-English Lexicon of the New Testament and Other Early Christian Literature*, Chicago, Cambridge, 1957.

Bang, *TTs*, 1920=J. P. Bang, "Var Paulus 'Mystiker'?", *TTs*, 1920, pp. 35—88; 97—128.

Barrett, *1C*=C. K. Barrett, *A Commentary on the First Epistle to the Corinthians*, London, 1968.

— *Past*=*The Pastoral Epistles* (NCB), Oxford, 1963.

— *Rm*=*A Commentary on the Epistle to the Romans* (BNTC) London, 1962.

Barth, I,=M. Barth, *Ephesians*. Introduction, Translation, and Commentary, 2 Vols. (AB), N.Y., 1974.

BDF=F. Blass—A. Debrunner—R. W. Funk, *A Grammar of the New Testament and other Early Christian Literature*. With Supplementary Notes by A. Debrunner, Revised and Translated by R. W. Funk, Chicago, 1961.

BDR=F. Blass—A. Debrunner—F. Rehkopf, *Grammatik des neutestamentlichen Griechisch*. Bearbeitet von F. Rehkopf, 14., völlig neubearb. u. erweit. Auflage, Göttingen, 1976.

Beasley-Murray, *BNT*=G. R. Beasley-Marray, *Baptism in the New Testament*, London, 1962.

B—C, *TWG*=J. Beekman—J. Callow, *Translating the Word of God*, Grand Rapids, 1974.

Behm, *TDNT*, I=J. Behm, Art. αἷμα, αἱματεκχυσία, *TDNT*, I, pp. 172—7.

Bengel, *Gn*=J. A. Bengel, *Gnomon Novi Testamenti*, Berlin, ²1855.

Benoit, *ET*=P. Benoit, "Leib, Haupt und Pleroma in den Gefangenschaftsbriefen" in *Exegese und Theologie*, pp. 246—79, Düsseldorf, 1965.

— *PQ*="Qumran and the New Testament" in *PQ*, pp. 1—30.

Berkhof, *CM*=H. Berkhof, *Christus en de Machten*, Nijkerk, 1952.

Bertram, *TDNT*, IX=G. Bertram, Art. φρήν etc., in *TDNT*, IX, pp. 220—35.

Beyer, *TDNT*, II=H. W. Beyer, Art. εὐλογέω etc., pp. 754—65.

Bieder, *MCM*=W. Bieder, *Das Mysterium Christi und die Mission*. Ein Beitrag zur missionarischen Sakramentalgestalt der Kirche, Zürich, 1964.

— *TZ*, 1955="Das Geheimnis des Christus nach dem Epheserbrief", *TZ* 11, 1955, pp. 329—43.

Bietenhard, *TDNT*, V=H. Bietenhard, Art. ὄνομα etc., in *TDNT*, V, pp. 242—83.

Bingham-Kolenkow, *II Bar*=A. C. Bingham-Kolenkow, *An Introduction to II Baruch*, 53, 56—74: Structure and Substance (mimeographed Harv. Diss.), 1971.

Blass, *GrNT*=F. Blass, *Grammar of NT Greek*. Transl. by H. St. John Thackeray, London, ²1905.

Boers, *NTS*, 1975—6=H. Boers, "The Form Critical Study of Paul's Letters: I Thessalonians as a Case Study", *NTS*, 22, 1975—6, pp. 140—158.

Boobyer, *TGG*=G. H. Boobyer, *Thanksgiving and the Glory of God in Paul*, Leipzig, 1929.

Bornkamm, *Apo.*=G. Bornkamm, "Lobpreis, Bekenntnis und Opfer" in *Apophoreta*, Fs. für E. Haenchen, (BhZNW), pp. 46—63, Berlin, 1964.

— *TDNT*, IV=Art. μυστήριον. μυέω, *TDNT*, IV, 802—28.

Bousset, *KC*=W. Bousset, *Kyrios Christos*, Göttingen, ²1921, rp. Nashville, 1970.

Bowker, *JTS*, 1974=J. W. Bowker, "Mystery and Parable: Mark IV. 1—20", *JTS*, 25, 1974, 300—17.

Brown, *ET*=R. E. Brown, "Second Thoughts. X. The Dead Sea Scrolls and the New Testament, *ET*, 78, 1966, pp. 19—23.
— *SB*=*The Semitic Background of the Term 'Mystery in the New Testament'*, Phil. 1968.
Bruce=F. F. Bruce, *The Epistle to the Ephesians*, London, 1961, rp. 1968.
— *BEQT*=*Biblical Exegesis in the Qumran Texts*, London, 1960.
— *Col*=*Commentary on the Epistle to the Colossians* (NICNT), Grand Rapids, 1957, rp. 1970.
— *Rm*=*The Epistle of Paul to the Romans*, (TNTC), 1963.
— *SC*="Jesus and the Gospels in the Light of the Scrolls" in *SC*, pp. 70—82.
— *STDSS*=*Second Thoughts on the Dead Sea Scrolls*, London, ²1966.
— *TRQT*=*The Teacher of Righteousness in the Qumran Texts*, London, 1957.
Brugmann, *ECG*=K. Brugmann, *Elements of Comparative Grammar of the Indogermanic Languages*, (Eng. Tr. Wright) 1895.
Büchsel, *TDNT*, IV=F. Büchsel. Art. ἀπολύτρωσις, in *TDNT*, IV, pp. 351—56.
— *ZNW*, 1949="'In Christus' bei Paulus", *ZNW*, 42, 1949, pp. 141—58.
Bultmann, *TDNT*, VI=R. Bultmann, *TDNT*, VI, Art. πείθω etc., pp. 1—11.
— *TNT*=*Theology of the New Testament*, 2 Vols., London, 1965.
Burton, *MT*=E. D. Burton, *Syntax of the Moods and Tenses of the NT Greek*, Edinburgh, ³1909.
Böhlig, *NS*=H. Böhlig, 'Εν Κυρίῳ, *Neutestamentliche Studien für G. Heinrici*, (UNT, 6), pp. 170—75, Leipzig, 1914.
Caird, *PP*=G. B. Caird, *Principalities and Powers*, A. Study in Pauline Theology, Oxford, 1956.
— *Rev*=*A Commentary on the Revelation of St. John the Divine*, (BNTC), London, 1966.
— *SE*, 1964="The Descent of Christ in Eph. 4: 7—11", *SE*, 2, 1964, pp. 535—45.
K. Callow, *DC*=R. Callow, *Discourse Considerations on Translating the Word of God*, Grand Rapids, 1974.
Cambier, *Bib.*, 47, 1966=J. Cambier, "Le Grand Mystère concernant le Christ et son Eglise, Eph 5: 22—33", *Bib*, 47, 1966, pp. 43—90.
— *ZNW*, 1963="La Bénédiction d'Ephésiens 1: 3—14", *ZNW*, 54, 1963, pp. 58—104.
Caragounis, *NovT*, 1974=C. C. Caragounis, "'Οψώνιον: A Reconsideration of its Meaning", *NovT*, 16, 1974, pp. 35—57.
Cerfaux, *NTS*, 1956=L. Cerfaux, "La connaissance des secrets du Royaume", *NTS*, 2, 1956, pp. 238—49.
— *RLC*, I="Influence des Mystères sur le judaïsme alexandrin avant Philon" in *Recueil Lucien Cerfaux*, I, Louvain, 1954.
— *SacPag* II="L'influence des 'Mystères' sur les Epitres de s. Paul aux Colossiens et aux Ephésiens", *Sacra Pagina* II, 1959, pp. 373—79.
Chadwick, *DLB*=J. Chadwick, *The Decipherment of Linear B*, Cambridge, ²1967.
Chafer, *ELDC*=L. S. Chafer, *The Ephesian Letter Doctrinally Considered*, Findlay, Ohio, 1959.
Champion, *BD*=L. G. Champion, *Benedictions and Doxologies in the Epistles of Paul*, Oxford, 1934.
Charles, *Rev*=R. H. Charles, *A Critical and Exegetical Commentary on the Revelation of St. John*, (ICC), 2 Vols., Edinburgh, 1920.
— *II Bar*=*II Baruch* in *AP*, II, pp. 470—526.
Clemen, *EMÄC*=C. Clemen, *Der Einfluss der Mysterien Religionen auf das Älteste Christentum*, Giessen, 1913.

172

Clinton, *SOEM* = K. Clinton, *The Sacred Officials of the Eleusinian Mysteries*, 1974.

Colpe, *JUK* = C. Colpe, "Zur Leib — Christi — Vorstellung im Epheserbrief", in *Judentum, Urchristentum, Kirche*, (BhZNW), pp. 172—87, Fs. für J. Jeremias, Berlin, 1964.

— *RS* = *Die Religionsgeschichtliche Schule*, (FRLANT N. F. 60), Göttingen, 1961.

Conzelmann = H. Conzelmann, *Der Brief an die Epheser* (NTD), Göttingen, [14]1976.

— *Kol* = *Der Brief an die Kolosser* (NTD), [14]1976.

— *TDNT*, IX = Art. χαίρω etc. in *TDNT*, IX, pp. 359—76, 387—415.

Coppens, *PQ* = J. Coppens, "'Mystery' in the Theology of St. Paul and its parallels at Qumran", in *PQ*, pp. 132—58.

— *SE*, 1973 = "The Spiritual Temple in the Pauline Letters and its Background", *SE*, 6, 1973, pp. 53—66.

Coutts, *NTS*, 1957—8 = J. Coutts, "Ephesians 1:3—14 and I Peter 1:3—12" *NTS*, 4, 1957—8, pp. 115—27.

Crowther, *ET*, 1970 = C. Crowther, "Works, Work and Good Works", *ET*, 81, 1970, pp. 166—71.

Cullman, *CT* = O. Cullman, *Christ and Time. The Primitive Christian Conception of Time and History*, London, 1962.

Dahl, *ALC* = N. A. Dahl, "Das Geheimnis der Kirche nach Eph 3:8—10" in *Zur Auferbauung des Leibes Christi*, pp. 63—75. Fs. für D. P. Brunner z. 65 Gbrtg., ed. E. Schlink—A. Peters, Kassel, 1965.

— *JP* = "Cosmic Dimensions and Religious Knowledge", in *Jesus und Paulus*, pp. 57—75, Fs. für Kümmel, eds. E. E. Ellis—E. Grässer, Göttingen, 1975.

— *STK*, 1945 = "Dopet i Efeserbrevet", *STK*, 21, 1945, pp. 85—103.

— *TZ*, 1951 = "Adresse und Prooemium des Epheserbriefes" *TZ*, 7, 1951, pp. 241—64.

Davies, *PRJ* = W. D. Davies, *Paul and Rabbinic Judaism*, London, [2]1955.

— *SNT* = "Paul and the Dead Sea Scrolls: Flesh and Spirit", in *SNT* ed. Stendahl, N.Y., 1957.

ΔΔ = Δ. Δημητράκου, Μέγα Λεξικὸν ὅλης τῆς Ἑλληνικῆς Γλώσσης, Ἀθῆναι, 1933—53, rp. 1964.

Debrunner, *TB* = A. Debrunner, "Grundsätzliches über Kolometrie im NT", *TB*, 1962, pp. 231 ff.

Decharme, *EM* = P. Decharme, Ἑλληνικὴ Μυθολογία, 2 Vols. (Trans. fr. the French of 1879), Athens, 1965.

Deden, *ETL* = D. Deden, "Le 'Mystere' Paulinien", *ETL*, 13, 1936, pp. 405—42.

Deichgräber, *GC* = R. Deichgräber, *Gotteshymnus und Christushymnus in der frühen Christenheit* (SUNT, 5), Göttingen, 1967.

Deissmann, *BS* = G. A. Deissmann, *Bible Studies*, Edinburgh, 1901.

— *ICJ* = *Die Formel 'in Christo Jesu'*. Teil II, Diss. Marburg, 1892.

— *LAE* = *Light from the Ancient East*, rp. Grand Rapids, 1965 ([4]1922).

Delling, *TDNT*, I = G. Delling, Art. ἄρχω etc. in *TDNT*, I, pp. 478—99.

— *TDNT*, VI = Art. πλήρης etc. in *TDNT*, VI, pp. 283—311.

Deubner, *AF* = L. Deubner, *Attische Feste*, Berlin, 1959. ([1]1932).

— *WEM* = "Zum Weihehaus der eleusinischen Mysterien", in *Abhandlungen der Deutschen Akademie der Wissenschaften zu Berlin*, Jhrg. 1945—6, 2, 1948, pp. 2—19.

Dewailly, *SEÅ*, 1966 = L.-M. Dewailly, "Den 'förtegade' hemligheten, Rom xvi. 25", *SEÅ*, 31, 1966, pp. 114—21.

De Wette, *EH* = W. M. L. De Wette, *Kurzgefasstes Exegetisches Handbuch zum Neuen Testament. Epheserbrief*, Leipzig, 1847.

Dibelius, *Kol-Eph-Ph* = *An die Kolosser, Epheser, an Philemon* (HNT), Tübingen, 1953.

Dieterich, *ME*=A. Dieterich, *Mutter Erde. Ein Versuch über Volksreligion*, Leipzig, Berlin, ³1925.

— *ML=Eine Mitrasliturgie*, Leipzig, 1903, ³1923.

Dodd, *Rm*=C. H. Dodd, *The Epistle to the Romans* (MNTC), London, 1932.

Doty, *LPC*=W. G. Doty, *Letters in Primitive Christianity*, Phila., 1973.

Drury, *JTS*, 1973=J. Drury, "Reexamination of Parable and Allegory in Mk", *JTS*, 24, 1973, pp. 367—79.

Dugmore, *ISDO*=C. W. Dugmore, *The Influence of the Synagogue upon the divine Office*, London, 1944—45.

Dunn, *BHS*=J. D. G. Dunn, *Baptism in the Holy Spirit*, London, 1970.

Dupont, *Gn*=J. Dupont, *Gnosis*, Paris, 1949.

Elbogen, *JG*=J. Elbogen, *Der jüdische Gottesdienst in seiner geschichtlichen Entwicklung*, Frankfurt/Main, ²1924.

Elliger, *SHK*=K. Elliger, *Studien zum Habakuk-Kommentar vom Toten Meer,* (BHTh) Tübingen, 1953.

Ellis, *PRI*=E. E. Ellis, *Paul and his Recent Interpreters*, Grand Rapids, 1961.

— *PUOT=Paul's Use of the Old Testament*, London, 1957.

Ernst, *PPC*=J. Ernst, *Pleroma und Pleroma Christi*. Geschichte und Deutung eines Begriffs der paulinischen Antilegomena (BU), Regensburg, 1970.

Farnell, *CGS*=L. R. F. Farnell, *The Cults of the Greek States*, 5 Vols., Oxford, 1886—1909.

FBK=P. Feine—J. Behm—W. G. Kümmel, *Introduction to the New Testament*, 14th rev. ed., trans. A. J. Mattill, Jr., Nashville, 1966.

Feuillet, *CS*=A. Feuillet, *Le Christ Sagesse de Dieu d'après les épîtres pauliniennes*, Paris, 1966.

Fischer, *TA*=K. M. Fischer, *Tendenz und Absicht des Epheserbriefes*, (FRLANT), Göttingen, 1973.

Flemington, *NTDB*=W. F. Flemington, *The New Testament Doctrine of Baptism*, London, 1948.

Flowers, *ET*, 1926—7=H. J. Flowers, "Pauls's Prayer for the Ephesians: a Study of Eph 1: 15—23", *ET*, 38, 1926—7, pp. 227—33.

Flusser, *ADSS*=D. Flusser, "The Dead Sea Scrolls and pre-Pauline Christianity", in *Aspects of the Dead Sea Scrolls* (SH), eds. C. Rabin—Y. Yadin, Jerusalem, 1958.

Foerster, *NTS*, 1958—9=W. Foerster, "Εὐσέβεια in den Pastoralbriefen", *NTS*, 5, 1958—9, pp. 213—8.

— *TDNT*, II=Art. ἔξεστιν etc. in *TDNT*, II, pp. 560—75.

Fohrer, *TDNT*, VII=G. Fohrer, Art. σοφία etc. in *TDNT*, VII, pp. 476—96.

Foucart, *ME*=P. Foucart, *Les Mystères d'Eleusis*, Paris, 1914.

Foulkes=F. Foulkes, *The Epistle of Paul to the Ephesians* (TNTC), London, 1963.

Frisk, *GEW*=H. Frisk, *Griechisches etymologisches Wörterbuch*, 3 Vols., Heidelberg, 1960—72.

Fuller, *NTC*=R. H. Fuller, *The Foundations of New Testament Christology*, 1965, rp. 1976.

Funk, *LHWG*=R. W. Funk, *Language, Hermeneutic, and Word of God*, N.Y., 1966.

Furumark, *Eran*, 1954=A. Furumark, "Ägäische Texte in griechischer Sprache", *Eran*, 52, 1954, pp. 18—60.

Galloway, *CC*=A. D. Galloway, *The Cosmic Christ*, N.Y., 1951.

Gaugler=E. Gaugler, *Der Epheserbrief* (ANS, 6), Zürich, 1966.

Geldenhuys, *Lk*=N. Geldenhuys, *Commentary on the Gospel of Luke* (NICNT), Grand Rapids, 1951, rp. 1968.

Gibbard, StEph=S. M. Gibbard, "The Christian Mystery", in StEph, pp. 97—120.

Gibbs, Bib, 1975=J. G. Gibbs, "The Cosmic Scope of Redemption according to Paul", Bib, 1, 1975, pp. 13—29.

— CR=J. G. Gibbs, Creation and Redemption: A study in Pauline Theology, Leiden, 1971.

Gnilka=J. Gnilka, Der Epheserbrief (HTKNT, 10:2), Freiburg, Basel, Wien, 1971.

— BZ, 1971="Das Kirchenmodell des Epheserbriefes", BZ, 15, 1971, pp. 161—84.

— ZJ="Christus unser Friede: ein Friedens-Erlöserlied in Eph 2:14—7", in Die Zeit Jesu, Fs. für H. Schlier, Freiburg, 1970.

Goodspeed, ME=E. J. Goodspeed, The Meaning of Ephesians, Chicago, 1933.

Goodwin, SMT=W. W. Goodwin, Syntax of the Moods and Tenses of the Greek Verb, London, 1889.

Grant, Gnost=R. M. Grant, Gnosticism. A Source Book of Heretical Writings from the Early Christian Period, N.Y., 1961.

Griffiths, IB=J. G. Griffiths, Apuleius of Madauros. The Isis Book (Metamorphoses, Book XI), (EPRO 39), Leiden, 1975.

Grosheide, 1C=F. W. Grosheide, Commentary on the First Epistle to the Corinthians (NICNT), Grand Rapids, 1953, rp. 1968.

Grundmann, PQ=W. Grundmann, "The Teacher of Righteousness of Qumran and the Question of Justification by faith in the Theology of the Apostle Paul", in PQ, pp. 85—114.

Guthrie, NTI: PE=D. Guthrie, New Testament Introduction: The Pauline Epistles, London, ²1968.

Hamilton, HSEP=N. Q. Hamilton, The Holy Spirit and Eschatology in Paul, Edinburgh, 1957.

Hammer, JBL, 1960=P. L. Hammer, "A Comparison of κληρονομία in Paul and Ephesians", JBL, 79, 1960, pp. 267—72.

Hansen, TTs, 1929=M. Hansen, "Omkring Paulus-Formel 'in Christus Jesus'", TTs, 10, 1929, pp. 135—59.

Hanson, UC=S. Hanson, The Unity of the Church in the New Testament. Colossians and Ephesians (ASNU 14), Uppsala, 1946.

Harder, PG=G. Harder, Paulus und das Gebet, Gütersloh, 1936.

Harrison, CR, 1914=J. E. Harrison, "The Meaning of the Word Τελετή", CR, 28, 1914, pp. 36—8.

— PGR=Prolegomena to the Study of Greek Religion, ²1908.

Hartman, PI=L. Hartman, Prophecy Interpreted. The Formation of some Jewish Apocalyptic Texts and of the Eschatological Discourse Mark 13 Par. (CB:NTS 1), Lund, 1966.

— SEÅ, 1974="Some Remarks on I Cor 2:1—5", SEÅ, 39, 1974, pp. 109—20.

Hauck, TDNT, VI=F. Hauck, Art. περισσεύω etc. in TDNT, VI, pp. 58—63.

Headlam=see Sanday—Headlam.

Hendriksen=W. Hendriksen, New Testament Commentary. Exposition of Ephesians, Grand Rapids, 1967, rp. 1975.

Hennecke—Schneemelcher, NTA=see NTA.

Hering, 1C=J. Hering, The First Epistle of St. Paul to the Corinthians, Transl. A. W. Heathcote—P. J. Allcock, London, 1966.

Hodge=C. Hodge, A Commentary on the Epistle to the Ephesians, Grand Rapids, rp. 1966.

Houlden, SE, 1973=J. L. Houlden, "Christ and Church in Ephesians", SE, 6, 1973, pp. 267—73.

HR=E. Hatch—H. A. Redpath, *A Concordance to the Septuagint and Other Greek Versions of the Old Testament.* 3 Vols., Oxford, 1897—1900.

IEE=Ἱστορία τοῦ Ἑλληνικοῦ Ἔθνους, Vol. I, 1970; Vol. II, 1971; Vol. III, 1973, etc., Ἀθῆναι,

Innitzer, *ZKT*, 1904=Th. Innitzer, "Der Hymnus in Eph. 1: 3—14", *ZKT*, 28, 1904, pp. 612—21.

Jannaris, *HGG*=A. N. Jannaris, *An Historical Greek Grammar*, rp. Hildesheim, 1968.

Jeremias, *LG*=G. Jeremias, *Der Lehrer der Gerechtigkeit*, Göttingen, 1963.

Jewett, *ATR*, 1969=R. Jewett, "The Form and Function of the Homiletic Benediction", *ATR*, 11, 1969, pp. 18—34.

Johansson, *STK*, 1940=N. Johansson, "Τὸ Μυστήριον τῆς Βασιλείας τοῦ Θεοῦ" (in Dannish), *STK*, 16, 1940, 3—38.

Jones, *StEph*=C. P. M. Jones, "The Calling of the Gentiles" in *StEph*, pp. 76—88.

Kaminka, *BEEA*=A. Kaminka, *Beiträge zur Erklärung der Esra-Apokalypse und zur Rekonstruktion ihres hebräischen Urtextes*, Breslau, 1934.

Käsemann, *RGG*, II=E. Käsemann, "Epheserbrief" in *RGG*, II, pp. 517—20, 3rd ed. 1956—65, 7 Vols.

Kelly, *Past*=J. N. D. Kelly, *A Commentary on the Pastoral Epistles* (BNTC), London, 1963.

Kennedy, *PMR*=H. A. A. Kennedy, *St. Paul and the Mystery Religions*, London, 1913.

Kerenyi, *ME*=K. Kerenyi, *Die Mysterien von Eleusis*, Zürich, 1962.

Kern, *GMKZ*=O. Kern, *Die griechischen Mysterien der klassischen Zeit*, Berlin, 1927.

— *RG*=*Die Religion der Griechen*, Vol. I, 1926; Vol. II, 1935; Vol. III, 1938. Berlin.

Kirby, *EBP*=J. C. Kirby, *Ephesians: Baptism and Pentecost.* An Inquiry into the Structure and Purpose of the Epistle to the Ephesians, London, 1968.

Körte, *ArcRW*, 1915=A. Körte, "Zu den eleusinischen Mysterien", *ArcRW*, 18, pp. 116—26.

Koskenniemi, *IPGB*=H. Koskenniemi, *Studien zur Idee und Phraseologie des griechischen Briefes bis 400 n.Chr.* Helsinki, 1956.

Kourouniotes, *ArchRW*, 1935=K. Kourouniotes, "Das eleusinische Heiligtum von den Anfängen bis zur vorperikleischen Zeit", *ArchRW*, 32, 1935, pp. 52—78.

— Ἀρχ Δ, 1930—5="Ἀνασκαφαὶ Ἐλευσῖνος", Ἀρχ Δ. 13—6, 1930—35 (Parartema).

— Ἀρχ Δ, 1933—5="Συμβολὴ εἰς τὴν οἰκοδομικὴν ἱστορίαν τοῦ Ἐλευσινίου Τελεστηρίου". Ἀρχ Δ, 16, 1933—35.

— Ἀρχ Εφ, 1937="Ἐλευσινιακὴ Δαδουχία", Ἀρχ Εφ, 1937, pp. 223—53.

— *El*=Ἐλευσινιακὰ 1, 1937.

— Mylonas, *AJA*, 1933="Excavations at Eleusis", *AJA*, 37, 1933.

Krämer, *WD*, 1959=H. Krämer, "Zur Wortbedeutung 'Mysteria'", *WD*, N.F. 6, 1959, pp. 121—25.

— *WD*, 1967="Zur sprachlichen Form der Eulogie Eph 1: 3—14", *WD*, N.F. 9, 1967, pp. 34—46.

Kuhn, *PQ*=K. G. Kuhn, "The Epistle to the Ephesians in the Light of the Qumran Texts", in *PQ*, pp. 115—31.

— *KQT*=*Konkordanz zu den Qumran Texten* (In Verbindung mit A. M. Denis, R. Deichgräber, W. Eiss, G. Jeremias, and H.-W. Kuhn) Göttingen, 1960.

Kühner-Blass, *AG*=R. Kühner—F. Blass, *Ausführliche Grammatik der griechischen Sprache*, Bd. I, Teil i. und ii., Hannover, Leipzig, ³1892.

— Gerth, *AG*=R. Kühner—B. Gerth, *Ausführliche Grammatik der griechischen Sprache*, Bd. II, Teil i. und ii. Hannover, Leipzig, ³1904.

Ladd, *JK*=G. E. Ladd, *Jesus and the Kingdom*, London, 1966.

176

Lagrange, *RG*, 1919=M.-J. Lagrange, "Les Mystères d'Eleusis et le Christianisme", *RB*, 16, 1919, pp. 157—217.

— *RB*, 1919="Attis et le Christianisme", *RB*, 16, 1919, 419—80.

— *RB*, 1925="'Mystères'. Quoi de plus alléchant que ce titre: 'Influence des Mystères sur le Judaïsme Alexandrin avant Philon", *RB*, 34, 1925, 150—52.

Larson, *MPS*=Mildred Larson, *A Manual for Problem solving in Bible Translation*, Grand Rapids, 1975.

Lebram, *AUV*=J. Lebram, "Μυστήριον Βασιλέως", in *Abraham unser Vater. Juden und Christen im Gespräch über die Bibel*, (AGSU), Fs. für O. Michel, Leiden, Köln, 1963.

Lee, *NovT*, 1970=J. Y. Lee, "Interpreting the Demonic Powers in Pauline Thought", *NovT*, 12, 1970, pp. 54—69.

Lee, *StEph*=E. K. Lee, "Unity in Israel and Unity in Christ" in *StEph*, pp. 36—50.

Lenski=R. C. H. Lenski, *The Interpretation of St. Paul's Epistles to . . . the Ephesians*, Minnesota, 1937, rp. 1961.

Lietzmann, *1—2K*=H. Lietzmann, *An die Korinther 1—2*. Erklärt (HNT 9), rev. W. G. Kümmel, Tübingen, ⁴1949.

Lightfoot, *CPh*=J. B. Lightfoot, *St. Paul's Epistles to the Colossians and to Philemon*, London, 1879.

— *Gal*=*St. Paul's Epistle to the Galatians*, London, ⁵1876.

— *Phil*=*St. Paul's Epistle to the Philippians*, London, 1913, rp. 1967.

— *NEP*=*Notes on the Epistles of St. Paul* (On Eph 1:1—14), London, 1895.

Lindemann, *AZ*=A. Lindemann, *Die Aufhebung der Zeit. Geschichtsverständnis und Eschatologie im Epheserbrief* (SNT 12), Gütersloh, 1975.

— *ZNW*, 1976="Bemerkungen zu den Adressaten und zum Anlass des Epheserbriefes", *ZNW*, 67, 1976, pp. 235—51.

Lobeck, *Agl*=C. A. Lobeck, *Aglaophamus. sive De Theologiae Mysticae Graecorum causis libri III idemque poetarum Orphicorum dispersas reliquias collegit*, Regimont, 1829, rp. 1968.

Lohmeyer, *Kol-Ph*=E. Lohmeyer, *Die Briefe an die Kolosser und an Philemon* (KEKNT), Göttingen, 1961.

— *TB*, 1926="Das Proömium des Epheserbriefes", *TB*, 5, 1926, pp. 120 ff. and 233 ff.

Lohse, *CPh*=E. Lohse, *A Commentary on the Epistles to the Colossians and to Philemon* (Herm.), Phila. 1971.

— *NTS*, 1968—9="Pauline Theology in the Letter to the Colossians", *NTS*, 15, 1968—9, pp. 211—20.

Louw, BT, 1973=J. Louw, "Discourse Analysis and the Greek NT", *BT*, 24, 1973, pp. 101—18.

LSJ=H. G. Liddell—R. Scott—H. S. Jones, *A Greek-English Lexicon*, Oxford, ⁹1940, rp. 1968.

Lüken, *SNT*=W. Lüken, *Schriften des Neuen Testaments*, Göttingen, ³1917.

Lyonnet, *Bib*, 1954=S. Lyonnet, "L'étude du milieu littéraire et l'exégèse du Nouveau Testament", *Bib*, 35, 1954, pp. 480—502.

— *RD*="La Bénédiction de Eph 1:3—14 et son arrière-plan judaïque", in *A la Rencontre de Dieu* (BFCTL 8), pp. 341—52, Memorial A. Gelin, Paris, 1961.

Maas, *TL*, 1913=M. Maas, "Die antiken Mysterien und ihre Beziehungen zum Apostel Paulus", *TZ*, 38, 1913, p. 125.

MacGregor, *NTS*, 1954=G. H. C. MacGregor, "Principalities and Powers: the Cosmic Background of Paul's Thought", *NTS*, 1, 1954—5, pp. 17—28.

Mack, *LS*=B. L. Mack, *Logos und Sophia. Untersuchungen zur Weisheitstheologie im hellenistischen Judentum* (SUNT) Göttingen, 1973.

Mackay, GO=J. Mackay, God's Order. The Ephesian Letter and this present Time, London, 1953.

Manson, JTS, 1936=T. W. Manson, "A Parallel to a New Testament use of σῶμα", JTS, 37, 1936, p. 385.

Marsh, JTS, 1936=E. Marsh, "The Use of Mysterion in the Writings of Clement of Alexandria with special Reference to his sacramental Doctrine", JTS, 37, 1936, pp. 64—80.

Martitz, TDNT, VIII=P. W. Martitz, Art. υἱοθεσία in TDNT, VIII, 397—8.

Marxen, INT=W. Marxsen, Introduction to the New Testament, Oxford, 1968.

Maurer, EvTh, 1951—2=Chr. Maurer, "Der Hymnus von Eph 1 als Schlüssel zum ganzen Briefe", EvTh, 11, 1951—2, pp. 151—72.

— TDNT, VII=Art. τίθημι etc. in TDNT, VIII, pp. 152—68.

McL. Wilson, GnNT=R. McL. Wilson, Gnosis and the New Testament, Oxford, 1968.

Merklein, CK=H. Merklein, Christus und die Kirche. Die theologische Grundstruktur des Epheserbriefes nach Eph 2: 11—18 (SB 66), Stuttgart, 1973.

— KAE=Das kirchliche Amt nach dem Epheserbrief (SANT 33), München, 1973.

Mertens, DLTTM=A. Mertens, Das Buch Daniels im Lichte der Texte vom Toten Meer (SBM 12), Würzburg, 1971.

Metzger, TC=B. M. Metzger, A Textual Commentary on the Greek New Testament, London, N.Y., 1971.

Meyer=H. A. W. Meyer, Kritisch-exegetischer Kommentar über das Neue Testament: Epheserbrief, Göttingen, 1853.

— EH=Kritisch-exegetisches Handbuch über den Brief an die Epheser (KEKNT), ed. W. Schmidt, Göttingen, ⁶1886.

Michaelis, TDNT, III=W. Michaelis, Art. κράτος etc. in TDNT, III, pp. 905—15.

Michel, TDNT, V=O. Michel, Art. οἶκος etc. in TDNT, V, pp. 119—59.

Milik, BE=J. T. Milik, The Books of Enoch. Aramaic Fragments of Qumran Cave 4. Ed. by J. T. Milik, with the Collaboration of M. Black, Oxford, 1976.

— HTR, 1971="Problèmes de la littérature Hénochique à la Lumière de fragments araméens de Qumrân", HTR, 64, 1971, pp. 333—78.

Milligan, GP=G. Milligan, The Greek Papyri. With special Reference to their Value for NT Study, 1912.

Mitton, EE=C. L. Mitton, The Epistle to the Ephesians, Oxford, 1951.

MM=J. H. Moulton—G. Milligan, The Vocabulary of the Greek Testament. Illustrated from the Papyri and Other non-literary Sources, London, 1930, rp. 1972.

Montgomery, Dn=J. A. Montgomery, A Critical and Exegetical Commentary on the Book of Daniel (ICC), Edinburgh, 1927.

Morris, APC=L. Morris, The Apostolic Preaching of the Cross, London, ³1965.

— 1—2Th=The First and Second Epistles to the Thessalonians, (NICNT), Grand Rapids, 1969, rp. 1970.

Moule, CPh=C. F. D. Moule, The Epistles of Paul the Apostle to the Colossians and to Philemon (CGT), Cambridge, 1962.

— IB=An Idiom Book of the New Testament, Cambridge, ²1968.

H. C. G. Moule, ES=Ephesian Studies, 2nd ed. recent rp. no date, London.

Moulton, Prol=J. H. Moulton, A Grammar of New Testament Greek. Vol. I: Prolegomena, Edinburgh, 1908.

Müller, MM=M. Müller, Messias og 'Menneskesøn' i Daniels Bog, Første Enoksbog og Fjerde Ezrabog, København, 1972.

Münderlein, NTS, 1961—2=G. Münderlein, "Die Erwählung durch das Pleroma: Bemerkungen zu Kol 1: 19", NTS, 8, 1961—2, pp. 264—76.

Murphy-O'Conor, *PQ* = J. Murphy-O'Conor (ed.), *Paul and Qumran*. Studies in New Testament Exegesis, London, 1968.

Murray, *Rm* = J. Murray, *The Epistle to the Romans*, 2 Vols. in one, Grand Rapids, 1968.

Mussner, *CAK* = F. Mussner, *Christus, das All und die Kirche*. Studien zur Theologie des Epheserbriefes, Trier, ²1968.

— *GE* = "Die Geschichtstheologie des Epheserbriefes" in *Studiorum Paulinorum Congressus Internationalis Catholicus* 1961. Simul secundus Congressus Internationalis Catholicus de re Biblica, completo undervicesimo saeculo post S. Pauli in Urbem adventum, (An Bib, 18, II, pp. 59—63) Romae.

— *PQ* = "Contributions made by Qumran to the Understanding of the Epistle to the Ephesians", in *PQ*, 159—78.

Mylonas, *AY* = G. E. Mylonas, "Early Christian Fathers on the Eleusinian Mysteries", *AY*, 1959.

— Αρχ Εφ, 1936 = Γ. Ε. Μυλωνᾶ, Ὁ ἐνεπίγραφος ἑτερόστομος ἀμφορεὺς τῆς Ἐλευσῖνος καὶ ἡ Ἑλληνικὴ γραφή, Εφ Αρχ, 1936, σσ. 61—100.

— *AJA*, 1932 = "Eleusis in the Bronze Age", *AJA*, 36, 1932, pp. 104—117.

— *AJA*, 1936 = "Eleusiniaka", *AJA*, 40, 1936, pp. 415—31.

— *EEM* = *Eleusis and the Eleusinian Mysteries*, Princeton, 1961.

— *E1* = "Προϊστορικὴ Ἐλευσίς", Eleusiniaka I, pp. 1—172, 1937.

— *HDSE* = *The Hymn to Demeter and her Sanctuary at Eleusis*, St. Louis, 1942.

— *IEE*, I = Ἡ Μυκηναϊκὴ Θρησκεία in *IEE*, I, 1970, pp. 298—301.

— *IEE*, I = Μεσοελλαδικὸς Πολιτισμός in *IEE*, I, 1970, pp. 126—31.

Neil, *INT* = S. Neil, *The Interpretation of the New Testament 1861—1961*, London, 1966.

Neugebauer, *EX* = F. Neugebauer, Ἐν Χριστῷ. *Eine Untersuchung zum paulinischen Glaubensverständnis*, Göttingen, 1961.

— *NTS*, 1957 = "Das paulinische 'in Christo'", *NTS*, 4, 1957, pp. 124—38.

Nida, *ESS* = E. A. Nida, *Exploring Semantic Structures* (ILGL), München, 1975.

— *TST* = *Toward a Science of Translating*. With special Reference to Principles and Procedures involved in Bible Translating, Leiden, 1964.

— Taber, *TPT* = C. R. Taber, *The Theory and Practice of Translation*, Leiden, 1969.

Nilsson, *ArchRW*, 1935 = M. P. Nilsson, "Die eleusinischen Gottheiten", *ArchRW*, 32, 1935, pp. 79—141.

— *GFR* = *Greek Folk Religion* (= *Greek Popular Religion*, 1940), New York, 1961.

— *MMR* = *Minoan-Mycenaean Religion*, Lund, ²1950.

Noack, *EBEH* = F. Noack, *Eleusis: die baugeschichtliche Entwicklung des Heiligtums*, Berlin, 1927.

Norden, *AT* = E. Norden, *Agnostos Theos*. Untersuchungen zur Formengeschichte religiöser Rede, Berlin, Leipzig, 1913.

O'Brien, *NTS*, 1974 = P. T. O'Brien, "Thanksgiving and the Gospel in Paul", *NTS*, 21, 1974, pp. 144 ff.

Ochel, *ABKE* = W. Ochel, *Die Annahme einer Bearbeitung des Kolosserbriefes im Epheserbrief in einer Analyse des Epheserbriefes untersucht*, Diss. Marburg, 1934.

Odeberg, *VU* = H. Odeberg, *The View of the Universe in the Epistle to the Ephesians* (AUL N. F. Avd. 1, Bd. 29, Nr. 6) Lund, 1934.

Oepke, *1—2Th* = A. Oepke, *Die Briefe an die Thessalonicher* (NTD), Göttingen, 1965.

— *TDNT*, II = Art. ἐν in *TDNT*, II, pp. 537—43.

Oesterley, *IBA* = W. O. E. Oesterley, *An Introduction to the Books of the Apocrypha*, London, 1935.

— *II Es* = II Esdras, 1933.

Olsson, *SMFG*=B. Olsson, *Structure and Meaning in the Fourth Gospel.* A Text-linguistic Analysis of John 2:1—11 and 4:1—42 (CB:NTS 6), Lund, 1974.

Palmer, *IMGT*=L. R. Palmer, *The Interpretation of Mycenaean Greek Texts*, Oxford, 1963.

Παπαχατζῆ, ΠΕΠ, I=N. Παπαχατζῆ, Παυσανίου Ἑλλάδος Περιήγησις: ᾽Αττικά. Εἰσαγωγὴ στὸ ῎Εργο τοῦ Παυσανία καὶ στὰ ᾽Αττικά, ᾽Αποκατάσταση τοῦ ᾽Αρχαίου κειμένου, Μετάφραση καὶ Σημειώσεις Ἱστορικές, ᾽Αρχαιολογικές, Μυθολογικές. (being Vol. I of X planned), ᾽Αθῆνα, 1974.

Parian Chronicle (=Jacoby, *MP*), see under Texts.

Percy, *PKE*=E. Percy, *Die Probleme der Kolosser- und Epheserbriefe*, Diss. Lund, 1946.

— *ZNW*, 1950—1="Zu den Problemen des Kolosser- und Epheserbriefes", *ZNW*, 43, 1950—1, pp. 178—94.

Persson, *ArchRW*, 1922=A. Persson, "Der Ursprung der eleusinischen Mysterien", *ArcRW*, 21, 1922, pp. 287—309.

PL=*Patristic Greek Lexicon*, ed. G. W. H. Lampe, Oxford, 1961—68.

Picard, *REG*, 1927=Ch. Picard, "Sur la patrie et les pérégrinations de Déméter", *REG*, 40, 1927.

— *RHR*, 1927="L'épisode de Baubô dans les Mystères d'Eleusis", *RHR*, 95, 1927, pp. 220—55.

— *RP*=*Les Religiones Préhelléniques*, Paris, 1948.

Pike-Pike, *Ling*, 1972=K. L. Pike—Evelyn G. Pike, "Seven Substitution Exercises for studying the Structure of Discourse", *Ling*, 94, 1972, pp. 43—52.

Piper, *JR*, 1958=O. A. Piper, "The 'Book of Mysteries' (Qumran I 27). A Study in Eschatology", *JR*, 38, 1958, pp. 95—105.

Plöger, *Dn*=O. Plöger, *Das Buch Daniel* (KAT 18), Gütersloh, 1965.

Pokorny, *EG*=P. Pokorny, *Der Epheserbrief und die Gnosis*, etc., Berlin, 1965.

— *ZNW*, 1962="Epheserbrief und gnostische Mysterien", *ZNW*, 53, 1962, pp. 160—94.

Porteous, *Dn*=N. W. Porteous, *Daniel.* A Commentary (OTL), London, 1965.

PQ=*Paul and Quamran.* (A Collection of papers previously published in various Journals), ed. J. Murphy-O' Conor, London, 1968.

Prestige, *GPT*=G. L. Prestige, *God in Patristic Thought*, London, 1964.

Pringsheim, *GEK*=G. H. Pringsheim, *Archäologische Beiträge zur Geschichte des eleusinischen Kults*, 1905.

Prümm, *ZKT*, 1937=K. Prümm, "Mysterion von Paulus bis Origenes", *ZKT*, 61, 1937, 391—425.

— *Bib*, 1963="Das neutestamentlich Sprach- und Begriffsproblem der Vollkommenheit", *Bib*, 44, 1963, pp. 76—92.

— *Bib*, 1956="Zur Phänomenologie des paulinischen Mysterion und dessen seelischer Aufnahme. Eine Übersicht", *Bib*, 37, 1956, 135—61.

Pryke, *SC*=J. Pryke, "Eschatology in the Dead Sea Scrolls", in *SC*, pp. 45—57.

Quell, *TDNT*, IV=G. Quell, Art. λέγω etc. in *TDNT*, IV, pp. 145—68.

Quispel, *GW,*=G. Quispel, *Gnosis als Weltreligion*, 1951.

Rabinowitz, *JBL*, 1952=I. Rabinowitz, "The Authorship, Audience and Date of the de Vaux *Fragment* of an Unknown Work", *JBL*, 71, 1952, pp. 19—32.

Rackham, *Acts*=R. B. Rackham, *The Acts of the Apostles*, London, 1901.

Ramsey, *PTRC*=W. M. Ramsey, *St. Paul the Traveller and the Roman Citizen*, London, [14]1920.

Reicke, *TDNT*, V=B. Reicke, Art. πᾶς, ἅπας in *TDNT*, V, pp. 886—90; 892—6.

180

Reid, *TT*, 1960=J. K. S. Reid, "The Phrase 'in Christ'", *TT*, 17, 1960, pp. 353—65.

Reitzenstein, *HM*=R. Reitzenstein, *Hellenistische Mysterienreligionen* nach ihren Grundlagen und Wirkungen, Darmstadt, rp. 1956 (^{3}1927).

Rese, *TZ*, 1975=M. Rese, "Die Vorzüge Israels in Röm. 9: 4 f. und Eph. 2: 12", *TZ*, 31, 1975, pp. 211—22.

— *VF*, 1970="Formeln und Lieder im NT", *VF*, 15, 1970, pp. 75—95.

Reumann, *JBL*, 1958=J. Reumann, "Stewards of God: Pre-Christian Religious Application of οἰκονόμος in Greek", *JBL*, 77, 1958, pp. 339—49.

— *NovT*, 1959="Οἰκονομία: 'Covenant'; Terms for Heilsgeschichte in Early Christian Usage", *NovT*, 3, 1959, 282—92.

— *NTS*, 1967="Οἰκονομία-Terms in Paul in Comparison with Lukan Heilsgeschichte", *NTS*, 13, 1966—7, pp. 147—67.

— *SE*, 1968="Heilsgeschichte in Luke: Some Remarks on its Background and Comparison with Paul", *SE*, 4, 1968, pp. 86—115.

— *UOGS*=*The Use of* οἰκονομία *and related Terms in Greek Sources to about A.D. 100, as a Background for Patristic Applications*, Diss. (on Microf.), Univ. Penna., 1957.

Richardson, *ITNT*=A. Richardson, *Introduction to the Theology of the New Testament*, London, 1958.

Riesenfeld, *BNT*=E. H. Riesenfeld, "Nytestamentlig Teologi", in *En Bok om Nya Testamentet*, pp. 359—455, ed. B. Gerhardsson, Lund, ^{3}1973.

Robertson, *Gr*=A. T. Robertson, *A Grammar of the Greek New Testament in the Light of Historical Research*, ^{4}1923, rp. Nashville, 1934.

— *PI*=*Paul and the Intellectuals*. The Epistle to the Colossians, rev. ed., Nashville, 1959.

Robinson=J. A. Robinson, *St. Paul's Epistle to the Ephesians*. A Revised Text and Translation with Exposition and Notes, London, ^{2}1922.

J. M. Robinson, *Apo*="Die Hodayoth-Formel in Gebet und Hymnus des Frühchristentums", in *Apophoreta* (BhZNW 30), pp. 194—235, Fs. E. Haenchen, Giessen, Berlin, 1964.

Roller, *FPB*=*Das Formular der paulinischen Briefe*. Ein Beitrag zur Lehre vom antiken Briefe, Stuttgart, 1933.

Rowley, *DM*=H. H. Rowley, *Darius the Mede and the Four World Empires*. An Historical Study of Contemporary Theories, Cardiff, 1935, rp. 1964.

— *WAI*=*Worship in Ancient Israel*. Its Forms and Meaning, London, 1967.

Rudberg, *PNT*=G. Rudberg, "Zu den Participen im NT" (CN, 12), pp. 1—38, Lund, 1948.

Rupp, *PP*=E. G. Rupp, *Principalities and Powers*, N.Y., 1952.

Russel, *MMJA*=D. S. Russel, The Method and Message of Jewish Apocalyptic 200 B.C.—A.D. 100 (OTL), Phila., 1964.

Ryrie, *BS*, 1966=C. C. Ryrie, "The Mysteria in Eph. 3", *BS*, 123, 1966, pp. 24—31.

Salmond=S. D. F. Salmond, *The Epistle of Paul to the Ephesians* (EGT Vol. 3), rp. Grand Rapids, 1967.

Sampley, *OF*=J. P. Sampley, *And the Two shall become One Flesh*: A Study of Traditions in Eph 5: 21—33 (NTS:M 16), Cambridge, 1971.

Sanday-Headlam, *Rm*=W. Sanday—A. C. Headlam, *A Critical and Exegetical Commentary on the Epistle to the Romans* (ICC), Edinburgh, ^{4}1900.

Sanders, *CH*=J. T. Sanders, *The NT Christological Hymns*. Their Historical Religious Background (NTS:M 15), Cambridge, 1971.

— *JBL*, 1962="The Transition from Opening Epistolary Thanksgiving to Body in the Letters of the Pauline Corpus", *JBL*, 81, 1962, pp. 348—62.

— *ZNW*, 1965="Hymnic Elements in Eph. 1—3", *ZNW*, 56, 1965, pp. 214—32.

SC=M. Black (ed.), *The Scrolls and Christianity* (*TC*, 2), London, 1969.

Scharlemann, *ConcTM*, 1969=M. H. Scharlemann, "The Secret of God's Plan. Studies in Ephesians: Study One", *ConcTM*, 40, 1969, pp. 532—44.

— *ConcTH*, 1970¹="Study Two", *ConcTM*, 41, 1970, pp. 155—64.

— *ConcTM*, 1970²="Study Three", *ConcTM*, 41, 1970, pp. 338—46.

— *ConcTM*, 1970³="Study Four", *ConcTM*, 41, 1970, pp. 410—20.

Schattenmann, *SNP*=J. Schattenmann, *Studien zum neutestamentlichen Prosa-hymnus*, München, 1965.

Schille, *FH*=G. Schille, *Frühchristliche Hymnen*, Berlin, 1965.

— *LG*=*Liturgisches Gut im Epheserbrief*, Diss. Göttingen, 1953.

Schlier=H. Schlier, *Der Brief an die Epheser*. Ein Kommentar, Düsseldorf, ⁷1971.

— *CK*=*Christus und die Kirche im Epheserbrief* (BHTh 6), Tübingen, 1930, rp. 1966.

— *MG*=*Mächte und Gewalten im Neuen Testament* (QD), Freiburg, 1958.

— *TDNT*, I=Art. γόνυ, γονυπετέω in *TDNT*, I, pp. 738—40.

— *TDNT*, III=Art. κεφαλή, ἀνακεφαλαιοῦμαι in *TDNT*, III, pp. 673—82.

— *ZK*=*Die Zeit der Kirche*. Exegetische Aufsätze und Vorträge, Freiburg, 1956.

— Warnach, *KE*=P. V. Warnach, *Die Kirche im Epheserbrief* (BKT:BC 1), Münster, 1949.

Schmauch, *IC*=W. Schmauch, *In Christus*. Eine Untersuchung zur Sprache und Theologie des Paulus (NF 9), Gütersloh, 1935.

Schmidt, *TDNT*, V=K. L. Schmidt, Art. ὁρίζω etc. in *TDNT*, V, pp. 452—6.

Schneider, *TSK*, 1932=J. Schneider, "'Mysterion' im NT", *TSK*, 104, 1932, pp. 255—78.

Schrenk, *TDNT*, II=G. Schrenk, Art. εὐδοκέω, εὐδοκία in *TDNT*, II, pp. 738—51.

— *TDNT*, IV=Art. λέγω etc. in *TDNT*, IV, pp. 144, 168—92.

Schubert, *FF*=P. Schubert, *Form and Function of the Pauline Thanksgivings* (BhZNW 20), Berlin, 1939.

Schürer, *GJV*=E. Schürer, *Geschichte des jüdischen Volkes im Zeitalter Jesu Christi*, 3 Vols., Leipzig, ⁴1901—09.

— *HJP*=*History of the Jewish People* (Eng. Tr. S. Taylor, P. Christie, from 2nd Germ. ed.), 1890.

Schweizer, *TDNT*, VIII=υἱός, υἱοθεσία etc. in *TDNT*, VIII, pp. 354—7; 363—92; 399.

Scott=E. F. Scott, *The Epistles of Paul to the . . . Ephesians* (MNTC), London, 1930.

— *Col*=*The Epistles of Paul to the Colossians . . .* (MNTC), London, 1930.

Simpson=E. K. Simpson, *Commentary on the Epistle to the Ephesians* (NICNT), Grand Rapids, 1957, rp. 1970.

SNT=*The Scrolls and the NT*, ed. K. Stendahl, N.Y., 1957.

Sophocles, *Lex*=E. A. Sophocles, *Greek Lexicon of the Roman and Byzantine Period*, N.Y., Leipzizg, 1893, rp. 1967.

Staerck, *RAC*, I=W. Staerck, Art. 'Anakephalaiosis' in *RAC*, I, pp. 411—4.

Stanton, *Glot*=G.L. Stanton, "The Oriental Background of the Compound γονυπετεῖν". *Glot*, 46, 1968, pp. 1—6.

Starcky, *RB*, 1956=J. Starcky, "Communication de J. Starcky", *RB*, 63, 1956, pp. 66—7.

Stauffer, *NTT*=E. Stauffer, *New Testament Theology*, London, 1955.

StEph=*Studies in Ephesians*, ed. F. L. Cross, London, 1956.

Stibbs, *MWB*=A. M. Stibbs, *The Meaning of the Word 'Blod' in Scripture*, London, ²1954.

Stier=R. E. Stier, *Die Gemeinde in Christo: Auslegung des Briefes an die Epheser*, Berlin, 1848—9.

Str—B=H. L. Strack—P. Billerbeck, *Kommentar zum Neuen Testament aus Talmud und Midrash*, Vols. I—IV (VI), München, 1922—8, (1959).

182

Stromberg, *STPT*=A. v. Stromberg, *Studien zur Theologie und Praxis der Taufe in der christlichen Kirche der ersten zwei Jahrhunderte*, Berlin, 1913.

Stuiber, *RAC*, I=A. Stuiber, Art. 'Doxologie' in *RAC*, IV, pp. 210—26.

Taber=see Nida—Taber, *TPT*.

Taylor, *Mk*=V. Taylor, *The Gospel according to St. Mark*, London, ²1966.

Tooley, *ScJT*, 1966=W. Tooley, "Stewards of God. And Examination of the Terms Οἰκονόμος and Οἰκονομία in the NT", *ScJT*, 19, 1966, pp. 74—86.

Traub, *TDNT*, V,=H. Traub, Art. οὐρανός etc. in *TDNT*, V, pp. 497—502; 509—43.

Travlos, Εφ Αρχ, 1951=J. N. Travlos, "Τὸ ἀνάκτορον τῆς Ἐλευσῖνος", Εφ Αρχ, 1951, σ. 1—6.

— *Hesp*, 1949="The Topography of Eleusis", *Hesp*, 18, 1949.

— *PDAA*=*Pictorial Dictionary of Ancient Athens*, London, 1971.

Trench, *SNT*=R. C. Trench, *Synonyms of the New Testament*, London, ⁹1880, rp. 1961.

Trevijano, *SE*, 1973=R. Trevijano, "Εὐλογία in St. Paul and the Text of Rom. 16:18", *SE*, 6, 1973, pp. 537—40.

Trinidad, *Bib*, 1950="The Mystery hidden in God (Eph. 1:3—14)", *Bib*, 31, 1950, pp. 1—26.

Turner, *Synt*=N. Turner, *A Grammar of NT Greek: Vol. III: Syntax*, Edinburgh, 1963.

V. d. Burg, ΑΔΟ=N. M. H. van der Burg, Ἀπόρρητα-Δρώμενα-Ὄργια. *Bijdrage tot de Kennis der Religieuze Terminologie in het Grieksch*, Amsterdam, 1939.

Ventris—Chadwick, *DMG*=M. Ventris—J. Chadwick, *Documents in Mycenaean Greek*, Cambridge, 1956.

Ventris—Chadwick, *JHS*, 1953="Evidence for Greek Dialects in the Mycenaean Archives", *JHS*, 73, 1953, pp. 84—103.

V. d. Lof, *ZNW*, 1962=L. J. Van der Lof, "Die Mysterienkulte zur Zeit Augustins", *ZNW*, 53, 1962, pp. 245—55.

Vielhauer, *GUL*=Ph. Vielhauer, *Geschichte der urchristlichen Literatur*: Einleitung in das NT, die Apokryphen und die apostolischen Väter, Berlin, N.Y., 1975.

V. Hofmann=J. C. K. von Hofmann, *Der Brief Pauli an die Epheser* (HSNT 6:1), Nördlingen, 1868—86.

V. Rad, *OTT*=G. von Rad, *Old Testament Theology*, 2 Vols., Edinburgh, 1968.

V. Roon=A. van Roon, *De Brief van Paulus aan de Epheziers* (PNT), Nijkerk, 1976.

— *AE*=*The Authenticity of Ephesians*, Diss. Leiden, 1974 (Trans. from the orig. Dutch, 1969).

— *NovT*, 1974="The Relation between Christ and the Wisdom of God according to Paul", *NovT*, 16, 1974, pp. 207—39.

Vogt, *SNT*=E. Vogt, "Peace among Men of God's good pleasure", in *SNT*.

V. Soden=H. von Soden, *Die Briefe an die ... Epheser* (HNT), Leipzig, ²1893.

— *ZNW*, 1911="Μυστήριον und Sacramentum in den ersten zwei Jahrhunderten der Kirche", *ZNW*, 12, 1911, pp. 188 ff.

Wagner, *PBPM*=G. Wagner, *Pauline Baptism and the Pagan Mysteries*, Edinburgh, 1967.

Walvoord, *Dan*=J. F. Walvoord, *Daniel*: A Key to Prophetic Revelation, Chicago, 1971.

Warnach, *KE*=see Schlier—Warnach.

Webster, *BICS*, 1954=T. B. L. Webster, "Pylos E Tablets", in *BICS*, 1, 1954, pp. 13—4.

— *Lat*, 1957="Hommages à Waldemar Déona", *Lat*, 28, 1957.

— *MH*=*From Mycenae to Homer*, London, 1958.

Wehrli, *ArchRW*, 1934="Die Mysterien von Eleusis", *ArchRW*, 31, 1934; pp. 77—104.

Weiser, *IOT*=A. Weiser, *Introduction to the Old Testament*, (Eng. Trans. from Ger. 1957) London, 1961, rp. 1969.

Weiss, *1K*=J. Weiss, *Der erste Korintherbrief* (KEKNT), Göttingen, ²1910.

— *TSK*, 1896=J. Weiss, "Paulinische Probleme II, Die Formel ἐν Χριστῷ 'Ιησοῦ", *TSK*, 69, 1896, pp. 7—33.

Wendland, *1—2K*=H. D. Wendland, *Die Briefe an die Korinther* (NTD), Göttingen, 1965.

Werner, *DSC*=E. Werner, *The Doxology in Synagogue and Church* (HUCA 19), Cincinnati, 1945—6.

Westcott=B. F. Westcott, *The Epistle to the Ephesians*, 1906, rp. 1950.

Westermann, *LGP*=C. Westermann, *Das Loben Gottes in den Psalmen*, Göttingen, 1954.

White, *FFBGL*=J. L. White, *The Form and Function of the Body of the Greek Letter*, etc. Diss. SBL, Montana, 1972.

Whiteley, *ET*, 1957=D. E. H. Whiteley, "Expository Problems; Eph 6: 12: Evil Powers", *ET*, 68, 1957, pp. 100—3.

Wilckens, *TDNT*, VII=U. Wilckens, Art. σοφία etc. in *TDNT*, VII, pp. 465—76; 496—528.

— *WT*=*Weisheit und Torheit*. Eine exegetische-religionsgeschichtliche Untersuchung zu 1 Kor 1 und 2 (BHTh), Tübingen, 1959.

Wilcox, *SC*=M. Wilcox, "Dualism, Gnosticism, and other Elements in the pre-Pauline Tradition" in *SC*, pp. 83—96.

Willi—Plein, *VT*, 1977=I. Willi—Plein, "Das Geheimnis der Apokalyptik", *VT*, 27, 1977, pp. 62—81.

Wilson, *SE*, 1964=R. A. Wilson, "'We' and 'you' in the Epistle to the Ephesians", *SE*, 2, 1964, pp. 676—80.

Winklhoffer, *GCW*=A. Winklhoffer, *Über die Kirche. Das Geheimnis Christi in der Welt*, Frankfurt/Main, 1963.

Wolfson, *Ph*=H. A. Wolfson, *Philo I—II*. Foundations of Religious Philosophy in Judaism, Christianity, and Islam, Cambridge, Mass., 1947.

Wood, *ET*, 1967=J. E. Wood, "Pauline Studies and the Dead Sea Scrolls", *ET*, 1967, pp. 308—11.

Young, *PD*=E. J. Young, *The Prophecy of Daniel*, Grand Rapids, 1949.

Zerwick=M. Zerwick, *Der Brief an die Epheser*, Düsseldorf, 1961.

Zijderveld, Τε=C. Zijderveld, Τελετή: *Bijdrage tot de Kennis der religieuze Terminologie in het Grieksch*, Purmerend, 1934.

INDICES

I. INDEX OF AUTHORS

Abbott 2, 30, 63, 65, 66, 67, 68, 71, 75, 76, 78, 79, 81, 82, 83, 84, 86, 87, 88, 89, 90, 91, 92, 93, 97, 98, 99, 100, 101, 102, 103, 104, 106, 108, 109, 110, 111, 112, 143, 147, 148

Adler 119

Alford 1, 63, 66, 82, 84, 87, 89, 93, 97, 100, 102, 104, 108, 109, 112, 147

Allan 66, 155, 156

Althaus 1

Anderson-Scott 1

Andresen 60

Anrich 19, 119

Arvedson 27

Audet 40

Bang 153

Barrett 1, 27, 28, 30

Barth, M. 36, 41, 45, 46, 47, 52, 53, 63, 65, 66, 67, 68, 71, 78, 79, 80, 81, 82, 84, 87, 89, 90, 93, 97, 100, 101, 102, 104, 106, 108, 109, 110, 111, 112, 147, 158, 159, 161

Beasley-Murray 46

Beekman (B—C) 54, 57, 58, 59, 60, 61, 62, 63, 64, 67, 69, 70, 82, 88, 93, 104, 138

Behm 91

Bengel 65, 84

Benoit 68, 130

Berkhof 158

Bertram 93

Beyer 39, 79, 80

Beza 84

Bieder 29, 30

Bietenhard 157

Bingham-Kolenkow 127

Blackman 39

Blass 9, 79

Boers 53

Böhlig 154

Boobyer 52

Bornkamm 9, 21, 25, 26, 28, 29, 30, 40, 119

Bousset 119

Box 127

Bowker 26

Brown 23, 26, 27, 28, 29, 30, 102, 103, 119, 121, 124, 127, 129, 130, 133, 134, 135

Bruce 1, 30, 65, 84, 93, 97, 102, 104, 108, 109, 130, 131, 132, 147

Brugmann 79

Büchsel 91, 153, 154, 156

Bultmann 110, 119, 120, 121, 157

Burton 64, 74, 86

Caird, 1, 28, 152, 157, 158, 159, 161

Callow, J. 54, 57, 58, 59, 60, 61, 62, 63, 64, 67, 69, 70, 82, 88, 93, 104, 138

Callow, K. 50, 58

Calvin 68, 84

Cambier 41, 59

Caragounis 10

Cerfaux 21, 26, 119

Chadwick, J. 3, 4

Chafer 1

Champion 39

Charles 25, 26, 127, 128, 129, 159, 161

Clemen 119

Clinton 14

Colpe 119, 126

Conzelmann 1, 80, 81, 89

Coppens 27, 29, 72, 119, 129, 130

Coutts 46, 47

Crowther 69

Cullmann 159

Dahl 36, 39, 45, 46, 47, 52, 53, 66, 75, 76, 84, 108, 109

Davies 117, 119, 131

Debrunner 41

Decharme 12

Deden 27, 134

Deichgräber 39, 41, 42, 44, 46, 47, 129

Deissmann 59, 60, 75, 87, 146, 152, 153, 154, 155, 156

Delling 67, 68, 159, 160, 161

Denis 24

Deubner 3, 4, 14, 16, 17, 18
Dewailly 28
De Wette 66
Dibelius 1, 39, 45, 80, 81, 84, 93, 108, 109, 147, 148
Dieterich 17
Dodd 1
Doty 60
Drury 26
Duensing 161
Dugmore 39, 44
Dunn 46, 50
Dupont 29
Elbogen 39
Elliger 133
Ellis 119, 135
Erasmus 84
Ernst 67, 68
Farnell 16
Feuillet 75
Fischer 42, 43, 47
Flemming 25, 161
Flemington 46
Flowers 52
Flusser 66
Foerster 30, 158, 159, 161
Fohrer 93
Forbes 161
Foucart 4, 14, 16
Foulkes 63, 66, 79, 84
Frisk 9
Fuller 119
Funk 29
Furumark 3
Galloway 158
Gaugler 1, 29, 39, 45, 47, 63, 66, 68, 81, 84, 87, 89, 90, 91, 92, 93, 100, 110, 111, 139, 147
Geldenhuys 1
Georgiades 42
Gerth 63, 97
Gibbard 142
Gibbs 139
Gnilka 1, 39, 41, 44, 46, 63, 66, 71, 78, 82, 83, 84, 87, 89, 90, 91, 92, 93, 97, 100, 108, 110, 121, 126, 129, 147, 149
Goodspeed 100
Goodwin 75
Grant, R. M. 121
Griffiths 33

Grosheide 1, 27, 28
Grundman 130
Guthrie, D. 39
Hamilton 62
Hammer 66
Hansen 153
Hanson 117, 126, 144, 161
Harder 52, 56
Harris, Z. S. 57
Harrison, J. 8, 15
Hartman 1, 123
Hauck 92
Headlam 108
Heidegger 155
Hendriksen 63, 66, 68, 110
Hennecke 161
Hering 29
Hodge 1, 81, 83, 84, 87, 93, 104, 108, 109
Houlden 142
Innitzer 41, 47
Jacoby 12
Jannaris 64, 79, 106, 108, 110
Jeremias, G. 130
Jewett 41
Johansson 27
Jones 142
Kaminka 127
Käsemann 45, 60
Kautzsch 24
Kelly 1, 30
Kennedy 27, 119
Kerenyi 5
Kern 3, 4, 9, 12, 17, 19
Kirby 46
Körte 17
Koskenniemi 60
Kourouniotes 3, 4, 15
Krämer 9, 42, 44, 84
Kuhn, K. G. 45, 88, 101, 119, 121, 129, 132
Kühner 9, 63, 79, 97
Kümmel 45
Ladd 1
Lamb 57
Langrange 21, 119
Larson 58
Lebram 126
Lee, E. K. 144
Lee, J. Y. 158
Lenski 83, 84, 108, 109
Lidzbarski 21

Lietzmann 28
Lightfoot, J. B. 1, 2, 30, 68, 75, 84, 97, 148
Lindemann 95, 100, 144, 146
Lobeck 17
Lohmeyer 1, 41, 47
Lohse 30, 130, 133
Louw 58
Lüken 46
Luther 84
Lyonnet 29, 41
Maas 119
MacGregor 157, 158, 159
Mack 21
Mackay 1
Manson, T. W. 68
Marsh 32
Martitz 87
Marxsen 45
Maurer 36, 42, 45, 46, 47, 84, 94, 161
McL. Wilson 120
Merklein 38, 39, 46, 49, 70, 71, 100, 119, 139, 140
Mertens 121, 130, 132, 133, 159
Metzger 1
Meyer, H. A. W. 66, 84, 93
Michaelis 161
Michel 95, 97
Milik 24, 25, 127, 129, 132, 133
Milligan 60
Mitton 1, 27, 28, 29, 30, 35, 98, 100, 101, 102
Montgomery 123, 160
Morfill 24
Morris 1, 91
Moule, C. F. D. 1, 30, 65, 108
Moule, H. C. G. 87, 97, 148
Moulton 64, 65, 79, 86, 106, 108
Müller 123
Münderlein 67
Murray 1
Mussner 30, 71, 95, 117, 119, 129, 144, 145, 147, 149, 157, 158
Mylonas 3, 4, 5, 12, 14, 15, 16, 17, 19, 119
Neil 121
Neugebauer 153, 155, 156
Nida 57, 58, 67, 75, 80, 87, 103, 104, 138
Nilsson 4, 5, 16, 17, 19
Noack 3, 4, 15, 16, 17, 19
Norden 44
O'Brien 52

Ochel 41, 47
Odeberg 147, 148, 149, 150
Oepke 154
Oesterley 127
Oliver 12
Olsson 57, 58
Palmer 4
Παπαχατζῆς 17
Percy 35, 38, 39, 41, 46, 66, 68, 84, 89, 93, 100, 139
Persson 4
Picard 4, 17
Pike, E. G. 57
Pike, K. L. 57
Piper 133
Plöger 123
Pokorny 46, 119
Porteous 121, 123
Prestige 97
Pringsheim 17
Prümm 28, 29, 32, 119
Pryke 132
Quell 85
Quispel 121
Rabinowitz 133
Rackham 86
Rahlf 125
Ramsey 86
Reicke 93
Reid 157
Reitzenstein 22, 119
Rese 41, 70
Reumann 94, 97
Richardson 120
Riesenfeld 126
Robertson 1, 60, 63, 64, 65, 67, 75, 76, 79, 80, 82, 86, 87, 101, 106, 108
Robinson J. A. 1, 30, 39, 63, 65. 66, 68, 71, 78, 79, 81, 82, 84, 87, 89, 90, 91, 92, 93, 97, 98, 100, 103, 106, 108, 110, 111, 112, 117, 119, 147
Robinson, J. M. 40, 52, 54
Roller 60
Rowley 39, 121, 123
Rudberg 63
Rupp 158
Russel 127
Ryrie 142
Salmond 1, 80, 81, 83, 84, 86, 87, 89, 90, 91, 92, 93, 97, 100, 102, 104, 108, 109, 148

Sampley 59, 97
Sanday 108
Sanders 36, 42, 43, 44, 45, 47, 49, 52, 54, 55, 71
Scharlemann 142
Schattenmann 42, 47
Schille 41, 42, 44, 46, 47, 129
Schlier 1, 28, 29, 30, 36, 39, 40, 41, 42, 45, 46, 47, 63, 65, 66, 67, 71, 74, 75, 78, 79, 81, 83, 84, 87, 89, 90, 91, 93, 95, 97, 99, 100, 101, 102, 104, 106, 108, 109, 110, 111, 117, 121, 126, 140, 143, 144, 146, 147, 148, 149, 150, 157, 158, 161
Schmauch 155
Schmidt, C. 120
Schmidt, K. L. 86
Schneemelcher 161
Schneider 22, 26, 29, 30
Schrenk 84, 88
Schubert 46, 49, 52, 53, 54, 55
Schürer 39
Schweizer, E. 87
Scott 1, 97
Seesemann 109
Simpson 63, 65, 66, 68, 81, 83, 87, 100, 104, 108, 109
Sophocles 108
Staerck 161
Stanton 74
Starcky 133
Stauffer 41, 47
Stibbs 91
Stier 66
Str.-B. 39, 161
Stromberg 46
Stuiber 39
Taber 57, 58, 80, 138
Taylor 1
Tooley 97
Traub 146
Travlos 3, 14
Trench 93

Trevijano 41
Trinidad 84
Turner 64, 65, 67, 86, 89, 108
V. der Burg 6, 7, 11, 15
Ventris 3
Vermes 130, 131, 132, 133
V. der Lof 33
Vielhauer 43
V. Hofmann 66
V. Rad 85
V. Roon 35, 41, 42, 44, 45, 46, 52, 53, 54, 60, 65, 76, 89, 97, 99, 100, 107, 118, 147, 148, 158, 160
Violet 127
Vogt 88
V. Soden 27, 30, 68, 84, 87, 126, 135
Wagner 119
Walvoord 123
Warnach 68
Webster 3, 4
Wehrli 16, 17, 18
Weiser 127
Weiss, B. 68
Weiss, J. 28, 154
Wendland, H. D. 1
Wendland, P. 120
Werner 39
Westcott 84
Westermann 39
White 60
Whiteley 157, 158
Wilckens 29, 93
Willi-Plein 121
Wilson 46, 52
Wilcox 131
Winklhoffer 142
Wolfson 21
Wood 119
Young 123
Zerwick 63, 66, 84
Ziegler 125
Zijderveld 4, 7, 8

II. INDEX OF REFERENCE WORKS

BAG   31, 64, 79, 82, 83, 86, 88, 91, 92, 96, 97, 99, 100, 103, 108, 111, 112, 153, 156

BDF   65, 80

BDR   63, 65, 82, 86, 89, 97, 107, 110

ΔΔ   10, 79, 96, 100, 147

FBK   45

HR   79

IEE   3, 4, 15, 42

LSJ   79, 97, 99

MM   83, 87, 106

MPG   8

MPL   74

III. INDEX OF PASSAGES

1. Biblical Passages

A. *Old Testament*

Gen
14: 19 f.   79

Deut
7: 6 ff.   85
32: 8 f.   159

III Kin (LXX)
1: 48   40, 79

II Chr
20: 26   39

Neh
9: 5   39

Jb
1: 9 ff.   150
1: 21   80
15: 8   121
19: 19   121
29: 24   121

Ps
8   67, 131, 160
25: 14   121
55: 15   121
64: 2   121
67: 15   147
71: 19   54
72: 18   40
72: 18 f.   79
83: 3   121
89: 7   121
111: 1   121
143: 1 f.   40
144: 1 f.   79

Prov
3: 32   121
25: 9   121

Isa
24: 16   121
29: 15   110
30: 1   110
43   131

Jer
6: 11   121
23: 18   121
23: 22   121

Ez
13: 9   121

Dan
2   124, 126, 128, 131, 132
2: 18   23, 123
2: 19   23
2: 19 f.   124
2: 20   124, 125
2: 21   122, 123, 125
2: 22   125
2: 23   93, 123, 125
2: 27   159
2: 27 f.   23, 124
2: 28   122, 123, 124, 125
2: 29   23
2: 30   23
2: 34   123
2: 34 f.   122
2: 35   125
2: 37   161
2: 37—8   125
2: 38   126, 161
2: 44   123
2: 44 f.   122
2: 46   23
2: 47   23

3: 24 f.   40
3: 26—33   48
3: 26—45   39, 48, 79
3: 45   48
3: 51 ff.   79
4   126
4: 17   122
4: 22   122
4: 23   147
4: 25   122
4: 28   122
4: 32   122
4: 35   122
5: 21   122
7   124, 126, 127, 128
7: 7 f.   127
7: 9   123, 161
7: 11   158
7: 11—4   158, 159, 160
7: 12   158
7: 13   123, 158
7: 13 f.   122
7: 14   122, 123, 124, 126, 158
7: 16   123
7: 17 f.   123
7: 18   123
7: 22   122, 123
7: 23 ff.   122
7: 23—7   123
7: 25   123
7: 26   158
7: 26—7   158, 159
7: 27   122, 158, 160
8: 23 ff.   122
10: 13   159
10: 20   159
10: 21   159

11:36	122
12:10	122

Am

3:7	121

Hab

2:1—2	131
2:3 b	132

B. *New Testament*

Mt

6:7	45
6:26	151
13:11	26
13:13	27
13:16	27
16:2 f.	151
24:9—14	123
27:46	81

Mk

4:11	26
6:46	81
13:9—13	123
14:16	80

Lk

1:46—55	40, 48
1:68	80
1:68—79	40, 48
1:73	48
1:76—9	40
2:29—32	48
8:10	26
9:57—62	58
10:18	150

Jn

3:13	147
20:17	81

Acts

1:11	151
2:5	151
26:28	100
26:29	100

Rm

1:5	98
1:8 ff.	54
1:16	50
1:21	54
1:25	80

1:28	82
5:12—21	58, 154
5:20	108
8:10	30
8:15	87
8:19 ff.	157
9:5	80
11:11	108
11:25	28
12:3	98
13:9	144
14:11	75
15:4	100
15:15 ff.	98
15:30 ff.	37
16:25	28
16:25 f.	34, 102

I Cor

1:6	82
1:25—8	139
1:26 f.	28
2:1	1, 28
2:7	108
2:7—16	102
2:8	139
2:9	129
4:1	28
5:7	82
6:17	30
9:17	97
13:2	27
14:2	27
14:15	27
15:22	153, 154
15:40	147
15:45—9	154
15:48—9	147
15:51	1, 2, 27

II Cor

1:3	80
1:3 ff.	40, 46, 54

1:3—11	53
4:15	54
5:7	150
5:10	100
9:8	80, 92
10:3 f.	151
11:31	80
12:2	151
12:3	156
13:5	30
14:16—9	54

Gal

1:12	99
2:7—9	98
3:4	97
4:5	87
4:19	30

Eph

1:3	41, 42, 48, 78, 80, 124, 144, 147, 150
1:3—4	42
1:3 ff.	40
1:3—6	41, 42
1:3—10	42, 47, 50, 52, 58, 59, 61, 62, 78
1:3—12	44
1:3—13	96
1:3—14	36, 39, 41, 42, 43, 44, 45, 46, 47, 49, 53, 60, 62, 67, 69, 72
1:4	48, 157
1:4 f.	149
1:4—6	41, 42
1:4—7	137
1:4—10	41, 47, 49
1:5	105, 156
1:5—8	42
1:6	62, 138

1 : 6—7   41
1 : 6—10   42
1 : 7   48, 90, 110,
            144, 157
1 : 7—8   42
1 : 7—10   42, 47
1 : 7—12   41
1 : 8   125
1 : 8 f.   140, 141
1 : 8—10   41, 49
1 : 9   29, 93, 100,
            110, 125, 139,
            140, 141, 156,
            157
1 : 9 f.   34, 100, 107,
            132, 141, 142,
            143, 157
1 : 9—10   42, 43, 125
1 : 9—12   42
1 : 9—13   43
1 : 10   47, 48, 49, 97,
            118, 125, 126,
            151, 155, 157,
            160
1 : 10—12   42
1 : 11   48, 49, 73,
            103, 124
1 : 11—2   42, 47, 50, 52
1 : 11—3   52
1 : 11—4   41, 42, 47, 49,
            50, 52, 61, 62
1 : 12   42, 62, 89, 138
1 : 13   47, 50, 52
1 : 13—4   41, 42
1 : 14   47, 48, 50, 52,
            62, 66, 73, 89,
            103, 138, 144
1 : 15   84
1 : 15 f.   54
1 : 15 ff. 52, 60, 74, 117
1 : 15—23   36, 62, 69, 72,
            74
1 : 16   64, 65, 75
1 : 16—8   65
1 : 17   51, 64, 65, 75,
            81
1 : 17 ff. 55
1 : 17—9   65
1 : 18   66, 73, 75, 89,
            103, 106, 107

1 18—22   125, 140
1 : 19   55, 62, 67, 88,
            107
1 : 19 f.   90, 145
1 : 20   51, 67, 69,
            147, 150, 151
1 : 20—2   126
1 : 20—3   62
1 : 21   67, 117, 157,
            161
1 : 21 f.   113, 145, 157
1 : 22   51, 67, 125,
            126, 145, 160,
            161
1 : 22 f.   118, 144
1 : 23   50, 51, 55, 67,
            117, 146

2 : 1   62, 69, 144,
            150
2 : 1 f.   145
2 : 1—5   69
2 : 1—7   68
2 : 1—10   68, 69
2 : 2   51, 145, 149,
            157, 161
2 : 2 f.   144
2 : 3   51
2 : 4   90
2 : 4—8   139
2 : 5   35, 69, 73,
            144, 150
2 : 5—6   69
2 : 5—8   51
2 : 6   51, 69, 73,
            144, 147, 150
2 : 7   138, 143
2 : 7—8   51
2 : 8   51, 69, 144
2 : 8—9   68, 69
2 : 10   54, 55, 68, 69
2 : 11   35, 69, 70
2 : 11—2   70
2 : 11—3   69, 72, 156
2 : 11—8   39, 139, 140
2 : 11—22   38, 72, 140
2 : 12   51, 70, 103
2 : 12 f.   103
2 : 12 ff. 139
2 : 12—9   73

2 : 13   51, 70
2 : 14   35, 69, 88, 103
2 : 14—6   71
2 : 14—8   71, 72, 139
2 : 15   88, 103, 156
2 : 15 f.   139
2 : 16   103, 139
2 : 16—9   140
2 : 19   66, 72, 73, 103
2 : 19—22   55, 71, 72
2 : 20—2   72
2 : 22   157

3 : 1   36, 52, 55, 72,
            74, 96, 111,
            142, 150
3 : 1—13   59, 72, 96, 142
3 : 1—4 : 22 36
3 : 2   51, 73, 74, 97,
            107, 147
3 : 2—7   73
3 : 2—9   139
3 : 2—12   74
3 : 2—13   36, 55, 96, 142
3 : 3   51, 59, 73, 93,
            105, 125, 139
3 : 3 b   140
3 : 3 ff.   142
3 : 4   29, 50, 51, 59,
            73, 93, 125,
            140, 141, 142,
            143
3 : 4 ff.   141
3 : 5   29, 51, 73, 93,
            125, 140, 142
3 : 5 f.   140
3 : 5 ff.   34
3 : 6   51, 66, 73, 142
3 : 7   73, 88
3 : 7 f.   98
3 : 7—8   98
3 : 8   73, 142
3 : 8 f.   142
3 : 8—12   73
3 : 9   2, 51, 59, 97,
            125, 141, 157
3 : 9 ff.   141
3 : 10   51, 73, 74,
            109, 118, 138,
            139, 145, 147,
            150, 157

3:11	51, 73, 157
3:13	51, 73, 74, 111, 142
3:14	55, 64, 73, 75, 96
3:14 ff.	52, 72
3:14—9	36, 55, 74, 75, 96
3:15	51, 75, 151
3:16	51, 75
3:16—7	75
3:16—9	75
3:17	30, 75, 84
3:18	75, 76
3:18—9	75
3:19	51, 76
3:20	51, 77
3:20—1	36, 39, 76
3:21	51, 77, 138
4:1	90
4:2	84
4:5	46, 51
4:13—4	51
4:6	51, 80
4:9	51, 151
4:9—10	35
4:10	51, 151
4:13	51
4:15	51, 84
4:16	84
4:17—25	51
4:19	28
4:20	110
4:21	35, 51, 97
4:22	35
4:23-6:20	36
4:25	35
4:29	51
4:30	51
4:32	82
5:2	84
5:5	51, 66
5:6	51
5:6—9	51
5:16	51
5:17	51
5:19	35, 51
5:27	51

5:29 ff.	156
5:32	2, 30, 32, 59
6:2	51
6:6	51
6:9	51, 149, 151
6:12	51, 147, 149, 150, 157
6:12 f.	145
6:13—6	145
6:14	51
6:15	51
6:16	51
6:17	51
6:18	51
6:18 ff.	28, 52
6:18—20	36, 37
6:19	28, 29, 51, 59, 93
6:19 f.	142
6:20	150

Phil

1:3 f.	64
1:3 ff.	53
1:29	74
2:10	75, 147
3:10	76
3:19	148
3:20	150

Col

1:3	64
1:5—6	35
1:9—20	45
1:13	90
1:16	148, 157, 161
1:20	35
1:22	84
1:23	97
1:24	74
1:25	97, 98
1:26	2, 29, 30, 102
1:26 ff.	34
1:27	30, 101
1:29	105
2:2 f.	30
2:9—10	35
2:10	145
2:15	143
2:23	35

3:20	35
4:2 ff.	37
4:3	28, 35
4:4	102
4:12	64, 75

I Th

1:2—5	53
1:2—3:13	53
1:3	64
2:13—4	53
3:9—13	53
5:23	37

II Th

2:7	27
2:8	27
2:9	27

I Tim

3:9	30
3:13	84
3:16	31

II Tim

4:18	147

Philm

4	64

Heb

1:3	139
1:24	151
3:1	147
4:14	151
5:12	46
6:4	147
6:12	103
6:17	103
7:26	151
8:1	151
8:5	147
9:7	91
9:22	91
9:23	147
11:9	103
11:16	147
11:28	91
12:22	147
13:22	100

I Pet
1: 3	80
1: 3 ff.	41, 46, 54
1: 3—9	48
1: 5	48
3: 18	110
5: 12	100

II Pet
2: 10	161
3: 14	84

I Jn
4: 19	82

Jd
8	161
24	84

Rev
1: 20	1, 26, 28, 31
5: 12	80
10: 6 f.	95
10: 7	28
12: 7—9	150
12: 9—10	150
12: 10	150
12: 12	145
13: 8	137
17: 3 ff.	27
17: 5	1, 27
17: 7	27, 28
17: 8, 9	28
17: 9—12	28
21: 16	75

2. Apocrypha

I Esd
8: 25	79

Jud
2: 2	22
13: 18	79
15: 31 f.	159

Tob
3: 11	48
3: 11—5	48
3: 12—5	48
8: 5—7	48
8: 7	48
8: 15—7	48
8: 17	48

12: 7	22
13: 1	40, 48
13: 1—18	79
13: 2—18	48
14: 1	40, 48

I Mac
4: 30	40, 79

II Mac
3: 31	146
13: 21	22

III Mac
6: 28	146
7: 6	146

IV Mac
11: 3	147

Wis
2: 22	23
6: 22	23
14: 5	22
14: 23	22

Sir
3: 19	23
22: 22	22
27: 16	22
27: 17	22
27: 21	22

3. Pseudepigrapha

Ahik	126
2: 53	24
5: 7	24
8: 37	24

Apoc Soph	161

Arist	
129	83

Asc Isa	148
1: 4	161
2: 2	161
6—11	151

II Bar
48: 3	24
60: 1	24
81: 4	24, 126, 127

III Bar
1: 6	24
1: 8	24
2: 5	24

I En
	126, 127
1—36	24
8: 1—4	25
8: 3	25
9	127
9: 6	25
10	127
10: 7	25
16	127
16: 3	25
37—71	127
45: 3	127
45: 3 f.	127
46	127
46: 3	127
46: 4 f.	127
47: 1 ff.	128
48: 2 ff.	128
48: 4	127

48: 4 ff.	128	81: 1 f.	129	Sib Or	126, 127	
48: 6	128	83—90	25, 128	3: 812	24	
49: 2	128	83: 7	128	4: 51	146	
49: 2 ff.	127	84: 2—6	48	4: 135	146	
49: 4	127, 128	84: 4	48			
51: 1 ff.	128	84: 5—6	48	*Test XII Patr*		
51: 3	25, 127, 128	90: 1	25	Test D		
51: 5	127	93: 2	129	6: 2	159	
52: 1—9	128	103: 2	129			
52: 2	128	103: 2 f.	25	Test G		
53: 3 ff.	128	103: 3	129	6: 5	24	
55: 4	128	103—104	129			
58: 1 ff.	128	104: 10	25, 129	Test J		
61: 9	128	104: 12	25, 129	12: 3	24	
61: 10	161	104: 12—3	26	12: 4	24	
62: 1 ff.	127, 128	106: 19	26, 129	12: 6	24	
62: 6—7	128	II En	126	16: 4	24	
62: 13 ff.	128	3: 21	151			
63: 1 ff.	128	20: 1	161	Test L		
63: 3	25	24: 3	24	2: 7—3: 8	151	
63: 3 a	25			2: 10	24	
63: 11 ff.	128	IV Ez	126	3: 8	161	
64: 2	128	10: 38	24, 25	7: 4	24	
65: 6	128	12: 11 ff.	127			
65: 11	128	12: 36	24	Test Z		
67: 4 ff.	128	12: 38	24	1: 16	24	
68: 2	128	14: 5	127			
68: 2 f.	128			Test Sol		
68: 5	128	Late Heb Test N		8: 2	161	
69: 8	128	8: 4 ff.	159	20: 15	161	
69: 15	128					
69: 29	127	Ps Sol		Vit Ad et Ev	126	
72—82	25	14: 5	24	21: 1	24	
				34: 1	24	

4. Rabbinic

Chag		Sh^emone Esre		(Eighteen Bened.)	
12	151		39, 40, 48		45
Mishn					
I.50	39				

5. Qumran

1QS		9: 18	130	11: 19	130
3: 23	130, 131	11: 3—4	133		
4: 6	130	11: 5	130	1QSa	
4: 18	130, 131	11: 7—8	66	I.9: 12 f.	66

1QSb		
4: 23	66	
CD		
3: 8	130	
3: 15	88	
1QH		
1: 11	130	
1: 13	130	
1: 21	130	
1: 29	130	
2: 1	130	
2: 1—9	130	
2: 13	101, 130	
2: 31—9	130	
4: 5—5: 4	130	
4: 27	130	
5: 5—19	130	
5: 20—7: 5	130	
5: 20—7	130	
5: 25	130	
5: 36	130	
7: 6—25	130	

7: 27	130
8: 4—40	130
8: 6	130
8: 11	130
9: 23	130
11: 10	130
11: 11 f.	66
12: 20	130
13: 2	130
13: 3	130
13: 13	131
1QHf	
50: 5	130
1QM	
3: 9	130
3: 27	133
4: 18	133
14: 9	130
14: 14	130
16: 11	130
16: 16	130

17: 9	130
1QpHab	
7	132
7: 2	131
7: 4—5	131
7: 5	130
7: 7—8	132
7: 13 f.	132
7: 13—14	132
1Q26	
1: 1	133
1: 4	133
1Q27	
1: 1, 2	130
1: 1, 2—4	133
1: 1, 3—4	133
1: 1, 3 ff.	133
1: 1, 5	133
1: 1, 7	133
13: 3	132

6. Christian Authors

Ambrosiaster
    84

Asterius
  Hom. X 16

Athenagoras
  Apol. 32: 1 15

Chrysostom
  Ad Eph. 29, 68, 81, 84,
              89, 90, 93,
              102, 104, 108,
              112, 117, 126,
              148

I Clement
  61: 2 146

Clemens Alexandrinus
  Protr.
    2   6, 9, 15, 16,
          17
    9   32
    12   32

Str.
  IV.3, 1 14
  V.11   16, 161
  VII.16 32

Didache
  11: 11   31

Diognetus
  4: 6   31
  7: 1 f. 31
  10: 7 31
  11: 2 31

Ephraim   84

Epilogus Mosquensis
  4   146

Epiphanius
  Haer.
    31: 5, 3 31

Eusebius
  Praep. Ev.
    9, 34 46

Gregorius Naz.
  Or. 39 8

Hermas
  Vis. 3.2, 5 75

Hippolytus
  Ad Noët. 4 32
  Phil.
    V   22
    V.7   6, 32
    V.7, 34 16
    V.7—8 32
    V.7—9 120
    V.8   16 18, 32
    V.20 2

Ignatius
  Eph.
    13: 2 146
    19: 1 31
  Magn. 9: 2 31
  Sm. 6: 1 146
  Trall.
    5: 1—2 146
    9: 1   146

Irenaeus
Ad Haer.
I.21, 4   32
(Proem.) 2 32

Justinus Martyrus
Dial.
40: 1   31
44: 2   31
74: 3   31
131: 2   31
134: 2   31
134: 5   31
138: 2   31
141: 4   31

Mart. Polycarpi
14: 3   146

Pelagius
Ad Eph.   84

Polycarpus
Phil. 2: 1   146

Syncellus   25

Synesius
Dion. 10   16

Tertullianus
Ad Nat.
2, 7   15

Theodorus Mops.
Ad Eph.   79, 84

Theodoretus
80, 93, 102,
148
Ther. I.72119

Theophylactus
Ad Eph.   81, 84, 102

7. Ancient Authors

Achilles Tatius
I.11   19

Aelianus
Frg.
12   17
58: 8   17, 18

Aeschylus
Frg.
218   17
302   17
479   6, 18
Pr. 398   74
Sept. Th.
179   5, 7

Alexander Trall.
V.4   22

Andocides
De Myst.
10   17
11   17
19 ff.   17
111   12

Apollodorus
Bib.
I.3, 2   6
II.2, 2   6
II.5, 12   6, 11
III.5, 1   6
III.14, 7 12

III.15, 4 12

Apollonius Rhodius
Argon.
I.920   5, 17

Apuleius
Met.
11: 5,
762   109
11: 23   33

Aristophanes
Av. 1073 f. 17
Ec. 442   11
Eq. 282   17
Pax
411—20 8
413—20 6
Pl. 1013   6
Ra.
320   17
324 f.   14
356   7
386   6, 8
386 f.   13
386 ff.   7
455 f.   18
457 ff.   18
887   18
1032 ff. 8
Th.
947 f.   7
948   6

Aretaeus
CD II.7   22

Aristoteles
EN
III.1, 17 17
Rh II.24, 2 6, 8

Athenaeus
III.98 d   9

Batrachomyomachia
303   8

Demosthenes
31   86
772   8
1463 ff.   60

Dinarchus
II.1   110

Diodorus Siculus
9
II.62, 8   17
V.49   18
V.49, 5   17

Diogenes Laertius
II.8, 101   17
VI.39   18

Epictetus
Diss.
I.12, 25   86

Eunapius
Vit. Soph.
52 ff.   12

Euripides   8
Ba.
20 f.   6, 8
32 ff.   7
72 ff.   8
78 ff.   7
Frg.
63   11
218   86
Hec. 1150   74
Hel. 1307   11
Hipp. 25   13
IT 1331   11
Rh.
942   8
943   11
Supp.
173   6
470   13

Firmicus Maternus
Err. prof.
rel. 22: 1   33

Galenus
13: 777   100

Herodotus
II.51   5, 6, 7
II.59   4
II.122 f.   4
II.156   4
II.171   4, 7
IV.79   7
V.61   5
V.30   110
V.83   11
VI.101   110
VI.135   11
VIII.65   6, 14
IX.94   11

Heraclitus
Frg. 14   5, 6

Herodianus
VIII.7, 4   13

Hesiodus
Th. 912 ff. 5

Hesychius   11, 15

Homerus
Il.   5
6: 129   146
6: 131   146
8: 116   74
Od.   5
5: 453   74
17: 484   146

Horatius
Od. III.2,
25 ff.   17

Hymn to Demeter
5, 13
203   13
273   6
273 ff.   6
337   13
439   13
474—9   6
475   13
478 f.   13, 18
480 ff.   18
481 f.   6
486   13

Hymn ad Pluto
15

Iamblichus
Myst. 7: 1   19
Protr. 2   14, 21

Isocrates
De Big.
6   17
347   17
Pan.
IV.31   12
IV.157   12, 14

Josephus
Ap. II.266   17

Libanius
Plethr. 6   19

Livius
31: 14   17
33: 14   18

Longinus
ΠΥ I.1   45

Lucianus
D Deor.
4: 3   146
Demon. 11   6
Herm. 4   6
Lex. 10   10
Pseudol. 5   6
Salt. 15   6, 15

Lysias
14: 42   17

Meleager
(Anth.
Pal. c.
Plan.)
12: 158   86

Menander
Inc. 168   21

Menander Protector
16 D   100

Mnesimachus
Frg. 11   21

Moschus
2: 21   146

Pausanias
I.2, 5   6, 17
I.36, 4   12
I.37, 4   6, 17
I.38, 2   14
I.38, 3   6, 12
I.38, 7   17
IV.33, 4   13
V.10, 1   6
IX.25,
5—9   6
IX.30, 4 f.   6
IX.30,
4—5   6
X.31, 9   18

Philo Judaeus
  Agr. 10   146
  Cher.
    XII.42   21
    XIV.48   21
    XIV.49   21
  De. Imm.
    XIII.61   21
    XIII.62   21
  Gig. 62   146
  Leg. All.
    III.168f. 146
  Migr. Abr.
    107 f.   79

Philostratus
  Vit. Ap.
    I.15   19
    IV.18   12

Phocylides
  Sent. 229 24

Pindarus
  Frg.
    114   18
    131   19
    132: 3 146
  Ol. III.41 7
  Pyth.
    IV.189 86

Plato
  Ap.
    19 b   146
    41 a   18
  Euthd.
    277 d   6
  Gor. 497 c 20, 21
  Leg.
    4: 713 c
    ff.   159
    5: 738 d 159
  Men. 76 e 20
  Phd. 69 d 18
  Phdr.
    249 a—
    250 c   20
    253 c ff. 20
    256 d   146
  Pol.   20

Res.
  363 c   18
  439 d ff. 20
Soph.
  238 c   11
Symp.
  201 d—
  212 a   20
  202 e   159
  210—
  211   20
Tht. 156 a 20
Tim.   20
  293 c   16

Plutarchus
  Alc.
    19—22 17
  Demetr.
    24   12
  Frg.
    24   2, 6
    212   6, 9
  Is.-Os. 4
  Mor.
    10 e   10
    21   6, 18
    22   16, 18
    107 e   21
    360 F   6, 15
    417 A   6
    422 C   6, 20
    956   83
    996 b   10
  Vit.
    711—2 6

Proclus
  Tim. 293 c 16

Pseudo-Homeric
  Batr. 303 7

Pseudo-Lysias
  VI.51   17

Sch.: Aristophanem
  Pl.
    845   14
    1013   14
  Ra.
    369   12, 14
    456   9

Sch.: Lucianus
  Lex. 10   10

Sch.: Sophoclis
  OC 1051 9, 11

Sopater   16, 17

Sophocles
  Aj.
    214   11
    837   13
  Ant.
    452   86
    1013   7
  Frg.
    943   6, 13
    753   18
  OC
    90   13
    458   13
    1050 ff. 17
    1051 ff. 17
  OT 301   11
  Tr. 765   5, 6, 7

Soranus
  Gyn.
    I.3   21
    I.4   21

Stobaeus
  Ecl. 4   15

Strabo
  IX.400   14

Suetonius
  Ne. C, 34, 12

Themistius 15

Theocritus
  Id.
    25: 5   146
    26   6

Thucidides
  VI.28   17

Xenophon
  Hell.
    I.4, 14   17
    VI.3, 6   11

8. Inscriptions

IG
I², 6: 93   14, 21
I², 6: 96   14, 21
I², 313:
144   14
II², 1672: 4 14

III, 713   11

OGIS
234: 11,
20 ff.   54

SIG
83   12
873: 9   11
885   14

9. Papyri

BGU
780, 2   100

P Flor.
296: 12   146

PGM
1: 130 f.   22

4: 719 ff.   22
4: 968—72 75
12: 313 ff. 22
13: 27   22

PML
10: 19   22

P Pap.   75

P Par.
574. 3042   146

SGUÄ
41: 66   146

10. Other Ancient Sources

Anecdoda Graeca
I, 273, 25   14

CAF
II, 442   21
III, 200   21

DMG   3

EG
261: 9 f.   146

Etym. Magnum
455, 10   8
595, 48   9

OF (Orph. Frg.)
37   8

OH
115   15

Orph. Frg.
247: 33 ff. 146

Parian Chron.
12

Suidas   8, 12, 18

11. Hermetica

CH
Ascl.
3: 32 b   146

Exc
12: 1   146
21: 2   146

Frg. 26   146
Poem   22, 120
Tract. XIII 120

12. Gnosticism

Gospel of Thomas
120

Gospel of Truth
120

Jeu (Book of)
120

Naasene Tractate
(Sermon) 22, 32, 120

Pistis Sophia
120

Unbek. altgnost. Werk
120

ERRATA

Page 6 line 10 read ἔρδω   instead of ἔρδω
  ,, 11 ,, 10 ,, ῎Αρρητον   ,,   ,, ᾽Απόρρητον
  ,, 12 ,, 38 ,, (Decharme   ,,   ,, Decharme
  ,, 33 ,, 14 ,, μύστης,   ,,   ,, μύστης
  ,, 54 ,, 32 ,, Thanksgiving   ,,   ,, Thankgiving

DATE DUE